MW00559180

Praise for *Is Social Justice Just?*:

"If I were putting together my dream team to organize a volume to answer the question, 'Is social justice just?', it would be Rob Whaples, Mike Munger, and Chris Coyne. And the dream team delivers! Anyone concerned with social justice will find this book makes him question his assumptions, rethink his premises, and think! They have assembled their own dream team of authors to provide insights from a variety of disciplinary perspectives that provoke thought, provide new perspectives, and make the reader want more."

— **Andrew P. Morriss**, professor, Bush School of Government and Public Service, School of Law, Texas A&M University

"In the world of public policy, words should mean something, not just sound like they mean something. The words 'social justice' are thrown around quite liberally these days, often with the assumption that their meaning is clear—but from the way these words are used, it's clear that their meaning varies from author to author and sometimes even from paragraph to paragraph in the works of a single author. Here a stellar cast of policy-oriented intellectuals faces this problem head on, attacking the problem of what 'social justice' ought to mean and why it matters. It's about time."

— **Steven Landsburg**, professor of economics, University of Rochester

"Social justice is an ambiguous concept that allows people to redefine justice to conform with their own biases. This volume clearly points out problems with the concept and offers a clear-headed analysis of the way the concept should be viewed, along with analyses of socially just policies."

— **Randall Holcombe**, DeVoe Moore Professor of Economics, Florida State University

"Though plenty of people have opinions about the importance of social justice, they seldom explain what they mean by the term. Is it a meaningful concept? If so, what constitutes social justice? Are there better and worse ways to pursue it? This collection of readings addresses those controversial issues and more. It is a timely contribution to an important debate."

— **Bruce Caldwell**, Research Professor of Economics; director, Center for the History of Political Economy, Duke University

"What principles of social justice will foster peace, cooperation, and mutual respect among highly diverse individuals within a decidedly pluralist society rather than foster exploitation, tribal conflict, coercive re-education, and the enhancement of arbitrary state power? From their own distinctive philosophical or economic perspectives, the contributors to *Is Social Justice Just?* converge toward the powerful conclusion that justice must be modest. It must protect each person's life, liberty, and property and not proclaim purportedly radiant social ends to which people's lives, aspirations, and fortunes are to be sacrificed."

    —**Eric Mack**, professor of philosophy, Tulane University

"With more clamor for 'social justice' in the public square today than serious inquiry into what social justice consists of, the essays in *Is Social Justice Just?* are timely and essential reading. Twenty-three scholars lay bare both the promise and pitfalls of initiatives that are taken under the social justice banner."

    —**J. Daniel Hammond**, Hultquist Family Professor (emeritus), Department of Economics, Wake Forest University

"*Is Social Justice Just?* brings together a remarkable collection of scholars who study one of the most controversial issues of our time, one that has created enormous divisions across social, political, cultural, economic, racial and religious lines. Each author deconstructs *social justice* using his own unique set of analytical tools, with the hope of creating a concept of justice that can help bring society back together. A broad consensus emerges from this process, as these scholars are individually led to a reconstruction of social justice focused on the sanctity and the beauty of each of us as individuals, individuals who have the same rights and freedoms and opportunities to create our own paths, while respecting the choices of others. Read this book, and you will look at our world with a very different and much more optimistic vision than you have now."

    —**Lee Ohanian**, professor of economics and director of the Ettinger Family Program in Macroeconomic Research, University of California, Los Angeles

"Readers of this book will be rewarded by the interdisciplinary perspectives on social justice from a distinguished group of contributors …"

—**Barry W. Poulson**, professor of economics (emeritus), University of Colorado

"In the zeitgeist of our times, social justice is just by definition, as well as by intuition and emotion. The articles in this book put the conventional wisdom to the test, with rational analyses from a number of different perspectives."

—**Pierre Lemieux**, economist, Department of Management Sciences at the Université du Québec en Outaouais (Canada)

"A popular intellectual sport is to classify individuals into this or that group and then to ask: Is this or that group 'owed' something by society? With such classifications typically guided by political considerations, the answer is very often 'yes.' And because 'owe' implies obligation, and because justice demands the fulfilment of all obligations, justice demands that society—in one form or another—pay up. Or so goes the argument for 'social justice.' The papers in this remarkable volume examine this argument from a variety of perspectives. It's a feature and not a bug of this collection that, no sooner are you convinced by one paper, then another paper turns your mind in a different direction."

—**Donald J. Boudreaux**, professor of economics, George Mason University

IS
SOCIAL JUSTICE
JUST?

INDEPENDENT INSTITUTE

INDEPENDENT INSTITUTE is a nonprofit, nonpartisan public-policy research and educational organization that shapes ideas into profound and lasting impact. The mission of Independent is to boldly advance peaceful, prosperous, and free societies grounded in a commitment to human worth and dignity. Applying independent thinking to issues that matter, we create transformational ideas for today's most pressing social and economic challenges. The results of this work are published in books; in our quarterly journal, *The Independent Review*; and in other publications and form the basis for numerous conference and media programs. By connecting these ideas with organizations and networks, we seek to inspire action that can unleash an era of unparalleled human flourishing at home and around the globe.

FOUNDER
David J. Theroux

CHAIRMAN AND CHIEF EXECUTIVE
Mary L. G. Theroux

PRESIDENT
Graham H. Walker

RESEARCH DIRECTOR
William F. Shughart II

SENIOR FELLOWS
Bruce L. Benson
Christopher J. Coyne
Ivan Eland
Williamson M. Evers
John C. Goodman
Stephen P. Halbrook
Steve H. Hanke
William Happer
Randall G. Holcombe
Lawrence J. McQuillan
Michael C. Munger
Benjamin Powell
Gregory J. Robson
Judy L. Shelton
William F. Shughart II
Randy T. Simmons
Alexander Tabarrok
Diana W. Thomas
Alvaro Vargas Llosa
James Tooley
Richard K. Vedder
Robert M. Whaples

ACADEMIC ADVISORS
Leszek Balcerowicz
WARSAW SCHOOL OF ECONOMICS

Jonathan J. Bean
SOUTHERN ILLINOIS UNIVERSITY

Herman Belz
UNIVERSITY OF MARYLAND

Peter J. Boettke
GEORGE MASON UNIVERSITY

Boudewijn R. A. Bouckaert
UNIVERSITY OF GHENT, BELGIUM

Allan C. Carlson
HOWARD CENTER

G. Marcus Cole
UNIVERSITY OF NOTRE DAME

Robert D. Cooter
UNIVERSITY OF CALIFORNIA, BERKELEY

Robert W. Crandall
BROOKINGS INSTITUTION

Richard A. Epstein
NEW YORK UNIVERSITY

George Gilder
DISCOVERY INSTITUTE

Steve H. Hanke
JOHNS HOPKINS UNIVERSITY

Victor Davis Hanson
HOOVER INSTITUTION

James J. Heckman
UNIVERSITY OF CHICAGO

Wendy Kaminer
AMERICAN CIVIL LIBERTIES UNION

Lawrence A. Kudlow
FORMER DIRECTOR,
NATIONAL ECONOMIC COUNCIL

John R. MacArthur
HARPER'S MAGAZINE

Deirdre N. McCloskey
UNIVERSITY OF ILLINOIS, CHICAGO

J. Huston McCulloch
OHIO STATE UNIVERSITY

Thomas Gale Moore
STANFORD UNIVERSITY

June E. O'Neill
BARUCH COLLEGE

James R. Otteson
UNIVERSITY OF NOTRE DAME

Thomas J. Peters III
AUTHOR

Charles E. Phelps
UNIVERSITY OF ROCHESTER

Daniel N. Robinson
GEORGETOWN UNIVERSITY AND
OXFORD UNIVERSITY

Paul H. Rubin
EMORY UNIVERSITY

Bruce M. Russett
YALE UNIVERSITY

Pascal Salin
UNIVERSITÉ PARIS-DAUPHINE

Vernon L. Smith
CHAPMAN UNIVERSITY

Joel H. Spring
QUEENS COLLEGE, CITY UNIVERSITY
OF NEW YORK

John B. Taylor
STANFORD UNIVERSITY

Richard E. Wagner
GEORGE MASON UNIVERSITY

Paul H. Weaver
FORTUNE

Todd J. Zywicki
GEORGE MASON UNIVERSITY

100 Swan Way, Oakland, California 94621-1428, U.S.A.
Telephone: 510-632-1366 • Facsimile: 510-568-6040 • Email: info@independent.org • www.independent.org

IS SOCIAL JUSTICE JUST?

Edited by Robert M. Whaples,
Michael C. Munger, and Christopher J. Coyne

FOREWORD BY JORDAN B. PETERSON

Preface by Nicholas Rescher

INDEPENDENT
INSTITUTE

Is Social Justice Just?
Copyright © 2023 by the Independent Institute

ISBN 978-1-59813-353-0

All Rights Reserved. No part of this book may be reproduced or transmitted in any form by electronic or mechanical means now known or to be invented, including photocopying, recording, or information storage and retrieval systems, without permission in writing from the publisher, except by a reviewer who may quote brief passages in a review. Nothing herein should be construed as necessarily reflecting the views of the Institute or as an attempt to aid or hinder the passage of any bill before Congress.

Independent Institute
100 Swan Way, Oakland, CA 94621-1428
Telephone: 510-632-1366
Fax: 510-568-6040
Email: info@independent.org
Website: www.independent.org

Cover Design: Denise Tsui
Cover Image: ER09 via Getty Images

Library of Congress Cataloging-in-Publication Data:

Names: Coyne, Christopher J., editor. | Munger, Michael C., editor. | Whaples, Robert M., editor.
Title: Is social justice just? / [edited by Christopher J. Coyne, Michael C. Munger, Robert M. Whaples].
Description: Oakland, California : Independent Institute, [2019] | Includes bibliographical references and index.
Identifiers: LCCN 2022037609 (print) | LCCN 2022037610 (ebook) | ISBN 9781598133530 (cloth) | ISBN 9781598133554 (epub)
Subjects: LCSH: Social justice--Moral and ethical aspects. | Equality. | Justice (Philosophy)
Classification: LCC HM671 .I75 2019 (print) | LCC HM671 (ebook) | DDC 303.3/72--dc23/eng/20220915
LC record available at https://lccn.loc.gov/2022037609
LC ebook record available at https://lccn.loc.gov/2022037610

Contents

    Injustice of Economic Inequality   205
    Andrew Jason Cohen

16 Classical Liberalism as the Fulfillment of the
    Egalitarian Ideal   219
    Axel Kaiser

17 Social Justice, Public Goods, and Rent Seeking
    in Narratives   233
    Vincent J. Geloso and Phillip W. Magness

18 Is Social Justice a Mirage?   243
    Stefanie Haeffele and Virgil Henry Storr

19 Social Justice, Antiracism, and Public Policy   253
    Robert M. Whaples

    Notes   265

    Bibliography   295

    Index   327

    About the Editors and Contributors   341

    Credits   347

Foreword

The Narcissists of Compassion

Jordan Peterson

AS NICHOLAS RESCHER points out in the preface of this new volume, the demands of those crying out for what has come to be known as "social justice" are, at minimum, incoherent and contradictory—so much so that they cannot even in principle be simultaneously satisfied. This conundrum might actually be the point of such cries, although making such a claim likely means giving the devil more than his due on the strategic front (never presume intent where incompetence is sufficient explanation). Here's an example of such incoherence: the clamor for social justice is part and parcel of the broader, or at least analogous and parallel, requirement for "diversity, inclusivity, and equity." Well, diversity means difference, and the most fine-grained differences (as those who additionally push the "intersectionality" mantra explicitly claim) are those manifested at the level of the individual, whose particularized combination of race, sex, "gender," socioeconomic class, education, etc., make that individual someone often literally unique.

A unique entity, by definition, has characteristics that are not shared by any other entity; it therefore possesses valuable and potentially immutable differences. In the current and foreseeable political climate, these characteristics are to be celebrated, or else the mob-fostered shaming begins. But it is impossible to understand how those differences can be deemed important, vital, and necessary while the demand that everyone be utterly equivalent in the outcomes assigned to them is also satisfied. If we allow the claim that differences in race and sex, etc., make a signal difference in perspective and, therefore, in their potential contribution to the broadening of both opinion and skill—else why celebrate diversity—then (this is not a claim I am willing to make, but will allow for now) those differences mean nothing if they don't mean a difference in outcome. It is precisely our lack of equality—of equivalence—that makes us, in our multiplicity, valid contributors to dialogue and process by the very tenets of the social justice/DIE (as well as classical) theorists, but it is that self-same lack of equivalence that is being fought on the equity front.

This problem can of course be solved by abandoning the principle of noncontradiction—the generally assumed certainty that it is unacceptable to claim that A can also be not-A—the sine qua non of any productive dialogue, thought, or general human interaction whatsoever. But perhaps no price is too high to pay when the goal is the universal reformation of human nature in the image of the requisite ideology (and when someone else will conveniently be paying).

And this is only one of the almost innumerable faults of the social justice movement, which is neither "social" (as it demands that subjectively defined identity be regarded as paramount) nor "just" (as justice demands the just treatment of individuals, defined and considered as individuals, and not the just treatment of "groups," which can be defined and recategorized without limit, which cannot suffer or be redeemed as groups, and which have never in the history of the Western thought that has made us all somewhat free and autonomous been the central and proper target of "justice").

In his introduction co-editor Robert Whaples cites Thomas Sowell: "Envy was once considered to be one of the seven deadly sins before it became one of the most admired virtues under its new name, 'social justice.'" This strikes right to the heart of the matter, as does much of what Sowell writes and says. Years ago, the great UK essayist George Orwell noted that the typical middle-class adherent of socialism (a doctrine that in some of its versions Orwell admired) did not so much love the poor as hate the rich. It is certainly the case that the desire to ensure that all are granted everything at once and in exactly the same measure is the desire that no one will ever have anything that everyone else can't have simultaneously. It is also certainly the case that if no one can have anything for themselves (something unique and different, which is what "for themselves" means), then no one can have anything at all. And finally, that is how the hypothetical equity paraded as the sole virtue is most likely to realize itself: all become equal in possessing nothing of value. That is the great enemy of achievement and abundance and productivity and generosity manifested by Maoist China and the Leninist-Stalinist USSR (and Cambodia, North Vietnam, East Germany, Poland, Czechoslovakia, Hungary, North Korea, Cuba, Laos, Albania, and Yugoslavia. But who's counting?). Envy is most truly the issue here when all the moral posturing is stripped away; and envy masquerading in virtue is a metavice, making mere envy look almost benign by contrast.

I would say, too, that another sin, so to speak, is also driving the social justice madness of crowd—something perhaps best conceptualized as a narcissism of compassion. There is perhaps nothing more important to people than their reputation: honest, trustworthy, productive, generous people are valuable producers and social partners and are sought out precisely for that value. The fact that such people exist, however—and that their value can be stored and measured, so to speak, in units of reputation—means that an enticing opportunity opens up on the psychopathic, narcissistic, and Machiavellian front. That opportunity is the ability (conjoined with the willingness) to make attributes of temperament that have little to do with the difficult balance that true virtue requires a loudly trumpeted and insisted-upon replacement for virtue. True virtue requires the integration of (at least) discipline, responsibility, maturity, love, truth, beauty, and a willingness to sacrifice. It may also require an admixture of compassion—the genuine compassion that makes service a moral necessity. But the mere passive and reflexive act of pity—"When I gaze upon something suffering, regardless of cause, I feel bad"—by no means justifies a claim to virtue, but that feeling and the sense of virtue that perhaps automatically accompanies it can be made into a powerful weapon and used as a shortcut to reputation, and that is happening repeatedly, to the widespread and increasing detriment of general psychological health, social stability, and truly productive and genuine peace. That is the rise of the great and terrible mother, all-encompassing and all-devouring, identified by the genius of Freud as one of the most ever-present dangers facing the emerging individual, and that Jung and his school (particularly Erich Neumann, in *The Great Mother* and *The Origins and History of Consciousness*) warned about as a threat to individual and social stability and sustainability in the most detailed and explicit possible manner.

The German philosopher Friedrich Nietzsche warned us of the tyranny of self-serving pity in word and image, prophetic and dire:

> Lo, this is the tarantula's den! Wouldst thou see the tarantula itself? Here hangeth its web: touch this, so that it may tremble.

> There cometh the tarantula willingly: Welcome, tarantula! Black on thy back is thy triangle and symbol; and I know also what is in thy soul.

> Revenge is in thy soul: wherever thou bitest, there ariseth black scab; with revenge, thy poison maketh the soul giddy!

> Thus do I speak unto you in parable, ye who make the soul giddy, ye preachers of equality! Tarantulas are ye unto me, and secretly revengeful ones!

> But I will soon bring your hiding-places to the light: therefore do I laugh in your face my laughter of the height.

> Therefore do I tear at your web, that your rage may lure you out of your den of lies, and that your revenge may leap forth from behind your word "justice."

> Because, for man to be redeemed from revenge—that is for me the bridge to the highest hope, and a rainbow after long storms.

> Otherwise, however, would the tarantulas have it. "Let it be very justice for the world to become full of the storms of our vengeance"—thus do they talk to one another.

> "Vengeance will we use, and insult, against all who are not like us"—thus do the tarantula-hearts pledge themselves.

> "And 'Will to Equality'—that itself shall henceforth be the name of virtue; and against all that hath power will we raise an outcry!"

> Ye preachers of equality, the tyrant-frenzy of impotence crieth
> thus in you for "equality": your most secret tyrant-longings
> disguise themselves thus in virtue-words![1]

The authors of the present volume dissect the tarantula and lay it bare, clarifying the definition of justice, assessing the relationship between true and false justice and economics from a variety of perspectives, criticizing the postmodern "intersectional" approach to jurisprudence, analyzing the issues from within a number of traditional philosophical schema, and making a case for public policy reform.

Perhaps their work will do something to protect us all from the poisonous fangs of the narcissists of compassion.

Preface
Is Social Justice Just?
Nicholas Rescher

SOCIAL JUSTICE, LIKE motherhood, is hard to oppose. And yet motherhood too has its problems. For even as it reaches along a wide spectrum of modes ranging from tenderness to tough love, so social justice calls for both safeguarding the weak and challenging the able. The complex desiderata at issue require the coordination of many gears that often do not mesh smoothly.

We are told that social justice requires equality. But this too is a many-sided factor. There is both equality of process and equality of product, and the two are, in many circumstances, incompatible. People can be equal before the law, but the laws themselves can be unfair and inequitable.

The ideal of equality also vividly illustrates the roadblock in the way of social justice created by the unavoidable tension between process and product. There often can simply be no fully just way of allocating burdensome tasks among the members of a group that only some of them are capable of performing.

Tradition has it that justice consists in "giving everyone their due" (*suum cuique tribunes*). But what is their due and who determines this—be it law, or custom, or "the powers that be"—can be problematic because all alike can be fractious and unreasonable.

It is not that we lack definitive beliefs about social justice, but rather that we have too many of them. Social justice, we are told, calls for

- treating everyone alike (with outcome or process equality);
- treating everyone fairly in line with uniform rules of procedure;

- treating everyone justly—that is, in line with their appropriate claims; and
- treating everyone as we ourselves would ideally like to be treated.

The awkward difficulty is twofold: (1) taken collectively, these principles are incompatible: each admits of circumstances when some of its requirements are met but some of the others violated, and (2) taken individually, these principles are untenable: each of them admits of intuitively unacceptable conditions where they themselves are nevertheless satisfied.

A familiar joke has the youngster who is asked what he wants to be when he grows up respond: "rich." But many pathways to riches are tainted (robbing banks, operating Ponzi schemes, etc.), while society has need of a vast variety of contributors in more modern roles (auto mechanics, salesclerks, etc.). No effectively functioning society can position everyone into the niche they ideally desire. Even if everybody's personal aims and aspirations are well served by their doing X, the best interests and needs of the community demand more non-X-ers than X-ers.

When people insist on doing what looks to be individually optimal, they may well create a situation that is collectively unfortunate. Individual desire often conflicts with communal need. We confront the paradox of balancing what people want and what people have to do in life—the tension between what is personally desired and what is communally benign.

Collective misfortune can result when people strive too ardently for their personal desiderata. Airplane crashes have resulted when passengers crowded to one side for sightseeing. Fatal melees have resulted when theatergoers sought to escape an incipient fire. Disastrous crushes have occurred at stores opening for special-opportunity sales.

What sorts of measures can countervail against this tension between individual and social advantage? The ultimate problem is overcrowding, rooted in a situation when individuals seek to achieve a benefit for themselves that cannot be accommodated at the level of generality. In essence, the difficulty is an interlace created by supra-demand due to scarcity. And the biggest stumbling block for social justice is scarcity. There is not, and cannot be, any sort of technical fix for resolving the conundrum of justly allocating insufficiency. And the counsel to avoid scarcity provides cold comfort, for even where a scarcity of goods is absent, a scarcity of talent and time may yet prevail.

But how this can be realized in a fair and reasonable way is a social engineering paradox. The standard way to prevent niche overcrowding is by access/entry control. In general, this can best be achieved by setting up eligibility conditions, qualification standards, competency requirements, and other such limitations to niche access. And these of course must be set up in a way that is—and is perceivable as—reasonable.

A great many of the basic conceptions of political economy (democracy, for example, or equality) are also of this nature. And such concepts are bound to lead to irresolvable frustrating controversy, seeing that the conflicting ideas can be rendered coherent only by sacrificing some of them, and because this can always be achieved in different ways, no one single resolution can ever be cogently represented as rationally compelling.

The realization of such an ideal may simply prove too much to ask of a society constituted by such imperfect beings as the humans we are. The reality of it is that injustice, like many other negativities—criminality, suicide, and self-delusion—cannot be expunged from human affairs. Experience suggests various ways for its diminution, but also teaches that its elimination is a utopian pie in the sky.

Perfection may well be out of reach for us. But improvement—doing better today than yesterday and better yet tomorrow—is (or ought to be) within our grasp.

To arrive at a viable conception of social justice, we must turn from the optimizing *via positiva* to the satisficing *via negativa* of a specification along some such lines as *treating everyone in line with procedures that avoid patently unacceptable outcomes in particular cases.* Such a fallback to negativity is the apparently unavoidable price of realism.

There are theoretically two modes of *fairness*:

1. *Egalitarian fairness*: to divide benefits and burdens among people *equally*, with identical shares for each. Such fairness consists in treating everyone alike.

2. *Desertic fairness*: to divide benefits and burdens differentially in due proportion to the desert of the individual. Such fairness consists in giving everyone their appropriate shares, their "just dues."

The second of course leaves open the question of how desert is to be adjudged, whether by need or by contribution (or some combination thereof). And there is no reason to expect agreement between the two. There are also distinct modes of *social justice* according to whether the pivotal ideal of the enterprise is regarded as being a matter of one of the following:

1. *Floor-elevating justice* (minimum maximization): improving the condition of the worst-off.
2. *Safety-netting justice* (deficiency minimization): ensuring that as few as possible fall beneath the level of acceptable minimality.

It is clear that in conditions of scarcity these can disagree. Thus, suppose an economy of scarcity with only ten resource units available for distribution among five participants. Here, floor-elevating justice would call for a distribution of two units apiece. But were three to be the level of minimal sufficiency, safety-netting justice would call for allocating three units to three of the parties—thus (regrettably) leaving two in the lurch.

Consider the following situation:

> We have to deal with a group of three ailing individuals. In order to survive, they each need a dose of two medicines, A and B. One dose of each is available for distribution. However, X already has a dose of A and Y a dose of B. What, then, is the fair allocation?

Theoretically, there are nine possible distributions of two items among three recipients. And in point of abstract fairness, a random choice among them will treat everyone alike. But this conformity to Principle I will leave Principles II and III unsatisfied. The situation regarding distributive justice in an economy of insufficiency is embarrassed by the fact that egalitarian distribution may put everybody below the basic level of adequacy.

So, scarcity creates real problems for equity. But so does abundance. For the Nobel laureate Kenneth Arrow and other mathematical economists have long established that the fair accommodation of interpersonal and intercommunal preferences poses incomparable difficulties.

As one surveys this book's cornucopia of thoughtful and informative reflections on social justice, one realization becomes almost inescapable: what one is addressing here is an immensely complex issue that combines plausible desiderata so varied in scope as to become collectively unrealizable. It is, in sum, a concept that calls for having its cake and eating it too. As the book's sober deliberations indicate, social justice invokes such a varied panoply of desiderata that collectively, it winds up asking for more than can possibly be had. It is inherently so multifariously demanding as to become an overall impossibility.

The overall lesson is clear: only under very favorable conditions of supply/ need balance can all of the desiderata inherent in considerations of justice and fairness possibly be achieved.

Realistically, the circumstances are more commonly such that we are caught up in what might be called a *desideratum conflict*—a teeter-totter situation where one aspect of a positivity can be augmented only at the cost of diminishing another. In a less comparative world, we have to be prepared to confront crucial cases where the various definitions of adequacy for ideas of equality, fairness, and justice remain at the level of unrealizable ideals. We have to be prepared for dissonance and conflicts where no optimal resolution is available and only unsatisfactory arrangements are on offer.

Matters of fairness and justice are critically affected by the state of the resources available for distribution. The crucial fact for the theory of distributive justice is the achievability of fairness and justice critically depends on the nature of the prevailing economy of means.

The possible better is all too often allowed to be enemy of the achievable good. By universally asking too much of our constitutional arrangement—in refusing to settle for realizable improvements that leave open the prospect— and perhaps even the need—for yet further improvement, we immobilize ourselves in avoidable imperfections.

How is this to be done? As the book's informative deliberations indicate, great thinkers from the days of Plato and Aristotle to the present have pointed the way and illuminated the goals in ways energized by the teachings of the religious traditions of East and West alike. The thoughtful deliberations of this book and its constructive recourse to the thought of the great minds that have preceded us highlight our opportunities for progress in working toward the more rational and just social order that all of us would welcome. And even though perfectionism is one of need, improvement mercifully is not.

Introduction
New Thinking about Social Justice
Robert M. Whaples*

WE ALL HUNGER to live in a just world. Most of us work constantly, in ways great and small, to promote justice.

But what *is* justice? The classic definition—the "constant and perpetual will to render to each what is due him"[1]—is a solid foundation on which to build. But what is *social* justice? At this point, there is considerable disagreement. For many, the term *social justice* is baffling and useless, with no real meaning. Most who use it argue that social justice is the moral fairness of the *system of rules and norms* that govern society. Do these rules work so that all persons get what is due to them as human beings and as members of the community? Shifting from the will of individuals in rendering justice to the outcome of the system of rules in achieving justice can be a dangerous leap. To some, it suggests that virtually every inequality arises because the rules of the game are unfair and that the state must intervene whenever there are unequal outcomes.

The dangers of this leap are the primary focus of *Is Social Justice Just?*, whose twenty-one authors accepted an invitation to "explore, reassess, and critique the concept of social justice—relating it to ongoing debates in economics, history, philosophy, politics, public policy, religion, and the broader culture." *Is Social Justice Just?* is vital because many thinkers pondering "social justice" have reached for something great but have failed in their grasp. Because of this gap, the term *social justice* has acquired considerable baggage. For some people, it encapsulates the highest aspira-

*Robert M. Whaples is professor of economics at Wake Forest University and editor of *The Independent Review*.

tions of everything that is right, but for others it embodies their darkest fears. Progressives often venerate the term, and it animates the core of their policy prescriptions, whereas classical liberals often see it as "inimical to the classical liberal tradition," as Vincent Geloso and Phillip Magness put it in their chapter. They warn that "social justice" has been fashioned into a cudgel used by those pretending to the higher ground in their militant rent seeking. Thomas Sowell admonished that "social justice" is merely a fig leaf for wrongdoing: "Envy was once considered to be one of the seven deadly sins before it became one of the most admired virtues under its new name, 'social justice.'"[2]

Social justice is certainly a vexed topic. Has the term been so badly mangled by the conflicts over its use that it should be abandoned? Many classical liberals have become so wary of it that they think it should be avoided. Too many using the term have talked (or screamed) past each other. Can the term *social justice* be rescued?

Confronting these problems, James Otteson argues that we should care about social justice, despite all its unavoidable definitional difficulties. In "Opting Out: A Defense of Social Justice," the first chapter of part 2, "How to Do (Social) Justice Right," Otteson begins by warning that social justice implies enforcement—that "the issue concerns not just differences of opinion about how resources should be allocated, what virtue requires, what public institutions we should have, or how people should be treated. Rather, the issue is that the use of the term *social justice* ... entails either applying coercive mechanisms to enforce one view over another or endorsing punishment for incorrect behaviors or outcomes."

Otteson continues that much advocacy of social justice is compromised by its failure to distinguish between inequality arising from (1) luck or (2) "deliberate choice[s] that the relevant agents *are* entitled to make" and inequality arising from (3) choices made by people who "*are not* entitled to make" those choices (emphasis added). Social justice advocates often run these three categories together: "[S]omething of which I disapprove has happened or is the case; therefore, remedies are required. And if remedies are not voluntarily forthcoming, then 'social justice' demands it—*justice* being the preferred term not only because it connotes both gravity and certitude (even self-evidence) but also because it licenses coercive enforcement if necessary."

As an alternative to confusion and coercion masquerading as fairness, Otteson draws on the insights of Adam Smith and other classical liberals:

> Smith argues that our natural desire to better our own condition leads us to seek cooperation with others in mutually beneficial ways ... [and that] this can happen only within a "well-governed society" ... whose public institutions protect "the life and person of our neighbour," each citizen's "property and possessions," and each citizen's "personal rights, or what is due to him from the promises of others." When those three pillars of justice are protected, I am forestalled from getting what I want from others by enslaving them, stealing from them, or defrauding them. Thus, my only recourse is to make offers of voluntary cooperation, which others are free to decline if they so choose.

Otteson extols Smithian justice, which "protects others' opt-out option, which disciplines me to consider their interests, not just my own; and my own opt-out option disciplines them to consider my interests, not just theirs. ... My need for your voluntary consent requires that in order to achieve my own goals I must consider your wishes, your desires and needs, and your values and obligations and constraints and that I must therefore show you respect. My own opt-out option means you must show me respect as well. A society that protects Smithian 'justice' therefore requires and engenders mutual respect."

Otteson concludes that it is fruitful to think about social justice as requiring the removal of formal restrictions placed on any individuals or groups that limit their ability to achieve a flourishing life as they themselves understand it. He endorses a "political and economic policy that rewards people for engaging in cooperative behavior and partnerships that provide benefit and value to others as well as to themselves—and that hence punishes or disincentivizes behavior that benefits one person or group at the expense of others." He concludes that a commercial society constrained by protections of liberal negative justice encourages *both* increasing material prosperity and morally improved relations among increasingly many people.

A Consensus on Social Justice

The arguments of the remaining contributors have considerable overlap with Otteson's chapter and with each other. This is salutary because in approaching a subject as important as justice, it is imperative to begin with fundamental principles and to assess what has worked and what has failed. Synthesizing their thoughts is a daunting task because each has so much to say.

If there is a consensus among our contributors, it is that the term *social justice* can be rescued and rehabilitated only when it stands on legitimate principles—principles that recognize each person as unique, unrepeatable, worthy of dignity, and endowed with the ability and right to direct his or her own life without harming others, while also noble enough to care deeply for the well-being of others. When each person is seen as unique and worthy of dignity, humanity won't be shattered into irreconcilably fragmented groups. If social justice is seen in this light, it involves working to ensure that the norms, laws, and legislation of society free people to do what is good for themselves and good for others—not enabling some to impose their wills upon those with less power but empowering everyone to flourish. This generally means not only working through political democracy, a market economy, and the organizations of civil society (especially the family) but also removing barriers that hinder the most vulnerable and those in danger of being forgotten or left behind.

The consensus includes a somber warning: even honest attempts to involve the state in redistributing resources to bring about more socially just outcomes can and often do rapidly decay into base rent seeking, so that resources and opportunities go to those who have political sway. The progression is even more rapid when the attempts to redistribute are less honest. Such interventions often undermine a free society and the progress it brings. As an example, free college tuition for everyone may sound worthwhile and generous, but it doesn't take long to notice that the major beneficiaries would be rent-seeking college administrators and faculty members and that there might be better ways to make higher education more affordable to students with limited financial means.

The consensus also attacks unwarranted privilege. Capitalism, centered on voluntary exchange and widespread opportunity, is a pillar of true social justice, but crony capitalism is not.[3] A just system must do no harm before it can walk the extra mile.

This consensus is in stark contrast to the most destructive branches of the modern social justice movement, which envision the economy, society, and politics as zero-sum games or, worse, see society as locked into a civil war between groups of oppressors and groups of victims. They see conflict everywhere rather than cooperation. They proclaim that the rules allow only a few to thrive. This rising rancor about "social justice" sits uncomfortably beside the exceptional standards of living and improvements in health, life expectancy, education, and self-reported well-being in the modern world. Because modern markets are a positive-sum game, material standards of living are at the highest level in human history and continue to rise. Absolute poverty is disappearing. The perverse reaction has been to turn a blind eye to success, ungratefully oblivious to how fortunate we are, and complain that some other person has more. Perhaps one of the greatest injustices of human history is that we now live the high life, standing on the shoulders of those who came before us and struggled in a world marked by brutal poverty. We have escaped their ubiquitous hardship in part because of their wise decisions, and we cannot help them, yet we pretend that we are the ones struggling in an unfair, unkind world. The "social justice" movement ignores these manifest, widespread gains and insists that the modern economy is one in which only a few players win because the deck is stacked. (Tell this to the owners of Sears and General Electric, but don't expect the lucky customers of the firms that have displaced them to pay attention.)

Animating much of the symposium is an unsuccessful conversation between John Rawls in *A Theory of Justice* (1971) and Friedrich Hayek in *The Mirage of Social Justice* (1976). The authors take very seriously Hayek's conclusion that "social justice" is a misguided, incoherent notion because there is no true morality to emergent outcomes that are unintended. However, they push Hayek and themselves to go the next step and explain how to respond to the broadening of the concept of social justice from mere monetary redistribution to wider questions about underlying institutions, privilege, and societal relationships.

New Thinking on Social Justice: How to Do (Social) Justice Wrong

Part 1 of *Is Social Justice Just?* begins by considering how to do justice—or social justice if you prefer the term—*wrong*. In "Social Justice versus Western Justice," Daniel **Guerrière**, the volume's harshest critic of modern social justice ideas, argues that most proponents of social justice equate justice with equality and aim at nothing less than reforming the "consciousness" of uncompassionate, irredeemable deplorables. The discovery, protection, and promotion of the uniqueness of the person is one of the great achievements of Western civilization. The ideals of modern social justice risk throwing this achievement away by unhuman means whose outcome is massive misery. Correctly grounded ideas of justice that are rooted in the ancient Greeks, Hebrews, and Romans suggest that pluralistic democratic capitalism is a better model of social justice.

The next two chapters identify two fundamental defects of modern social justice—one tied to its theory, the other to its practice. In "Social Justice, Economics, and the Implications of Nominalism," R. Scott **Smith** shows that a key assumption of modern social justice is nominalism—the theory that only particular things exist, that there are no real universal, identical, shareable qualities. Smith argues that nominalism undermines justice and economic practice. By taking ethics as nominal, modern social justice theory reduces justice to power.

In "The Mantle of Justice," Adam G. **Martin** explains that the most fundamental pathology of modern social justice is "justice creep," which expands the range of issues over which we are supposed to feel resentment. But "justice is a blunt moral instrument. ... [W]hen dealing with complex, nuanced issues, it may consume valuable moral resources or even lead us to misdiagnose problems entirely." According to Martin, either outcome is very worrying, especially with respect to issues of poverty and economic inequality. Resentment may get people "on the streets or into the voting booth," but it doesn't "equip [them] to deal with such issues in a constructive manner. ... The mantle of justice is weighty."

Jacob T. **Levy** notes in "Social Injustice and Spontaneous Orders" that classical liberals have self-consciously moved toward an embrace of social justice in Rawls's sense and have adopted a wider range of concerns such as "identity" and "oppression." Unfortunately, Levy points out, we are surrounded by many injustices—injustices that provide grounds for legitimate complaint—that *cannot* be remedied. "Social justice" has bitten off more than it can chew. We need to prioritize the mitigation and prevention of true *injustices* in our political-moral thinking rather than continue to exceed our grasp in reaching for unobtainable "social justice."

In "Hayekian Social Justice," Kevin D. **Vallier** determines that Rawlsian social justice is too radical and unreachable. Contractarian approaches that aim to reconstruct society from scratch are untenable. We need Hayekian humility when considering social reform because of our own fallibility and the cautionary track record of social engineering from the ground up. Piecemeal, marginal reform may be more reasonable. There may be an important role for a constrained state in assisting the disadvantaged—incrementally working to maximize average well-being with a utility floor—but not a massive state whose core mission is redistribution.

Continuing the critique of Rawls, Daniel J. **D'Amico** points out that there are significant "knowledge problems from behind the veil of ignorance." The Rawlsian social justice framework implies that social outcomes are capable of being designed and strategically manipulated through democratic deliberation. However, comparative social science demonstrates a much broader swath of workable institutional types than the Rawlsian vision accommodates. D'Amico uses the case study of traditional Inuit society to discuss how there are simply too many substantial knowledge problems hiding behind the veil of ignorance.

In "To Give Each Man His Due: The Folly of Dworkin's Jurisprudence of Social Justice," William J. **Watkins** Jr. explains that in modern Western jurisprudential thought, the ideal of justice seldom exists apart from "social justice." The political system creating statutes and regulatory instruments and a legal system interpreting and molding the products of the political branches are both expected to embrace social justice. This view was popularized by Ronald Dworkin with his concept of law as integrity. Dworkin shows no hesitation in elevating unelected and unaccountable judges to the apex of the political order. He places the people, their representatives, and fundamental law under the feet of the judges. Borrowing a phrase from Frédéric Bastiat,

Watkins argues that Dworkin makes law "the tool of every kind of avarice, instead of being its check" on arbitrary power. In contrast, Roman civil law and the church's law both recognized justice as giving each man his due. Both also condemned the plunder of another's property and demanded extraordinary amounts of restitution. These principles seeped into the fabric of Western society and inform our historical reverence for the private-property order. Watkins warns that our society will give way unless we recapture ancient principles of justice honored by both the civil magistrates and the church from the classical Roman period to the Middle Ages and into the early modern period. We cannot endure ideas about social justice from men like Ronald Dworkin and still maintain a free society. We must choose and choose wisely.

Finally, starting with a simple example of two people trading, Anthony **Gill** considers a definition of social justice that appeals to many—the idea that gains from trade between a buyer and a seller will be equal—in his chapter "An Exchange Theory of Social Justice: A 'Gains from Trade under Uncertainty' Perspective." Numerous problems immediately arise, including what price(s) should hold when preferences vary, the impact of uncertainty about costs and preferences, and the dynamic nature of competition. "Notions of social justice that are rooted in a particular equitable distribution chase a ... benchmark that doesn't exist or, at least, doesn't last for long."

New Thinking on Social Justice: How to Do (Social) Justice Right

In Part 2, Otteson's chapter "Opting Out: A Defense of Social Justice" is followed by ten other chapters on how to do justice—or social justice if you prefer the term—right. The first four of these follow Otteson by focusing on the ideas of prominent philosophers and theologians. (Of course, virtually all the volume's chapters explicitly or implicitly draw heavily on the ideas of great thinkers, as well.) The final six chapters present ideas about how we can empower people to build a just society on their own and by reforming public policies.

James R. **Stoner** Jr. explains in "Civil Society and Social Justice: A Prospectus" that social justice needs to restore an Aristotelian and Thomistic anthropology without succumbing to the statist trap laid by Wilhelm Hegel.

Social justice must recognize the basic individual rights out of which civil society developed (life, liberty, property, exchange, and communication). The state, the family, and civil society need to flourish in their own realms, without the state dominating all.

In "Social Justice: Intersecting Catholicism, Citizenship, and Capitalism," John A. **Moore** argues that social justice "must encompass spiritual and civic elements that go well beyond a simple materialist response." He agrees with Michael Novak that social justice is "the capacity to organize with others to accomplish ends that benefit the whole community."[4] True social justice emerges as a bottom-up "experience that encompasses an individual's legal and social status in a society of citizens, all of whom possess rights and responsibilities, and where work is recognized as beneficial and dignified"—rather than a top-down experience where "the state rather than the individual takes responsibility for dispensing social justice." Top-down social justice "lacks a soul." It claims to have broadened the playing field in the search for justice, but it has instead only constricted the field.

Like Moore, Martin **Schlag** examines the Roman Catholic Church's social teachings, in "Social Justice or Preferential Option for the Poor?" He asks why Pope Francis speaks of the "preferential option for the poor" rather than of "social justice." The key, Schlag argues, is that Francis wants a cultural revolution that places the human person, not money, at the center. He does not believe in a top-down approach but seeks justice in the periphery, in the faithful people of God. Pope Francis understands exclusion as the source of poverty: "there is no worse material poverty ... than the poverty which prevents people from earning their bread and deprives them of the dignity of work." Schlag argues, however, that it is sad and counterproductive that this preferential option for the poor has long sailed under the flag of anticapitalism, which has led to a neglect of what businesses and corporations can do to overcome poverty and improve the economic system.

A third point of view on social justice and Christianity comes in D. Eric **Schansberg**'s "Biblical Christianity and Social Justice." Christians worship a God of justice and righteousness—who does not show favoritism and defends the poor and needy in the face of affliction and oppression. Accordingly, believers must also defend the poor, the needy, and the defenseless. Helping the poor on a voluntary basis—individually or through a body like the church—

is laudable if done well. However, Schansberg argues that "there is no biblical license to advocate the force of government to redistribute income, even to the poor." Coerced redistribution seems to violate the Eighth Commandment: "You shall not steal." Because the primary causes of poverty today are poor decisions by individuals and poor policies by their governments, Christians should educate people about the consequences of poor decisions and oppose unjust policies. Likewise, the Bible is active in condemning bribery—which effectively occurs when special interest groups use money to manipulate outcomes in political markets. Beware of government, which the Bible portrays at its best as "a necessary evil" to restrain evil.

How can people build a just society on their own, in their day-to-day interactions? In "The Myth of Social Justice," Pascal **Salin** argues the merits of *inequality*. He warns that when those in power use coercion to take resources from some people to redistribute them to others, they undermine universally held moral principles in attacking legitimate property rights. Salin points to a supreme irony: when "I sell 10 dollars of tomatoes against 10 dollars of wheat … what I buy is more valuable for me than what I am selling. What each of us seeks, in his dealings with others, is an *inequality* in subjective values. And one can achieve his own objectives, incommunicable to others, only because individuals are *not* the same, because they do not have the same scales of value" (emphasis added)—they are unequal in their capabilities, preferences, and information. Human beings derive their specificity and even their dignity from their differences. "Inequality thus means not that some are making profits at the expense of others, but, on the contrary, that they provide services to others. In this sense the inequalities are 'requested,' they are even the condition for social cooperation between people. … The obsession with equality becomes destructive of civilization and it is not surprising if the revolutions on behalf of equality led to the worst inequalities, those coming from the inequality of power."

In a similar vein, Andrew Jason **Cohen** argues that protecting consensual trade—and allowing the inequalities that come with it—is the core of social justice, even for those whose hearts "bleed" with concern for the plight of the less fortunate, in his chapter, "Bleeding Heart Libertarianism and the Social Justice or Injustice of Economic Inequality." History demonstrates that markets bring more wealth for all. Should we bemoan the possibility that markets also likely bring inequality? Cohen concludes, quoting Harry Frankfurt, that from "the point of view of morality, it is not important that everyone should have the same. What is morally important is that each should have enough." Markets have reduced absolute poverty and eliminated the attendant suffering—they often deliver more than enough. But haven't markets also been abused by the wealthy to enrich themselves at the expense of others? Yes, they have. However, this happens when rent seekers use the power of *government* to capture the economy. "Why do markets go awry?" The "main cause of markets misfiring is the perversion of law, perversion of the government."

Like Cohen, Axel **Kaiser** argues that economic science offers enough theoretical and empirical arguments to support the thesis that what is most beneficial to the less privileged of society is a system in which the means of production are private property, and in which competitive markets and limited government prevail. He sees "classical liberalism as the fulfillment of the egalitarian ideal." The greatest mistake of egalitarians has always been to believe that centralized rather than decentralized systems allow the best possible use of the knowledge scattered in society to achieve universal well-being and higher levels of meaningful equality. Egalitarians compound this mistake by relying on organized coercion in the attempt to reach their unreachable end. The moral alienation of egalitarianism consists precisely in sacrificing actual individual well-being for the sake of an aesthetic preference motivated by envy.

Individuals can work toward a just society on their own, but important public policies may need to be reformed along the way. In "Social Justice, Public Goods, and Rent Seeking in Narratives," Vincent J. **Geloso** and Phillip W. **Magness** are much more supportive of modern social justice approaches. They argue that classical liberals should be amenable to attempts to salvage part of the new social justice discourse because undeniable invisible forces at play have led to lesser outcomes for certain groups. Hindering "relational" equality is one way of erecting rent-preserving entry barriers for favored groups. Classical liberals must work to dismantle barriers to entry—formal and informal—for excluded groups. Geloso and Magness illustrate both the concept of "rent seeking in narratives" and the idea that cementing relational inequality may work against both minorities and majorities by examining racism toward black Americans in the nineteenth century and discrimination aimed at the French Canadian population of Quebec in Canada.

In "Is Social Justice a Mirage?," Stefanie **Haeffele** and Virgil Henry **Storr** tackle this question in the volume's penultimate chapter. Hayek argues that social justice "has no real meaning within the context of a free society" and that "advancing reforms based on social justice will undermine a free society and progress." He contends that the market is like "a game with rules of conduct as well as winners and losers," and that although the outcome may be unfortunate, it is not "just" or "unjust." Haeffele and Storr argue that this view ignores a major criticism from modern social justice advocates. If the referees prefer some players over others, the game is rightly considered unjust. When the socioeconomic system favors powerful market and government actors, social injustices can occur, and it is appropriate and even obligatory to consider reforms that limit favoritism.

In the final chapter, **I address** an important aspect of social justice in "Social Justice, Antiracism, and Public Policy." How can one justly combat racism? I use Ibram Kendi's (2019) influential best-seller *How to Be an Anti-racist* as a springboard. What antiracist policies can help put all groups on an equal footing? Rather than scrapping capitalism, which Kendi sees as racism's "conjoined twin," I consider a range of antiracist policies. These include reforming education, curtailing abortion, implementing a universal health care tax credit, taming police unions, eliminating restrictive zoning laws, funding a basic income guarantee or "baby bonds," ending agricultural subsidies, encouraging fracking, and forswearing corporate bailouts and crony capitalism. However, all of these policies have substantial limits, and the antiracist challenge goes well beyond government policy. To achieve the goal of seeing all people of every group as fully human, justice requires us to recognize that we have been created to love one another as children of the same God and to reject as sinful the idea that one group or one individual is superior to another.

Our authors have spent untold hours and years wrestling with ideas about the nature of social justice, looking for inspiration, and building on the ideas of modern giants such as Adam Smith, John Rawls, F. A. Hayek, and Michael Novak, as well as on the ideas of ancient thinkers from Aristotle to Jesus of Nazareth. Their chapters thus provide much light for marking out surer paths toward greater social justice.

PART I

How to Do
(Social) Justice Wrong

I

Social Justice versus Western Justice

Daniel Guerrière*

IN THE DEMOCRATIC socialist's lexicon, the term *social justice* designates what he aims to achieve: an egalitarian social, political, and economic configuration of the modern state—indeed, of humankind. In "a society deeply pervaded and structured by social oppression," he defines himself as the warrior fighting for this ideal.[1] His indictment of "capitalism" has sounded the same for more than a hundred years. About twenty years ago, the president of the American Sociological Association urged, "[S]ocial justice requires resource equity, fairness, respect for diversity, as well as the eradication of existing forms of oppression. Social justice entails a redistribution of resources from those who have unjustly gained them to those who justly deserve them, and it also means creating and ensuring the processes of truly democratic participation in decision-making. ... It seems clear that only a decisive redistribution of resources and decision-making power can ensure social justice and authentic democracy."[2] This is no small task, for every kind of social interaction is at stake: "In the end, social justice entails a restructuring of the larger social frameworks of social relations generally."[3] Indeed, the task is, in the Marxian locution, "the reform of consciousness."[4] No metric for the success of this project is evident, though the means for it is obvious: total control. This account of "social justice" is synecdochic for the democratic socialist vision as a whole, however it names itself—progressivism, American liberalism, socialism. The opponent of this vision is, of course, deplorable and irredeemable, whereas its advocate is compassionate.

---

*Daniel Guerrière is professor emeritus of philosophy at California State University at Long Beach.

A synonymous term in this lexicon is *equality*. This equality goes beyond what the ancient Greeks already articulated—formal equality, political and legal. According to this articulation, all the citizens of a polity are equal as citizens: no one is more or less a citizen than anyone else. And all citizens are equal before the law: the court shows neither deference toward the mighty nor partiality for the lowly. In contrast, though a metric is again not evident, the equality pursued by democratic socialism is general. Any inequality that is not explicitly chosen by the person is identical to dominance and subordination by others and is thus a moral outrage. Wherever the egalitarian may focus his attention at the moment, there is inequality to be found and therefore oppression to be eradicated. Wherever persons may differ—whether in social status, economic class, political power, educational attainment, sexual persuasion, race, ethnicity, gender, citizenship, maternity—there is a potential source of egalitarian passion. All the philosophers prestigious for the democratic socialist agree: though equality is unprovable, redistribution of resources into equality for all is the principal aim of government.[5] The great moral task is to reorganize all societies into regimes wherein all are "free and equal"—that is, wherein social justice prevails. The opponents of redistribution are greedy, oppressive, and even fascistic, while the proponents are compassionate.

The burden of this chapter is threefold: to refute the democratic socialist version of equality, to critique its version of justice, and to adduce a tenable sense of "social justice."

I. Refutation

It is easy to refute egalitarianism, even in its own terms. *Equality is entirely compatible with evil.* All may be free and equal—and evil. Equality by itself is no guarantee of justice or of any other virtue. Insofar as equality and social justice are identical, this argument also refutes social justice.

II. Critique

A critique is a delineation of limits. This critique aims to show how justice and equality interrelate, how far they imbricate. A critique that aims to penetrate to the foundations is philosophical, and so this critique will be. Because the concept of social justice arose in Western civilization, the strategy here will be *ressourcement*—that is, a recall of the sources of the Western practice and conception of justice so that the place of social justice or equality in it may be discerned.

III. Tenable?

A. Foundations

Western civilization inherited both the practice and the concept of justice from the ancient Greeks, the ancient Hebrews, and the Romans. For all three, human justice had been only the human alignment with cosmic justice. The preconceptual awareness of this cosmic justice is the foundation for the later concept of justice as a human endeavor.

As in all early civilizations, the Greeks recognized an all-encompassing Order, a Cosmos, a Whole, in which humanity only participates. Humankind discerned this Order prior to their differentiation of it into divinity and world, society and individual.[6] Although chaos keeps threatening to break in, the Cosmos is an order wherein all things are measured out as what and how they are. Insofar as everything keeps within its own bounds and does not trespass upon others, this Order is called, by the ancient Greeks, *dikē*, "measuring-out," "balancing-out"; it is the allotting to each its own, the apportioning, no more and no less. And insofar as the Order is the guide for human conduct, it is called, again, *dikē*, "justice," "righteousness."[7] In other civilizations, this originary Order and hence standard for human conduct come to expression in their basic words—for example, *ma'at* in Egyptian, *kittu* in Akkadian, *asha* in Avestan, *arta* in Old Persian, *'adl* in Arabic, *rita* in Sanskrit, *dao (tao)* in Chinese, *dō* in Japanese, *sydyk* in Phoenician, and *tsadaq* in Hebrew.[8] However the Order be named, discernment of it is common to humankind; likewise is the acceptance of it as the measure for man.

The Hebrews inherited the idea from their Near Eastern neighbors and developed it in a distinctive way. Gradually, as the god YHWH separated from the mere cosmos and at once disputed and finally nihilated all the other gods, the cosmic *tsadaq* became "the *tsadaq* of YHWH." The Septuagent rendered *tsadaq* as *dikaiôsynê*, whence "the righteousness/justice of YHWH."

It is YHWH who restores righteousness to the world order after its violation by man, and man may again become righteous by attunement to the laws of YHWH.[9] Paul of Tarsus adds that ordinary humans can do nothing to restore the *dikaiôsynê* of YHWH; only "the Messiah" could effect the restoration. The Latin Fathers of the Church later rendered *dikaiôsynê* as *iustitia*, "justice."

Thus, when the Greek and Hebrew traditions intersected in the Roman Empire, the Hebrew and Christian undertones of the term *dikaiôsynê* gave the quest for the Greek virtue of justice a religious resonance—a matter of ultimate concern.

Chaos—the wild and the waste, Leviathan and Hydra, monster and desolation— always threatens to return. The struggle against it is perpetual. However, if anything should indeed violate its bounds, if there should be a lapse into disorder anywhere, order will eventually prevail. This is so, too, for human action; the just fate will be measured out, necessarily though unpredictably, to anyone who violates the true order even if this fate be delayed to postorganic existence.

Every member of the sociocultural order is to act within bounds, not to grasp for more than his allotment, to allot to others whatever is proper to them. Man, in order to fulfill his destiny within the great Order, must correspond to it; he must respond to its exigencies. To do so is to live in reality, to live according to the truth, to live righteously. To refuse to do so is, in Greek, hubris (presumptuousness)—the pretense that the measure is reducible to oneself. To act disorderly is to live a lie, to enact a fantasy, to destroy one's own reality.

In the evolutionary paradigm, orderly conduct is, at the minimum, that behavior that allows the culture to maintain itself as a distinctive unit and, at best, to flourish. Every culture has a word for such behavior: *right, straight, just.*[10]

But a further distinction is apposite. For ancient man, the just and the lawful are the same; the words for the two in all languages are the same (e.g., L. *ius*, F. *droit*, G. *Recht*). It takes considerable experience and reflection to overcome this identity. Originally, the law (Gr. *nomos*) is both "the normal/customary" (its social function) and "the normative/obligatory" (its moral import). The law dictates the right (Gr. *dikaios*; L. *iustus, rectus*; F. *juste*, *droit*; G. *recht, gerecht*) conduct. The ancient Greeks were able to shatter this conceptual density. Only on condition that one can distinguish between the law and the just can one then conceive abstractly justice as a virtue.

B. Definition

Among the Greeks, it was Plato and especially Aristotle who forged the concept of justice. A collection of lectures summarizes it: the *Nicomachean Ethics*, book 5.[11] Here Aristotle, heir to the poets, dramatists, historians, and Plato, theorized the laws and the practices of the Greeks.[12] The concept that he forged became the Roman one and eventually the Western. Aristotle took for granted three civilizational achievements.

First is the domestication of the *lex talionis*, the law of retaliation ("Do unto others the wrong that they have done unto you," "Like for like," "An eye for an eye," "Get even"). Like the later Hebrews, the Greeks had already transcended this law, as witnessed in the *Oresteia* of Aeschylus. Aristotle is explicit.[13] The *lex talionis* had been the basic moral principle of ancient kinship societies and their attempt to maintain cosmic balance.

Second is the realization that "justice" is not a societal structure or condition, which is always a datum; any just or unjust social condition is an institution of the acts of individuals, hence posterior to just or unjust conduct. If no one acts justly or unjustly, there is no just or unjust social structure. Justice, as Socrates realized, is, before anything else, an interior disposition to act justly and then the just act (dramatized in the *Republic*[14]). A social, political, or economic configuration may be just or unjust only insofar as it is the deliberate consequent of voluntary behavior.

Third is the acceptance of the equality of fellow citizens of the polity. For the classical Greeks, these fellow citizens were the adult, free males of one's own clan, tribe, or polis. This equality is not, of course, an equality of ability, intelligence, temperament, ambition, attraction, interests, possessions, merit, moral worth, luck, or "life chances" in general. Indeed, everyone has relations in which he is special, transequal, to others; favoritism is universal.[15] Later, once the uniqueness of persons is recognized in Christianity, their simple equality becomes morally impossible, for the unique is precisely that which has no equal. *Uniqueness precludes equality.* Hence, persons may be equal only *with respect to* something. Persons as citizens are equal as citizens and, as such, enjoy equality under the law. Gradually, of course, this political and legal equality, through the mediation of Christianity, was extended beyond males of a certain group to others—for example, women.

Aristotle distinguishes, as does Plato, between two genera of *dikaiôsynê*: the general sense, designating the whole of human virtue, "righteousness,"[16] and the strict sense, "justice."[17] In both senses, *dikaiôsynê* concerns interactions between and among "equals"—that is, free adult males in the polity. The interaction between them and their nonequals (women, children, slaves, aliens) is governed by justice in a looser, metaphoric sense.[18]

In the strict sense, justice falls into three species:

1. dispensational, dispensive, (ad)ministrative, allocative, "distributive" (*dianemêtikon*, L. *distributiva*);[19]

2. redressive, rectificative, remedial, restorative, restitutional (*diorthô-tikon*), or amendatory, conducive to improvement, "corrective" (*epanorthôtikon*);[20] and

3. transactional, commercial, economic (*emporikon*), or "reciprocative" (*anti-peponthôtikon*).[21]

The medieval thinkers assimilated the third into the second and then called the resultant species "commutative" (L. *commutativa*). Confusion may arise but is avoidable.

The first type of justice is distributive or allocative justice.

It concerns how the social whole (the polity), represented by its stewards (statesmen), distributes or divides the benefits—possessions, control, and esteem—that depend on one's fellow men and especially on their wealth (accruing to the public treasury by taxes, tribute, tolls, gifts, or slavery). Examples of what can be allocated are safety/security/protection (the sine qua non of government, *the* public good, including the redoubt and the walls); money from the treasury for public goods (e.g., the marketplace, the temple, the roads); but especially *timês* ("honor," recognition, esteem, honorary post and the honorarium attached thereto). Because the first two kinds of benefit were obvious, the major issue was the third. Examples of honorary positions are general, architect, minister, theatrical producer, jurist, disabled veteran, priest, flutist. The major problem was, as always, "the lust for more" (*pleonexia*, insatiableness, badly rendered as "greed")—the desire of the vulgar (*phaulous*) to get as much as they can from the public treasury, regardless of desert.[22]

The statesman, through whom all the members of the polity act, is to effect the distribution/allocation *not* according to the principle of simple equality but according to merit/desert/worth (*axis*). Merit is determined according to excellence in *performance* and *contribution* to the purpose of the polity (moral excellence). "The polis is the partnership [*koinonia*] of the clans and the villages in a perfective and self-sufficient life, which, as said, is the happy and noble life; the political community [*koinonia*] must therefore be deemed to exist for the sake of noble actions. Hence, those who contribute most to an association [*koinonia*] of this kind have a greater share in it"—that is, should receive the greater reward.[23]

Hence, the definition of *distributive justice* is clear: "All agree that justice in distributions [from the common weal] must be based on desert [*axia*] of some sort. ... Justice is therefore a certain proportion/analogy [*analogia*], ... proportion being the equality of ratios, involving at least four terms."[24] The terms are, in the simplest case, the two persons between whom a comparison is made and the two shares/portions between which a comparison is made. "The ratio between the shares will be the same as the ratio between the persons."[25] What is equivalent (*isotês*) is neither the persons nor the portions but the two ratios. The dictum here is "To each according to his merit."[26]

The abstract formula for justice is the geometric proportion/analogy:

$$A:C :: B:D$$

Person A by his merit is due some degree of honor C in the same proportion as person B by his merit is due a different degree of honor D. A is to C as B is to D; the ratios between A and C and between B and D are equal. "Thus the just also involves four terms at least, and the ratio between the first pair of terms is the same as that between the second pair."[27] The general who saves the polis deserves a greater portion than the hoplite under him; the disabled veteran deserves support, whereas the lazy bum deserves shame.

This proportionate share is neither too much nor too little; it is the mean between the erroneous extremes. "The principle of distributive justice, therefore, is the conjunction of the first term of a proportion with the third and of the second with the fourth; and the just in this sense is a mean between two extremes that are disproportionate, since the proportionate is a mean, and the just is the proportionate."[28]

The second species of justice is corrective or redressive.

It concerns how one private party interacts with another regarding a single issue, whatever their status otherwise. Once the interaction is complete, one side may claim to have lost something by the action of the other, who has thereby gained something. Examples are defrauding, injuring, and slandering. The terms *gain* and *loss* come from voluntary commercial exchange but are here used analogously. Whatever is gained or lost is not necessarily the same matter (e.g., one may win office by the destruction of another's reputation). Justice here is righting the wrong, restoring "wholeness" to the victim, reestablishing the original condition, redressing a grievance. It is more than simply vengeance according to the *lex talionis*; under the law of retribution, after all, justice would be the equality of condition (e.g., two eyes equally blind).

Once a legal action is brought, the two parties are equal under the law. "The law looks only at the nature of the damage, treating the parties as equal, and merely asking whether one has done and the other has suffered injustice, whether one has inflicted and the other has sustained damage. Hence, since the unjust is here the unequal, the judge endeavors to restore equilibrium."[29] In the model case (e.g., fraud), the judge, who is "ensouled justice,"[30] takes away the wrongful gain of the one and restores it or a substitute to the other. The justice here treats the litigants as equal under the law; no one is more or less a litigant than anyone else; in other words, the judge is impartial, an umpire. This is what "fairness" means—the same rules for all. "Fairness," already recognizable by the pubertal mind, is known universally.

The embodied justice makes the two sides "equal" again. Justice is not a geometric proportion but rather an "arithmetic analogy [*analogia*]."[31] "The judge tries to make them equal by the penalty/loss that he imposes, taking away the gain."[32] The punishment is to be commensurate to the advantage (*keidos*) that the convicted had intended to gain by his wrong. A penalty is not revenge, "getting even." Justice is incremental addition and subtraction, an arithmetically analogous adjustment, in order to make both parties' new condition equivalent to the original one. This equivalence is not an equality of condition, for the original condition was a condition of difference (which the criminal sought to change). "Thus, the equal [to the original condition] occupies the middle position between the more and the less. But gain and loss are a more and a less, respectively, in opposite ways; more good and less evil are gain, and the reverse is loss. The median between them, as we saw, is the equal—which, we assert, is just. The just as a corrective is, therefore, a mean between loss and gain."[33] The relevant equality/equivalence/comparability (*ison*) here has nothing to do with distribution.

Clearly, a trial, therefore redressive justice, presupposes an allegation of injustice. Hence, a standard of justice must already be operative, governing the interrelations of one legal individual to another. Aristotle has no particular term for this sense of justice. The Christian theologians of the West gave it the name *commutativus*, "commutative." A *commutatio* is an exchange or interchange.

However, an unfortunate confusion arises here. The medievals assimilated Aristotle's third species of justice into this second one—understandably, because his third species, like this one, governs the interrelations of private parties, albeit commercial ones. They then specified a different third species of justice: so-called legal or general justice, which governs the relations of the individual to the social whole. As the opposite of distributive justice, this general justice may be called "contributive" justice. It concerns such matters as military and other public service, taxation, and loyalty. The individual must render to the whole its due.

In reverse, then, the government, acting on behalf of the whole, must not require of the individual more than that due; such a requirement would be unjust, an instance of pleonexia (e.g., confiscatory taxation). This kind of justice, proper to the governors, deserves its own name—perhaps "constraintive justice." For, those who wield governance—because they exercise legitimate power or the threat thereof—are especially dangerous to their fellow men and therefore need to be constrained. Government, like fire, is a good servant but a terrible master.

The third species of justice in Aristotle is the commercial or economic.

It concerns how traders exchange goods or services to their mutual benefit. The classical Greek took for granted that citizens and others, in seeking to live together, do not abide by the *lex talionis* but rather "repay good with good."

And it is precisely this "exchange," this mutual contribution, "that binds them together."[34] Prior to exchange, the earliest human bands, like the primates, engaged in violent competition and even warfare over scarce resources (which included the females).[35] Once the inequality of resources was accepted and the transformation of them into unequal wealth was normal, peaceful exchange could arise. "But in associations [*koinonioi*] of exchange, the just is what binds them together: reciprocity according to proportion/analogy [*analogia*], not according to equality."[36] Justice here is "reciprocal proportion/analogy [*antipeponthôs analogos*]" or proportionate/analogous reciprocity.

How is proportionate reciprocity to be determined? Well, "nothing prevents the product of one from being worth more than the product of the other," and for the exchange to take place, the products (or services) must be weighed on some scale ("equalized").[37] How much of the one product is worth how much of the other? What quality of the physician's care is worth which quantity of the shoemaker's boot? This "equivalence" is established by mutual agreement. "Thus, if analogous equivalence [*isos*] be worked out first [by the traders], and then reciprocation takes place," justice shall have occurred; "but if this is not done, the exchange is not equal, and the association does not continue."[38] If the parties agree to an exchange, they are to that extent just toward each other.

The abstract formula for analogous reciprocity is an inverse proportion. Less of a product or service worth more gets in exchange more of a product worth less. The more and less are, again, established by mutual agreement. Of course, evaluations by the traders will differ according to the different markets (supply and demand) in space and time; hence, the concretion of justice will also differ in space and time.

Given the species of justice, the place of equality in the pursuit of justice is clear. Justice is not equality of condition—which, given uniqueness, is impossible in any case. Justice is to render to each what is due to him, whether in the distributive, redressive, or commercial sense. It is to measure out according to proportion, analogy, and ratio. In distributive justice, equality contracts into the equality of ratios. In redressive justice, equality is proper to the actions of "ensouled justice" (the judge): before the trial, he grants the parties equal status to bring or to defend a case; during the trial, he is neutral between them; and after a conviction, he aims to render the victim whole again. In commercial justice, equality means the condition of mutual freedom in exchange, of which no third party may change the parameters.

Given concurrence on the definition of justice and on its concretion in law, a problem arises.[39] Norms are formally universal propositions. But persons and cases, although typical, are unique. Hence, the *spoudaios* (morally mature person) realizes that the generality of the norm has to be adjusted for particular cases. The general form of the law may become formal rigidity, and justice requires an adjustment of the formality to the particular circumstance. Plato had already articulated the problem.[40] As Aristotle says, "Law is always a general statement, yet there are cases that it is not possible to cover in a general statement. ... This does not make it a wrong law; for the error lay not in the law or the law-giver, but arises in the nature of the case."[41]

The *spoudaios* discerns the degrees of responsibility and the other variables that make the case unique and then determines how the generality has to be "corrected" in order to effect justice. "This is the essence of the equitable [*epie-ikês*]: it is a corrective of law where law is defective because of its generality."[42] Equity (*epieikeia*), then, "is justice of a special sort."[43] Aristotle theorized the Greek practice.[44] Today, however, egalitarians seize the term *equity* when they cannot make the term *equality* sound plausible.

The Aristotelian definitions became normative in the West. Cicero takes for granted that justice is "to grant to one his own [*suum cuique reddere*]."[45] Roman law, as in Justinian's collections, understood justice in this way: *suum cuique tribuere*.[46] The classical Western definition of justice is *suum cuique reddere/tribuere*, "to render/to grant to one his own." Thomas Aquinas put it, *reddere unicuique quod suum est*, "to render to each what is his."[47]

In summary, justice is the disposition *suum cuique reddere mutatis mutandis*, "to grant to each his due," with the necessary adjustments having been made. Equality is subordinate to justice and takes on concretion according to the species of justice.

C. Equality

Egalitarianism is the ideology of equality—that is, the principle that equality of condition for all would be social justice, and vice versa. The relevant condition is various, according to the ideologue's current interest.

Beyond its roles in justice, what could "equality" be? Equality is the abstract exchangeability or substitutability of one for another, the irrelevance of the difference between the one and its other, the suppression of everything that makes the one different from the other. When unique persons find that equality may serve the interests of inherently unequal persons, they may adopt the principle of equality. The egalitarian, however, deems it to be the fundamental principle of human relations and judgment. Outside the sphere of its utility, however, the principle of equality leads to absurdity: aesthetic relativism, either moral relativism or the *lex talionis*, emotional indifference, economic stasis, and a loveless life.

Human beings are each unique. To be unique is to be individual to such a degree that one is irreplaceable, unsubstitutable, nonexchangeable. Uniqueness excludes equality. The discovery, protection, and promotion of the uniqueness of the person is one of the great achievements of Western civilization.[48] Because the principle of equality abstracts from that by which one is different from another, it ignores the unique self. Therefore, any morality that takes equality as its basic guideline is not a morality for humans. The ideal of social justice as equality is unhuman, not to say inhumane.

But what about the "self-evident" truth that "all men are created equal"? How can unique persons be equal to one another? They can be equal in a *functional way*: with respect to some condition, some "third." For example, the workers may earn equivalent wages; the teams play under rules that are the same for both; the mother divides the pie equally among her children; each citizen has one vote. Unique persons may be considered in relationship to one another and reduced to an equal condition in function of one another: how one is treated is a function of how the other is treated. Equality does not rise to the level of uniqueness. In the Declaration of Independence, "all men are created equal" in the sense that all "are endowed by their Creator with certain unalienable rights," which governments are created "to secure." Men are equal *with respect to* certain rights.

The limitation of functional relations is evident. The criminal reduces his victim to a mere function of his impulse; the socialist reduces his current "oppressed class" to a mere function of his self-definition as the "liberator" of the oppressed. Functional relations may or may not subserve uniqueness.

Tenable?

The only ways in which large sectors of humankind have arrived at a rough equality of condition are the Four Horsemen of Leveling: massive mobilization warfare, transformative revolution, state collapse, and catastrophic plague. In other words, by a destruction of the fortunes of the rich.[49] Social justice—that is, general equality—is massive misery. But it is the cocaine of the democratic socialist.

Beyond arbitrary stipulation, however, can there be any tenable sense of "social justice"? Beyond vacuity, what can "social" add to "justice"? Three possibilities obtain.

First, it may mean what it did in its original provenance, Catholic "social thought" and specifically papal encyclicals.[50] Here it means the congeries of political institutions and laws that encourage social peace and, vaguely, economic welfare—but according to the principle of subsidiarity.

Second, it could mean what Plato discerned of the well-ordered polity. That polity has (three) parts: the leaders/guardians; the guardians' auxiliaries, naturally robust and energetic; and the common workers. If each does its own function well, then the whole is just (*diakaios*).[51] In complex societies, the socially just would be a regime of liberty wherein each person may develop himself as far as his finite condition will allow: the "pursuit of happiness."

Third, the term *social justice* may name the disposition and action to associate with others in civil society in order to advance the welfare of those who in the circumstances cannot by themselves achieve a welfare contributive to the welfare of the whole.[52] This association requires vigilance, discernment, judgment, prudence, initiative, trust, perseverance. It enlarges social networks but restricts politics. Its variations are indefinite: siblings organize to care for their superannuated parent; three mothers in a church cooperate to homeschool their children; the wealthy fund a municipal orchestra. There is nothing coercive about this "social justice." Tenable "social justice" is pluralistic democratic capitalism.

2

Social Justice, Economics, and the Implications of Nominalism

R. Scott Smith*

THE SOCIAL JUSTICE movement (SJM) is galvanizing attention to a number of issues, such as racism, discrimination based on sex or gender, environmental exploitation, and economic justice. In terms of the latter, one aspect that SJM proponents have targeted is disparities in the distribution of wealth, as reflected, for example, in the increasing gap between the wealthy and the poor, arguing that these disparities are due to discrimination of an immoral kind.[1] Yet, interestingly, some key philosophical assumptions behind social justice as it is advocated in the SJM have rarely been discussed, let alone assessed. These assumptions include critical theory (CT), with its commitments to materialism and historicism. In addition, CT is wed to *nominalism*, roughly the theory that only particular things exist; unlike in *realism*, in nominalism there are no universal, literally shareable qualities in reality.

With its emphasis upon justice, the SJM necessarily intersects with the field of ethics. Yet in the history of Western ethics since at least the sixteenth century there has also been a decidedly nominalist influence. Moreover, with its interest in just distributions of wealth, the SJM has major implications for economics. Yet economics also has been shaped by nominalism, at least in the way economics tries to operate as a science, for science has been deeply affected by nominalism through the Scientific Revolution.

Although it may seem to some that as a metaphysical theory nominalism may be irrelevant to the *practice* of economics and even to the recognition of injustices, nonetheless I argue that justice, economic practice, and the SJM actually presuppose a different view of what is real from nominalism. Nomi-

*R. Scott Smith is professor of ethics and Christian apologetics at Biola University.

nalism undermines justice itself and even economic practice. Thus, ironically, because of its nominalist disposition the SJM actually cannot hope to give us social justice, including in economics.

To help accomplish this task, first I survey the philosophical assumptions in the SJM, with a focus on CT and its assumed nominalism. Second, I draw connections between the SJM's appeal to justice and how justice has been understood in light of the history of Western ethics since the time of Thomas Hobbes (1588–1679). In short, ethics (and thus justice) basically has been treated nominalistically, a move that reduces justice to power, as Friedrich Nietzsche (1844–1900) foresaw. Third, I explore the importance of nominalism in economics, particularly in light of its influence upon science.

Then, fourth, I assess the impact of nominalism on social justice by examining how nominalism undermines justice. I also show how nominalism subverts economics. Thus, with its dependency upon nominalism, the SJM undercuts itself. However, I then explore a counterargument that even if my philosophical arguments are cogent, nonetheless we still can engage practically in economics and recognize injustices quite successfully. If so, then it seems my philosophical objections might be suited simply for abstract theorizing and ivory-tower disputes. As a concluding suggestion, social justice, including in economics, is not indifferent to ontology. There must be a different theory of what is real other than nominalism that can account for the reality of justice and the practice of economics, one that will constrain and shape the many cries for justice coming from the SJM.

Some Key Philosophical Assumptions of the SJM

One of the central theories informing the SJM is CT, which began in the Frankfurt School in Germany. The school brought together many German philosophers and social theorists working in the western European Marxist tradition, including Max Horkheimer (1895–1973) and Herbert Marcuse (1898–1979). CT draws upon the belief that disparities are due to immoral discrimination, usually against groups of people. To achieve social justice, these groups need to be liberated from their oppression by the powerful. SJM supporters focus on social structures and systemic evils embedded within them, which oppress people.

For Horkheimer, a CT seeks "emancipation from slavery," domination, and oppression, with the goal of liberating humans "to create a world which satisfies the[ir] needs and powers."[2] More than just a philosophical theory, CT aims to be *both* prescriptive *and* descriptive by drawing upon the social sciences and philosophy in social inquiry. Philosophy provides its contribution by organizing and defining problems from empirically gathered resources toward the objective of "decreasing domination and increasing freedom in all their forms."[3]

Like Karl Marx (1818–83), Horkheimer sees reason as historicized, which stresses the "historical situatedness of each individual consciousness as a particular moment."[4] CT is a nominalist theory, for historicism emphasizes particulars and rejects the reality of universals. As such, CT focuses on discrete, historical particulars (not abstract, universal ideas or principles), which determine cultural phenomena.

As a historicist, Horkheimer denies that we can access reality directly. We instead always work from our situated, historically located standpoints, being unable to transcend them and gain direct access to reality. Thus, all our knowledge is *aspectual*, having been drawn from contingent, limited, and particular vantage points.

Also like Marx, Horkheimer embraces materialism in ontology. Foreshadowing more contemporary arguments, he claims that "materialism requires the unification of philosophy and science."[5] In addition, Horkheimer sees individual humans as concrete particulars and not in terms of a universally common nature. Their freedom is grounded in their holistic relation to social totality and nature.[6] Humans seem to be holistically embedded in nature, as though they are nothing but material beings.

So far we have seen how CT stresses the nominalist emphasis upon particulars. Yet nominalism has some additional features that distinguish it from realism. First, I explore realism. Consider two Red Delicious apples. On a realist view, the two apples *literally share the same qualities*: both have the same nature, and both have the same red color instanced in them. Or consider two people who have the character quality of being just. On Aristotle's realist virtue ethics, they literally share the same virtue, justice, which is instanced in both of their souls. These shareable qualities are called *universals*: each one is one thing in itself, yet it can be instanced (be present) in many individuals.

So, for example, there is a quality of justice, yet this very same quality can (and should) be instanced in many people. For this reason, a universal often is called a "one-in-many." Plato's universals (the "forms") *are metaphysically abstract;* that is, they *themselves* are not located in space and time as such. Justice, redness, and "appleness" are examples of his universals. Nevertheless, they can be instanced in many particular humans or apples, respectively. Furthermore, there seem to be essential natures to universals, for there is an essence to each instance of these qualities that makes them all that kind of thing.

In contrast, nominalism denies that universals exist. Only discrete, particular qualities and things exist. Although we may use a *word* to speak of two just humans, they literally do not share the identical quality. Moreover, on nominalism, properties are not metaphysically abstract; thus, all things are located in space and time. As such, we would expect what is real to be empirically observable. Moreover, on nominalism, particular things are just *one* thing (i.e., metaphysically they are *simple*). In contrast, on realism, particular just humans are a *complex* unity of a universal (justice) and a particular (human$_1$, human$_2$) that instances the universal.

It should not surprise us, then, to see that CT also stresses nominalism in ethics. Because all knowledge is drawn from particular, socially embodied settings, and because humans are particular beings who are embedded holistically in nature and those settings, ethics, too, is socially based. It is not based on universally valid moral principles or virtues that exist objectively in themselves. There are instead many discrete actions that we group together, yet they do not share anything literally the same except perhaps a word we use for them (for example, *justice*).

This nominalist approach to ethics and thus to justice in particular is not unique to CT. Rather, it fits with a decidedly nominalist turn in Western ethics, starting at least with Hobbes and continuing through the present.

Nominalism in Ethics

Hobbes influenced the Scientific Revolution with his mechanical atomism and nominalism.[7] Given his ontology, goodness and badness need to be defined mechanistically and atomistically. For him, motions *toward* something cause our desires for it, and what causes desire in us is good. In contrast, motions *away* from something cause aversions to it in us, and so that thing is evil (chaps. 6 and 15). Yet, given his nominalism, these interests and desires are particulars to each individual. There is no universal, objectively real moral property such as justice that is applicable to all people.

Hobbes also rejected rights and justice as "inalienable," arguing instead that they are creations of the sovereign.[8] If justice were inalienable, then it would seem to be a universal and transcend our particularity. Yet, consistent with his nominalism, Hobbes's rights are human products and thus are contingent and historically located.

After Hobbes, David Hume (1711–76) rejected any literal identities between two or more things, even experiences. Moreover, for him, reason is slave of the passions; reason does not tell us what is moral or move us to action.[9] He instead treated morals as particular *sentiments*. So moral statements would seem to be just expressions of feelings. Justice, then, would not be a subject of rationality. Moreover, as a nominalist, Hume saw the sentiments and passions as highly individualistic.

Immanuel Kant (1724–1804) continued on the nominalist path, even though he thought our maxims should be *willed* to be universal for all. For him, morals command us absolutely and thus are what he called "categorical imperatives." Despite this belief, he did not embrace a form of realism. He believed "all our knowledge begins with experience," yet experience tells us only how something appears to us.[10] Further, what we experience by the senses is contingent. If so, then it seems there are no knowable, universal, necessary features to all our experiences. Because, according to Kant, all of our experiences seem to be particular, Kant, too, seems to be a nominalist.

After Kant, the utilitarians, Jeremy Bentham (1748–1832) and John Stuart Mill (1806–73), followed. Consistent with nominalism, they tried to develop their ethical theories in light of empiricism. On utilitarianism, we determine the rightness or wrongness of a particular action based on its net utility. As a result, there are no intrinsically valid moral principles or virtues; their moral status depends completely on the sum of the consequences. Further, utilitarianism has no place for universals as moral properties, for we cannot know immaterial, metaphysically abstract moral principles by the five senses. Thus, morals are not objectively real. They are just particular principles that we *treat* generally.

Historically, the next major set of moral theories that arose in the West was naturalistic. Although these theories accept the reality of natural, physical facts, they must reject any intrinsically moral facts, including any morals on a realist interpretation. Moreover, as naturalist Wilfrid Sellars claims, "a naturalist ontology must be a nominalistic ontology."[11]

Naturalists suggested many ethical options that fit with nominalism. For example, Nietzsche rejected Kant's universalizability of morals, arguing instead that our claims about reality, including ethical ones, just reflect "our artificial (though convenient) *linguistic-conceptual shorthand* for functionally unitary products, processes, and sets of relations," including identities.[12] Indeed, our appeals to universal morals actually reflect our will to power, a view that CT has adopted.

Although we may consider many different examples of naturalism, there is a pattern among them. Christine Korsgaard expresses this pattern well when she admits that because brute reality is material, there is just matter and what we *count as* good and valuable. We do this by imposing our concepts and willings upon matter.[13] Thus, morals end up being our constructs, and as such they are located in space and time and are not intrinsically moral. Thus, they are nominal.

Ethical relativism also clearly is nominalist, for it rejects any universally valid morals. Morals are just particulars, applicable to individuals or cultures if they accept them as such. Moreover, ethics done in light of the postmodern turn also reflects nominalism's emphasis on historically located particulars. For instance, Alasdair MacIntyre asserts there is no rationality or language as such. He also raises the prospect that there are rival conceptions of justice, each of which is particular to some tradition.[14] Nor is there a universal vantage point from which we can know reality directly. There are only particular standpoints from which we access and understand reality.[15]

Thus far, we have seen the nominalist emphasis in CT, which the SJM embraces, as well as the general nominalist trend in Western ethics. On these views, it seems justice is a particular moral virtue of a historically located, particular group of people. Moreover, if ethics, justice in particular, is just about how we impose our concepts upon brute reality, then it seems Nietzsche was right after all: ethics is all about our impositions of power. Now I turn to an exploration of how nominalism affects economics, which is crucial for the SJM's calls for economic justice.

Nominalism in Science and Economics

Supporters of the SJM raise many concerns about economic justice. However, in so doing, they presuppose that we can make sense of the practice of economics. To address the question of the adequacy of nominalism to preserve and account for economics, I now explore how nominalism has affected science and thus economics as it tries to operate as a science.

Before the rise of the Scientific Revolution, the Scholastics followed Aristotelianism and emphasized metaphysics, with its commitment to the reality of universals and essential natures. Owing in part to this commitment, Aristotelianism fit with a more a priori, deductive approach to science. However, in the sixteenth and seventeenth centuries the Scientific Revolution introduced several key shifts. First, natural philosophers rejected Aristotelianism, developing instead a more a posteriori, observational approach. Second, Pierre Gassendi (1592–1655), Johannes Kepler (1571–1630), and Hobbes welcomed *mechanical* philosophy, on which the universe is a large-scale machine. Third, Gassendi, Hobbes, and others adopted Greek *atomism*, according to which atoms are ultimate and the material world is constituted by them. Gassendi and Hobbes also followed in the direction of William of Ockham (1287–1347), embracing nominalism. Thus, on this family of views, atoms are particular, material things without any universals or an essence to them.

The *mechanical atomists* of the period combined these two views. They included scientists such as Galileo Galilei (1564–1642); Francis Bacon (1561–1626) and Robert Boyle (1627–91), both of whom were nominalists; and Isaac Newton (1642–1727), who was a nominalist in mathematics.[16] However, many in this era bracketed a "spiritual" world from their atomism. The spiritual could include, for instance, minds, souls, angels, and God. For Boyle, mechanical philosophy could not explain our spiritual faculties.

A further distinction arose from Galileo's and Boyle's views. Matter has only *primary* qualities, including size, shape, location, and quantity. This distinction relegated other qualities, such as colors, tastes, and odors, to being merely subjective qualities in an observer's mind. Or they could be just words we use, a move in keeping with nominalism. These *secondary* qualities, along with Aristotelian universals, would be very hard to reconcile with what mechanical atomism taught as real, a result closely fitting with nominalism.

So the new scientific methodology embraced empirical observation of concrete, particular material things, which was due in part to nominalism's influence. Today, the effects of these shifts are still being felt, with an assumed nominalism and naturalism in science.[17] Moreover, in order to maintain the prestige that has been granted to science, scientific practice must be done according to today's orthodoxy, *methodological naturalism*.[18] On that view, scientists must bracket any immaterial entities or agents and focus just on empirically observable entities, causes, and effects. Thus, methodological naturalism fits with an assumed nominalism.

It should be no surprise that insofar as economics has tried to function as a science, these influences upon science and scientific methodology should affect economics as well. For one thing, according to the received "fact–value split," whereas science gives us knowledge of facts, ethics and religion give us mere opinions. Thus, one influence upon economics is a pressure to separate itself from ethics. An example of this is the Cambridge School, which, under the influence of John Neville Keynes (1852–1949), separated economics from morality.[19] For another, the mathematical approach taken to economics by Alfred Marshall (1842–1924) contributed to its being more technical and scientific.[20]

In light of the influence of nominalism, it should not surprise us that economists often focus on empirically observable, quantifiable results, causes, and effects. Moreover, although economists may generalize their findings by how they conceive of them, nonetheless on nominalism their findings cannot be objectively existing, universal principles or laws, for then they would have essential natures, which would not fit with orthodox science and its assumed nominalism.

In this expository portion of my argument, I have tried to show how nominalism has a deep influence upon the SJM through CT and ethics. I also have explored how nominalism has shaped science and thus economics significantly. Now I turn to assess the implications of nominalism for justice and economics.

Assessing Nominalism for Justice and Economics

Nominalism and Justice

According to nominalism, there are only particular things. Indeed, particulars are metaphysically *simple*: they are just *one* thing. In contrast, universals are a one-in-many, and when universals are instanced in particulars, these particulars become *complex* entities.

Now let us consider an objection to nominalism. Because a nominalist particular (e.g., justice$_1$) is simple (it is just one thing), there cannot be distinct grounds in it for its individuation (the "1") and qualitative content (justice). Yet it seems that is how nominalists speak of properties as *particular qualities*. Because the individuator and the quality of a particular cannot be ontologically different, it seems we can eliminate either one without loss of being.

Let us apply this finding to justice. If we eliminate the individuator, then we have justice, but it seems to be a general, abstract quality, just like with universals. Alternatively, if we eliminate the quality, we are left with just an individuator, yet it individuates nothing. However, that makes no sense; we do not find bare individuators in reality. They always individuate *something*. Nevertheless, because the distinction between the individuator and the quality is not metaphysically real, but just a distinction we make by our reason, we can eliminate the quality without any loss in reality. By extension, nominalism cannot sustain *any* qualities, *including justice*.

This explanation fits with what we have seen in the development of Western, nominalist ethics. On it, ethics *has* to be something we construct. Thus, nominalism leads to what Nietzsche and others realized: that all our moral claims are just our constructs. Without any objectively real, universal standards to which to appeal, our constructs can easily reflect our will to power, which is drawn from our limited, perspectival knowledge. Coupled with actual injustices perpetrated by people in positions of power, this realization seems to lend much credence to the claims made by the SJM.

Nevertheless, nominalism has a far more devastating impact on ethics, justice in particular. Simply put, there is no room for justice to exist, even as our construct, for justice has qualities. Furthermore, on nominalism, all qualities whatsoever can be eliminated, including all other moral ones and even any qualities assigned to us as people. Therefore, there is no room for us to exist, much less as just people. Yet that implication radically undermines the SJM's objectives.

Further, if ethics is basically about power, and if on CT we are either oppressors or the oppressed, then it seems necessary that our constructs will be power moves. Unfortunately, that conclusion triggers another problem. On CT, it seems cycles of violence and rampant injustice will never end. Those who are oppressed and yet later are liberated will turn into oppressors, for there is no other option. Then those who are newly oppressed will need to be liberated, and so on, with no end to injustice and violence. Justice will be crushed.

Finally, SJM proponents realize correctly that people should embody justice and that people oppressed by injustices should be freed from them. The latter realization presupposes that people *should* be treated with dignity. However, nominalism eviscerates that moral principle of its content. Nor, according to nominalism, would there be anything about us that is worthy of moral protection; at best, that we should be treated with dignity is simply our construct. As with justice, it seems human dignity cannot be sustained on nominalism.

So nominalism undermines justice and other moral principles and qualities, along with us as moral subjects. By relying heavily on nominalism, promoters of the SJM actually undercut their entire position.

Nominalism and Economic Reasoning

What, then, are the prospects for economics on nominalism? As we might suspect, economics, too, will be undermined. Not only would there not be any economists or even people engaging in exchanges, there would also not be any observable qualities to be studied or exchanged. Moreover, as we will see, there are effects upon the very ability to reason economically.

Consider examples of reasoning in the works of Alfred Marshall and John Maynard Keynes (1883–1946). Marshall believed that economics should be understood primarily mathematically. Keynes addressed probabilistic reasoning employed by science. Concerned with how to justify the "innumerable arguments in science ... which are believed to be rational in some sense, but which are not deductively conclusive," he attempted to develop "a logical conception of probability in which probability was concerned with logical relations between propositions, the typical case being that of an argument in which the premises lend only *partial* conclusion."[21]

In addition, Marx embraced a historicist approach. Yet he rejected G. W. F. Hegel's (1770–1831) appeal to the historical development of ideas, arguing instead that history is the succession of modes of production. Drawing upon his historicism, materialism, and his observations and interpretations of capitalism in his period, Marx predicted that communism would be the final synthesis of human development.

These are but a few examples of reasoning in economics. However, now let us consider nominalism's impact on principles of reasoning themselves. Consider the principle of noncontradiction (PNC): something cannot be both p and $-p$ (not p) at the same time and in the same sense. Marx seems to presuppose the PNC in his dialectic of thesis, antithesis, and synthesis.

Now, on nominalism, one and the same PNC cannot be invoked in a discussion; there would be just PNC_1, PNC_2, PNC_3, and so on. Moreover, there would be (at best, it seems) just a series of empirically observed sensory phenomena that we *conceive of* as instances of the principle. Accordingly, PNC and other first principles would be "no longer laws of being, of reality, but only of phenomena."[22] Furthermore, because nominalism cannot sustain actual qualities in the world, then there simply would not even be p, $-p$, or even the PNC. Therefore, although Marx seems to treat his dialectical process as a universally valid one, yet on nominalism that claim cannot be sustained.

The same kinds of problems seem to repeat themselves for other principles of reasoning. Although generally inductive reasoning is a good principle to follow, nominalism seems to undermine it, including J. M. Keynes's use of it. Induction involves an inference from observed instances to predict the likelihood that the next instance shall be like the former ones. However, that inference does not seem justified on nominalism, for there would not be any qualities to compare.

Consider, too, Marshall's application of mathematics to economics, such as in his use of supply-and-demand curves. However, the very ability for one factor to influence the other depends on there being *real* qualities and features at work in a real market. Without them, there are no things upon which supply and demand can exert their influences. There would not even be any supply or demand because there would not be any products or people on nominalism taken consistently.

This discussion serves to make a general point: if nominalism is true, then our abilities to reason will be undermined, which subverts economic practice. Moreover, without any real qualities in the world to be observed, nominalism would make economics impossible. Combined with the finding that nominalism also eviscerates moral principles and virtues, including justice and respect for human dignity, this discussion indicates that nominalism thereby destroys the possibility for any kind of justice, including in economics, which undercuts SJM proponents' many claims.

So what can said in response to the assertion that a nominalist foundation weakens the SJM? To that question I now turn.

Objection: The Practical Irrelevance of Nominalism for Economic Justice

Despite the severity of these criticisms of nominalism and their implications for economics and justice, surely there remains a *practical* objection to this *principled* line of reasoning. Quite simply, because we are able to do good economic work and recognize clear cases of (in)justice, what practical difference does this assessment make? It seems the problems posed by nominalism are just the result of mere theory and metaphysical speculations that are irrelevant practically for economic justice.

By way of response, I grant that, practically speaking, we can do economic analyses and recognize clear cases of (in)justice, whether anyone ever created the theory of nominalism or not. However, these practical abilities would not be possible if nominalism were true. That realization should make us pause, for, as we have seen, social and economic justice, as advocated by SJM proponents, depends significantly on CT, the reigning view of what counts as scientific orthodoxy, as well as on contemporary ethical theories, all of which are intertwined with nominalism.

Conclusion: Implications for Social Justice

Social justice, in particular economic justice, is not indifferent to ontology. There must be a view of what is really different from nominalism that can account for the reality of justice and the practice of economics. It is beyond the scope of this chapter to make a full-blown, positive case for realism about universals,[23] so I highlight a few examples that are vital for social and, in particular, economic justice.

First, SJM advocates want others to realize that there are indeed *actual* injustices, something that anyone should be able to recognize and not merely what SJM proponents interpret as being unjust from their contingent, historically situated viewpoints. Indeed, they presuppose there is universal content to justice that makes these actions unjust. Second, SJM proponents presuppose that their concepts can be received and understood by others. Yet this good expectation presupposes that these concepts are universals. Third, realism about universals helps explain the presumed human dignity that each person should enjoy, which is presupposed in CT and the SJM.

These points offer a few suggestive lines for further inquiry into the reality of universals. Nevertheless, for a viable and sustainable case for social and even economic justice to be made, it cannot be wed to nominalism.

3

The Mantle of Justice

Adam G. Martin*

F. A. HAYEK famously argues that the concept of social justice is incoherent.[1] His argument is inseparable from his theory of spontaneous order. Spontaneous orders are distinct from planned organizations in that they lack central direction and have no coherent set of goals.[2] Individuals and individual business firms can act toward a given end. Justice applies to the conduct of these individuals and organizations. If the word *social*, when appended to *justice*, means "interpersonal," it is redundant.[3] Justice is always social in this sense. But the "catallaxy," or market order, is a process of individuals and groups who frequently have incompatible goals and motivations interacting with one another. If the word *social* refers to the outcomes of this sort of spontaneous process, *social justice* becomes meaningless.

Because economic distributions are not products of human design, they can be neither just nor unjust. Justice and injustice apply to conduct. Any given distribution of economic rewards or resources is the result of a multitude of both just and unjust actions. No one controls the distribution of rewards or resources in a market economy. So claiming that a distribution is unjust is problematic because no identifiable individual or group can be said to have caused the purportedly unjust outcome. The concept of social justice "does not belong to the category of error but to that of nonsense, like the term 'a moral stone.'"[4]

*Adam G. Martin is political economy research fellow at the Free Market Institute and assistant professor of agricultural and applied economics in the College of Agricultural Sciences and Natural Resources at Texas Tech University.

Table 1. Justice Creep

Adjective 1 *Justice*	Number of Google Scholar Citations
social justice	1,960,000
environmental justice	155,000
economic justice	105,000
global justice	75,600
racial justice	53,800
gender justice	35,300
climate justice	17,700
international justice	14,000
health justice	11,100
food justice	9,300
spatial justice	8,260
ecological justice	7,570

Note: Excludes the word *court* so as not to count articles about the International Court of Justice.

Hayek's attempt to cut the legs out from under social justice talk has spectacularly failed. Academic institutions have become centers of social justice talk through curricula and other student services. Harvard, for example, offers a graduate certificate in social justice. In reaction to some of these trends, *social justice warrior* has become a pejorative reference to activists concerned with inequality. Over time, however, social justice has come to mean more than merely fairness in economic distributions. Modern social justice talk is broader, addressing issues of race, gender, and sexuality and discussing forms of social inequality beyond distributions of wealth, income, and other resources.[5]

We might refer to this phenomenon as "justice creep": the language of justice is applied to an ever-expanding universe of moral evaluations. Table 1 reports a list of adjectives appended to the noun *justice*, each of which returns at least five thousand hits on Google Scholar.[6] The term *social justice* is still king, with more than 1.9 million hits in the scholarly literature. And a cursory examination of any of this literature makes it clear that these other justices are typically treated as species of social justice: they focus on the outcomes of social systems rather than on the justice of individual conduct. So although

Hayek's critique has failed to substantially shift scholarly opinion, if he is right, his claims are more relevant than ever.

Hayek's rejection of social justice has also received substantial pushback or qualification in recent years from friendly thinkers who (at least nominally) embrace his concept of spontaneous order. In my reading of this literature, these responses take three primary forms:

- *Planned Spontaneity*: Spontaneous orders can be created and modified intentionally and so are subject to complaints about injustice.
- *Specific Complaints*: A theory of social justice can ground complaints about particular rules within a broader system of rules.
- *Mere Semantics*: Social justice is a normative standard all its own and need not have any relation to justice as Hayek conceives of it.

This chapter explores these challenges to Hayek's argument in order to determine which are successful. Although I do provide examples, I focus on the types of claims rather than on specific texts for two main reasons. First, there are common themes across different arguments. Second, there is no apparent agreement among Hayek's friendly critics about the substance of social justice. What matters—and what makes Hayek still relevant—is that social justice concerns the outcomes of spontaneous processes. For each of these responses, I ask (1) whether the response gets Hayek's view of spontaneous order correct and (2) whether it successfully identifies a source of *injustice*. Ultimately, I defend the contemporary relevance of Hayek's arguments, in part on the grounds he endorses but also in part on Smithian grounds about the nature of justice.

Planned Spontaneity

In the preface to *The Mirage of Social Justice*, volume 2 of *Law, Legislation, and Liberty*—the very book in which Hayek mounts his full assault on social justice—Hayek states suggestively that his own thought has some affinity with that of John Rawls.[7] The Planned Spontaneity response takes this ball and runs with it. This response accepts that central planning of economic activity is undesirable or impossible or both. But the *institutions* that govern economic activity *can* be designed. Institutions include the rules that constitute markets such as property rights and contract law. Social justice is an evaluative standard for judging the design of such institutions. Do these institutions, in their current form, adhere to principles of justice?

John Tomasi articulates this view most directly. He refers to spontaneous order as a "strategy for social construction."[8] Because individual rules can be constructed, so can "*whole systems* of rules."[9] Tomasi goes so far as to claim that all political societies manifest this sort of intentionality in the design of their institutions.[10] In doing so, he attempts to fully wed Hayek to Rawls, who famously claims that "society is a cooperative venture for mutual advantage."[11] Economists typically ask whether such rules are efficient. But it is also perfectly coherent to ask whether the rules of such a venture are fair or unfair, just or unjust. Social justice is the justice of the system of rules itself.

This response misunderstands the relationship between society and state. The state is an organization—or a network of organizations—that exists within society.[12] It does not sit outside the social order, passing edicts from above. Political institutions are nested within and entangled with social, cultural, and economic institutions that influence how they operate. Hayek distinguishes bottom-up *law* from top-down *legislation* to make precisely this point.[13] To be sure, the state is a "big player" in society that often has a decisive impact. But to point out that political institutions can be designed as a way of salvaging a distributive view of social justice is to ignore that institutions always interact with other institutions as well as with ecological and psychological factors.

Society is *not*, contra Rawls, a cooperative venture. The system Rawls lays out might make sense for such a venture, but the logic he applies is that of an organization rather than an order. It resembles a worker cooperative rather than a Hayekian catallaxy. Society is an ecology of enterprises,[14] joint ventures that may be political or economic, religious or philanthropic, and that relate to each other in both competitive and cooperative ways. The state is a part of this ecology, not separate from it. It does not sit outside the social order with access to some Archimedean lever with which to implement social goals, even in an indirect fashion. The man of spontaneous system is still a man of system and makes the same error.

Specific Complaints

The Specific Complaints response tries to avoid this problem. Rather than claiming that social justice can be used to critique an entire system of institutions, it focuses on reforming particular rules or bundles of rules. Gerald Gaus articulates this sort of view. He recognizes that Hayek's critique of social justice is inseparable from his concept of spontaneous order and that such extended orders operate through the interaction of rules that have various sources.[15] Gaus argues that although the complexity of a spontaneous order creates a problem for arguments about the justice of distributions, there is less of a problem when discussing the justice of particular institutions. This view seems to be much closer to Hayek's original intention than the Planned Spontaneity response.[16]

Interaction effects between rules are complex but do not defy any prediction whatsoever.[17] This means that deliberate changes in the rules—although possibly fraught with peril—can in principle improve the functioning of a spontaneous order. These sorts of specific changes are also sometimes within the state's power. Reforms to particular rules can be pursued purposefully, and the state is a big enough player to effect many such changes. Gaus mentions social justice only in passing, but this approach could ground a promising conception of the idea: social justice is a normative criterion applied to institutions themselves. It grounds complaints against particular institutions.

"An unjust law is no law at all." This ancient motto captures the force of this response. Most hold, against some of Hayek's stronger statements, that laws themselves can be unjust. One popular view is that a law is unjust if it contradicts some higher law: natural law, human rights, or divine law. A consistently Hayekian view on law has a hard time taking these sorts of claims at face value because Hayek takes on the views of David Hume and Adam Smith in thinking that law is a product of human action.[18] If law is a creation of human beings and justice means conformity to laws, what does it mean for a law to be unjust? Hayek does passingly offer one answer to this question:

> It is sometimes said that, in addition to being general and equal, the law of the rule of law must also be just. But though there can be no doubt that, in order to be effective, it must be accepted as just by most people, it is doubtful whether we possess any other formal criteria of

justice than generality and equality—unless, that is, we can test the law for conformity with more general rules which, though perhaps unwritten, are generally accepted, once they have been formulated.[19]

An unjust law, in Hayek's view, is one that violates the principles that make for good law: equality and generality. Laws that establish legal hierarchies or discriminate between individuals can be called unjust. Maybe, then, a Hayekian could accept *social justice* as a sort of metaphor for justice in conduct, applied specifically to unjust laws. But this step might not be necessary. In the case of unjust legislation, an identifiable group of individuals has clearly acted unjustly—namely, the legislators. A clear example of such a law is the Fugitive Slave Act of 1850. I single out this act not because it is the most harmful aspect of the slave system (far from it), but because it is an obvious case of a single, specific law that caused harm. By making it easier for the institution of slavery to be upheld, this legislation—even on top of the complex of rules that made slavery possible—distinctively impeded the realization of legal equality. But in this case *injustice* is not a metaphor. The Fugitive Slave Act was unjust *simplicitur*. So what does *social* add to *justice* here? Plain old justice will do.

We can push this line of reasoning a bit further. What about a law that is spontaneous in origin rather than the result of legislation? Laws that emerge from the bottom up can also create legal hierarchies or involve discriminatory treatment. Customary legal systems often include status distinctions such as slaves and masters. The practice of slavery typically involved a body of related laws that did not have a clear legislative body as their author. Where there are no legislators, who has acted unjustly in the spontaneous creation of such laws? I posit that there is at least one identifiable group in many cases: law enforcers. Whether judges, constables, or vigilantes, those who enforce unjust laws can be said to have acted unjustly.

Even though there are many laws that propped up slave systems, altering them individually or as a bundle does not require reinventing society from the ground up. Again, it is unclear in this case what work the modifier *social* is doing. Principles of justice in conduct, combined with appeals to principles of legal equality and generality, can already cover these cases. How big can a bundle of rules get before Hayek's critique kicks back in? I do not aim to answer that question here. But clearly at some point there is no identifiable group of agents that can pull the rug out from under a bad set of rules. Because large-scale social systems are unplanned and unplannable, justice simply does not apply.

Thinking about enforcement raises the question of a more difficult case: social norms. Social norms are rules that do not have defined enforcers.[20] But norms may disadvantage some groups. As noted earlier, pointing out such norms is the growth market in the world of social justice. Who has acted unjustly in the generation of such norms? If the answer is "anyone who acts on them," then we are back to justice in conduct. But social justice advocates typically claim that the norms themselves or their distributive results are unjust. I do not claim to have a definite or satisfactory answer to this question. A Hayekian may simply bite the bullet and argue that these norms are simply not matters of justice. This assertion does *not* imply that divergent social outcomes or discriminatory norms are immune from normative evaluation and critique. Rather, it simply raises the possibility that justice may not be the right normative standard for making such claims. This leads us to the last response to Hayek.

Mere Semantics

If a social norm disadvantages some individuals through no fault of their own, perhaps we cannot identify a culprit. So what? The norm is still a bad one. This is the essence of the Mere Semantics response to Hayek. One way of rescuing the idea of social justice is to accept that it has no direct relation to justice as Hayek understands it. Social justice is simply different in kind from what Hayek thinks of as justice. That difference does not make social justice incoherent; it simply makes social justice different.

Jason Brennan provides the best example of this sort of argument, largely by omission.[21] He does not discuss the relationship between justice in action and social justice, nor does he meditate on the importance of spontaneous order for such claims. He instead argues that social justice is simply a standard by which institutions are judged. He focuses on whether institutions are justified, not whether any identifiable group has acted unjustly. He does not attempt here to square this idea with Hayek's Smithian view of justice in action. To deny the coherence of social justice so defined would thus be a definitional mistake because social justice is different in kind from justice in action. As long as institutions can be evaluated according to some normative principle, then social justice has a clear meaning.

This argument is decisive in one important way. It is perfectly coherent to think that we should judge social institutions according to their results. This is true whether they are spontaneous in origin or not. If we are willing either (1) to expand the concept of justice well beyond what Hume, Smith, and Hayek placed within it or (2) to deny that social justice is a species of justice, Hayek's argument is irrelevant. He could be right or could be wrong about the relationship between justice in conduct and social justice, but his claim has no force to anyone who does not want to ground evaluations of outcomes or institutions in his definition of justice.

Russell Hardin makes this point more explicitly when he analyzes the strategic structure of different moral problems. Hardin's goal is to examine how interactions between individually choosing agents create moral dilemmas and to assess how various institutions and norms address those dilemmas. Some moral dilemmas are defined by small-number, face-to-face interactions, whereas others come into play with large numbers of agents. When Hardin models distributive justice, he explicitly scales up his model of beneficence.[22] That is, distributive justice—concern for how well-off the disadvantaged are—is simply beneficence on a large scale. The problem that institutionalizing beneficence solves is different in kind from the problem that "justice as order" (Hayek's rules of just conduct) solves. The point is not that duties of beneficence are unimportant or should not involve institutional solutions, but only that the problems solved by distributive justice on the one hand and justice and conduct on the other are different in kind.

If social justice is different in kind from justice in conduct, why not use the language of beneficence? Or mercy? Do the semantics matter? On one level, the answer is no. In strictly academic communication, when words and phrases are carefully defined and terms of art abound, it probably does not matter whether we describe our standards for institutions in terms of justice or beneficence. The term *justice* has taken on innumerable meanings in the history of political philosophy, probably because it serves as a sort of moral trump card. We can hold people morally blameworthy for failures to be kind or to moderate their passions, but we cannot compel them to act unless it is a matter of justice.[23] To say that a problem is not a matter of justice seems to indicate that it is less important.

But social life is not an academic seminar. I want to raise two concerns with the Mere Semantics response to Hayek. First, justice creep comes at the cost of nuance in our moral language, obfuscating important distinctions between moral concerns. Second, justice talk in particular relies on and instigates resentment. These two concerns are rooted in a hypothesis: moral talk matters. It affects our understanding of both moral problems and appropriate solutions and thus exerts some influence on the quality of our social morality. This hypothesis may be incorrect—it may be that moral talk merely mirrors our underlying moral sentiments and judgments—but there are good reasons to consider it plausible. The language we use to make demands on one another or to understand our own responsibilities touches virtually all aspects of our social morality. Language is the medium through which moral praise and blame are assigned.[24] Words constitute social rules, which express which actions are permitted, forbidden, or required.[25] And language is clearly important for developing and communicating moral theories, which may modify those practices.[26]

Justice creep impoverishes our moral language. Morality is not reducible to justice, beneficence, utility, propriety, happiness, or any other singular and simplistic formula. Moral claims are heterogeneous and interact in complex ways. Moral values often complement one another, but they also sometimes conflict. Justice and mercy can butt heads. Politeness and honesty can stand opposed. Moral pluralists, virtue ethicists, moral psychologists, and even economists recognize this basic insight. Equity or efficiency: on the margin, which should we side with? It depends. The norms and strategies we deploy to deal with one moral problem are different from those that are appropriate to another problem.

My aim here is not to argue for any particular list of virtues or moral principles. Rather, it is to point out that our varied moral language grows out of varied forms of interaction. Navigating these interactions thus requires a varied moral tool kit. It is probably no accident that empirical approaches to moral inquiry tend to be pluralist.[27] Even Hardin, who defends a straightforward utilitarian view of the *foundations* of morality, recognizes that differences across social contexts make social morality *effectively* pluralistic.[28] Collapsing important distinctions between moral categories can lead us astray in a complex world.

One objection to my claim is this: social justice rhetoric is an established practice. So, by my own argument, isn't it ipso facto serving some important function? I agree that social justice rhetoric serves an important function for its practitioners, to which I return later. But Hayek's argument about social justice is in part based precisely on a rejection of this claim. As individuals, we never encounter system-level phenomena such as "capitalism" or "society."[29] These phenomena are mental reconstructions that allow us to better understand activities and information that we do have access to. Social justice talk—when it addresses system-level phenomena—is guided not by an experience of society-scale phenomena but primarily by its advocates' mental models.[30] Talk about mental models can continue for decades or even centuries despite being mistaken, especially in academia. The moral talk that Adam Smith discusses, by contrast, concerns interactions that take place in everyday life. It is adapted to navigating human interaction in a situation of tight feedback and real consequences.

Smith's keen understanding of the varieties of moral judgment underwrites my second concern:

> Resentment seems to have been given us by nature for defence, and for defence only. It is the safeguard of justice and the security of innocence. It prompts us to beat off the mischief which is attempted to be done to us, and to retaliate that which is already done, that the offender may be made to repent of his injustice, and that others, through fear of the like punishment, may be terrified from being guilty of the like offence. It must be reserved, therefore, for these purposes, nor can the spectator ever go along with it when it is exerted for any other.[31]

For Smith, justice is a virtue rooted in the emotion of resentment. It becomes a virtue when it is appropriately tempered in its degree and directed toward acts that harm others. Accusations of injustice are invitations to feel resentment. Modern evidence from experimental economics is consistent with Smith's point, which sees "altruistic punishment" as key to enforcing rules that enable cooperation.[32] More recent experiments conducted by Vernon Smith and Bart

Wilson have more explicitly tested Smith's view of moral sentiments such as resentment, finding them largely on target.[33]

Justice talk invites resentment into our moral lives. Resentment can easily blossom into feelings of anger or outright hatred. Sometimes anger is appropriate. Anger at Jim Crow laws and various rules propping up the slave trade is well placed. Smith argues that justice, rooted in resentment, is the sine qua non of civil society.[34] Society can carry on, albeit coldly, without beneficence, but it cannot function without widespread observation of rules of justice. But justice creep expands the range of issues over which we are supposed to feel resentment. It also explains why advocates of social justice sometimes treat calls for civility as a suspect form of "tone policing."[35] Civility is not an appropriate response to injustice.

The connection to our moral emotions reveals a functional reason to appeal to justice over and above its intellectual status as a moral trump card. Resentment and anger are powerful motivating forces for mobilizing collective action. This, I posit, is a plausible explanation of the power and ubiquity of justice talk. It is effective not because we directly experience large-scale social phenomena, but because it works to motivate individuals to protest, vote, and engage in other forms of collective action. This function is of course not limited to social justice talk. Justice talk is plentiful across most political ideologies. I will not take to the streets because of a perceived lack of beneficence. But I will march for justice.

Justice is a blunt moral instrument. But when dealing with complex, nuanced issues, it may consume valuable moral resources or even lead us to misdiagnose problems entirely. This is especially worrying when it comes to addressing issues of poverty and economic inequality. When social scientists examine such issues, many important causes are—compared to justice talk—rather boring. For example, Matthew Rognlie argues that trends in the changing share of capital and labor income are driven entirely by housing prices.[36] Dealing with economic inequality thus involves attention to issues such as zoning, restrictions on multifamily housing units, and the mortgage-interest tax deduction. Economists often point out that the causes and remedies for such perceived problems depend on technicalities such as the elasticity of supply or demand. It is difficult to organize a march about elasticity.

Resentment fueled by justice talk might get feet on the streets or into the voting booth, but it is not going to equip us to deal with such issues in a constructive manner.

This is not to say justice has no role in these discussions. When considering, for example, the economic disadvantages of African Americans, issues related to the criminal justice system loom large. But to load every challenge facing disadvantaged groups onto justice is to adopt a narrow moral view of complex, interrelated problems. Vincent Ostrom, meditating on a science of citizenship appropriate to self-governing, free societies, issues an important and unfortunately timely warning about this trend: "These powers [of the state] can only work with the development of a culture of inquiry in which conflict can be addressed in a problem-solving mode of inquiry rather than in a way that provokes fight sets where threats and counterthreats easily escalate into violent confrontations. Rhetoric about rage and outrage is the language of violent confrontation, which is not an appropriate prelude to inquiry and the exercise of problem-solving capabilities."[37]

Conclusion

This chapter has assayed three responses to Hayek's critique against social justice. The Planned Spontaneity response falls flat, fundamentally misunderstanding the nature of spontaneous order and the relationship between state and society. The Specific Complaints response is mostly correct and what I imagine Hayek had in mind when thinking about institutional evaluation. My only question is whether the adjective *social* adds anything to the noun *justice* in such evaluations. The Mere Semantics objection succeeds by simply bypassing Hayek's concerns. Hayek's argument against social justice can be defined away. But should it?

The mantle of justice is weighty. It should not be conferred lightly because doing so comes at a substantial cost. My argument is not that problems diagnosed under the heading of "justice" are not problems at all or that they are somehow less serious than problems of justice. Many of them are quite grave indeed. Rather, my aim has been to point out the danger of restricting our moral tool kit to justice, thus obscuring potential causes and solutions to these issues. Justice creep impoverishes our moral talk by eliminating important distinctions between moral principles and by giving pride of place to a very blunt principle at that. And in recent years justice talk has proven to be an engine of resentment and conflict. Hayek's warning is as relevant as ever.

4

Social Injustice and Spontaneous Orders

Jacob T. Levy*

Hayek's Critique and Its Legacy

IN *THE MIRAGE OF SOCIAL JUSTICE,* the second volume of *Law, Legislation, and Liberty,* F. A. Hayek developed an argument against "social justice," describing it as a "mirage," the pursuit of which would be both futile and destructive.[1] The argument was unfortunately timed. It was published a few years after John Rawls put out *A Theory of Justice* (1971) but did not engage that book in any serious way. Hayek merely commented that he thought his differences with Rawls were "more verbal than substantial."[2] Perhaps this was true, and Hayek's book-length indictment of social justice was therefore largely irrelevant to the debate about justice that came to dominate political philosophy and theory in the English-speaking world after 1971. Perhaps it was false, possibly because Hayek knew Rawls's work from the 1960s better than he knew *Theory* and did not realize how much Rawls had revised his views. In that case, Hayek *might* have had arguments that could have blunted the appeal of Rawls's account, but because he did not understand the disagreement and confront it head-on, those arguments did not enter mainstream debates.

Apart from the question of what was in Hayek's mind, there are questions here about how to interpret both Rawls and Hayek. The apparent gap between them can be narrowed by noting Hayek's long-standing if understated support for social insurance and basic income maintenance provided according to impersonal rules and by emphasizing the continuous elements in Rawls's

---

*Jacob T. Levy is Tomlinson Professor of Political Theory at McGill University.

thought from the 1960s on—namely, the identification of justice with impersonal rules identified ex ante rather than with individual outcomes ex post. But the substantive political commitments that both thought were informed by their theories remained distant.

In any case, Hayek's arguments on this question have generally been ignored in theoretical debates about justice, and when they have been subject to serious scrutiny, they have mainly been found wanting.[3] Hayek seems to have thought that the pursuit of social justice required, indeed consisted of, ex post redistribution to particular persons or interest groups, a distributive scramble of all against all. Because this appears not to be true of universal social insurance or state welfare provided according to impersonal rules of means testing and is certainly not true of Rawls's theory of "property-owning democracy" and rules of justice applied at the level of an overall institutional order, Hayek's argument has been taken to fall flat.

And, indeed, in the past decade or so classical liberal scholars self-consciously inspired by Hayek have moved toward an open *embrace* of social justice in Rawls's sense. John Tomasi pathologizes the rejection of social justice as akin to an allergic overreaction: "social justicitis."[4] In his search for a reconciliation between Rawls and Hayek, the objection to social justice is an obstacle that must be removed. Jason Brennan and Tomasi identify an emerging school of thought, "neoclassical liberalism," as the view that encompasses "classical liberalism's commitment to robust economic liberties and property rights as well as modern or 'high' liberalism's commitment to social justice."[5]

The phrase *social justice* was not in particularly widespread use during the long era of Rawlsian dominance in political philosophy, although Rawls himself occasionally used it. The terms *distributive justice* and simply *justice* were more common, which only aggravates the sense that Hayek's critique was marginal to the prominent debates. Around the same time that these Hayek-influenced scholars were embracing Rawlsian "social justice,"[6] the phrase began to find a great deal more uptake, mainly outside of political philosophy circles. "Social justice" in this sense addresses a range of topics, some of which political philosophy tends to treat under concepts such as "identity," "recognition," and "oppression."[7] Social justice in this sense remedies not poverty or maldistribution but racism, sexism, and similar phenomena that are understood as partly political, partly economic, and partly cultural. This understanding seems to leave behind not only Hayek's critique but even the latter-day Hayekians' rejection of it in favor of a more Rawlsian view. Hayek's theory thus comes to look doubly marginal, a dead end on the way to a destination that is not there anymore anyway.

I think this conclusion is the wrong one to draw, however. In this chapter, I suggest that there is something importantly true in Hayek's understanding of justice. The traditional understanding on which Hayek built is the conceptual core of the idea of justice that is easily lost sight of in contemporary political philosophy. Hayek can help us keep the rules of just conduct in mind and thereby avoid much confusion. But Hayek was wrong (and untrue to the tradition) to try to restrict the concept of justice entirely to the rules of just conduct. Indeed, his own contributions to social theory make it more difficult to rule out social justice in the way he aimed to do. The understanding of spontaneous or emergent social orders that forms such a crucial part of Hayek's intellectual legacy helps us make sense of the idea of social justice and of why the rules of just conduct have never wholly exhausted that idea. I also suggest that this understanding of social justice can capture both the Rawlsian sense of *distributive justice* that has lately been adopted by some scholars in the classical liberal tradition and the widespread vernacular sense of attention to the oppression and misrecognition. The relationship between the microlevel rules of just conduct and social justice as a normative evaluation of emergent orders unifies the two senses of the concept. I conclude with some remarks on Hayek's account of the dangers of pursuing social justice and on a possible theoretical remedy for them.

Ius and the Rules of Just Conduct

Hayek argued that justice is an inappropriate standard of evaluation for outcomes that are not planned and that the results of spontaneous or emergent processes are not in themselves either just or unjust. Justice and injustice are attributes of deliberate actions; justice consists of individual actors' observance of rules of just conduct. In Hayek's view, the use of this normative category, justice, to describe large-scale social outcomes is a superstitious anthropomorphication: imagining a blameworthy actor where there is none. The classical liberal theorist Anthony de Jasay turned the same basic idea into a more full-throated critique of Rawls and his followers, characterizing theories that view "justice as a matter of social choice rather than, as in the traditional approach, a quality of individual acts" as a category mistake, erroneously treating "justice as something else"[8]—fairness or universalizability or impartiality.

This view has its roots in the oldest and most widespread understanding of justice in the Western tradition: rendering unto each what is due him. In Plato's *Republic*, Cephalus defines justice as telling the truth and paying one's debts.[9] The paying of debts in particular is probably the paradigmatic case of a rule of just conduct, the obvious example of rendering to someone else what is due to him. It moreover has the double moral and juridical sense that characterizes justice: repayment is an obligation under the positive law, and it is so *because* the law recognizes the underlying duty. The honoring of contracts is a broader way to think about this concept of justice. Note that contracts combine truth telling with the discharge of a debtlike obligation; a breach of contract means that the promise the contract codified has turned out to be a lie.

Aristotle subsequently saw the value in joining the justice of honoring voluntary obligations under private law to the justice of respecting the prohibitions of the criminal law.[10] It is unjust to steal or kill and unjust to break a contract or repudiate a debt, and in either case the legal system will try to do justice by restoring the disrupted equilibrium through restitution, compensation, and punishment.

In the Roman tradition that came to dominate European thinking on justice, *ius* is "law" and "lawfulness," "right" and "rightfulness." Justice is a juridical and judicial virtue (and the terms are, obviously, etymologically related, as is *jurisdiction*). Just verdicts from a judge render unto each party what is rightfully due to each. To act unjustly is to commit an injury—*iniuria*, "injustice"—which calls for a judicial remedy. And when Thomas Aquinas sought to reinfuse Roman law with Greek morality, to characterize justice as paradigmatically a virtue of individual persons, as Plato and Aristotle did, the resulting hybrid was the definition of justice as *the constant and perpetual will to render to each what is due him*, to be the kind of person who will render just verdicts as a judge or who as a private person will pay one's debts and refrain from committing injuries.[11]

Adam Smith famously endorsed a version of this understanding of justice in *The Theory of Moral Sentiments*, equating justice with rules of just conduct with which one complies mainly by refraining from the kinds of injuries that are justifiably punishable:

> Mere justice is, upon most occasions, but a negative virtue, and only hinders us from hurting our neighbour. The man who barely abstains from violating either the person or the estate, or the reputation, of his neighbours, has surely very little positive merit. He fulfils, however, all the rules of what is peculiarly called justice, and does every thing which his equals can with propriety force him to do, or which they can punish him for not doing. We may often fulfil all the rules of justice by sitting still and doing nothing.[12]

As Allan Beever argues, this core meaning of justice, the commutative justice associated primarily with private law and with the horizontal obligations among private persons to render each other his or her due, has been increasingly "forgotten" and obscured in modern political philosophy.[13] Consider the strange intellectual path that led to G. A. Cohen's purported "rescuing" of justice from John Rawls.[14] Like David Hume, Rawls identifies justice as an attribute of institutions and laws suitable for coordination and coexistence under conditions of scarcity and limited altruism. But whereas Hume uses this understanding to explain the core private-law rules of just conduct, Rawls uses it to build a conception of distributive or social justice that includes limits on the permissible inequality in a society. But he does so while recognizing the link to Hume and the tradition. His conception of "justice as fairness" is explicitly a modification. He takes the legalistic normativity that characterizes property and contract law and, as he thinks, generalizes it through a contractarian thought experiment into a normativity that governs public institutions as well. We agree on the terms of a private-law contract before knowing who will later face the temptation to breach it. That fair-decision procedure becomes the core of Rawls's thought that just institutions are those that would be chosen before knowing who would be advantaged by them. (It is this impulse that Hayek rightly recognized as shared between Rawls and himself.)

But in the decades that followed, many readers came to misunderstand the principles of justice Rawls derived from the fair-decision procedure, his hypothesis that we should link justice to fairness in this way. Rawls's influence (here as elsewhere) was so great as to obscure recognition of his own ideas' history and precursors, until it was common to simply *identify* justice with fairness or with Rawls's particular principles, the limits on inequality in particular. And against that background, Cohen challenges precisely the legalism and institutionalism of Rawls's view, insisting that they turned his theory into one of mere "rules of regulation" and not *justice*.[15] If justice demands equality, then it cannot be premised on limited altruism and cannot be restricted in scope to juridical and enforceable norms. Justice demands an ethos of equality promotion in daily life. Rawls's difference principle allows inequalities if they were necessary to increase the absolute well-being of the worst-off because, for example, those whose work creates widespread economic benefits need to be compensated for it. Although this is not a traditional rule of just conduct, it is part of a theory of justice because all would agree to it in a fair-decision procedure.

Cohen breaks the link to the traditional views entirely without noticing that he has done so; justice forbids the talented from making the outrageous demand for unequally high compensation, and it demands that they put their talents to work for the betterment of all. If humans have such limited altruism that this is unworkable, so much the worse for humans, who may lack the capacity for justice. The legalism of justice, its roots in *ius*, disappears altogether. Cohen perversely moves justice back to the individual level, but not in order to reemphasize the rules of just conduct. Rather, he takes the idea of justice Rawls developed for public institutions based on a kind of metaphorical extension from *ius* and imports *them* to the level of individual morality.[16]

Cohen's work has been tremendously influential, doing a great deal to shape the research agenda of political philosophy as it begins to emerge from the decades of Rawlsian dominance. This influence makes it all the more important to reengage with Hayek and with the tradition of thinking about *ius* that he represents. Understanding Hayek's theory of justice would be valuable even for Rawlsians seeking to understand the older view to which Rawls's view remains tethered and from which Cohen's is completely detached.

Justice and Spontaneous Orders

All of that being said, the core of the idea of justice is not the *whole* idea. *The Republic* is not, after all, a book-length examination of the rightness of Cephalus's understanding of justice but rather a rejection of that view in favor of an understanding that includes the right ordering of the self and the right ordering of a polity. Alongside the commutative or corrective justice of honoring obligations between private individuals and responding to violations of them, Aristotle identified *distributive justice* as a part of the concept of justice. Persons are owed things not only by other persons but also by public institutions, and it is a matter of justice that they receive what is due to them in that sense as well: a proportionate rather than disproportionate share of the tax burden, a due measure of public honor, a due portion of political power, and due access to public places and benefits. This view is not, to be sure, the modern understanding of *re*distributive justice,[17] but neither is it reducible to the individual-level rules of just conduct, and it cannot be satisfied by Smithian inaction.

Indeed, Hayek acknowledged that there are questions of justice at stake in "shares in the services of government services, and [perhaps] for an equal share in determining what government shall do"[18]—that is, precisely the kind of access to public benefit and political power that Aristotle identified with the distributive branch of justice. (And here it is worth remembering that the account of publicly provided social insurance Hayek gestured at several times over his career indicated that the public services at stake might be substantial.) Hayek likewise characterized the rule of impartial and disinterested law as a demand of justice. These concessions are in apparent tension with the emphasis of the rest of *The Mirage of Social Justice* and, I think, have not received as much attention as they should have. Although Hayek was not explicit on the point, I think that he supposed *public* distributive justice to be reconcilable with his theory because it involves actors making decisions, decisions that can be identified as just or unjust depending on whether they are made justly or unjustly. (The evaluation of such actions includes concepts such as "impartially or partially" and, again, resembles the core contractarian impulse in Rawls's theory.) What Hayek insisted can*not* be judged against the standards of justice are outcomes that are unplanned and undecided, those that emerge in a spontaneous order such as the marketplace. It is to this exclusion that I now turn.

Around the same time that Hayek published *The Mirage of Social Justice*, Robert Nozick was arguing forcefully against treating goods or wealth as "manna from heaven," available for legitimate distribution in accordance with the distributor's theory of distributive justice. "Things come into the world already attached to people having entitlements over them"[19]—determinate, particular people. The image here is, appropriately for Nozick, Lockean. Either I have mixed my labor with the world and produced a new thing to which I have an entitlement, or I have reached voluntary contractual relationships with others (agricultural workers I have hired, perhaps) to do so on my behalf, retaining for myself the entitlement to the new good.

This cannot be, however, all there is to say about the matter, in part precisely because a market economy is a spontaneous order and, like all such orders, is very much more than an aggregation of its component microscale elements. To put it in different terms, it has been well known at least since Joseph Schumpeter that entrepreneurial innovation and technological development throw off tremendous positive externalities, creating much more wealth than the entrepreneur himself or herself will capture. Indeed, it is not uncommon to find that the key original entrepreneurs receive only a very short-lived economic reward, if indeed they receive any at all. That this should be so is an aspect of Schumpeterian creative destruction; a productivity-enhancing innovation has knock-on effects throughout an economic order in ways that cannot possibly be internalized by the innovator, no matter how dense and controlling intellectual property law becomes. The more profound and transformative an innovation, the more widely it reshapes an economy, and the *more* impossible it is to track down, monetize, and capture all of the associated benefits.

Those large economic benefits are not manna from heaven; they were brought about by human action. But they were not brought about by human design, and there are no determinate, particular people who have a powerful moral entitlement to them. I think Hayek fundamentally understood this notion but used it to emphasize the *absence of injustice* in market losses. The particular entrepreneur, investor, or worker whose incumbent line of work is wiped out by the destruction in "creative destruction" can't be said to have been injured because no particular person did the injuring. This is true enough as far as it goes, but it is no *more* true than that a growing market economy sees the creation of a great deal of wealth to which no particular actor has a decisive claim in prelegal justice to own.

I repeat: this conclusion does not mean that the proceeds of economic growth are the "manna from heaven" Nozick described. The idea that the only choices are goods that come into the world under an ownership-like kind of decisive and unique moral entitlement and "manna from heaven" is just the fallacy I mean to criticize. Nozick's view was aggregative: all stuff comes into the world under entitlement, and stuff that doesn't do so must come from some mysterious source. An emergent order is not aggregative; it is more than the *sum* of its parts even though it is made up of nothing but those parts. (A diamond is not a pile of coal dust.) This is not a mystical or holist view about social organisms; it is just a restatement of the idea of a spontaneous order Hayek did so much to develop. And I do not think he would have disagreed so far; his view was not Nozick's. He consistently thought of the economic results of market processes as *neither just nor unjust*, whereas Nozick would have had to characterize them as just if they have arisen from just ownership and just exchanges.

Now, recall that Aristotle paired what I have been identifying as the core concept of commutative justice with *corrective* justice—that is, with remedies for injustice. And consider how individual-level injustices work in a spontaneous order.

Emergent phenomena are highly sensitive to small changes in initial conditions. They are somewhat *unpredictably* so, but that does not make it impossible to understand the relationship in retrospect. In a market economy, comparative advantage and the division of labor mean that very small differences in upstream talents or skills can lead to huge downstream differences in specializations. This need not but can mean huge differences in vulnerabilities: to state violence, to private violence, to natural disasters, or simply to the destructive side of creative destruction. And the original differences in talents, skills, or capital may have been triggered by an earlier injustice. Sometimes this earlier injustice will have been one of the great historical injustices: slavery or expropriation. But sometimes it will have been something smaller and subtler: an unjust educational system that segregated on the basis of race or was more concerned with stamping out a minority's religion or language than with enhancing their capacities; an excessively restrictive intellectual-property regime that generated large rents; or, a crucial example Hayek used, a legal system with a pronounced class bias over time. Hayek suggested that "the most frequent cause" of a need for legal reform

> is probably that the development of the law has lain in the hands of members of a particular class whose traditional views made them regard as just what could not meet the more general requirements of justice. There can be no doubt that in such fields as the law on the relations between master and servant, landlord and tenant, creditor and debtor, and in modern times between organized business and its customers, the rules have been shaped largely by the views of one of the parties and their particular interests— especially where, as used to be true in the first two of the instances given, it was one of the groups concerned which almost exclusively supplied the judges.[20]

As Adam Smith put it, the class bias in traditional lawmaking was so pronounced that it could generate a very reliable rule of thumb: "When the regulation, therefore, is in support of the workman, it is always just and equitable; but it is sometimes otherwise when in favour of the masters."[21]

Hayek acknowledged the need for legal reform and for reform in the name of justice. But he did not consider the ways that the initial injustice might multiply through an economy and did not entertain the idea of rectification or correction for the attendant injustices. Once we leave behind the merely aggregative understanding of an economy, the injustices become extremely difficult to calculate, and the remedies complex to imagine. Most simply, if at some point in the past the thumb on the scales of justice in favor of employers, landlords, and creditors meant that some social groups had access to capital that could compound in their favor, and others disproportionately lived in debt that compounded to their detriment, initial injustices might have led to greatly magnified inequalities over the generations. Such compounding is admissible in considering remedies for private-law injustices; that is, the initial injustice cannot be made good years later by repaying only the initial amount.

At a larger-scale social level, the remedies may be difficult to calculate, but *there is plainly a problem of justice at stake.*

But even compounding interest is a relatively simple case. The real complexities arise through such cases as comparative advantage and the resulting concentrations of skills and human capital. Thanks to some earlier initial injustice—an unequal educational system that left excluded some and left them largely illiterate—one part of a population specialized in manual labor, where their comparative advantage lay compared to their literate neighbors. Comparative advantage works to the absolute improvement of all concerned, but only so long as there is some demand for what each group is able to produce. If technological advancement leaves the manual laboring group's specialized work close to valueless in exchange, then what? When the disadvantaged group says, "We would not have concentrated all of our human capital in this now defunct specialization if not for the initial injustice," how shall we respond?

I cannot answer the question about what to do here; advancing a positive theory of social justice is well beyond the scope of this chapter. But I think the *question* has to be understood as a question of justice. It is the core idea of corrective justice applied to the complex setting of a spontaneous order. The answer may well be "This situation is too complex to be justiceable or remediable," but that is not the same as saying, "There is no problem of justice here." It is rather only to say, "Not all injustices will be addressed." And at that point, we have left behind Hayek's world in which the outcomes of a spontaneous order cannot be attributed to any decision maker who might be judged unjust and have instead entered the world described in Judith Shklar's rejoinder that *what misfortunes and injustices to respond to* is a matter for identifiable decision makers, who might themselves be blamed for injustice.[22]

Some readers will object that a claim that is too complex to be remediable in a court of law cannot be a claim of justice because the concept of "justice" precisely means moral claims that are legitimately coercively enforceable. As with the similar concept of "right" or "rights," the legalism of *justice* as a word and a concept easily connects to the idea of legitimate enforceability. To render to others what is due them, understood as paying one's debts, is a central case of an enforceable obligation. But even if there is considerable overlap between "rendering to others what is due them" and "legitimately enforceable claims," they are not the same concept and come apart in plenty of cases. "To do someone an injustice" is a venerable way of describing a false disparagement of them and need not imply anything legally actionable or coercively reparable. It can occur in a private argument between two people, invisible to the law of defamation or customs of violent redress, such as dueling. It is a way of saying not that "you have violated an enforceable obligation" but that "you have given less credit, offered more blame or criticism, than is due." (We might recognize the intuitive appeal of Rawls's famous pairing by noting that the more current way to express the thought would be "that's unfair" or "in fairness to me or that person. ...")

To put the relationship between justice and enforceability in Adam Smith's terms,

> [W]e feel ourselves to be under a stricter obligation to act accord-
> ing to justice, than agreeably to friendship, charity, or generosity;
> that the practice of these last-mentioned virtues seems to be left in
> some measure to our own choice, but that, somehow or other, we feel
> ourselves to be in a peculiar manner tied, bound, and obliged, to the
> observation of justice. We feel, that is to say, that force may, with the
> utmost propriety, and with the approbation of all mankind, be made
> use of to constrain us to observe the rules of the one, but not to follow
> the precepts of the other.[23]

That is, the relationship of justice to enforceability is a conclusion that follows from the character of justice as a moral demand; it is not part of the *definition* of justice. An injustice that cannot be remedied is not a contradiction in terms; the human condition may well be such that we are surrounded by such injustices. But the unremedied injustice is at least a ground for legitimate *complaint*. And so it matters that we are able to recognize the amplification of initial injustices through the complex workings of an emergent order as its own kind of injustice.

Social Injustice without Individual Injustice?

The next question is whether microlevel injustices are *necessary* to be able to generate a claim of injustice against the eventual outcomes of the spontaneous order. For an example to suggest otherwise, one that will bridge the case of distributive social injustice with that of oppressive social injustice, consider Thomas Schelling's famous model of white flight as a perverse spontaneous order: "[T]he interplay of individual choices, where unorganized segregation is concerned, is a complex system with collective results that bear no close relation to individual intent."[24] On the reasonable view that it is not a violation of the rules of just conduct to sell my house and move for the sake of my own family's financial well-being, a black family moving to a previously all-white neighborhood may trigger a cascade of sales and a spiral of falling property values without attributing an injustice to the local whites. Indeed, it may do so without even individual-level racial prejudice on the part of the local whites if they believe that *other* whites suffer from such prejudice or even if they believe that other whites believe this about other whites. Certainly it does not take *much* racial prejudice to trigger the cascade that leads to persistent racial segregation, and even a population of whites whose first preference might be to live in a racially diverse neighborhood will carry out white flight to avoid their worst-case scenario of living in an overwhelmingly black neighborhood with a collapse in property values. Again, as with comparative advantage, small shifts in initial conditions (a little bit of racial prejudice or even an uncertain belief in a widespread little bit of racial prejudice) can have very large effects on the ultimate pattern.

Of course, in the real world, the ex ante existence of all-white neighborhoods was a symptom of enforced discrimination and segregation that violated any ordinary sense of justice, but the dynamic Schelling models does not depend on that fact. The white homeowners, acting individually within the boundaries of the rules of just conduct, may have been led as if by an invisible hand to the creation of a pattern that was no part of their intention: a pattern whereby black homeowners were systematically set back in their attempts to invest in rising home values, and members of a rising black middle class were shut out of the social benefits provided by middle-class neighborhoods. In the real-world case, this is a story about how injustices persist and propagate through a complex order; in the model, it is a story about how patterns of systematic disadvantage can emerge even in the absence of an initial seed of injustice. An emergent or spontaneous order can display characteristics that its component elements do not display; this is what distinguishes the spontaneous order from an aggregation. Injustice can be one of those characteristics.

Social Justice and Oppression

Consider now the term *social justice* in the sense in which it is most often used today: the remedy for or absence of *oppression*, in Iris Young's sense,[25] which is the combination of political, economic, and social disadvantage that faces those who stand outside a society's dominant understanding of full membership—women; gays and lesbians; persons with disabilities; members of disadvantaged ethnic, religious, and racial groups; and so on. Social justice so understood is characteristically concerned with *structural* disadvantages. We are now in a position to make sense of this idea: such structural disadvantages are more than the sum of individual acts. Cultures, like economies, are spontaneous and complex orders, as Hayek often emphasized with the example of language.

Under conditions of uncertainty, even a small minority of police officers committing unjust violence against members of racial minorities or a small minority of men committing sexual assault against women is enough to multiply into a pervasive sense of unease and fear that limits the opportunities and freedom of many, most, or all members of those targeted groups. Individually minor slights or expressions of stereotypes—so-called microaggressions, not one of which rises to the level of an actual *aggression* or injustice—can multiply into a pervasively exclusionary atmosphere and culture. What feels to one actor like a minor and not-unjust act—crossing the street away from an oncoming black pedestrian, stopping to leer or whistle at a passing woman—can multiply into social and cultural effects that keep members of the affected groups from being able to enjoy their distributively just access to public space.

Again, to describe the resulting patterns of social and cultural exclusion as unjust is not to immediately call for their coercive remedy. And—crucially—it is not to call for the individual actions that make up the pattern to be criminalized, the conclusion often feared by those who are most critical of this understanding of social justice. The whole pattern may exhibit an injustice that the individual actions do not exhibit, and part of the value of being able to diagnose such a pattern—say, structural racism—is the ability to understand that it is not primarily about identifying lots of individual persons as racially prejudiced. Oppression and exclusion can be emergent phenomena, and we need not read them back into the souls of the individual actors any more than we read a desire for general prosperity back into the souls of the individual actors in Adam Smith's original illustration of the invisible hand.

In the short space available here, I don't pretend to decide which theory of social justice, in either sense, is correct. I don't offer answers to the questions regarding which economic distributions or which patterns of racial and gender disadvantage are just or unjust. I aim only to show that the *questions* are legitimate and unavoidable and cannot be dismissed as a category mistake. They do not require, as Hayek supposed, a superstitious anthropomorphization of society, treating it as subject to unified and centralized decision-making. Indeed, the understanding of social orders we gain from Hayek (and from Smith before him) can help us to comprehend social injustice *better* than someone in the grip of such a superstition can.

Of Tyranny and Injustice

I conclude by returning to the fear of tyranny that runs through Hayek's critique. Believing as he did that social justice must mean trying to undo the results of impersonal processes, treating those processes just as though they were deliberate and planned actions, he saw a short path from the pursuit of social justice to the progressive subjection of human action to lawless and arbitrary state power. Although this fear is apparently misplaced when directed against social insurance policies in the world or in Rawlsian theory, it is not groundless. There are *ways* of understanding and seeking social justice that can lead to such consequences.

The best response to this worry, it seems to me, is not to abandon the idea of social justice. After all, there are ways of understanding ordinary *ius* that can lead to terrible, violent, and tyrannical consequences, too. Justice, in its traditional juridical sense, can be too harsh and exacting, calling forth the moral urge to offset it by equity or moderation. (Think of *A Merchant of Venice*.) Rather, I would suggest that we proceed as Judith Shklar recommended: prioritize *injustice* over justice in our political-moral thinking.[26] The point of viewing justice as a general normative category for thinking about social orders is not to provide a blank canvas on which utopian blueprints can be drawn, blueprints that will then tempt monomaniacal political actors to ruthlessly implement them. Rather, it is to provide a way to perceive, describe, and diagnose experiences of being wronged. This is how Adam Smith thought we learn a sense of justice: by perceiving injustices and reflecting on the wrongness of them. Working in this direction means that those who pay the price for any given remedy or program of reform do not disappear from view. Our problem is not to create the socially just society once and for all, but to perceive and, where possible, to mitigate or prevent injustices here and now, whether they be individual or social.

Acknowledgments: For valuable research assistance, I thank Emma Ebowe, Chloe Batista, Michael Church Carson, Sejeong Park, and Alex Byrne.

5

Hayekian Social Justice

Kevin D. Vallier*

DESPITE F. A. HAYEK'S apparent rejection of the very idea of
social justice, this chapter develops a theory of social justice *from entirely
Hayekian components*. Hayek recognizes two concepts of social justice—local and holistic. Local social justice identifies principles that can be used to
judge the justice of certain specific economic outcomes. Hayek rejects this
conception of social justice on the grounds that specific economic outcomes
are not created by moral agents, such that social justice judgments are a category mistake, like the idea of a "moral stone."[1] But if one understands social
justice as the principles that ought to govern the social order as a whole, as
John Rawls did,[2] then Hayek is on board. Hayek agrees with Rawls that we
cannot use contractarian principles to evaluate particular economic outcomes,
and he supports Rawls's attempt to identify the general principles that should
govern social systems.[3]

I argue that Hayek can be understood as adopting a principle of social
justice that Rawls respected but rejected—namely, the principle of restricted
utility.[4] Restricted utility combines increasing a society's average utility with
establishing a utility floor below which no one will fall. So the Hayekian
principle of social justice is this:

> Society should be governed by the system of general rules that we can
> predict will maximize average utility with a utility floor.

---

*Kevin D. Vallier is associate professor in the Department of Philosophy at Bowling
Green State University.

Hayek does not seek to restructure all of a society's rules at once, however, so Hayekian social justice does not license us to reconstruct society from the ground up. Rather, the principle is a guide for engaging in "immanent criticism" of particular rules.[5] We should improve on our present order by asking whether particular rules are ones that we can predict will maximize average utility with a floor. So the application of Hayekian restricted utility is much more limited than the application of Rawls's justice as fairness. Yet it has considerable merit as a principle for just social reform. Hayek's commitment to immanent criticism thus leads to the following principle of reform:

> Social and legal rules should be reformed by asking whether a new rule will predictably increase average utility and/or secure a utility floor for all members of the public.[6]

Restricted utility thereby provides a principled basis for feasible social improvement, which we can use to approach, but perhaps never reach, a fully socially just society.

I begin by reviewing Hayek's critique of social justice to identify the form of social justice he embraces. I examine some passages in Hayek's corpus that suggest a contractarian framework for selecting principles of justice. I then advance a Hayekian contractarian argument for restricted utility and address a tension between the principle of restricted utility and Hayek's commitment to immanent criticism. I end by examining which political and economic institutions are socially just. Hayek's arguments for liberal constitutional rights, free-market capitalism, constitutionally limited democracy, and a modest welfare state help to show that these four institutions satisfy a principle of restricted utility. Thus, Hayekian contractors should endorse them. This means that Hayekian social justice requires liberal democratic welfare-state capitalism, and we should accordingly reform social and legal rules with the aim of establishing that politicoeconomic regime.

Hayekian Social Justice

Principles of social justice, Hayek argues, are meant to evaluate particular economic outcomes as just or unjust. But evaluating outcomes as just or unjust implies that these outcomes are produced by moral agency, exercised either well or poorly. Valid principles of social justice therefore imply that we can judge, say, particular distributions of income as just or unjust *because* one or more moral agents deliberately ordained the outcome. However, if, as Hayek thought, particular economic outcomes are not deliberately produced by moral agents, but rather by spontaneous order, then particular economic outcomes cannot be evaluated as just or unjust *in principle*. Such evaluations of justice and injustice are incoherent, like evaluating a stone as moral or immoral. The notion of a "moral stone" is absurd because a stone can be neither moral nor immoral.[7]

Let's assume for the rest of the chapter that this critique of social justice succeeds. Interestingly, even if the critique succeeds, Hayek allows that we can morally evaluate the justice of rules that govern society as a whole. As John Tomasi notes, Hayek thinks "[a] commitment to the ideal of a free society as a spontaneous order is compatible with the affirmation of some external standard of *holistic* evaluation, including a standard that expresses distributional concerns."[8] To illustrate, consider Hayek's assessment of Rawls's approach to identifying principles of justice:

> [T]here *unquestionably* … exists a genuine problem of justice in connection with the deliberate design of political institutions. … I have no basic quarrel with an author who … acknowledges that the task of selecting specific systems or distributions of desired things as just must be "abandoned as mistaken in principle, and it is, in any case, not capable of a definite answer. Rather, the principles of justice define the crucial constraints which institutions and joint activities must satisfy if persons engaging in them are to have no complaints against them. If these constraints are satisfied, the resulting distribution, whatever it is, may be accepted as just (or at least as not unjust)." This is more or less what I have been trying to argue.[9]

Hayek is explicit that we can make justice judgments about the rules governing the system as a whole. That is *unquestionable*. My aim here, then, is to develop a Hayekian conception of holistic social justice rather than *particularistic* social justice.

I should caution that Hayek rejects the Rawlsian approach to deliberately designing political institutions, as discussed later in this chapter. Holistic social justice furnishes a method of improving the rules of social systems piece by piece, but it is social justice all the same.[10]

Hayek's Contractarianism

In this section, I explain Hayek's contractarian basis for adopting a principle of holistic social justice. Hayek is not a utilitarian or even a consequentialist. In fact, he rejects consequentialisms because he rejects any demand for justification where "our morality is justified just to the extent, say, that it is directed toward the production of, or striving after, some specific goal such as happiness."[11] Gerald Gaus argues that, for Hayek, utilitarianism manifests "a constructivist delusion that we can have adequate knowledge of the overall consequences of our actions and so can design systems to optimize good consequences."[12] So if we are trying to determine which moral theory Hayek can use to formulate a principle of social justice, we cannot appeal to utilitarianism as the most fundamental criterion of normative evaluation.

Hayek adopts a variant of Kantian contractarianism in *The Mirage of Social Justice*, despite the fact that in *The Constitution of Liberty* he criticizes the social contract tradition as rationalistic, claiming that civil society was not "formed by some wise original legislator or an original 'social contract.'"[13] Contractarian approaches do not have to construct society from scratch based on an original agreement; they can instead be used to evaluate rules piecemeal. And this is what we see in Hayek. He claims that legal rules are legitimate when they "command general assent."[14] They must survive Immanuel Kant's test, which we employ by "asking whether we can 'want' or 'will' that such a rule be generally applied."[15] Hayek thought that consistently applying the test of Kantian assent will "amount to a test of compatibility [of a rule] with the whole system of accepted rules," so Kantian contractarianism furnishes the best test for aligning social rules with each other and organizing them into a hierarchy.[16]

Robert Sugden has argued that Hayek is a contractarian based on several passages in *The Mirage of Social Justice* where Hayek emphasizes the moral importance of agreement.[17] For instance, Hayek points out that although in the Great Society people "do not know each other" and so have "no agreement on the relative importance of their respective ends," they can agree "on means which are capable of serving a great variety of purposes and which each hopes will assist him in the pursuit of his own purposes."[18] Similarly, he stresses that people can agree to use "multi-purpose instruments" to assist each other in pursuing their own ends.[19] He sells liberal institutions as a basis for agreement and mutual benefit but rarely claims that we should have certain institutions because they maximize some aggregate good. This is the language of contractarianism, not of utilitarianism.[20]

Hayek never fleshes out the details of his Kantian contractarianism. It does appear, however, that he thinks the social contract is formulated from behind a modest veil of ignorance that, following Rawls, denies contractors information that would lead them to adopt biased or socially inefficient arrangements. However, according to Hayek, the veil of ignorance is not imposed as a moral constraint, as it is according to Rawls, but by the fact that we cannot predict the outcomes of the rules we choose and so cannot bias them in our favor. In choosing holistic social systems, we cannot predict what "the share of each will be,"[21] which means that we should generally seek to increase the share of wealth and liberty available to each. And, again, we should select rules as though we "knew that our initial position in it would be decided purely by chance."[22] In this way, Hayek's view better resembles the veil-of-ignorance device adopted by James Buchanan and Gordon Tullock.[23]

The best objection to interpreting Hayek as a contractarian is that contractarianism requires that we select entire social systems based on a comparison of their overall results and then have contractors agree to abide by the rules of the social systems that have the best results. But Hayek says that such comparisons are generally impossible. It is for this reason I believe he developed the standard of evaluation that he calls "immanent criticism"[24]: "The test by which we can judge the appropriateness of a particular rule will always be some other rule which for the purposes on hand we regard as unquestioned."[25] We evaluate social and legal rules by taking some rules as given and looking for ways to improve others piecemeal. Hayek illustrates the concept of "immanent criticism" by appealing to judicial reasoning, which aims to make the common law coherent through metarules governing judicial decision making. Common-law judges do not legislate from scratch but rather modify and improve existing practices through a method of gradual reform.

Hayek motivates the need for immanent criticism as follows:

> The effects of any person's action will depend on the various rules which govern the actions of his fellows. The "consequences of one's actions" are not simply a physical fact independent of the rules prevailing in a given society, but depend very largely on the rules which the other members of society obey; and even where it is possible for one to discover a new rule which, if generally adopted, might be more beneficial for all, the rules which the others in fact follow must be among the data from which he will have to derive his belief in the more beneficial character of the new rules which he proposes.[26]

We face general informational limitations in predicting the consequences of general rules. We must therefore evaluate them by how well they fit with other rules in the system that we take as fixed in the course of evaluation.

The Principle of Restricted Utility

It seems as though Hayek selects principles of holistic social justice through a Kantian contractarian procedure for immanent criticism. On this basis, perhaps we can determine which principle of holistic social justice he adopts or at least might have adopted. It is clear enough that Hayek thinks social justice involves doing all we can to increase the chances of a person selected at random, but there is some evidence that he would conjoin that imperative with providing a floor below which no one can fall. This suggests he accepts what Rawls calls the "principle of restricted utility," where average resources are maximized subject to a floor.[27] Let's review the passages in Hayek's work that support my claim. First, he argues that "[a] policy of using the spontaneously ordering forces therefore cannot aim at a known maximum of particular results, but must aim at increasing, for any person picked out at random, the prospects that the overall effect of all changes required by that order will be to increase his chances of attaining his ends."[28] Here Hayek says that policy should not and cannot aim at a *known* maximum but should still increase as much as possible each person's prospects in achieving his or her ends. We should evaluate rules by their utility, but carefully and incrementally toward an unknown maximum. Second, when Hayek speaks of choosing a person at random, he is arguably advocating that we increase *average* utility because random selection should sample representative persons over time. "[T]he rules of just conduct can affect only the chances of success of the efforts of men, the aim in altering and developing them should be to improve as much as possible the chances of anyone selected at random."[29] Here Hayek says that *justice* requires greatly improving, if not maximizing, the chances of a person selected at random. That sounds a great deal like an average-utility principle extended over time. Hayek also seems to think that we establish fairness by focusing on a person selected at random. The system of rules in this case cannot be rigged because "it must be unknown who will benefit by such an abstract rule and how much different persons will benefit."[30] Hayek even says that we will achieve "the best results if we abide by a rule which, if consistently applied, is likely to increase everyone's chances" by encouraging people to follow rules of conduct so "as to make as large as possible the aggregate product of which they will get an unpredicted share."[31]

In the latter passage, Hayek speaks of maximizing an aggregate product, which makes him look as if he is utilitarian *and* as if he is claiming that we know what a maximum aggregate looks like and how to achieve it. But, as we have seen, utilitarianism is not the moral theory most consistent with Hayek's thought; contractarianism is. Further, given that the limitations of our cognition is a central theme in Hayek's work, he does not think we are in a position to realize the utilitarian principle, nor can we know how to maximize aggregate utility, nor do we know what society would look like if we did. Hayek thinks instead that the rules of justice are those that our best social science tells us will tend to increase the life prospects of society as a whole, where the selection of a random person is a proxy for average utility. The aggregate is not foreordained or foreknown but rather discovered and approached gradually over time.

The principle of restricted utility includes average utility *and* a floor. Although Hayek says much less about the floor than about average utility, he seems to embrace a floor in his argument for a basic minimum income. Here is a central passage: "[T]he assurance of a certain minimum income for everyone, or a sort of floor below which nobody need fall even when he is unable to provide for himself, appears not only to be a wholly legitimate protection against a risk common to all, but a necessary part of the Great

Society in which the individual no longer has specific claims on the members of the particular small group into which he was born."[32] Hayek's use of the term *legitimacy* is imprecise and may only somewhat overlap with the use of the term in contemporary political philosophy,[33] but it looks as though he is saying that welfare-state measures are legitimate in the sense that governments are morally permitted, if not morally required, to pursue those measures to maintain a free society. We should pursue poverty relief not only because it is beneficial and welfare increasing but also because it is just. Thus, it looks as though Hayek thinks we commit injustice if we maximize average utility but ignore those whose prospects are poor. He thinks that a minimum income may be a *necessary* part of the Great Society because it helps to achieve basic minimum of ends satisfaction through poverty reduction. A minimum income also helps to secure something like equality of opportunity, which we can infer from Hayek's claim that persons should not have to depend on their small group for social advantage. So, again, Hayekian social justice seems to include some kind of minimum-utility floor below which no one should fall.

The restricted-utility principle raises a puzzle about how to trade off maximizing average utility and maintaining a floor when the two priorities conflict. Hayek never addressed this question in print, as far as I know, probably because he thought that a free society satisfies both parts of the principle.

Restricted Utility as Immanent Criticism of an Evolved Order

My proposal in this chapter is that Hayek in effect offers a contractarian argument that restricted utility is the prime principle of holistic social justice. But my proposal reveals a puzzle in Hayek's thought. Hayek both endorses holistic social justice and insists that we review particular parts of our social order through *immanent* criticism. But how can we use a standard of immanent criticism to evaluate a social system as a whole? And how do we use a holistic principle to evaluate and improve particular social rules? The holistic principle requires that we evaluate the system as a whole, whereas immanent criticism requires evaluating particular rules.

Here is one way to resolve the tension. When someone calls a particular social rule into question, we can evaluate that rule according to whether it *contributes* to maximizing average utility or to maintaining a utility floor or to both. We do not have to assess the whole social system's average utility or its provision of a utility floor. We can instead assess particular rules by their social scientifically predicted impact on restricted utility. That determination is going to be very difficult in some cases, but we can nonetheless experiment with new rules to figure out how to make improvements. Hayek does think, however, that we can make rough estimates of the effects of modest social reform, even given our cognitive limitations. Thus, if the change has surprising negative effects that we can identify, further reform is called for. Restricted utility thereby serves as a standard of immanent criticism. This approach is better than adopting no principle of social justice, which would effectively abandon the development of any principled basis for evaluating social and legal rules. Thus, contractors should adopt restricted utility as the foundation of immanent criticism.

Liberal Democratic Welfare-State Capitalism Is Socially Just

Now we must determine which institutions realize Hayekian social justice. In this section, I review Hayek's preferred political and economic institutions and explain why contractors might embrace those institutions after they use a principle of restricted utility to evaluate them. We will see that Hayek's familiar arguments for liberal constitutional rights, free-market capitalism, constitutional democracy, and a modest welfare state explain how these institutions satisfy the restricted-utility principle. The generic rationale is that these four institutional forms help people use their knowledge to satisfy each other's ends and make new discoveries about how to live together. Each of us alone is too ignorant of the many factors "on which the achievement of our ends and welfare depends."[34] As a consequence, our institutions should encourage each person to "make the fullest use of his knowledge, especially of his concrete and often unique knowledge of the particular circumstances of time and place."[35]

Liberal Constitutional Rights. Hayek was first and foremost a liberal committed to a constitutionally limited government that respected basic negative liberties in accord with general rules that apply equally to all.[36] We must keep coercive power in check by defining a protecting private sphere of individual activity and limiting state power.[37] The rule of law is especially essential for preserving a free society. On Hayek's conception of the rule of law, all persons have a right to be treated as equals by the legal, administrative, and political institutions in their society. Failing to respect the rule of law and the freedom it secures can lead to tyranny, wherein professional administrators become "the main rulers of the people."[38] When this occurs, restricted utility is limited because social discovery and improvement is limited. As a consequence, protecting negative liberties through the rule of law should greatly increase restricted utility over time. Recognizing this link, contractors should agree to constitutionally protect basic freedoms.

Free-Market Capitalism. Hayek's endorsement of constitutional liberties extends to the right of private property. Socialist regimes, those that violate private-property rights, will face many difficulties, primarily inefficiency, social conflict, and abuses of power.[39] The parties to a social contract, then, will choose capitalism to realize restricted utility because socialist systems will reduce utility for all and lead people to combat and control one another. These weaknesses are shared by quasi-socialist regimes as well, though to a lesser extent.

Constitutionally Limited Democracy. Hayek embraces democracy for instrumental reasons: "[T]he basic principles of democracy are the only effective method which we have yet discovered of making peaceful change possible."[40] Democracy serves as a "sanitary precaution protecting us against an abuse of power" because "it enables us to get rid of a government and try to replace it by a better one."[41] Democracy is, as such, "one of the most important safeguards of freedom."[42] Even so, Hayek is concerned that an unlimited democracy may undermine the rule of law and create tyranny.[43] The powers of any "temporary majority" must be limited to avoid giving too much power to administrators.[44] On these grounds, constitutionally limited democracy should satisfy restricted utility. Democracy, so long as it is constitutionally limited, will preserve peace, check bad governments, and help to secure basic rights, providing both increases in well-being over time and protection of the vulnerable. Contractors should, therefore, adopt constitutionally limited democracy.

A Modest Welfare State. In *The Road to Serfdom* Hayek defends a number of government activities, including monetary countercyclical policy, transportation infrastructure, and regulation of commercial practices, such as limiting work hours, establishing health and safety regulations, restricting poisons, stopping deforestation, preventing harmful agricultural methods, and restricting noise and smoke pollution; government would also subject natural monopolies to price control, provide insurance for natural disasters and health care, and deliver a basic minimum income.[45] In *The Constitution of Liberty*, Hayek explains that he wants government to prevent depressions, to protect unions, to provide pensions and medical care, and to finance public education, among other things.[46] He stresses throughout his work that the "old formulae of laissez fair [*sic*] or non-intervention do not provide us with an adequate criterion for distinguishing between what is and what is not admissible in a free system."[47] Free societies must have welfare states to avoid severe deprivations. Hayek does worry that a social safety net might get out of control,[48] but a welfare state should nonetheless improve restricted utility, especially by establishing a utility floor.

There is a worry that redistribution required by the welfare state may reduce average utility by taxing richer citizens and so make production more costly. Contractors must therefore formulate some kind of trade-off rate between restricted utility's two priorities and then embrace the policies that the trade-off rate requires.

In sum, then, Hayekian contractors will embrace a principle of restricted utility. Liberal constitutional rights, capitalism, constitutionally limited democracy, and a modest welfare state best satisfy that principle. Thus, when we engage in immanent criticism and seek to reform our society's social and legal rules, our aim should be to reform our way in the direction of the liberal democratic capitalist welfare state. In doing so, we will establish Hayekian social justice.

6

Knowledge Problems from behind the Veil of Ignorance

Daniel J. D'Amico*

RELATIVE TO THE prominent influence of the Rawlsian framework, F. A. Hayek's forceful critique of social justice has been largely overshadowed. This is not surprising because Hayek's bold proclamation that social justice is essentially meaningless was likely penned prior to his closer reading of Rawls.[1] Hence, those committed to Rawlsian social justice today perceive Hayek's argument as a sort of straw man rather than as a deep or foundational engagement.

I argue that much of Hayek's initial skepticism was warranted and remains prescient even amid the more nuanced Rawlsian framework. Rawls's theory is not a moral prescription for specific institutional changes; it instead aims more modestly to identify the margins from which we may assess the relative moral qualities of different institutional communities. In other words, Rawls is concerned primarily with how we know which sets of rules and public policies are more just compared to others.

My central claim is that the Rawlsian framework does not succeed in this more-mild aspiration. To assess the *relative* moral conditions of different institutional systems requires comparative institutional analysis beyond the capacities of the Rawlsian paradigm. In short, Rawls does not sufficiently address the epistemic challenges inherent to the processes of institutional design or selection. In result, Rawls may succeed in providing some good reason(s) for why social equality bears moral relevance, but his paradigm provides no

*Daniel J. D'Amico is associate director of the Political Theory Project and lecturer in economics at Brown University.

meaningful way to assess the relative moral value of social equality or any other normative value against other reasonable moral standards.

In essence, the idea of the veil of ignorance is a conceptual attempt to mitigate individual citizens' biases. It seems obvious that any individual would prefer rules that privilege her own personal interests, but what sorts of institutional rules would a person select if she were conveniently blind to her own identity or socioeconomic status within a community? What rules would reasonable citizens choose from behind a "veil of ignorance"? Rawls argues that such agents would be risk averse and would thus prioritize those institutions that ensure the well-being of the least well-off. Rawls labels this situation "the maximin condition." Hence, the veil of ignorance is thought to vindicate a general normative commitment to social equality.

Rawlsians and Hayekians draw contrasting policy inferences from the two thinkers' respective theories. Rawlsians interpret the insights from the veil of ignorance to justify stronger institutional commitments to redistributions and social safety nets than are currently observed. Hayek, although not principally opposed to public welfare programs, tends to emphasize the epistemic challenges inherent to central planners while designing and implementing such programs.[2] Furthermore, Hayek's commitment to generality places strong normative limitations on the potentials of progressive redistributions.

I believe that the disagreements of policy across Rawlsians and Hayekians are more than skin deep. Rather than merely reflecting the alternative biases of these two thinkers or the biases of their respective followers, these divergences stem from core differences in how the two models understand the positive operations of society and specifically the processes of institutional design and selection therein. In short, the Rawlsian framework implies that social outcomes, like material distributions, are capable of being designed and strategically manipulated through democratic deliberation. In contrast, Hayek's insights and more contemporary findings of social science suggest a far more limited potential for democratic deliberation to effectively reshape inequality via institutional manipulations. In Kantian terms, "ought implies can." Hence, normative policy implications that are justified on Rawlsian grounds break down if such outcomes are not systematically governable by designed efforts and then break down further if such efforts conflict with other normative commitments of high moral weight.

Comparative social science today demonstrates a much broader swath of institutional types than the Rawlsian vision accommodates. In short, different communities confront some similar and some unique social problems, but such problems are often distinctly shaped by the particular conditional factors faced across diverse societies. Hence, the intentions and functions that motivate collective choices toward the design and maintenance of institutional norms also vary across communities. Such institutional functions are difficult if not impossible to fully comprehend let alone predict from a purely theoretical vantage or behind a veil of ignorance.

Attempting to ascertain the normative dimensions of a particular social norm apart from the real social context within which it was developed is comparable to asking what is the just price for a particular commodity. It could very well be that an equilibrium price in a particular social setting was brought about by morally dubious procedures or actions, but such information alone tells us virtually nothing about how to actually obtain more morally desirable outcomes or at what morally reasonable consequence.

To demonstrate this limited potential of the Rawlsian framework, I investigate Inuits' historical social norms as a useful case study. "Inuit" is the current name used to refer to the indigenous peoples once commonly referred to as "Eskimos" in the present-day Arctic areas of Canada, Greenland, and Alaska. A variety of sociological and ethnographic reports provide consistent qualitative descriptions of individual life, legal customs, and social norms common among Inuits prior to the mid-twentieth century.[3] Although Rawlsians may object that the veil-of-ignorance paradigm was intended to assess the normative qualities only of advanced Western democracies, I select the Inuit case specifically because its vast differences from contemporary developed contexts highlight some specific limitations of the Rawlsian framework and its associated inferences in that certain Inuit social norms seem to explicitly violate Rawlsian standards of social equality while promoting alternative social outcomes of dire normative relevance.

Although it is true that historical Inuit social norms were vastly different from Western norms, this case suffices to demonstrate a variety of key theoretical insights regarding how institutions are understood to evolve, operate, and change. First, institutional forms that relate to and shape legal, political, and economic outcomes are often deeply embedded in local conditional factors and long-run historical processes therein. Second, particular outcomes such as wealth distributions are the result of multiple different institutional types coexisting and interacting through time. Institutions across political, economic, legal, and cultural dimensions of a community tend to come in interdependent bundles. Hence, third, institutional forms cannot be transported or manipulated across societies without practical consequences, some with inescapable normative relevance. Insofar as these principles of institutional dynamics are generalizable and persist throughout more contemporary and traditional settings, any normative theory of social institutions such as Rawlsianism must take them into account.

Hence, I argue that there remains strong reason to embrace the boldness of Hayek's original critique of social justice. The relationship between social institutions and the distribution of wealth in a community is as complex and as socially contingent a relationship as the emergence of different equilibrium price levels across different market environments. It makes little conceptual sense to ask what the just price of a particular good or service is apart from such contexts, just as it is meaningless to ask whether German is more moral than French. Each price level, like each language, evolved within its relative climate as a product of individuals aiming to ameliorate the unique costs and challenges they faced when communicating. Importing or displacing particular norms across contexts inevitably entails social consequences of significant moral concern.

Thus, the supposed normative weight and supposed objectivity of the maximin condition lack meaning without a comparably objective assessment of its normative worth relative to other reasonable values. This does not require or justify a commitment to moral relativism or nihilism; it merely demonstrates the strict epistemological limits of the Rawlsian paradigm. The Rawlsian framework essentially comes full circle back to a deductive and conceptual comparison across normative standards rather than to a successful mechanism to infer objectively the relative moral weights across different social institutions.

In the next section, I briefly summarize the Rawlsian framework. Following that, I explain the epistemological limits of the Rawlsian framework via Hayekian knowledge problems. Then I examine a case study of historical Inuit social institutions to highlight the practical limits of the Rawlsian paradigm, before offering concluding remarks.

The Rawlsian Veil of Ignorance

It is not possible to provide a fully nuanced or detailed re-creation of the Rawlsian framework within the constraints of this chapter. However, a rudimentary but accurate summary will suffice for our purposes.

At its core, the Rawlsian project was focused on ascertaining the relative moral qualities across different societies. Different individuals harbor alternative normative beliefs and are motivated toward biased interests. Given such proclivities, how can we know objectively what social policies and rules are just? In this vein, Rawls's work was a step of tremendous progress in political philosophy because, first, it recognized the epistemic challenge posed by special interests and, second, it provided a framework intended to cope with this obstacle.

Rawls's setup is straightforward. Imagine which institutional system a reasonable citizen would prefer were she ignorant of her own identity and status within any system. Rawls thus interprets this framework to imply some commitment to material equality because reasonable citizens would likely seek to hedge against the risk of being among the worst-off members of a community. Hence, Rawls proclaims the maximin condition as the inference that reasonable citizens would support social policies that prioritize the well-being of the lowest socioeconomic classes.

Again, many infer that Rawls's argument provides a strong justification for policies aimed at ensuring the well-being of the poor. Hence, many Rawlsians favor more intensive forms of social safety nets and redistributions than currently observed in modern capitalist contexts. However, the framework itself (and Rawls's personal inferences therefrom) remains more agnostic regarding the particular institutional demands of the veil of ignorance. In other words, the framework is not necessarily geared toward advising real public policies but is rather more narrowly intended to identify objective proxies for gauging the normative value of different social institutions.

In short, Rawls implies that societies ought to be morally judged against the standard of how well they provide for their poorest members. I should state clearly that I am not interested in challenging the idea that the treatment of the poor is a reasonable standard from which to assess a community's moral qualities; rather, I intend to challenge the idea that the Rawlsian framework is a strong or effectively objective justification for prioritizing the well-being of the poor above and beyond other normative values.

The Epistemic Limits of Choosing from behind a Veil

Although conceptually ingenious, the Rawlsian framework inevitably confronts two epistemological challenges, or what Hayekians refer to as "knowledge problems." First, even if the framework is modeled accurately and without bias, conceptual agents choosing from behind a veil of ignorance lack the forms of tacit knowledge inherent to the procedures of real institutional decision-making. Reasonable agents may harbor and express a preference for equality or a targeted concern for the least well-off, but they lack the ability to know how to practically achieve such ideals via institutional design or manipulation. Furthermore, they lack the capacity to recognize how any strategic attempt to instantiate such values may conflict with some desirable social outcomes or other normative ideals. Thus, we can see that the supposed objectivity of the maximin condition is maintained only in the absence of any knowledge or appreciation of real institutional opportunity costs.

In the second challenge, related to the first, Rawlsian theorists face a knowledge problem when modeling the preferences of reasonable citizens choosing from behind the veil. By what assurances do theorists know which normative conditions are specifically those that reasonable citizens would prefer? By what standard of objectivity can we know that the maximin condition is not merely reflective of the imbued biases of the theorists themselves? What is to be said for other normative values? Although we may have reason to believe that there is some objective moral weight to the maximin condition thanks to the Rawlsian paradigm, we have no ability to assess this normative weight against competing moral values.

There is no explicit reason for why the maximin condition is the only or even the most relevant margin for differentiating the conditions of justice across social systems apart from the presumption that material equality is what unbiased reasonable citizens would demand. Though the Rawlsian framework provides reason to recognize some normative weight for the absolute welfare of the poor, it remains distinct from a full-throated argument that the well-being of the poor ought to be prioritized above other normative values. This is a particularly damning observation in that virtually any normative institutional ideal can be afforded some positive moral weight via the veil of ignorance.

The veil of ignorance is capable of ascertaining only a single dimension of institutional outcomes at a time. In other words, the two hypothetical societies viewed through the veil of ignorance are essentially identical apart from the material conditions of the poor. In such a situation, it does seem reasonable that, all other things being equal, a society with better living conditions for the poor is morally desirable relative to other societies. However, any normatively desirable social outcome can be similarly isolated and heralded. Hence, the Rawlsian framework alone falls short of providing an objective reason for privileging one normative ideal above others.

It is important to note that the general commitment to social equality can and often does conflict with other reasonable normative commitments. Whereas Tomasi highlights the normative ideal of self-determination as potentially compatible with Rawlsian implications,[4] I focus on the inevitable tension between the maximin condition and a normative commitment to the pursuit of excellence and/or technological progress.

When considered alone, the prioritization of the well-being of the poorest classes seems reasonable, but so too can other normative ideals be upheld for justifiable reasons in the absence or unawareness of any exclusivity with other normative commitments. Just as someone's moral commitments to attend to the well-being of the poor is likely supported by good reasons, so too can someone else have justified reasons for normatively heralding the institutional conditions that provide for the opportunities of technological breakthroughs and personal excellence, what Nicholas Capaldi and Gordon Lloyd refer to as a commitment to "the technological project."[5] Technological progress through history and across social environments is correlated with nearly every marker of human well-being and perceived happiness.

The technological project can pass a Rawlsian impartiality standard when we control for wealth distributions, just as the maximin condition can pass when we control for technological progress. Suppose a reasonable citizen is choosing from behind the veil across two societies with the same levels of well-being for the least advantaged, but the two communities differ only with regard to their levels of technological advancement. Reasonable citizens would likely prefer the more advanced community and its associated institutions. Again, this preference may tell us something about an inherent moral worthiness of technological progress, as viewed by reasonable and impartial citizens. However, it reveals nothing about the normative value of technological progress compared to a prioritization of the well-being of the poor.

By forcing an engagement between the Rawlsian maximin condition and the technological project, I can showcase the limitations of the Rawlsian framework when normative values conflict. How generalizable the inferences from the veil of ignorance are depends on how well commitments to the maximin condition can supersede other normative values.

Rawls is aware that the maximin condition could conflict with other normative preferences. Hence, he is unwilling to uphold a universal commitment to material equality in all social circumstances. Reasonable, unbiased citizens would be unlikely to prefer a social environment wherein they endure worse absolute conditions but smaller relative gaps of wealth. Few would opt to live in a community where a normative commitment to equality means that everyone is equally poor. Rawls explicitly rejects such equality; his argument accepts large spreads of inequality so long as a more unequal society also contains a superior absolute condition for the poor.

But Rawls's emphasis on the absolute conditions of the poorest in society does not abate concerns regarding the potential trade-offs across conflicting normative values. For example, suppose an individual upholds a commitment to the technological project as the primary margin from which to normatively assess a social community. Such an individual may concede the intuitive appeal of the Rawlsian maximin condition when it is viewed in isolation from other normative values, but she would likely be willing to trade off the absolute conditions of the poorest classes within an individual community if the potentials for pursuing technological excellence were sufficiently large. It seems intuitive to prefer Society A over Society B, when the poor living within A are substantially better off than B, all other things equal. It is less intuitive that Society A would still be preferable to B if B possesses tangibly superior technological advancements and opportunities for similar pursuits despite the poor enduring only slightly worse conditions than in Society A.[6] Would a reasonable citizen prefer to live in a society without the Internet where the poorest households enjoy incomes of $30,000 per year or in a society with the Internet and household incomes of $25,000 per year among the poor? The answer does not seem obvious. Legitimate reasons can undergird each preference.

Empirical attempts to test the Rawlsian framework affirm the presence of these types of trade-offs. Ordinary participants are often willing to deviate from the maximin condition. In short, when confronted with an experimental version of the Rawlsian veil, subjects tend to prefer the existence of larger middle classes even when such distributions entail worse absolute conditions for the poorest classes.[7] Migratory trends can be thought of as another evidentiary case to think about how real individuals assess the desirability of different social systems.[8] Consistently across times and cultures, individuals often move from relatively equal but low-income environments toward more unequal but wealthier contexts. Most international migrants are similarly motivated by economic opportunities despite high rates of inequality in destination countries.

The preceding comparison helps to highlight the critical need for dynamism in political philosophy. Although it is convenient to simplify the idea of material well-being as a household income in constant dollar terms, such simplification does a great disservice to understanding the ways that individuals actually behave in society, how economic inequality actually occurs, and how individuals design and select the institutional environments they desire to live in. Real people do not identify as a member of a fixed socioeconomic demographic, nor do they assess their willingness to reside in a community according to national Gini coefficients. Many citizens normatively herald real societal institutions with reference to more dynamic components. Which community has more opportunity for one's future and one's children's futures often takes precedent over animosities about material inequality.

Comparative Institutional Analysis and the Veil of Ignorance: The Inuits

The Rawlsian paradigm obfuscates how individuals within a community actually participate in institutional design and selection. Different communities confront a variety of social challenges, many of which are unique and particular to their specific conditions of time and place. Hence, individual citizens within a given community must make institutional decisions and take actions that often prioritize responses to those challenges above and beyond other normative values. Many seemingly immoral or even inhumane institutional practices can actually be seen to provide necessary social functions when their evolutionary design and selection processes are better understood.

In the previous section, I focused on the potential tensions that may arise between the Rawlsian maximin standard and technological progress in a modern institutional setting. In this section, I take seriously the other extreme end of economic performance: mere subsistence and survival. Whereas one may infer a reasonable prioritization of the maximin standard above the possible increased production of advanced technologies, inescapable normative tensions become more obvious when the stakes are more severe and the viable existence of the community is placed in jeopardy.

In this section, I briefly survey some qualitative but representative descriptions of historical Inuit social institutions, culture, and legal norms. The Rawlsian paradigm typically limits its applicability to advanced Western democracies, but social cases beyond such boundaries provide a variety of conceptual insights via comparative analytics. In particular, they demonstrate that the operational dynamics of institutional evolution and change occur consistently across both modern and nontraditional environments. Such operational features are not unique to the Inuit context; similar research provides institutional descriptions across other nontraditional contexts, including primitive tribes,[9] organized criminal syndicates,[10] frontier communities,[11] and many others. In short, across both traditional modern developed contexts and nontraditional social environments, a variety of principles of institutional dynamics bear relevance.

Though the particular institutions in historical Inuit society are vastly different from institutions in other societies—the contemporary United States, for example—those different institutional outcomes adhere to similar causal dynamics and operational principles. In short, individuals tend to invest in social institutions of governance via collective actions in the face of high or rising costs of conflict. Such institutions can take shape as formal governments or informal social norms or both, each having the potential to serve as a substitute in the absence of the other. I chose to focus on Inuits because their particular norms explicitly violate the maximin condition and social equity and thus provide a unique opportunity to challenge the Rawlsian paradigm directly.

Traditional Inuit life prior to its integration with and displacement by the developed world in the early twentieth century was far removed from the material abundances of industrialization, with even more exaggerated material constraints than commonly observed within other primitive societies. The harsh environment of the frozen tundra provided sustenance resources only through narrow channels of large game-hunting and fishing endeavors.[12] Hence, resolving collective-action problems to maintain cohesive and effective group production efforts was often a matter of life and death for the entire community. If the tribe could not cohesively work together, everyone would starve and freeze. The direct threat from climate coupled with the inherent logistic challenges of reliable social coordination thus permeated almost all social customs and institutional norms across Inuit tribes.

Many of the most clichéd norms of Inuit culture have some grounding in reality. It is true that Inuits had many more words for snow than other languages do and that "eskimo kisses" (*kunik*), though slightly different from merely rubbing noses, were a genuine cultural practice because one's face tended to be the only exposed part of the body to express signals of intimacy and trust.[13] Hence, one can easily recognize that the particular conditional factors of Inuit society had a strong influence on even nonmaterial cultural norms that emerged therein.

Because Inuit tribes were so critically dependent on working cohesively as a group to hunt, fish, and construct shelter, violent conflict, especially among young, strong men, was extremely costly. If the two strongest men fought and injured each other, the net productivity of the tribe was significantly curtailed. This connection had a direct effect on both the Inuits' rituals of conflict resolution and their sexual cultural norms. Physical altercations, proprietary disputes, and conflicts surrounding sexual infidelity were resolved via nonviolent norms that heavily leveraged cultural practices of song and dance.[14] Disputants were expected to voice and perform their grievances. Tribal members sided with and supported the most compelling and engaging performer. Furthermore, polygamy and adultery were consistently observed as acceptable and stable social norms.[15] In short, social institutions were aimed to strongly discourage, avoid, and swiftly resolve physical conflicts.

The pervasive influence of geographic conditions on social institutions conforms with a secondary insight provided by institutional theory: institutions tend to have long evolutionary histories and cannot be seamlessly decoupled from their surrounding institutional complements without altering the general patterns of social outcomes associated with the institutional basket. In other words, institutions come in clusters. Rules that directly relate to legal and/or political processes often relate and interact with conditions, rules, and policies more relevant to economic and cultural conditions. Hence, it is difficult and sometimes impossible to reshape specific social outcomes, such as inequality, without disrupting a variety of other social and cultural processes, many of them with significant moral relevance.

The iconic Inuit practice of essentially euthanizing the elderly (no longer practiced but a prominent feature when Inuits were first encountered and studied in the latter part of the nineteenth century) brings this issue to light. At first glance, the idea of exiling elderly members of a society (an essential death sentence in their particular climate) seems morally repugnant and obviously so. More puzzling from an external vantage is the sense of duty and obligation reported by the elderly when conforming to this practice. Replicating such a custom in an advanced Western democracy would be almost impossible to rationalize or morally justify. However, a closer investigation and appreciation of the unique societal challenges of historical Inuit society makes such normative condemnations far more complicated and less certain.

Again, resource constraints for Inuits were extremely strict. Hence, the evolution and persistence of senicide can be seen as a necessary function of tribe sustenance. Submission to this norm was not determined by age but rather by when one's production-to-consumption ratio fell below one. If you consumed more than you produced, you risked the tribe's health and well-being because surplus production was scarce. Furthermore, it is interesting to consider the likely outcomes of an institutional change motivated by the maximin standard imposed into the Inuit context. A social security system akin to that of modern Western societies with forced savings rates and redistributions from the young to old would likely have condemned a historical Inuit tribe to death and starvation.

Conclusion

I have argued that the Rawlsian paradigm does not achieve its intention to identify margins from which to objectively assess the relative moral value of different social institutions. I identified two critical forms of knowledge problems inherent to the Rawlsian paradigm. First, Rawlsian theorists do not know with objective certainty that the normative standards they presume reasonable agents will hold, such as the maximin condition, are accurate. Hence, we are still left with the challenge of how to assess the relative moral weights across different reasonable but conflicting moral standards. Second, agents choosing from behind the veil do not know what real intentions or normative priorities actually motivate real individual citizens and real institutional decision makers. Hence, institutional changes justified via the Rawlsian veil of ignorance tend to be shortsighted regarding their full practical consequences and the normative implications of those consequences.

Though the Inuit case study appears far afield from the case of advanced Western societies, I selected it because in it the institutional tensions and consequences of imposed institutional changes are most obvious. But the same principles of institutional operation consistently hold within contemporary developed contexts. In short, modern institutions and social outcomes are also deeply embedded with their local conditional factors and long-run evolutionary histories. Social outcomes as varied as economic performance, rates of military conscription, the degree of regulated labor markets, welfare spending, government ownership of banking, and incarceration rates have been shown to carry strong and robust correlations with long-run embedded markers of historical institutional choices. In short, key institutional decisions were made during episodes of social conflict long ago. Such instances of conflict varied significantly across different social environments and legal systems, and such differences altered the selection of different institutional types. Furthermore, such institutional differences are associated with significantly different patterns of social outcomes today.[16] It is also well established that transporting singular institutional types such as labor policies or financial regulations across these categories of institutional clusters may disrupt the functional components of other surrounding institutions within the imported social environment.

7

To Give Each Man His Due:

The Folly of Dworkin's Jurisprudence of Social Justice

William J. Watkins Jr.*

IN MODERN WESTERN jurisprudential thought, the ideal of justice seldom exists apart from "social justice." A political system creating statutes and regulatory instruments and a legal system interpreting and molding the products of the political branches are both expected to embrace social justice. Those that do not, we are told, are counterfeit and unworthy of recognition. This view was popularized by Ronald Dworkin with his concept of law as integrity.

Following the logic of Dworkin and his disciples, a state embracing Wilhelm von Humboldt's nightwatchman vision of a minimalist government is morally indefensible. Its lack of mechanics permitting redistribution of resources renders it unjust. The concept of law in a Humboldtian state is logically a variant of legal positivism or natural law, both of which Dworkin spent his career inveighing against.

This chapter argues that the mainstream position popularized by Dworkin is incongruent with a historical understanding of justice that has shaped Western jurisprudential thought. In fact, the modern enthrallment with social justice runs counter to classical principles of actual justice that have defined the West from its inception. Only an accurate understanding of justice's essence can return us to a path of political and legal integrity and supply the foundation for liberty in a limited state.

---

*William J. Watkins Jr. is a research fellow at the Independent Institute and president of the Greenville, South Carolina, Lawyers Chapter of the Federalist Society.

What Is Social Justice?

Of course, before accepting or rejecting social justice we need an understanding of what this politically charged term encompasses. One of the clearest discussions of social justice comes from the United Nations' International Forum for Social Development. After a three-year study "for the purpose of promoting international cooperation for social development and supporting developing countries and social groups not benefitting from the globalization process," the Forum published *Social Justice in an Open World: The Role of the United Nations.*[1] This publication is especially helpful for its honesty in definition and description that often matches its advocacy for global redistribution of wealth. In the background discussion, the report recognizes the novelty of social justice and its foreignness to traditional understandings: "[u]nlike justice in the broad sense, social justice is a relatively recent concept, born of the struggles surrounding the industrial revolution and the advent of socialist views ... on the organization of society."[2]

With parentage established, the report offers a simple definition: "Social justice may be broadly understood as the fair and compassionate distribution of the fruits of economic growth."[3] The report expresses doubt that full income equality is possible, but postulates that to achieve an acceptable range of inevitable inequality, "strong and coherent redistributive policies conceived and implemented by public agencies" are necessary.[4] On the international level, the United Nations, if it is to be an instrument of justice, "must work to restore the integrity and appeal of social justice, interpreted in the contemporary context as distributive justice."[5]

Further reference to "social justice" in this chapter should be understood in accordance with the above definition provided by the United Nations. At its essence, it is government apportionment of property and resources to those deemed worthy or in need by authorities.

The Roman Legacy

To understand the historical Western idea of justice, classical Roman law is a necessary starting point. With the accomplishment of codification in Europe and Anglo-American pride in the common-law system, moderns have lost appreciation for the debt owed to the jurisprudence of ancient Rome. Goethe accurately described Roman law as much like a duck. At times it is clearly visible swimming and preening on top of the water. At other times we lose sight of the duck as it dives for food in the depths. But in either case, the duck is present. Roman law might be on a deep and protracted dive as we traverse the twenty-first century, but its principles are foundational to Western society and remain with us.[6]

But Roman law would not be known to us absent Justinian's desire in the 530s to reclaim the best of classical Roman jurisprudence and to reconquer the heartland of the fallen Western empire. Justinian was the emperor of the eastern Roman Empire from 527 to 565. He was the last emperor to be a native Latin speaker and is often described as the last Roman. Justinian commissioned Tribonian, a Byzantine lawyer and scholar, to compile various Roman legal sources and edit them to remove any inconsistencies. The result was the *Corpus Juris Civilis*. The heart of this work and what would be most influential was the *Digest*. This was a compilation of the writings of the Roman jurists who advised parties to litigation as well as the judges in disputes. The writings of the jurists were unparalleled for their deductive and analogical reasoning.

Justinian's armies left copies of the *Corpus Juris Civilis* on library shelves in their unsuccessful attempts to reconquer modern Italy. The collapse of the Western empire had left the descendants of the Romans and their Germanic invaders without an educated class that could appreciate, understand, and use Justinian's work. Learning did eventually reemerge and when the *Digest* was "rediscovered" in the 1070s, it led to a revival of European legal culture. Law—a combination of Roman civil law and the church's canon law—became the superstructure of Western society. This *ius commune*, or common law, shaped European ideas about law and justice as it was interpreted and used by myriad schools of thought including the glossators, commentators, humanists, and German historical school.

In his *Institutes*, a primer for students beginning their study of law, Justinian gives the classical definition of justice. "Justice is the set and constant purpose which gives to every man his due."[7] He further emphasizes this in his summary of the law, a kind of Roman Shema: "The precepts of the law are these: to live honestly, to injure no one, and to give every man his due."[8] Clearly, Justinian sees justice as an individualized concept and not primarily institutional. (These statements about justice are also found in the *Digest* and are attributed to the great Roman jurist Ulpian,[9] who wrote in the early 200s and served as praetorian prefect, which was the highest imperial office and involved advising the emperor and serving as his chief legal officer.)

But does one's due encompass a right to property held by another? Considering the texts that follow this description of justice and law, one must say no. Justinian teaches that robbery is theft and that the person "who deals with the property of another ... against that other's will" earns the moniker of "robber."[10] The robber, Justinian pronounces, is "an audacious thief" deserving the scorn of Roman society.[11] Robbers are liable, he further instructs, for four times the value of the object taken.[12]

Justinian's order of fourfold restitution has a biblical basis. This was the repayment required by Jewish law when a robber stole a sheep and was found guilty.[13] It is also the amount that Zacchaeus, the chief tax collector, promised to return to his victims once he was confronted by Christ and repented of his sins.[14]

The Church and Justice

It should not surprise us to find biblical principles embedded in much of Roman law. In 312, Constantine converted to Christianity and made many reforms favoring the Christian church. Historian N. R. Needham observes that Constantine "made Christian bishops into part of the Empire's legal structure, by decreeing that in a civil law dispute, the two parties could take their case to the local bishop, if they so desired, and the bishop's decision would have all the force of law."[15]

With the fall of the Western empire in 476, the church became the "main custodian of the Roman legal tradition" and was said to live by Roman law.[16] Anyone hoping to advance in the church needed a familiarity with Roman law because it was seen "as an integral part of the Roman heritage" and "a necessary part of a sound education."[17]

A critical part of *ius commune* was the law of the church. While throughout its history the church has ministered to the poor and urged the prosperous to aid the destitute, the church has also supported the institution of private property and opposed theft. St. Augustine, for example, believed that private property was a necessity in a fallen world and that it is willed by God.[18] Aquinas considered private property as inhering in the definition of justice, which he understood, in the spirit of Justinian, as rendering to each man his due. American sociologist Rodney Stark unequivocally sums up the views of these two giants of the church: "Augustine, Aquinas, and other major theologians taught that the state must respect private property and not intrude on the freedom of its citizens to pursue virtue."[19]

Pope John XXII, during the church's internal Franciscan conflict in the 1300s, rejected claims that property should be held in common and instead argued that God had given Adam dominion over the Earth prior to the creation of Eve. Common ownership, John reasoned, could not exist in a world occupied by one individual; therefore, he saw private property as something of a creation ordinance. He declared it "erroneous and heretical" to claim that Christ and the apostles had no possessions in response to Franciscan claims that only a total forsaking of property could lead to piety.

Theologians of the Reformation continued in this line of reasoning. Ralph Barton Perry argues that much of the main body of Puritan doctrine—especially regarding property—continued in the medieval tradition.[20] In his study of the Eighth Commandment, John Calvin begins by echoing Justinian and observing that because injustice is "an abomination to God, we must render to every man his due."[21] The commandment's prohibition of theft "requires every man to exert himself honestly in preserving his own" and forbids longing after the property of others.[22] Contrary to modern social justice advocates, Calvin teaches that "what each individual possesses has not fallen to him by chance, but [by] the distribution of the sovereign Lord of all."[23] Consequently, "no one can pervert his means to bad purposes without committing fraud on a divine dispensation."[24]

In sum, Roman civil law and the church's law both recognized justice as giving each man his due. Both also condemned the plunder of another's property and demanded extraordinary amounts of restitution. Simply replacing the item taken was not enough. These principles seeped into the fabric of Western society and inform our historical reverence for the institution of private property. Indeed, the various right-to-acquire clauses found in early American state constitutions, while certainly having a Lockean lineage, would not exist absent the principles in *ius commune*. "All men have certain natural, essential, and inherent rights," declares the 1784 New Hampshire constitution, "among which are, the enjoying and defending life and liberty; acquiring, possessing, and protecting, property."[25] Vanderbilt's Professor James W. Ely Jr. observes that "because property ownership was associated with liberty and happiness" many of the early state constitutions included provisions to safeguard property rights and affirmed the freedom to obtain property.[26] Justinian would have certainly approved.

Law as Integrity

Ronald Dworkin was one of the most influential scholars of the twentieth century. He held dual appointments at New York University and Oxford. From these elite schools in the United States and the United Kingdom, Dworkin "influenced a generation of English and American law students, law professors, and even judges."[27] Dworkin is perhaps best known for his theory of law as integrity, which owes much to John Rawls and his advocacy of equality in his theory of the original position.[28] At base, Rawls asserted that rational individuals, if acting behind a veil of ignorance regarding their abilities, preferences, and other bias-identifying features, would choose a system fostering the greatest possible equality and thus the maximum benefit to those least advantaged.

In framing the argument, Dworkin defines justice as a condition of well-being within society.[29] Much like Rawls, who saw justice as institutional rather than individualistic, Dworkin posits that the creation and maintenance of well-being depends upon government initiatives, including the redistribution of resources. "Ordinary politics shares with utopian political theory certain political ideals," Dworkin elucidates, "ideals of a fair political structure, a just distribution of resources and opportunities, and an equitable process for enforcing the rules and regulations that establish these."[30] Dworkin summarizes these principles as "fairness, justice, and procedural due process."[31] It bears emphasizing that Dworkin's justice is integrally connected to redistributionism. "If we accept justice as a political virtue we want our legislators and other officials to distribute material resources and protect civil liberties in order to ensure a morally defensible outcome."[32] A neglect of social justice renders a regime morally indefensible in Dworkin's framework.

This view of social justice as a moral requirement for the good society explains Dworkin's antipathy toward legal positivism and natural law. The former, in the main, sees law and morality as separate entities.[33] According to legal positivist scholar H. L. A. Hart, a central goal of positivism is to "provide reliable public standards of conduct which can be identified with certainty as matters of plain fact without dependence on controversial moral arguments."[34] Morality need not be part of law for it to be binding, although most positivists accept that morality may be part of law if co-opted into the applicable rule of recognition or master rule (in the United States, this would be the Constitution).[35]

Natural law theory, according to Australian legal philosopher John Finnis, is a set of principles of practical reasonableness used in evaluating human institutions. At base, it is "a reasonableness in deciding, in adopting commitments, in choosing and executing projects, and in general in acting."[36] The first principles of natural law are "pre-moral" yet self-evident.[37] This irks Dworkin and he finds a pre-moral practicable reasonableness "unpersuasive" in determining accurate statements of the law.[38] Modern natural law theories embodied in the work of Finnis and his adherents fall short for Dworkin, inasmuch as modern natural law does not focus on determining the legal soundness of positive laws, but rather the general promotion of the common good.

At bottom, Dworkin sees Finnis's natural law theory and Hart's positivism as unnecessarily handcuffing his ideal jurist, Judge Hercules, a character of Dworkin's intellectual imagination. Under law as integrity, Dworkin demands that Judge Hercules (and lesser aspirants wearing the black robe) make judicial decisions "that he believes best from the standpoint of political morality as a whole."[39] Judges must reject clear rules and instead find the implicit moral principles beneath the rules and apply the principles to achieve the best account of the community's legal doctrine. But Dworkin does not confine judges to principles, but instead insists that they should also consider "justifications of policy."[40] Although policy is typically associated with the legislative branch, Dworkin believes that policy making is not off limits to the judiciary.

Competing theories of law (positivism or natural law) limit the judiciary's discretion in what Dworkin calls constructive interpretation. By being at liberty to determine what the community's morals are and ought to be, a judiciary modeled on Judge Hercules wields enormous power. It writes the story of society, via constructive interpretation, to place society in the most positive and progressive light.

Dissenting Voices

Fortunately, Dworkin is not the last word on justice, although his views remain in vogue in American universities and law schools. One noteworthy dissenting voice is Robert Nozick. In his *Anarchy, State, and Utopia*, which was an early libertarian response to Rawls, Nozick challenges the core of social justice. Citizens, Nozick argues, should not be treated as children "who have been given portions of pie by someone who now makes last minute adjustments to rectify careless cutting."[41] In the real world, "[w]hat each person gets, he gets from others who give to him in exchange for something, or as a gift."[42] To invest government with the power to direct distribution does away with a minimalist state and puts government in a position to terrorize and violate the rights of the people. In a free society, "there is no *central* distribution, no person or group entitled to control all the resources, jointly deciding how they are to be doled out."[43]

In dealing with justice, Nozick posits the entitlement theory in which the justice of property holdings is measured in historical terms.[44] So long as a person justly acquired an original holding, he is justly entitled to the use and fruits of the holding. The person is also entitled to transfer the holding by sale or gift, and the new recipient is entitled to the same rights as the original holder. Just holdings, in Nozick's view, leave the state no room for manipulation and interference with voluntary acquisitions and exchanges. But in a society wedded to principles of social justice, the state's "continuous interference with people's lives" is necessary.[45]

Friedrich von Hayek similarly saw the danger of social justice. In *The Constitution of Liberty*, Hayek urges that justice "ought to be confined to the deliberate treatment of men by other men."[46] Social justice, on the other hand, is addressed to "society" and not individuals.[47] While individuals are participating in the market and respecting the rights of others, Hayek contends that they should be free from any government concern about the distribution of wealth or incomes because the results of a spontaneous order "cannot be just or unjust."[48]

Once government concerns itself with these matters, a great danger is unleashed. According to Hayek: "The principle of distributive justice, once introduced, would not be fulfilled until the whole of society was organized in accordance with it."[49] Leaving men even a small window to operate freely, Hayek believed, would be intolerable to the planners and thwart their ultimate objectives. The result of such an organization is "a kind of society which in all essential respects would be the opposite of a free society—an authority that decided what an individual was to do and how he would do it."[50]

The Nightwatchman State and Morality

Under principles of justice, can a minimalist or nightwatchman state exist in a just society? The answer, of course, depends on one's definition of justice. Approaching the matter from Dworkin's law as integrity versus Justinian's injunction to give each man his due yields very different answers. Ultimately, we must choose between competing sets of principles: one of recent birth and socialist parentage, and the other dating back to the Roman *ius commune.*

In making our examination of the minimalist state and its relation to morality, we will use the work of Wilhelm von Humboldt because of its clarity and influence on later classical liberals. Ludwig von Mises, leader of the Austrian School of economic thought, described Humboldt as one of the five architects of modern classical liberalism. In distilling Humboldt's primary contributions to libertarian thought, historian Ralph Raico points to "his ideas on the value of the free, self-sustaining activity of the individual, and of the importance of the unhindered collaboration—often unconscious—of the members of society."[51]

Humboldt was a German humanist, founder of the University of Berlin, and a delegate to the Congress of Vienna. His correspondents and friends included Goethe, Schiller, and Madame de Staël. Intellectual historian J. W. Burrow describes Humboldt as "the lost leader of the Prussian liberal constitutionalists."[52] The posthumous publication of Humboldt's *The Limits of State Action*, written in the early 1790s, greatly influenced J. S. Mill's *On Liberty*, as evidenced by Mill's multiple quotations from the Prussian's work.

In examining the proper role of government, Humboldt desires that man reach his true end, which he describes as "the highest and most harmonious development of his powers to a complete and consistent whole."[53] The indispensable condition for such development was freedom. Only when enjoying broad liberty can a man cultivate his energies and individuality for the betterment of self and society. Humboldt reaches these conclusions regarding man's purpose by applying the "immutable dictates of reason."[54]

If man were free to develop, Humboldt believes that the result would be a great diversity of talents that would benefit civilization. Government interference and direction, on the other hand, would cause people to resemble one another and their activities to overlap. In the end, the active energy of individuals is suppressed as well as their moral character. Regarding the latter, Humboldt predicts that men would decline to help fellow citizens in need and would instead abandon them to "the solicitous aid of the State."[55] With this, the warmth of free and voluntary society is replaced with the cold calculations of government actors.

To counter government inertia toward homogenization of citizens and the loss of morals, Humboldt offers the following formula: "the State is to abstain from all solicitude for the positive welfare of the citizens, and not to proceed a step further than is necessary for their mutual security and protection against foreign enemies; for with no other object should it impose restrictions on freedom."[56] Humboldt has no false illusions that men are angels. He understands that some members of society will use freedom to plunder the property of their fellows and to encroach on others' rights. To prevent this, government is necessary but should only act in the role of a nightwatchman.

The society outlined by Humboldt could be based on or implemented in multiple ways. For example, one could argue (as Humboldt did) that such a society is an exercise in practicable reasonableness. Thus, it is in accordance with natural law. Or it could be the result of a majority, frustrated with government interference, that enacts positive laws on the classical liberal model. But whether based in natural law, positive law, or a combination of the two, Dworkin's legion of disciples and his mythical Judge Hercules would consider the experiment with a nightwatchman model as unjust and morally indefensible because of the absence of "social justice." Judicial and other forms of resistance would be necessary to return society to a state of well-being.

What have we wrought that modern views of justice render a classically liberal society morally defective and beyond the pale of choice? To give each person his due—a cardinal rule of the *ius commune*—is alien to our society, one in which a rich past is forgotten. A reckoning is in order and long overdue.

First, we must directly challenge the idea that redistribution is moral. It is not. In examining the truth behind law as integrity, the opening lines of Frédéric Bastiat's great work come to mind: "The law perverted! The law—and, in its wake, all the collective forces of the nation—the law, I say, not only diverted from its proper direction, but made to pursue one entirely contrary!"[57] Dworkin makes law "the tool of every kind of avarice, instead of being its check" on arbitrary power.[58] Moderns should not be shy about embracing Bastiat's simple definition of true law: "the collective organization of the individual right to lawful defense."[59] In this we have a clear rule to counter Dworkin's intellectual gymnastics that put social justice as the indispensable principle for the good society.

Second, we must recoil at Dworkin's preferred role for the judiciary. Dworkin claims that in every legal case there is one right answer. Judges determine this one right answer by fabricating a political and moral theory congruent with underlying principles found in past practice set forth in the Constitution, statutory law, and case law. This does not mean that judges must honor past precedent—the legal doctrine of *stare decisis*—or give the words of statutes or the Constitution their plain ordinary meaning. If the judge concludes that a past decision or statute is incongruent with fundamental societal principles such as social justice, he is free to ignore established law in reaching the one right answer.

Dworkin shows no hesitation in elevating unelected and unaccountable judges to the apex of the political order. He places the people, their representatives, and fundamental law under the feet of the judges. Judges for Dworkin are no different from Platonic Guardians—an elite class of citizens responsible for the management of society. Such a view is hardly surprising for a man educated at Harvard and Oxford, and teaching in the left-leaning intellectual bubbles of New York City and London. Dworkin thinks nothing of undermining the American tenet of popular sovereignty and the British precept of parliamentary sovereignty. Both must give way to the reign of judges.

And our society will give way unless we recapture ancient principles of justice honored by both the civil magistrates and the church from the classical Roman period to the Middle Ages and into the early modern period. We cannot endure social justice and still maintain a free society. We must choose and choose wisely.

Conclusion

Ronald Dworkin unabashedly argues that the nightwatchman state, because it lacks a dedication to social justice, is immoral. This contention, based on a novel theory of justice, is contrary to foundational principles of Western society. Classical conceptions of justice focus on the individual and giving each person his due. Dworkin's institutional concept of social justice treats people as categories: haves and have-nots. Historical considerations on how an individual has acquired property or resources are ignored. Judges are empowered to rewrite clear rules based on principles of social justice that Dworkin sees as the highest expression of a society's ideals.

What is truly immoral is Dworkin's insistence on what Bastiat called legalized plunder. Dworkin sets Judge Hercules up to be a robber, an audacious thief. Rather than an ideal jurist, Hercules should be considered a wrongdoer and one who should make a fourfold restitution to a society that he has robbed of legal certainty and self-governance in making its own rules. Such a result would be just, in the historical and classical sense of the word.

An Exchange Theory of Social Justice:

A "Gains from Trade under Uncertainty" Perspective

Anthony Gill*

ON THE ISLAND of Despair, Robinson Crusoe has little practical concern for social justice until Friday comes along. Once Friday arrives, both he and Crusoe face two important decisions. First and foremost, should they interact with one another?[1] Second, if they agree to interact, how will the benefits (and costs) of those interactions be distributed between them? The second question depends on the first: if either party *freely* chooses *not* to interact, no exchange occurs, and there are no gains from trade to be divided. If the first question is answered in the affirmative, then the second question comes into play, and issues of social justice arise. What is the most socially just distribution of the surplus that accrues from trade? Should the gains from trade be distributed equally between the two, or shall one party receive more of the net benefits than the other? If one party does receive more of the benefits, will this unequal condition persist over time, or might the gains eventually equalize?

And if the net benefits from interaction do equalize, how is this accomplished—via voluntary action or coercion? Although the Crusoe–Friday scenario is hypothetically simple, answers to these questions have implications for larger societies and shape the way we coordinate anonymous (and quasi-anonymous) trade, raising the question of what the most socially just means of coordination is.

---

*Anthony Gill is professor in the Department of Political Science at the University of Washington.

This chapter addresses these questions and argues that social justice should not be conceived in terms of distributional outcomes due to the uncertain and changing nature of individual preferences. Such uncertainty clouds the process of negotiating gains from trade between individuals, both in the short term and the long term. Concepts of social justice that rely on precise distributional outcomes of resources, in particular material wealth, increase the likelihood of potentially unjust misallocations because of the innate difficulty in gauging the diverse and changing preferences of individuals. Rather, I argue that social justice within a world of ambiguity and change should rest upon providing the greatest number of opportunities for individuals to exchange (or refuse to exchange). This conceptualization of social justice, although rooted in distributional concerns, rests upon a procedural definition of interaction as opposed to an outcome-based notion. Although not a comprehensive vision of what social justice entails, this perspective represents an important part of the discussion. Due to space limitations, this chapter does not examine directly broader conceptualizations of social justice that encompass obligations and duties,[2] though the framework presented does suggest possible avenues for future exploration in those areas.

A Restrictive Notion of Social Justice

Defining social justice comprehensively is no easy task. Numerous definitions exist, ranging from those emphasizing equality of opportunity to others favoring equality of outcome. The point of this chapter is to demonstrate that a distributive concept of social justice resting upon equality of outcome (or "fairness") is difficult, if not impossible, under situations of diverse preferences and uncertainty. Although equity is a noble goal, efforts by a third-party government to reduce inequity in distribution may lead to inefficient and less-equitable outcomes than those that emerge from voluntary trade over time. I argue that social justice instead rests upon the ability to *search and discover* fair outcomes in a world characterized by uncertainty and constant change (with respect to both preferences and prices). Although an optimal degree of distributional fairness might not obtain under this process-driven definition of social justice, opportunities to search and discover the terms of trade are better able to adjust to changing preferences and prices and will tend to converge toward distributional justice even if never reaching it.

To make this argument, I begin by conceding that the notion of social justice has a distributional component that relies on two criteria. First, social justice requires a Pareto efficient set of interactions such that no person is made worse off in a bilateral interaction. Admittedly, this restrictive assumption sets aside issues of negative externalities imposed on third parties. It also ignores matters of public goods and public choice (i.e., voting). If a theory of social justice cannot apply in situations of bilateral exchange, it will have difficulty with multilateral (cooperative) exchange. The goal of distributional justice in a large society of diverse preferences is quixotic in that any type of public choice (including those designed to provide pure public goods) will result in some individuals being made worse off. The second criterion is that distributional justice increases as the gains from trade within a bilateral interaction tend toward equitable distribution. The distribution need not be perfectly equal, but our chosen institutional structure—be it market or government—should push the distribution in that direction. This criterion sits with the commonsense notion of "share and share alike" taught to children and emphasized in distributive versions of social justice.[3] Granted, the "share and share alike" principle is not a market mechanism but is taught to children in a top-down hierarchical structure known as the family (or school system). However, individuals do take this inculcated norm into the marketplace at some point and to some extent.

This restricted definition subsumes the notion that individuals have equal rights in terms of free choice and property, a criterion that is impossible to satisfy in reality given differences in individuals' capabilities and existing sociopolitical institutional structures. It is an ideal, but one that serves to advance the discussion. The latter realization leads to a pessimistic conclusion that pure and lasting social justice can never be reached, but our quixotic search for social justice can at least be tempered by the goal of continually searching for better solutions among potential horrible ones.

Justice with Known Reserve Prices

Let me begin my examination of social justice from an exchange perspective by returning to Crusoe and Friday, remembering that they have two sequential choices to make: (1) whether to engage in exchange of goods, services, or time;[4] and (2) upon agreeing to exchange, how to share the costs and benefits of their transactions. Examining the gains from trade provides us leverage on how these choices are made and to what extent they are just. Gains from trade (i.e., consumer and producer surplus) can accrue if two parties have overlapping reserve prices for buying and selling. A reserve buy price is the highest price someone will pay to receive some good or service. Alternatively, a reserve sell price is the lowest price an individual will accept to part ways with his produce. Reserve prices reflect an individual's willingness to transact with another person and help answer the first choice facing Crusoe and Friday. Reserve sell prices set higher than a buyer's reserve buy price implies the two individuals will choose not to interact. If I refuse to pay more than $500,000 for a house, I will not enlist an agent selling million-dollar mansions. Forthwith, a person with an infinitely high reserve price is destined to become a hermit, a Crusoe who turns his back on Friday.

For rhetorical simplicity, figure 1 presents the gains from trade between two individuals, Friday and Crusoe. Friday is willing to sell a fish at a minimum price of $4 to Crusoe. As a thinly rational individual, Friday will accept any offer higher than that amount. At any price lower than $4, Friday would choose not to trade with Crusoe. Now assume two different preference states for Crusoe, A and B, which may be the same individual at different times. Crusoe A, with a higher reserve price, desires fish more than Crusoe B does. Crusoe in general (A or B), being thinly rational, would prefer to receive the fish at a zero price, but Crusoe A is willing to spend up to $8 for the fish, whereas Crusoe B (who is in less of a mood for seafood) would offer $2 at most. In the case of B, the reserve buy price for Crusoe ($2) is lower than Friday's reserve sell price ($4); thus, in this situation the two individuals would refuse to interact with one another and go their separate ways. Forcing Crusoe B to buy the fish at $4 or Friday to sell the fish at $2 would impose a cost of $2 on either party with no corresponding gain to their two-person society. A world with a net loss of utility resulting from a forced transaction would seem, under common sense and according to the criteria annunciated earlier, to be socially unjust.

If we are dealing with Crusoe A, however, any exchange between $4 and $8 would yield a net benefit of $4—the difference between Crusoe A's reserve

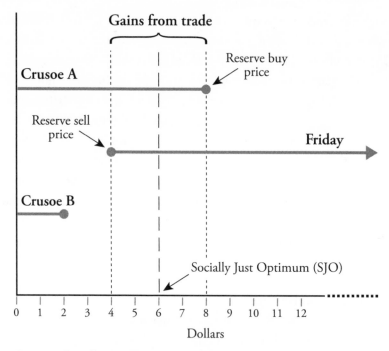

Figure 1. Socially Just Optimum with known reserve prices.

buy price and Friday's reserve sell price. The question arises as to how the $4 in gains from trade will be divided. The most equitable option would be a sale price of $6, wherein each party captures $2 of the surplus. I define this point as the Socially Just Optimum (SJO), wherein society is better off and all gains are distributed equally, perfectly meeting both criteria of the earlier definition. Movement away from the SJO, either toward the seller or toward the buyer, but within the overlap of reserve prices, remains just in that both parties are benefiting, albeit not equally. A sale price of $7 provides Friday with $3 in gains from trade, leaving Crusoe with $1 in surplus; both parties are better off than had the trade not occurred, albeit Friday is benefiting more. To summarize, any transaction resulting in gains from trade is socially just,[5] and an equitable distribution of the surplus represents optimum social justice because it satisfies the criteria of Pareto improvement *and* equality.

If reserve prices are clearly known and truthful, if participants are free to negotiate, and if a repeated relationship is anticipated or desired, the exchange may gravitate toward the SJO (i.e., evenly split surplus). If one party (Friday) desires to have an ongoing relationship with the other (Crusoe), he will gladly offer his fish at a price at or lower than the $6 SJO as a way to signal that he is a generous merchant worthy of continued interaction. Consider the commonplace use of "introductory prices" for new customers of a business as a means of reducing uncertainty and building trust.[6] The other party (Crusoe), however, should also signal generosity and exchange at a price at or higher than Friday's reserve sell price so as to remind Friday that he is a worthy customer who values good service, a situation reminiscent of tipping to ensure future personalized service at a tavern.[7] With both individuals trying to signal generosity and given that negotiating imposes transaction (time) costs, it is rational simply to split the surplus equally.[8] If transaction costs are high and reserve prices known by all, it also makes sense to split the gains from trade evenly.

From a normative standpoint, ethical codes across a wide array of cultures have emphasized the importance of sharing the fruits of transactions equally.[9] The Golden Rule, urging individuals to do unto others as they would have others do unto them, is common across religious traditions such as Buddhism (Udanavarga 6:18), Judaism (Leviticus 19:18), Christianity (Matthew 7:12), Islam (An-Nawawi's Forty Hadith 13), and Confucianism (Analects 15:23). Adam Smith conceived of an "impartial spectator" who guides individuals to think about their decisions as if they were watching the interactions of two other parties in a disinterested manner.[10] The "impartial spectator" observing Friday and Crusoe would expect an equal division of the surplus if reserve prices were transparently known. The anarchist Michael Taylor,[11] building upon the anthropology of primitive tribes, emphasizes the importance of reciprocity within small communities. Brian Skyrms bolsters Taylor's point by using evolutionary game theory to demonstrate that fair division of resources is an optimal strategy in bilateral, iterated ultimatum and dictator games.[12] In other words, when people choose to interact with one another (the first choice), and future interactions are anticipated, individuals will tend to settle on a fair division of the gains from trade. Repeated, voluntary interactions with known reserve prices will gravitate toward the SJO.

Social Justice under "Large" Societies and Diverse Preferences

To this point, we have examined social justice in a society of only two individuals and under known reserve prices. Admittedly, this society is not a big one; thus, meeting the criterion for the Socially Just Optimum in it would be fairly easy. But what if the society were larger—say, ten thousand people?[13] If the reserve prices of all individuals in this larger nation were identical, known, and truthful, the argument regarding social justice given earlier would hold: the SJO would represent prices that evenly split the surplus for two individuals for any and all transactions. Such a world is a central planner's ideal society in that all equitably just solutions are determined easily.

Alas, several problems arise in larger societies that affect our underlying assumptions and consequent analysis. First, preferences are unlikely to be identical. As population increases, so does the diversity in preferences. Second, discovering these diverse preferences becomes difficult and time-consuming. In other words, the discovery of reserve prices—both buying and selling—becomes increasingly costly. Businesses often invest substantial resources in market research and engage in trial-and-error experimentation to discover individuals' reserve prices and to develop creative ways to price discriminate across different buyer preferences. Consumers, conversely, usually do not invest resources into knowing sellers' reserve prices and frequently have wildly inaccurate notions of various industries' profit rates.[14] Overcoming uncertainty and asymmetric information is one of the biggest challenges facing interpersonal exchange in large economies.[15]

A third problem complicates the issue of knowing reserve prices even amid small populations—individual preferences are not stable and may be unknown even to consumers themselves. An individual who prefers fish one day may develop an allergy and despise it the next. Furthermore, when new products and services are introduced, individuals may have only a hazy idea what their reserve prices are for those things. Sellers are in a slightly better position in terms of knowing their own reserve prices given that they deal with reasonably predictable costs (e.g., raw materials, wages). Nonetheless, fluctuating input costs and changes in government policy also generate uncertainty for them. Finally, the aforementioned assumption about truthful reserve prices seems untenable because rational individuals have a proclivity to misrepresent their true reserve price in order to get a better deal in negotiations. Anyone who has negotiated the price of an automobile will attest to this, and sending false signals is often the "art of the deal" in business. Although misrepresentation may affect long-term trustworthiness, situations that shorten time horizons or the ambiguity of being discovered may prompt such behavior. The added complication of not knowing others' time horizons or perceptions of discovery further clouds the ability to ascertain exact reserve prices.

Let us first consider a world of diverse preferences. Figure 2 presents a "large" society consisting of one seller (X) among many buyers with different reserve prices (A, B, C, D). Assume that all reserve prices are truthful and known. In this world, the SJO (i.e., equally shared gains from trade) between A and X is $9 because A has a reserve buy price of $14 and X a reserve sell price of $4. Both receive $5 of the surplus. However, if Seller X offers his good only at the price of $9, satisfying the SJO requirement with Buyer A, Buyer B, who has a reserve buy price of $12, will receive only $3 of the surplus, whereas Seller X will capture $5 of it. Moreover, at a seller-offered price of $9, two consumers (C and D) are excluded for capturing any surplus because their reserve buy prices are below this level. Given the known reserve buy and sell prices, there are gains from trade to be made for all transactions between X, on the one hand, and A, B, and C, on the other, but the SJO for transaction AX would yield more surplus for X ($5) than for B ($3) in transaction BX and exclude the Pareto optimal transaction AC from occurring at all.

A Pareto optimal move to include Buyer C into the potential range of transactions by lowering the seller-offered price of $8 would increase the total buyer utility to $34 (the sum of A, B, and C's reserve prices), and Seller X would capture $12 of surplus by selling at $8. The $8 price represents the SJO price for Buyer B in that the gains from trade are equally divided between B and X ($4 each). Granted, at a sell price of $8, Buyer A benefits more than B or C, although all parties are better off (or at least not excluded from a transaction). Both Buyer B and Buyer C may believe that the $8 transaction is an "optimally unjust" situation in that A receives more benefit than they do, even though the $8 transaction is broadly just by the definition given earlier—all parties benefit from the transaction, though not all benefit equally. Remember

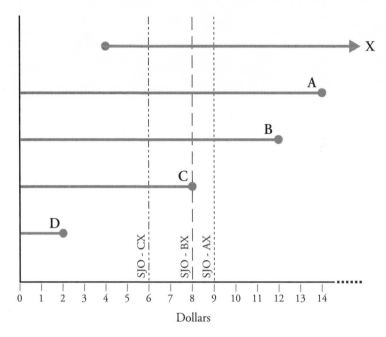

Figure 2. Socially Just Optimums with diverse reserve prices.

that we are in a world of known and truthful reserve prices, so this clarity may provoke some resentment in the sharing of gains from trade.

One means of mitigating potential resentment is for Seller X to offer a different price to each buyer based on each one's known and truthful reserve buy prices and to set it at the SJO for each consumer. As such, transaction AX would occur at $9, BX at $8, and CX at $6. Not surprisingly, if this were the case, an incentive for both A and B to misrepresent their reserve prices arises so that they can also get the lower price of $6 and surreptitiously capture more of the surplus. Alternatively, Seller X could modify her product with "ornamental baubles" or other pricing techniques so that there is a little bit of extra added or subtracted value to the good.[16] Of course, doing this would likely result in altering the reserve sell price of the good to the seller because the effort of ornamenting a product is not cost free. Nonetheless, figure 2 provides a theoretical case that the specter of "monopoly pricing" may not be as serious a problem as is commonly assumed by "trust-busting" advocates. A single seller in a world of known, truthful, and diverse reserve prices has an incentive to capture additional profit by modifying offered prices so as to maximize the

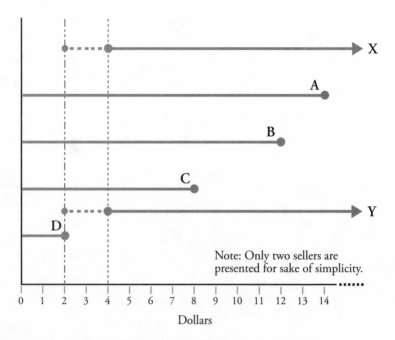

Figure 3. Gains from trade with multiple sellers and diverse buyer
preferences.

gains from trade; in such a situation, consumers benefit, and society is better
off. Although this outcome may not hit the Socially Just Optimum for every
individual and, interestingly, may leave more of the surplus to be captured by
some consumers, it does yield greater benefit for society as a whole. In other
words, free exchange is socially just by Pareto standards, albeit it may not be
optimally just by the requirement of perfect equity.

Another manner in which prices can be made to reflect the SJO is to allow competitors to enter the market. Figure 3 represents a world with many
competitive sellers, each with a similar reserve sell price. (Only two sellers
are presented in figure 3 for the sake of simplicity.) Realizing that gains from
trade can be captured with lower prices and with known and truthful reserve
prices, sellers such as Y can profit by taking less in the overall gains from trade
by catering to those with lower reserve buy prices. Thinly rational buyers who
seek to maximize their surplus will gravitate toward the lower sale price (as-
suming equal transaction costs between buying from X and buying from Y).
The standard model of competitive free markets would lead sellers to bid down

the price to their reserve sell price, resulting in consumers gaining the most in the gains from trade. Although consumers benefit disproportionately, the exchange still remains socially just. Moreover, any seller wishing to increase his take in the gains from trade has an incentive to innovate in such a way as to lower his reserve sell prices, which generally implies lowering costs by using resources (capital and labor) more efficiently, a Pareto-optimal move for society. This innovation is represented by the dashed lines for sellers in figure 3 and may result in the inclusion of buyers who were previously excluded from market transactions.

The important lesson of figures 2 and 3 is that in a world of diverse preferences (i.e., reserve prices) an equitable division of the gains from trade is unlikely to occur even though everybody will be better off than had trade not occurred at all. Seeking optimal (equitable) fairness is not socially efficient, and if overall wealth is a desired social goal, one need not worry about perfect equity.

Social Justice and Entrepreneurship under Uncertainty

Although diverse preferences in "large" societies complicate the goal of reaching perfect equity even under known and truthful reserve prices, the added problem of uncertainty and change makes the drive toward the SJO even more untenable. Figure 4 presents a world of uncertainty wherein reserve prices are vague and represented by "fuzzy clouds." Buyers facing new products may not have a strong sense of the value of these new things until they try them or see others consume them. Moreover, what might be highly valuable one day (represented within the right side of the "fuzzy cloud") may be of less desirability another day (the left side of the "fuzzy cloud"). Preferences change, and our desire for ice cream may be much less in the dead of winter than on a hot summer afternoon. The exact reserve buy price for any consumer exists within that cloud and is constantly shifting, largely unknowable to the seller and perhaps even to the consumer.

The seller's reserve price is slightly less ambiguous, particularly to the seller given the opportunity costs of producing the good. Competition with other sellers in the market also incentivizes each merchant to bid down prices to their lowest level lest the merchant lose sales to rivals. Nonetheless, buyers

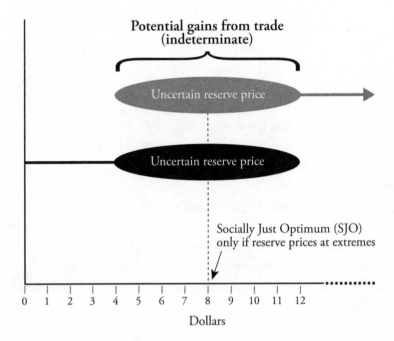

Figure 4. Gains from trade with uncertain reserve prices.

will not know with any certainty what the seller's lowest possible price is and therefore will be unable to evaluate accurately whether they are getting an equal, greater, or lesser share of the surplus.[17] So long as buyers are getting a price at or below their reserve buy prices, they can be happy knowing they are better off than prior to the transaction (or at least not worse off). Perhaps this uncertainty is all for the good in that it may dampen the resentment and envy that arise when buyers believe they are not capturing an equal or greater share of the gains from trade relative to the seller or other buyers. Less envy may indeed be a public good unto itself.[18]

What is immediately obvious is that not knowing where any of the consumers' reserve prices are at any given time makes it impossible to set prices at the SJO. In figure 4, a price set at $8 may be the SJO if the buyer's actual reserve price is $12 and the seller's reserve price is $4 (at the extreme boundaries of the two "reserve price clouds"). However, if the reserve price for either is elsewhere in the reserve price clouds, there is no guarantee that $8 is the equitable SJO price. In the aggregate, there may be some probabilistic degree of stability, and sellers are constantly trying to determine where to price goods and services via trial and error and other forms of marketing research, particularly with respect to routine and common products where competition is fierce (e.g., whiskey, bread). At best, price setting is educated guesswork, indicating that entrepreneurship may be as much art as it is science.[19] And while sellers have a difficult time offering an SJO price under conditions of uncertainty, third-party regulators of prices will have an even more difficult time. Efforts to set "socially just" prices for "necessary" commodities during emergencies (e.g., antigouging laws) can easily miss the mark and lead to significant unintended and harmful consequences. Reserve buy prices are most likely to shift upward during times of greater necessity, but they are not likely to shift upward equally for everyone. Although ostensibly designed to favor "needy" consumers, a "socially just" set price that is much lower than every reserve buy price will not incentivize buyers to truly evaluate their need for goods (relative to other consumers in the bidding process) and will prevent sellers from searching for a more optimal price. Gains from trade, at the end of the day, will not go to those who desire them most and who are willing to experiment entrepreneurially to supply them.

With uncertainty and diverse preferences reigning and the near impossibility of determining an SJO price under such conditions, are we left any hope that resources can be allocated justly between individuals in society? First, it is important to realize that so long as voluntary trade occurs and gains from trade are realized, we are achieving justice from an economic-exchange perspective. Under exchange, both parties are benefiting. But with diverse preferences and uncertain knowledge of reserve prices, is it possible to reach the Socially Just Optimum of equitably shared gains? If the goal is exactitude in equity, the answer is no, particularly over the long term. However, given that under known and truthful reserve prices, buyers and sellers will tend toward the SJO, it seems reasonable to assume that these individuals will also look for opportunities to search for and discover equitable distributions. This locates the notion of social justice in the process-driven realm of institutional opportunities and incentivized entrepreneurship.

As Adam Smith notes, humans have a "propensity to truck, barter, and exchange."[20] The opportunity to barter and exchange opens the possibility for experimentation for both buyers and sellers. Not only does such opportunity extend the market, a primary concern for Smith,[21] but the ability to interact freely allows negotiation over the gains from trade and allows both buyers and sellers to determine the most just prices for themselves based on changing conditions. Attempts to regulate and set rigid prices eliminate the ability to experiment and negotiate. Under uncertainty about reserve prices and in a world of changing and diverse preferences, cementing one specific price in place eliminates the possibility of adjustment toward the SJO (even if it can never be reached). Notions of social justice that are rooted in a particular equitable distribution quixotically chase a benchmark that doesn't exist or, at least, doesn't last for long. Rather, it is the opportunity to search and discover, to barter and exchange, and to explicitly and implicitly negotiate that allows society to strive for social justice. The opportunity to exchange, in other words, is the pathway for Crusoe and Friday and for all those who follow them to turn the Island of Despair into one of mutual prosperity.

Conclusion: A Framework for Broader Considerations

As noted at the outset, the space allowed for this chapter makes it impossible to cover every aspect of social justice. I have focused here on one small component of the broader concept—the distribution of social wealth (as derived from the gains from trade) and the opportunity to discover equitable and voluntary allocations in a world of diversity and uncertainty. Any theory of social justice that is interested in finding beneficial allocations must primarily take into account the freedom to discover an ever-changing and uncertain optimum. The freedom to search, experiment, discover, and negotiate is part of a necessary process that cannot be divorced from the eventual distribution. By ignoring liberty and the discovery process, and by advocating institutions designed to determine a preordained distribution of goods and services at any point in time, change and uncertainty will undoubtedly lead society away from a Socially Just Optimum as gains from trade are reshuffled.

The emphasis here on the gains from trade between buyer and sellers admittedly excludes important considerations such as the provision of public goods. Although public goods are conceived of in collective terms rather than in terms of bilateral exchange, the gains-from-trade perspective allows us to think about how the cooperative provision of such goods benefits individuals in different ways. It should be noted that not all individuals benefit equally from a public good despite the criteria of nonexcludability and nonrivalness. The individual who owns more property benefits more from the public good of "law and order" than someone who is destitute or has the skills of larceny. Thinking about the diverse and uncertain reserve prices individuals have for public goods sheds light on how to distribute possible contributions to the commonweal. This exchange perspective can also provide insight into concerns over duty and obligation, in particular our social responsibility to individuals who have high reserve buy prices but whose lack of resources excludes them from obtaining necessary goods such as food and shelter. A focus on exchange and reserve prices sheds light on the potential facts that not all individuals in need have the same preferences and that trying to promote means of discovering varying reserve prices for different life necessities will help allocate resources in a more efficient and just manner. An entrepreneurial market for charity is best for rescuing individuals from the Island of Despair.

PART II

How to Do (Social) Justice Right

A.

Use the Insights of Philosophers and Theologians

9

Opting Out:
A Defense of Social Justice

James R. Otteson*

BECAUSE "SOCIAL JUSTICE" allegedly makes the mistake of maintaining that the "results of the spontaneous ordering of the market" are instead the result of "some thinking being [having] directed them," F. A. Hayek argues that it is worse than a conceptual error: it is "nonsense, like the term 'moral stone.'"[1] Hayek may have thought he put a stake through the heart of all talk of social justice, yet reference to and use of the term *social justice* have not abated since he wrote these words; if anything, they seem to have increased. Hayek has a point that neither formal nor informal institutions enforce themselves and that the patterns of choice and allocation of resources that we see in fact result from the decisions of individuals—who are therefore individually, not collectively, accountable. Nevertheless, his insistence that we may criticize only individuals' particular decisions, not the overall results of many individuals' decisions, seems like idiosyncratic preference—in other words, prescriptivist, even rationalistic. The meaning of terms is determined by their use, and although we may stipulate a term's meaning based on consistent use or for the sake of argument, no one has the authority to fix, once and for all, the meaning of any term. Unfortunately for Hayek, then, the discussion of social justice is not closed.

In this brief chapter, I propose to do three principal things. First, I provide a bit of background for why discussions of social justice often seem inconclusive. I then indicate why we should care about social justice, despite recurring definitional difficulties, and point out what I take to be some confusion in

*James R. Otteson is the John T. Ryan Jr. Professor of Business Ethics at the University of Notre Dame.

discussions of social justice. Finally, I draw on some arguments David Hume and Adam Smith offer in support of a commercial society to propose and defend my own conception of social justice.

Background on Social Justice

Hayek's discussion of social justice seems to generate a problematic not unlike what Plato describes in *Euthyphro*. Socrates was on his way to stand trial for impiety and corruption of youth, a trial for which, if found guilty, he could face anything from fines to exile to execution—and, of course, Socrates was ultimately convicted and put to death. The philosophical action of *Euthyphro* centers on Socrates's discussion of the notion of piety with the young man Euthyphro. Euthyphro is bringing his father up on charges of impiety—which could have similarly grave potential outcomes for his father if convicted—and so Socrates suggests that because Euthyphro is taking such an extraordinary step regarding his own father, then Euthyphro must know what impiety is. Socrates professes not to know what piety and impiety are, and because he, too, is facing a charge of impiety, he proposes to make himself Euthyphro's "pupil" in the hopes of coming to understand exactly what he is up against.[2] There ensues an examination of several possible definitions of piety and impiety, all of which are found wanting. The dialogue ends with Euthyphro tiring of the embarrassment he suffers at Socrates's hands for not being able to produce a sound definition. Though Socrates wants to continue the discussion, Euthyphro decides simply to leave, and the dialogue ends inconclusively.

In later writings, Plato would articulate explicitly what is implicit in *Euthyphro*—namely, that for each term there is a single eternal essence, an Ideal or Form, from which the term gets its meaning and to which all proper uses of the term must refer.[3] If one is skeptical, however, about the existence of Platonic unchanging transcendent anchors for terms, then Hayek's criticism of the use of the term *social justice* begins to ring hollow. It sounds more like a plea to use *justice* the way he would prefer because he prefers not to use *social justice* at all. Fair enough, but others might have different preferences.

Nevertheless, there seem to be two recurring problems facing contemporary discussions of social justice. The first is that there is in fact no generally accepted, standard definition of the term. People apply the term *social justice* to many different things and to different kinds of things, so in arguing about it, they often end up talking past each other. The second and potentially weightier problem is that many of the various applications of the term do connect to and rely on one particular aspect of a standard conception of justice—namely, that it implies enforcement. So the issue concerns not just differences of opinion about how resources should be allocated, what virtue requires, what public institutions we should have, or how people should be treated. Rather, the issue is that the use of the term *social justice*, like the use of *impiety* in Socrates's time, entails either applying coercive mechanisms to enforce one view over another or endorsing punishment for incorrect behaviors or outcomes. The latter problem raises the stakes of the discussion: if something is a failure of social *justice*, then that means someone should be punished or made to pay. But if we are considering taking the significant step of punishing people or making them pay, then the former problem—definition—becomes more acute as well: we had better know what we are punishing or making them pay for.

Why Care about Social Justice?

There are many things one might find disagreeable in the world; some of them one might even consider unjust. An example of the latter might be the presence of large inequality: some countries are richer than others, and some people are richer than others. In some cases, the differences in wealth are huge: one hundred to one, one thousand to one, and even greater. A natural question is "Why?" Why are some countries richer than others? Why are some people richer, so much richer, than others?

But the question "Why?" has at least two senses. It might mean "How come?" and it might mean "What for?" The two are not the same thing. "How come?" asks for a *process explanation*: What are the historical mechanical or chemical or biological (etc.) causes that brought the situation, circumstance, eventuality (etc.) in question into being? By contrast, "What for?" asks for an *intention explanation*: Why did people do what they did?[4] The former, in other words, typically asks for a descriptive, empirical explanation involving no intent; the latter asks for a purposeful explanation of intent. The former, not being subject to rational action or autonomous judgment, admits of no moral judgment: it just is. (Why does the Earth revolve around the sun? Because of gravity. Why is there gravity? Because there is.) The latter is the result of someone's—or of several someones', sometimes acting in concert or coordination, sometimes not—taking deliberate action that he or she or they could have chosen not to take: it is a result of moral agency and thus admits of moral judgment. (Why was the bank robbed? Because that person or those people chose to rob it.)

It is important to keep these two categories of "why" questions separate. Otherwise, one runs the risk of categorical confusion. It can lead us to ask the "What for?" behind blind physical processes (processes, in other words, for which there is no "What for?") and to ascribe purpose and intention where none exists. Sometimes things happen unpredictably and unforeseeably, and no one is to blame (or credit). Why did the tornado strike here? Why did the hurricane strike then? Why did the flash floods hit exactly when the group of Thai soccer players happened to be hiking, stranding them inside a flooded cave? If by asking "Why?" we want to know the physical causes of what happened, these causes can often be retrospectively reconstructed. Sometimes, however, we are seeking an intentional, purposive answer to "Why?" though none exists. Sometimes our desire to find someone to blame for what has befallen us or others is so strong that we impute deliberate reasons even when none exists. Telling someone "it was bad luck" seems weak and unsatisfying, so we often find ourselves inclined to target some person, persons, or Person to blame or credit.[5]

Discussions of social justice often betray conflation of or equivocation between these two different kinds of answers to the question "Why?"[6] They identify things that are displeasing (at least to their advocates) and ask, "Why?" Why is there so much inequality? Why do some deserving people not get what they deserve? These questions are fair, reasonable, and important to ask. The problem is that they are only the first level of question. The next is: Do deliberate human action and intentional choice explain and account for what we see, or was it luck? And if it was the former, was it the result of choices that the individuals involved were entitled to make, as free and responsible moral agents? We therefore have three categories: (1) luck; (2) deliberate choice that the relevant agents are entitled to make; and (3) deliberate choice that the relevant agents are not entitled to make. Only category (3) comprises the two elements required for negative moral judgment—the result of deliberate human agency and choice, choice the agents should not have made—and thus only category (3) warrants moral condemnation. Any claim to injustice hence must demonstrate that the situation in question results from category (3). In such a case, *social* injustice would be the collective or aggregate results of individuals' choices that they should not have made.

It is important to note, however, that such a case is different from a collective action problem, in which circumstances are such that people are incentivized to choose differently from how they otherwise would wish to, resulting in a signature of effects they did not want. In case (2), the overall results might not be what a third party prefers, but the first and second parties chose what they wanted and were entitled to choose. Third parties might face an externality—an effect on or change in their circumstances—that they did not choose or would not have chosen, but that by itself does not yet rise to the level of (punishable) injustice. If Jack and Jill decide to marry, but Joe wants to marry Jill, Joe's circumstances have now changed for the worse as a result of Jack and Jill's choice; unless an extenuating circumstance is present (such as a promise to or contract with Joe), however, Joe has no grounds for demanding compensatory action.[7] In case (3), the "social" aspect might arise from the presence of many people making choices they should not have made. In that case, the qualifier *social* before *justice* would indicate more widespread similar instances of injustice.

Much advocacy of social justice is compromised by its failure to distinguish category (3) from categories (1) and (2) or its failure to properly discount instances of (3) for the admixture of (1) or (2) or both. It often runs them all together: something of which I disapprove has happened or is the case; therefore, remedies are required. And if remedies are not voluntarily forthcoming, then "social justice" demands it—*justice* being the preferred term not only because it connotes both gravity and certitude (even self-evidence) but also because it licenses coercive enforcement if necessary.[8] If, however, there are many similar acts of injustice, and if, moreover, they are encouraged or condoned by one's culture or institutions, then we may reasonably call such instances "social injustice" and seek not only to remedy the particular instances but also to condemn and even seek to change the culture and institutions.

Early Arguments for Social Justice in a Commercial Society

One way to think about what might constitute a conception of social justice builds on arguments in favor of a liberal political order and a commercial society that early political economists made. David Hume, for example, argues that commercial society encouraged an "indissoluble chain" linking industry, knowledge, and humanity. He claims that luxury is not necessarily a vice: "if a man reserve time sufficient for all laudable pursuits, and money sufficient for all generous purposes, he is free from every shadow of blame or reproach."[9] His argument is that the desire for luxury is really the desire to "enjoy ... those pleasures which are the fruit of [one's] labour."[10] This desire leads one to work hard—that is, to be industrious—to achieve those pleasures. But this labor requires one to develop skills, expand one's knowledge, and thereby increase the stock of knowledge of mechanical and other arts. Importantly for Hume, this desire also leads people to engage and develop their sociability. Because human beings are relatively limited in their natural gifts—they have no wings, fur, or claws, for example—the primary way for them to get what they want is by cooperating with other humans. And the best way to cooperate with others is to offer them something in return, which requires us to think not only of our own wants and desires but also of others' wants and desires. Hume argues that thinking of others leads us, even unwittingly, to become "more sociable."[11] The more cooperation in which we can engage, the more of our desires we stand a chance of satisfying; and we stand a better chance of getting others to cooperate with us if we act sociably rather than antisocially. Hume writes that people thus "flock into cities; love to receive and communicate knowledge; to show their wit or their breeding; their taste in conversation or living, in clothes or furniture."[12] "Particular clubs and societies are every where [*sic*] formed: Both sexes meet in an easy and sociable manner; and the tempers of men, as well as their behavior, refine apace."[13] On this basis, Hume concludes: "Thus *industry, knowledge,* and *humanity* are linked together by an indissoluble chain, and are found, from experience as well as reason, to be peculiar to the more polished, and, what are commonly denominated, the more luxurious ages"[14]—that is, in commercial societies.

According to Hume, commerce also disperses wealth "into numberless hands," who "employ it in the purchase of the common necessaries of life,"[15] thereby increasing their prosperity. This increasing prosperity not only "serve[s] to the ornament and pleasure of life," which is a benefit to individuals, but is moreover "advantageous to society; because, at the same time that they [that is, the ornament and pleasure of life] multiply those innocent gratifications to individuals, they are a kind of *storehouse* of labour, which, in the exigencies of state, may be turned to the public service."[16] Thus, wealth can enable a country to better address large-scale public necessities, such as infrastructure, disaster relief, and even, when necessary, war. And Hume believes that the benefits of commerce reach beyond national borders: "I shall therefore venture to acknowledge, that, not only as a man, but as a BRITISH subject, I pray for the flourishing commerce of GERMANY, SPAIN, ITALY, and even FRANCE itself."[17] Even France! Hume continues: "I am at least certain, that GREAT BRITAIN, and all those nations, would flourish more, did their sovereigns and ministers adopt such enlarged and benevolent sentiments toward each other."[18] Hume's argument thus has two main parts. First, commerce and trade, including in particular trade with people from other countries, lead to increasing material benefit and prosperity for all concerned because they are positive-sum transactions. Second, regular and mutually beneficial exchange with others softens our antagonisms toward them and can incline us to view others—even people from other countries, who speak different languages, have different cultures, and practice different religions—as opportunities instead of as enemies. This is Hume's "enlarged and benevolent sentiments."

Adam Smith makes a similar argument, as evidenced in the famous "invisible hand" passage from *The Wealth of Nations*.[19] There Smith argues that our natural desire to better our own condition leads us to seek cooperation with others in mutually beneficial ways—that is, ways that benefit others at the same time that they benefit ourselves. Now, according to Smith in *Theory of Moral Sentiments*, this can happen only within a "well-governed society," which Smith defines as one that protects "justice"—that is, a society whose public institutions protect "the life and person of our neighbour," each citizen's "property and possessions," and each citizen's "personal rights, or what is due to him from the promises of others."[20] When those three pillars of justice are protected, I am forestalled from getting what I want from others by enslaving them, stealing from them, or defrauding them. Thus, my only recourse is to make offers of voluntary cooperation, which others are free to decline if they so choose. Smithian justice protects others' opt-out option, which disciplines me to consider their interests, not just my own; and my own opt-out option disciplines them to consider my interests, not just theirs. Thus, each individual's desire to improve his own situation leads him, by an "invisible hand," to "promote an end which was no part of his intention"—namely, to benefit others, indeed "to promote the publick interest."[21] This argument for Smith is also twofold. First, individuals' cooperative exchanges lead to increasing individual and overall prosperity. Second, the requirement that exchanges must be cooperative and thus voluntary leads to mutual respect. If I cannot coerce you or mandate that you exchange with me—that is, if you retain your opt-out option—then I must understand that my interests and preferences do not trump yours, that I am not more important than you. My need for your voluntary consent requires that in order to achieve my own goals I must consider your wishes, your desires and needs, and your values and obligations and constraints and that I must therefore show you respect. My own opt-out option means you must show me respect as well. A society that protects Smithian "justice" therefore requires and engenders mutual respect.

As both Hume and Smith well understood, however, a commercial society is not perfect. People make bad choices, even by their own lights, and they buy and sell things they should not.[22] They can be persuaded and even duped by persistent salespeople or clever marketing or be exploited by asymmetrical knowledge.[23] Commercial activity can lead to negative externalities, collective-action problems, and environmental degradation.[24] There will be material inequality.[25] Commercial society's "creative destruction" is not only creative but also destructive—of community and of a sense of belonging, no less than of wealth.[26] Yet commerce, trade, and exchange have, as Hume and Smith predicted, improved our lives in many important ways. Billions of human beings now lead lives that their forebears could only have dreamed of. We live longer, healthier, and freer than ever before; in many parts of the world, the scope of opportunity is unprecedented; global rates of violence are at all-time lows; and the consensus against violence, racism, sexism, xenophobia, and other forms of discrimination is spreading.[27] Things are not perfect, and the improvements worldwide have been uneven, but by almost any objective measure conditions in the world are arguably better now overall than they have ever been, and there is considerable reason to be optimistic that the future will be yet better—with more improvement in the lives of ever more people.[28]

Perhaps even more important, however, is the dignity that such a society recognizes in each individual. Under the conception of "justice" endorsed by Smith, the only exchanges, trades, and partnerships allowed are those that are mutually voluntary. If each of us possesses an opt-out option—the right to say "no, thank you," and go elsewhere—then no one, not even the least among us, may be coerced or mandated into a transaction that he or she does not want. That means that for any transaction to be successfully executed, each party must recognize—and respect—the other's wishes, preferences, and values. Jeff Bezos, currently the richest person in the world,[29] might be able to offer me $1 billion to work for him, but as long as I can say "no, thank you," and go elsewhere if I so choose, our agency is immediately leveled, and we meet each other as peers. Protecting this sacred right to decline any offer or proposal is respecting people's dignity as free and equal moral agents. Indeed, one might argue that the bedrock moral principle of liberal political economy is both recognizing and exercising the right to say "no."

A Proposed Conception of Social Justice

One way to think about social justice, then, is as requiring, first, the removal of formal restrictions placed on any individuals or groups that limit their ability to achieve a flourishing life as they themselves understand it. A second step would be endorsement of political and economic policy that rewards people for engaging in cooperative behavior and partnerships that provide benefit and value to others as well as to themselves—and that hence punishes or disincentivizes behavior that benefits one person or group at the expense of others. As conceived by Hume and Smith, a liberal political regime that protects the widest scope of liberty of all its citizens that is compatible with the equal liberty of everyone else seems a plausible way to accomplish or at least work toward the first of these goals; a properly functioning market economy seems a plausible way to accomplish the second.

What neither a liberal political regime nor a properly functioning market economy addresses, however, or at least not directly, is two remaining central concerns of many uses of social justice—namely, inequality and informal obstacles to achievement. Regarding inequality, I suggest a lexical priority: as long as there are some people who still face formal, legal restrictions—that is, as long as there are some individuals or groups who are accorded differing and reduced legal rights and privileges than others in society due to what should be irrelevant factors about them (such as race, sex, etc.)—then rectifying that different treatment is the first priority and takes precedence over concerns about material inequality. Only once everyone has the same maximally extensive package of rights and negative liberties protected should we turn our attention to whatever concerns remain about inequalities in wealth.[30] My argument for this priority is that interference with people's negative liberties—the rights to be free from uninvited third-party interposition in their persons, to use their own justly acquired property as they see fit, and to order their lives according to their own schedules of value—is more destructive of people's abilities to achieve flourishing lives of meaning and purpose than anything else. When some may intrude into others' lives and coercively mandate or restrict their decisions, then a crucial part of their human identity, their moral agency, has been compromised. Thus, the first duty of any morally defensible liberal polity should be the default recognition of its citizens as full and equal moral agents capable of creating and entitled to create a life of meaning and purpose for themselves. Nothing else matters until this is the case.

Once that formidable task has been accomplished, I suggest that many worries about material inequality—though not all—will evaporate. A great inequality of wealth by itself cannot confer special power on the wealthier party as long as the less-wealthy party retains an opt-out option and the right to say "no, thank you," to any offer, request, or suggestion. Inequalities in wealth rise to a level warranting political redress only when they are combined with an authority to mandate choices against others' wills—but that, then, is an infraction of justice; the inequality itself is inert until it is joined with a coercive apparatus. Once the authority to coerce is eliminated, there may be other moral worries about material inequality that can arise—for example, the ability to seduce people into making unwise, or "noxious,"[31] choices with the lure of money—and we can safely turn our public attention to such cases once everyone's basic negative rights and liberties are formally recognized and protected.

The remaining part of many social justice concerns, then, consists of informal obstacles to achievement. Perhaps a society has mores, conventions, or prejudices that, although not enacted formally through law or other public institutions, nevertheless are sufficiently widespread to result in disfavored individuals or groups having fewer opportunities than other (favored) individuals or groups. Given the lexical priority for which I have argued that individuals' negative liberty should enjoy, any redress of informal obstacles to achievement must be pursued without infringing on this negative liberty. In most cases, that will mean that we should not use the coercive apparatus of law or policy to address them—in other words, they are not part of justice.

What recourses would that leave us, then? There are primarily two. First, the powers of speech, suasion, and association that the liberal polity ensures us. That is, we can condemn, including publicly, the mores, conventions, and prejudices that restrict the range of options available to the disfavored groups. We can make and publicize arguments demonstrating the moral failings of such informal restrictions. And we can refuse to participate in or cooperate or partner with organizations or projects or individuals who harbor or act on the objectionable prejudices. We can take our skills, our abilities, and our money elsewhere.

The second recourse we have to deal with such informal restrictions is the growing opportunities we have in a commercial society. One thing that happens in a properly functioning market economy is that people become wealthier. As wealth increases, our dependence on any one person or group for acquiring the goods and services we need and want and for partnerships and associations that contribute to the construction of lives of meaning and purpose decreases. In other words, wealth gives us options and therefore expands our independence. If this person will not hire me or if this company will not sell to me or if this group will not associate with or admit me, there are hundreds, even thousands, of others that will. In a perhaps surprising way, a market economy can enable people to capitalize on others' prejudices—benefiting the former for refusing to indulge society's prejudices and costing the latter for indulging theirs. This is especially important for the less advantaged in society, who often enjoy fewer options. As their wealth increases, their ability to chart a course for their lives that is consistent with their values—and that will include declining to associate, partner, or cooperate with organizations or people whose values are inconsistent with their own—increases. For the least advantaged in society, this greater ability can make a tremendous difference in their life prospects.

Conclusion

In a free society such as that envisioned by a Humean/Smithian liberal political order and market economy, people would not be formally (legally) punished for having prejudices or for refusing to partner with others, sell to others, hire others, and so on as a result of their prejudices. Respecting all citizens' equal moral agency would entail respecting their right not only to believe what they wish to believe but also to make choices that we disagree with—even choices we find reprehensible. But it does not require that we condone those choices or, perhaps more important, support or enable them with our time, talent, or treasure. Perhaps the single most important right that social justice should endorse and advocate for is what I have called the "opt-out option": the right to say "no, thank you," to any person, no matter how rich or privileged, and to any offer, any proposal, any request, any demand. We may not command that others choose and behave the way we might prefer, but if we are secure in our persons, properties, and voluntary agreements, then we may dissent from approving or supporting others whose behavior and choices are inconsistent with our own schedules of value.

No human society will ever be perfect, of course, because it is composed of, administered by, and created by imperfect human beings. Perhaps the best that can be hoped for, then, is a relatively better society or perhaps even a least-bad society, given our imperfections. What a commercial society constrained by protections of liberal negative justice proposes is both increasing material prosperity and morally improved relations among increasingly many people: formal equality, though allowing material inequality, will encourage prosperity and better moral relations. Perhaps that is true social justice, and a system of political economy that encourages increasing prosperity for all (especially the least advantaged) and respects the dignity of each individual—captured in particular by recognizing and respecting everyone's opt-out option—might constitute a conception of social justice worth defending.

Civil Society and Social Justice:
A Prospectus

James R. Stoner Jr.*

IN A RECENT article about the thought of Antonio Rosmini, one of two nineteenth-century Italian priests credited with coining the term *social justice*, Robert Kraynak asks

> why Rosmini invented the term "social justice" when he had at his disposal similar expressions from Aristotle and Aquinas. They defined justice as the constant will of rendering to others their due, and they viewed justice as the social virtue par excellence because it deals with relations to other people, not merely to oneself. Hence, Aristotle and Aquinas had no need to speak of social justice because the phrase would be redundant. Instead, they divided justice into two kinds: (1) general or complete justice and (2) particular or partial justice.[1]

I have more to say about Aristotle and Aquinas later, but let me now propose to answer Kraynak's question: Luigi Taparelli and Rosmini invented the new term because they had to deal with a new phenomenon uncovered by modern social and political theorists: civil society. This term, *civil society*, developed among seventeenth- and eighteenth-century thinkers in Great Britain and France to describe the commercial order that was emerging in Europe and was soon to encompass the entire world.[2] Entailed in this description was the recognition that the locus of production was not or was not optimally the household or the estate, but an indefinite network linked together by mar-

*James R. Stoner Jr. is Hermann Moyse Jr. Professor and director of the Eric Voegelin Institute in the Department of Political Science at Louisiana State University.

kets. Moreover, although states were needed to protect rights of ownership and enforce contracts of exchange, the expansion of wealth often depended on commercial relations that crossed state borders, and even within those borders state action was often more apt to suppress than to foster growth. By the time Rosmini coined the term *social justice*, this newly discovered phenomenon, civil society, already had a new science dedicated to its study: political economy.

In this brief chapter, I elaborate on the relation of social justice to civil society by reference to well-known texts, specifically Aristotle's *Politics* and *Ethics* and Hegel's *Philosophy of Right*, commenting on each author's insights and errors. After this secular accounting, I discuss the Catholic Church's attempt to invoke Thomistic natural law in developing its own social teaching, noting the latter's tendency to be swallowed up by Hegelian progressivism. Finally, I sketch a prospectus for thinking about social justice in the context of the modern world.

Aristotle and Economics

Aristotle introduces the *Politics* according to his genetic method, outlining the stages of human community from the household to the village to the city (polis), which he describes as already the complete community. Although the account at first appears historical, Aristotle makes clear that his point is analytical: the city is actually prior because it is complete, the community that makes possible human happiness. He famously concludes that this priority means the city exists by nature and that man is by nature a political animal.[3] The household includes the relations of the family (husband and wife, parents and children) as well as the relation of master and slave. Aristotle's discussion of the latter is notoriously difficult, raising the question of whether slavery is natural (and therefore, presumably, just) or merely conventional and concluding that it is mostly the latter but nevertheless useful, even necessary, for the heads of household to have the leisure for political action.[4] A discussion of acquisition follows the discussion of slavery and is likewise ambiguous or problematic. What Aristotle calls the natural modes of acquisition are either relatively primitive (herding, hunting, fishing, and agriculture) or startling (piracy, including wars to capture slaves). He calls unnatural those modes that depend on the invention of money, such as making a profit from exchange and especially from loaning money at interest; although money itself is not natural, he concedes, it is a necessary invention.[5] The Scholastic tradition read Aristotle's analysis of banking as condemnatory, but within a few lines he appears to endorse a liberal study of moneymaking and to recommend that cities take note of monopoly practices as a means to secure needed funds.[6]

What Aristotle's translators call the "village," which might also be translated as the "neighborhood," is mentioned only briefly in the *Politics*, in contrast to the household and the city, which are treated at much greater length. Indeed, when explaining that men are political because they are rational and engage with one another in speech about the advantageous, the good, and the just, Aristotle concludes that agreement about these things characterize a household and a city, leaving the village or neighborhood out.[7] Is the village where the market is to be found? Perhaps, but Aristotle does not say. Acquisition is part of household management, suggesting the household is the essential locus of trade as well as production, though the city is clearly involved in regulating trade, not least with other cities. Discussing the virtue of justice in *Nicomachean Ethics*, Aristotle gives an account of justice in exchange that remains a classic treatment of the topic.[8] Like punishment for crime, justice in exchange is a form of "arithmetic justice," where things of equal value change hands. Distributive justice, by contrast, is "geometric" or proportional, where the goods of the city, chiefly honors and offices, are distributed according to desert.

Wealth plays an important role in Aristotle's analysis of political life: it is, he suggests, a valid claim to rule because the city needs equipment, though it is hardly an exclusive claim, much less the highest claim, and the regime ruled by the wealthy, oligarchy, is after tyranny the worst of the six regimes. It is characteristic of Aristotle's realism that he thinks most cities oscillate between democracy and oligarchy, rule by the poor and by the rich, and that he thinks the most practicable political improvement would be to find a balance between them, a mixed regime he calls by the generic name *polity*, made stable if fortunes are also mixed so that neither the rich nor the poor predominate, but rather the middle class. Throughout the *Politics* and the *Ethics*, Aristotle is clear that acquisition is for the sake of use, that wealth is meant to serve virtue—in other words, that securing mere life is for the sake of the good life and that the "good life" means not a life of wealth and fame but a life of virtue, the genuine source of human happiness. In fact, Abram Shulsky, who catalogs the difficulties in Aristotle's account of slavery and acquisition, concludes that Aristotle's intention in remaining obscure must have been rhetorical, to guide his readers toward virtue and away from unlimited accumulation of wealth.[9] In short, Aristotle recognizes wealth as a good and even defines two virtues—liberality and magnificence—that involve the proper use of wealth, even great wealth in the latter case. But in his usual list of goods—external goods, goods of the body, goods of the soul—wealth is the least noble, however necessary as a condition for the others.

The Discovery of Civil Society

Fast-forward now to the nineteenth century, when it became clear to all that European society had become vastly different from society in Aristotle's time. In economic terms, this change was actually a recent development. The feudal world of manor, town, and kingdom was recognizably analogous to Aristotle's household, village, and polis, if on a scale corresponding to the emergent political form of the nation. Then, by the growth of commerce and manufacture, a process similarly described by thinkers as disparate as Adam Smith[10] and Karl Marx,[11] towns grew to be cities and achieved economic preeminence. Although the laws of the state sometimes facilitated this change in that it depended on enforcement of the rights of property and the obligations of contract, the state did not plan the transformation, and in the case of the French Revolution, of course, the new classes enriched by economic change upended the monarchy. There had developed a new way of thinking about wealth, too, encapsulated, for example, in the writings of John Locke,[12] a view that posited the equal natural rights of individuals, that emphasized the role of human labor and ingenuity in the creation of external value, and that affirmed rights of ownership independent of state distribution. This meant that there would be no limit on the accumulation of wealth, and the state's role became the protection of property, an aspiration less ennobling than the promotion of virtue but more measurable and precise.

In *Philosophy of Right*, the German philosopher Georg Wilhelm Friedrich Hegel sought to rewrite Aristotle for this modern world.[13] If we leave aside for now his account of the dialectic, Hegel identifies the three moments in what he calls the "ethical life"—by which he means not virtue in the soul but right order in the world—as the family, civil society, and the state. The family is not exactly the Aristotelian household: it has no slaves, nor are servants of any sort described as part of its structure, and the family itself is defined by the marriage of a man and a woman and the offspring that result—what we call today the "nuclear family," for Hegel makes clear that the family dissolves as the grown children marry and begin families of their own.[14] Nor is the state quite the same as the polis, for its concern is with actualizing freedom, not promoting virtue; its constitution is defined by the Crown, the executive, and the legislature, only the last of which includes the social classes or estates; and its sovereignty in relation to its peers in international law is part of its identity, as is its place in world history. The state encompasses but does not exactly include the church, Hegel remarks, for the latter is institutionally separate, appealing as it does to the religious feeling of the people, whereas the state embodies reason.[15]

Hegel makes clear that "the creation of civil society is the achievement of the modern world."[16] Civil society presupposes the state, which determines its laws—Hegel treats judges when discussing civil society, not the state—but it is distinct from it. Civil society is the realm where individual subjectivity has free play, where interests and desires are pursued; it is the sum of relations of concrete persons, the person described by Hegel as being "a totality of wants and a mixture of caprice and physical necessity."[17] Like Adam Smith and others, Hegel recognizes that the multitude of individuals seeking their own ends form a kind of whole: "In the course of the actual attainment of selfish ends—an attainment conditioned in this way by universality—there is formed a system of complete interdependence, wherein the livelihood, happiness, and legal status of one man is interwoven with the livelihood, happiness, and rights of all."[18] Human needs are dynamic, not merely natural, so they grow after the satisfaction of primitive needs and altogether replace them in an advanced society. Although individuals have equal rights, the inequality of talents and skills and the numerous contingencies of inheritance and opportunity inevitably mean that civil society is suffused with differences, which become differences of social class, described at first as agricultural, business, and civil service, with the business class subsequently divided into craftsmen, manufacturers involved in mass production, and traders. Although the young resist choosing a particular line of work, society depends on such choices, and men eventually come around to them, developing a certain esprit de corps with others who share their work and often organizing themselves into corporations, particularly insofar as civil society pulls men outside their families and weakens their personal security. Hegel supposes a general regime of "freedom of trade and commerce in civil society,"[19] but he allows that activities and prices can be subject to what he calls "police" or what we might call regulation, and he notes that the public authority has a role to play in caring for the poor. Without analyzing the business cycle, he nevertheless is aware that there are times of expansion and times when the masses' standard of living is threatened—recommending that "they might be given subsistence indirectly through being given work, i.e., the opportunity to work," rather than handouts so as not to "violate the principle of civil society and the feeling of individual independence and self-respect in its individual members."[20] He recognizes as well the dynamic character of international trade: "This inner dialectic of civil society thus drives it—or at any rate drives a specific civil society—to push beyond its own limits and seek markets, and so its necessary means of subsistence, in other lands which are either deficient in the goods it has overproduced, or else generally backward in industry, etc."[21]

Hegel is not a critic of civil society or of capitalism in the sense that he thinks it is fundamentally unsound and replaceable—he ridicules those who think societies and their constitutions can be designed arbitrarily—but he does think the state is clearly superior to civil society in the order of things and is capable through its laws and regulations to manage its failings. "The state is the actuality of the ethical Idea," he writes, or, equivalently, "the actuality of concrete freedom."[22] Whereas civil society results from subjective desire, the state embodies objective, rational duty, and Hegel locates human freedom in claiming one's duty as one's own, not in pursuing particular desires, at least not when they conflict with the duties of citizenship. Although indeed charged with protecting rights, the state as Hegel describes it is not a limited nightwatchman, but an active patron of human freedom. For example, universities are established by the state, and Hegel is proud that professors are civil servants; he does not include in civil society, as we might, a host of voluntary associations, including churches and schools, that are independent of the state and more closely integrated with the world of business than with the state. It is easy to see why Hegel is the darling of advocates of the administrative state still today, not to mention why Marx was a sort of Hegelian, for all his criticisms of Hegel and his radicalization of the Hegelian dialectic.[23] Both see civil society as a creation of the modern world, differing only as to whether it is something that can be managed or something that must be overcome. Neither Hegel nor Marx, to my knowledge, uses the term *social justice*.

Papal Encyclicals

The term *social justice*, as I mentioned at the outset, arose in Catholic social thought as it developed in the nineteenth century. In Rosmini's *Constitution under Social Justice*, a projected constitution for a unified Italian state, the term seems to refer particularly to the proper balance of social classes in the institutions of government and to reject the majoritarianism of the French Revolution.[24] Rosmini's argument thus seems consonant with Hegel's account of the constitution in the *Philosophy of Right*, and in fact Rosmini wrote a book with the same title.[25] There is no mention of Hegel in the *Constitution under Social Justice*, no doubt because Hegel's anthropology, not to mention his theodicy, was at odds with Christian teaching. When the Catholic Church, influenced by Taparelli and Rosmini, writes authoritatively upon civil society in *Rerum novarum*,[26] it turns instead to Thomas Aquinas, whose own authority on questions of social order is Aristotle. Not in that document but in conclusions sometimes drawn from it, the ironic consequence of ignoring Hegel has been that in practice those seeking to implement Catholic social teaching end up promoting the Hegelian state. What I mean to suggest is that by attending to the social analysis of civil society Hegel presents—which builds upon the liberal social and political thinking of the centuries that preceded him—one might more profitably develop an account of social justice that restores Thomistic and Aristotelian anthropology without succumbing to the statist trap.

The common title of Pope Leo XIII's encyclical, *Rerum novarum*, comes, as is traditional in papal documents, from the encyclical's first words, carefully chosen to convey the subject matter that follows. The "new things" (rendered in the English version as "revolutionary change") it focuses on are found "in the vast expansion of industrial pursuits and the marvelous discoveries of science; in the changed relations between masters and workmen; in the enormous fortunes of some few individuals, and the utter poverty of the masses; the increased self-reliance and closer mutual combination of the working classes," to which Pope Leo appends "the prevailing moral degeneracy," which was, of course, hardly new.[27] The four elements listed clearly belong to modern civil society as Hegel describes it, and the balance of the encyclical exhorts reform, particularly by encouraging the formation of Catholic workers' unions and by reminding owners of their duties to those they employ. From the beginning, socialism is denounced because private property is said—going beyond Aristotle and Aquinas, by the way[28]—to follow from natural law. The family is treated as natural, too, and in fact natural law ensures the right to property in the head of the family so that he can provide their material sustenance. The state is described as responsible for the protection of the rights of all classes (or both classes, for Leo writes principally of the rich and the workers) and therefore in particular the rights of the working class, rights that include the "natural right" of association as well as the rights of the family. The thrust of the encyclical is to see that the state protects workers in their right to unionize and bargain with their employers for fair wages and decent working conditions, not to insist that the state take these matters into its own hands. Moreover, there is of course much about the Catholic Church's work for the poor and its role in facilitating workers' associations.

Leo does use the term *civil society*, writing at one point that "[c]ivil society exists for the common good, and hence is concerned with the interests of all in general, albeit with individual interests also in their due place and degree."[29] But he does not seem to treat it as something new, as Smith and Hegel do, much less as something different in kind from the state, in fact writing in the sentence after the one just quoted that civil society is a "public society" and quoting Aquinas on the "commonwealth." And although Leo writes of justice throughout, he does not use the term *social justice*, which apparently first appears forty years later in a papal encyclical, *Quadragesimo anno*,[30] issued to commemorate and elaborate upon *Rerum novarum*.[31] Civil society in the sense that I have been using the term begins to receive attention in Pope John Paul II's encyclical *Centesimus annus*, which praises "initiative and entrepreneurial ability," notes that "the modern business economy has positive aspects," and acknowledges that "the free market is the most efficient instrument for utilizing resources and effectively responding to needs."[32] John Paul proposes "a society of free work, of enterprise, and of participation" not as an alternative to market society, but as its perfection, "the market be[ing] appropriately controlled by the forces of society and by the State, so as to guarantee that the basic needs of the whole of society are satisfied."[33] Whether this appreciation of market society remains regnant in Catholic circles might be doubted in light of the recent encyclical prompted by environmentalist concerns.[34]

On the one hand, it is not surprising that the Catholic Church looked askance at the emergent theory of civil society. The theory's first analysts were often its advocates, and they seemed to elevate self-interest over charity on the scale of virtues—or, rather, to subordinate virtue in all its forms to self-interest understood as an anthropological fact. Explaining human obligation solely in terms of individual rights seemed likewise to undercut human communities and the bonds of family, faith, and nation that placed duties before rights in the moral life and placed what was given before what could be chosen. On the other hand, rights adhere to persons, and the elevation of the person was now seen—indeed, was seen even by Hegel—to be a distinctive contribution to human civilization of Christianity or of Judaism and Christianity, these religions understanding every person to be made in the image of God and destined to be judged for all eternity. Moreover, the community of the faith, for both Christians and Jews, transcends the boundaries of states and makes possible relations of trust that are independent of political enforcement, critical to the expansion of commerce in the face of hostile state action. My point, though, is not to ask whether, were there a choice, civil or commercial society ought to be established by a regnant state, but to consider whether this society, having emerged, ought to be recognized as a natural development and as a good. My hypothesis is that this is so: as the polis emerged naturally and later was accepted by the Catholic Church as a good—even though it was sometimes perverted, its essence was to be just—so civil society should be recognized as a valuable human development, separate in principle from the state but essential for the satisfaction of human needs and desires. And if this hypothesis is correct, then the next step is to ask how we ought to think about social justice as the specific virtue of this specific order of human affairs.

A Prospectus for Defining Social Justice

Here are my initial suggestions. First, social justice includes recognizing the basic rights of individuals out of which civil society developed: the rights to life, to personal liberty, and to property, including rights of exchange and communication. Because I am accounting civil society as one moment in the order of things, not as a replacement for the state but as its companion, so to speak, it should be acknowledged that the protection of these rights will depend upon the state, and so it should be supposed that their definition will vary from state to state. Because I also noted at the outset that civil society and certainly the commercial economy cross state boundaries, it would be appropriate that there be internationally recognized human rights—though, to be just, an international order of human rights ought to respect not only civil society but also the claims of the family and the state. The rights would be equal rights, granted as they are to persons as such, but it is an obvious empirical fact that the free exercise of rights typically leads to unequal outcomes, if only because people value different goods differently. Inequality of wealth is not a concern of that aspect of social justice focused on rights, unless such inequality of wealth hinders others' rights.[35] Regarding rights to opportunity, of course, it sometimes does, so there is room for judgment in different states as to how to ensure genuine opportunity to the less advantaged without crushing enterprise and initiative with administrative burdens.

Second, social justice would include just arrangements within the various associations and institutions of civil society. As these associations and institutions vary in scope and purpose, so the principles of justice within them would vary: authority and reward within a firm are different from authority and reward within a school, and they are in turn different within a club. Because these associations are voluntary—the characteristic fact of civil society is that its relations are chosen and terminable—the general presumption ought to be that each association or institution establishes its own pattern, though I suppose social norms might emerge that confine the range of possibilities. There might also be circumstances—for example, the lingering effects of caste oppression—where the state might intervene to override institutional or associational autonomy, as in laws against racial discrimination in the United States. Like regulation for the sake of equal rights, regulation for the sake of institutional justice ought to be occasional, not comprehensive. The market has a way of punishing those who ignore social norms but can also provide room for those whose views are unpopular at a certain point in time.

Finally, social justice ought to include limits on the reach of its own principles, on the one hand in the name of the family, on the other in the name of the state. As the sovereign that makes and enforces law and provides protection against foreign danger, invasion of rights, and material desperation, the state encompasses all citizens and demands of them certain duties—established by majoritarian consent if the government is democratic but enforceable even against dissenters. A just state is a limited state, to be sure—it ought, naturally, to provide sufficient liberty for civil society—and it ought to establish a constitutional government, but it is a different kind of association from the voluntary associations of civil society and operates under different principles. Likewise, the family, as a natural unit that has a purpose independent of the state and of civil society, needs to be understood and protected on its own terms, which, rooted in biology, are different from those of either civil society or the state. To force it to conform to the principles of civil society is as mistaken and unjust as to force civil society to be subject to the family, as was the great injustice of feudal times.

Although I have adopted Hegel's tripartite division—family, civil society, and the state—I have not subordinated one to the other as he did with his dialectical logic, issuing in the dominance of the state. Nor have I followed Aristotle in asserting the priority of the city to the village and the household, not least because what he incorporated in the polis has been divided between civil society and the state and because the household, too, was changed by the abolition of personal slavery. As for the church, in keeping with the argument that the question of human order is a question that needs first to be addressed in human terms or, in other words, that the family, civil society, and the state can be defined as natural goods, I have intentionally not subordinated it either to the state (as in Hegel) or to civil society, as in those theorists who treat churches simply as forms of civil association. Is not the church's calling to be, so to speak, orthogonal to the whole arrangement, forming and transforming the persons who inhabit families, who live in society, and who govern the state, while offering its guidance concerning justice and its example concerning love in each realm?

Social Justice:

Intersecting Catholicism, Citizenship, and Capitalism

John A. Moore*

I refuse to accept the idea that the "isness" of man's present nature makes him morally incapable of reaching up for the eternal "oughtness" that forever confronts him. ... I have the audacity to believe that peoples everywhere can have three meals a day for their bodies, education and culture for their minds, and dignity, equality and freedom for their spirits.

—**Martin Luther King Jr.**, Nobel Peace Prize acceptance speech,
December 10, 1964

We hold these truths to be self-evident, that all men are created equal, that they are endowed by their Creator with unalienable Rights, that among these are Life, Liberty and the pursuit of Happiness.—That to secure these rights, Governments are instituted among Men, deriving their just powers from the consent of the governed.

—U.S. Declaration of Independence

This process of Creative Destruction is the essential fact about capitalism.

—**Joseph Schumpeter**, *Capitalism, Socialism, and Democracy*

WITHOUT DOUBT, SOCIAL justice is one of the most politically charged issues in American politics today. Social justice essentially looks toward attending to the needs of individual citizens. Contemporary commentators and activists see social justice through a variety of different perspectives. Although most current American policies address the material needs of less-fortunate citizens, this chapter argues that any effective approach

---

*John A. Moore is professor in the Department of Finance and Economics at Walsh College.

to the social justice question must also encompass spiritual and civic elements that go well beyond a simple materialist response.

Any consideration of social justice should address the whole of each individual human experience rather than simply the redirection of the goods and services of economic production. Social justice is about individual human beings, not about the distribution of economic output. This is precisely why consideration of individual life purpose, political activity, and economic well-being potentially serves as a useful lens to consider how social justice can be achieved as fully as possible in light of humanity's inherent limitations.

Technical dictionary definitions of the term *social justice* include examples such as "a state or doctrine of egalitarianism" (*Webster's*) or "justice in terms of the distribution of wealth, opportunities and privileges within a society" (*Oxford Dictionary*). However, these technical definitions do not necessarily provide clarity given the number of competing interpretations. For example, Michael Novak notes that "[s]ocial justice is really the capacity to organize with others to accomplish ends that benefit the whole community."[1] He adds that "[o]ne happy characteristic of this definition of the virtue of social justice is that it is ideologically neutral. ... [However,] we must rule out any use of 'social justice' that does not attach to the habits (that is, virtues) of individuals. Social justice is a virtue, an attribute of individuals, or it is a fraud."[2] At the opposite end of the spectrum, Catholic theologian Gustavo Gutiérrez states in his work *A Theology of Liberation* that "[c]harity is today a 'political charity.' ... [I]t means the transformation of a society structured to benefit a few who appropriate to themselves the value of the work of others. This transformation ought to be directed toward a radical change in the foundation of society, that is, the private ownership of the means of production."[3]

Novak's and Gutiérrez's definitions represent starkly different interpretations of social justice. Novak's view rests upon a broader definition of social justice that addresses the needs of community members in terms of a state of well-being that is both tangible and intangible. Crucially, he considers the process to successfully achieving social justice as a voluntary one premised on free will exercised by the individual within the parameters of a market economy. Gutiérrez, in contrast, views justice in almost purely economic terms. He entertains the position that social justice might likely be incompatible with capitalism. He also asserts that coercive redistribution of economic wealth is justified in the name of attaining social justice.

How has social justice been viewed in the past? If we look far back in history, we find a world contending with great uncertainty. Attaining the basic human needs of food, shelter, and clothing was far from easy. Famine occurred with great frequency, and there was more violence. In this context, many great thinkers categorically rejected a materialist explanation for both justice and ultimate human happiness. Aristotle in *Nicomachean Ethics* and Boethius in *Consolation of Philosophy* spoke to the question of human happiness. Aristotle concluded that a contemplative life is the pathway to personal happiness and fulfillment rather than fame, honors, or wealth.[4] Boethius determined that happiness must come from within one's heart and soul and that one's own experiences of earthly power are of no importance as one faces one's own death.[5]

In light of this brief introduction, how can we achieve social justice within the context of the American experience? Even as the United States has experienced significant economic, demographic, social, and cultural changes since its founding, there remain strong strands of continuity within our traditions of individual life purpose, politics, and economics. In the American experience, these three traditions have been more specifically represented by Judeo-Christian thought, concepts of citizenship, and the impact of capitalism.

All three of these "continuities" have evolved over time, but their foundational impact on the present American way of life remains quite strong. Even as fewer Americans belong to organized religious denominations and fewer regularly attend church services, the nation continues to reflect a significant Judeo-Christian worldview in its attitudes and behavior. Present American views on citizenship and the mutual responsibilities between government and citizens to each other remain foundationally similar to ideas circulating during the early-republic era even as Supreme Court decisions, constitutional amendments, and presidential addresses have shaped those ideas to be more inclusive and more clearly defined. Although the United States has never practiced unbridled laissez-faire capitalism, even in the wake of the New Deal and the Great Society, it remains fundamentally capitalist in its economic structure.

Catholicism

Catholicism has deeply influenced American thought and culture since the nineteenth century. Today the largest single religious denomination in the United States is Roman Catholicism. The Catholic Church has addressed the issue of social justice, and its proclamations have had an impact both in the United States and throughout the world.

Two significant Catholic papal encyclicals address the related issues of social justice and capitalism. Pope Leo XIII issued *Rerum novarum* in 1891, and Pope John Paul II issued *Laborem exercens* ninety years later in 1981. At the heart of both documents are considerations of the human experience and right relationships in the world. *Rerum novarum* was written at a time when the Second Industrial Revolution was in full swing in western Europe and the United States and large numbers of workers were migrating from farm to factory. A significant number of workers were experiencing a dramatic change in working conditions.

In *Rerum novarum*, Leo XIII condemned both the prevailing capitalism and socialism. In critiquing capitalism, he noted that "a small number of very rich men have been able to lay upon the teeming masses of the laboring poor a yoke little better than that of slavery itself." However, Leo did not see socialism as an acceptable remedy. He charged that "socialists, working on the poor man's envy of the rich, are striving to do away with private property, and contend that individual possessions should become the common property of all. ... [T]hey are, moreover, emphatically unjust, for they would rob the lawful possessor. ... [E]very man has by nature the right to possess property as his own."[6]

The pontiff addressed issues of inequality. He commented that "[t]here naturally exist among mankind manifold differences of the most important kind; people differ in capacity, skill, health, strength; and unequal fortune is a necessary result of unequal condition."[7] However, in the eyes of the church, these differences did not amount to simply a world of competing winners and losers. Leo insisted that "[a]s for riches and the other things which men call good and desirable, whether we have them in abundance, or are lacking in them—so far as eternal happiness is concerned—it makes no difference; the only important thing is to use them aright. ... It rests on the principle that it is one thing to have a right to the possession of money and another to have a right to use money as one wills. Private ownership, as we have seen, is the natural right of man."[8]

Although Leo clearly endorsed the concept of private property, he also clearly addressed the *voluntary* moral *obligation* to concern oneself with the well-being of others. He declared that, "[t]rue, no one is commanded to distribute to others that which is required for his own needs or that of his household. … But, when what necessity demands has been supplied, and one's standing fairly taken thought for, it becomes a duty to give to the indigent out of what remains over."[9] This exhortation to look out for others, however, was not intended to completely alleviate the frailties and challenges of the human experience or to establish material equality. Leo noted that "[a]s for those who possess not the gifts of fortune … poverty is no disgrace, and that there is nothing to be ashamed of in earning their bread by labor."[10]

Leo described a worldview of the human experience that transcends simple materiality. He asserted that "the true worth and nobility of man lie in his moral qualities, that is, in virtue; that virtue is, moreover, the common inheritance of men, equally within the reach of high and low; rich and poor; and that virtue, and virtue alone, wherever found, will be followed by the rewards of … happiness."[11] In Pope Leo's view, the quest for human fulfillment and happiness was ultimately dependent more on the egalitarian distribution of virtue than of possessions.

Almost a century later, John Paul II supplemented Leo's commentary, offering in *Laborem exercens* an updated view of the nature of work by noting that "[man] is *called to work*. … [M]an's life is built up every day from work, from work it derives its specific dignity, but at the same time work contains the unceasing measure of human toil and suffering."[12] He added that "the general situation of man in the modern world … calls for the discovery of the *new meanings of human work* … [and] it indicates that the social question must be dealt with in its whole complex dimension."[13]

Clearly, further technological advances were a major part of this new world. John Paul acknowledged that "man's work has today in many cases ceased to be mainly manual, for the toil of human hands and muscles is aided by *more and more highly perfected machinery* … [but] even in the age of ever more mechanized 'work,' *the proper subject of work continues to be man*."[14] John

Paul's primary concern with postindustrial economies centered on the dangers of materialism. He stated that "from the beginning of the industrial age, the Christian truth about work had to oppose the various trends of *materialistic and economistic* thought. ... [T]he *danger* of treating work as a special kind of 'merchandise,' or as an impersonal 'force' needed for production ... *always exists*, especially when the whole way of looking at the question of economics is marked by the premises of materialistic economism."[15]

A number of recent Catholic authors have taken issue with the foundational positions of both *Rerum novarum* and *Laborem exercens*. Andrea Tornielli and Giacomo Galeazzi quote Pope Francis's exhortation *Evangelii gaudium*, in which he stated that "some people continue to defend trickle-down theories which assume that economic growth, encouraged by a free market, will inevitably succeed in bringing about greater justice and inclusiveness in the world."[16] They conclude that "we are facing not only a financial-economic crisis or a stock market crisis due to speculative investments but first and foremost a crisis of *humanity*, one dominated by consumerism and one reduced to its needs alone."[17] They add that contemporary capitalism calls "for the total freedom of markets, while any willingness on the part of nations to assume responsibility for the common good in order to protect the people 'discarded' by the economy that 'kills' is labeled as state control."[18]

Angus Sibley further explores this theme of distorted economic distribution when he states that "Catholic social teaching emphasizes the doctrine of the *universal destination of goods*, which means ... every human being [should] have at least a basic sufficiency of this world's goods. ... Today, the majority of Americans ... are suffering a kind of oppression by a minority group, the very rich, who contrive to capture most of the benefits of American growth, leaving the rest to put up with static or declining incomes, high unemployment or underemployment, and increasingly precarious, frustrating, and overstressful jobs."[19]

However, many authors take the opposing view that the encyclicals discussed are fully compatible with free markets. Maciej Zięba maintains that John Paul's writings limit the state to "guaranteeing the rights and safety of working people."[20] In Zięba's view, the pope did not find inherent bad in a capitalist economy but rather critiqued capitalist societies "on the error of believing that economic reality is the only reality—what he [John Paul] calls the 'absolutizing' of life. He reminds us that 'the economy in fact is only one aspect and one dimension of the whole of human activity.'"[21]

Gabriel Martinez provides a specific counterargument to Sibley, noting that "there is abundant evidence of a high correlation between economic growth and the average incomes of the poorest fifth of society."[22] The studies he cites do not prove causality, but they identify empirical examples where the poor have experienced an improvement in their economic condition while living under capitalism. Sibley's charge that capitalism "kills" is certainly a hyperbolic overreach.

The heart of Catholic teaching on social justice hearkens back to the past. Just like Aristotle and Boethius, the church views justice with a far greater emphasis on personal conduct. Although it is crucial that all human beings should have access to basic needs, the purpose of life should be far more attached to spirituality than to materialism. The encyclicals tacitly endorse economic activity as inherently good.

In the twenty-first-century United States, Catholic teaching contends with the fruits of the Enlightenment and the Industrial Revolution. Americans are awash with material prosperity and a culture that fully embraces conspicuous consumption. Many Americans see social justice as an issue that revolves solely around income inequality and a need to provide a certain minimum basket of goods and/or services to less-fortunate citizens. The countercultural message from the church declares that the greatest benefit from a genuine application of social justice derives from the spiritual gains to both the providers and the beneficiaries of good works.

Citizenship

Citizenship concerns both the rights and obligations of individuals within a political community. The U.S. Founding Fathers were deeply concerned that a successful experiment in representative government required "virtuous" citizens. They consciously built checks and balances into the Constitution and ratified the Bill of Rights because of their cautious views about the deficiencies of human nature.

The historian Gordon Wood notes that "[p]erhaps everyone in the eighteenth century could have agreed in theory no state was more beautiful than a republic, whose whole object was the good of the people."[23] The Founders were keenly aware that there was a risk in any political structure where sovereignty rested in its citizenry. Wood further states that "[i]n a republic, however, each man must somehow be persuaded to submerge his personal wants into the greater good of the whole. This willingness of the individual to sacrifice his personal interests for the good of the community—such patriotism or love of country—the eighteenth century termed 'public virtue.' A republic was such a delicate polity precisely because it demanded an extraordinary moral character in the people."[24]

An entire section of Adam Smith's work *The Theory of Moral Sentiments* addresses the subject of virtue. Smith declared that "[t]he man who acts according to the rules of perfect prudence, of strict justice, and of proper benevolence, may be said to be perfectly virtuous. But ... his own passions are very apt to mislead him. ... [T]he most perfect knowledge, if it is not supported by the most perfect self-command, will not always enable him to do his duty."[25] Smith, like the Founding Fathers, acknowledged the shortcomings of human nature.

In the *Second Treatise*, John Locke defined the key rights of human beings under the social contract to be "life, liberty and property."[26] Thomas Jefferson's final draft of the Declaration of Independence accepted Locke's premise subject to the politically expedient rephrasing "life, liberty and the pursuit of happiness." Both Locke and Jefferson believed that rights can only be "natural." Rights, as understood by Locke and Jefferson, link to concepts of individual happiness and fulfillment more so than economic outcomes.

One of the great problems in modern American politics is confusion concerning what constitutes a right, and this confusion spills over into talk about social justice. Rights derive from the nature of human beings and their relationship to the world. As a consequence, issues such as health care and education should not be viewed as rights. They may represent issues for acceptable or unacceptable public policy, but they are not rights because they do not derive from nature. Rather, they derive from human use of ingenuity and technology.

It can be argued that contemporary American society is not in a virtuous state. Public political discourse reflects a discontent traceable to a creeping shift in what are perceived as rights. The rise of progressivism since the early twentieth century has consciously been accompanied by an expanding demand for material-oriented "rights." As a consequence, the current government-sponsored economic redistribution and assistance would have been unimaginable to the Founders.

E. F. Schumacher characterizes some of the challenges that modern economies present to societies. He writes that

> we can say today that man is far too clever to be able to survive without wisdom. ... [T]he hope that the pursuit of goodness and virtue can be postponed until we have attained universal prosperity and that by the singleminded pursuit of wealth, without bothering our heads about spiritual and moral questions, we could establish peace on earth, is an unrealistic, unscientific and irrational hope. ... [N]ow that we have become very successful, the problem of spiritual and moral truth moves into the central position.[27]

Schumacher concludes that "[t]he cultivation and expansion of needs is the antithesis of wisdom. It is also the antithesis of freedom and peace. Every increase of needs tends to increase one's dependence on outside forces over which one cannot have control, and therefore increases existential fear. Only by a reduction of needs can one promote a genuine reduction in those tensions which are the ultimate causes of strife and war."[28]

From a political perspective, social justice in the United States today is concerned primarily with economic distribution. This preoccupation with material matters strays away from the prevailing sentiment at the founding, that personal virtue is a key element to a sound nation. Schumacher's comments identify the fact that technology and consumerism are factors that need to be tamed by a renewed focus on wisdom and virtue in our present times.

Capitalism

Capitalism has greatly benefited humankind. The impact of capitalism on global economic prosperity since the publication of Adam Smith's work *Wealth of Nations* in 1776 has been transformative. In the middle of the eighteenth century, all parts of the world had to worry to some degree about the three essential needs—food, clothing, and shelter, with the greatest of them being food. Famine was a risk even in the leading world economies into the late eighteenth century and persists within certain regions of the world today.

Capitalism, as Joseph Schumpeter points out, is inherently disruptive because it encourages innovation and facilitates change.[29] Entrepreneurs constantly seek out better and more efficient economic activities that consumers find beneficial. This characteristic creates winners and losers on a daily basis. It is more egalitarian in terms of providing opportunity than it is toward the output of economic activity. Nonetheless, its chaotic nature has produced incredible leaps in the material well-being of the world over the past two and a half centuries.

Deirdre McCloskey has pointed out that in the aggregate the spread of capitalism and the technological gains accompanying it have improved global economic well-being.[30] She notes that since 1800 freedom has spread, the world population has grown sixfold, and per capita consumption has increased about eight and a half times. The vast majority of Americans in the twenty-first century possess more material comfort than anyone in the world just a few centuries earlier.

Israel Kirzner notes that "[t]he question of social justice under capitalism is seen as the question of its distributive justice. [However,] in reality the entire notion of distribution is a flawed one, and the identification of the question of justice as being one of distributive justice is, consequently, equally flawed and quite misleading." He adds that "[g]oods are not first produced and then distributed, as would be the case in a socialist state. Individual incomes are earned *simultaneously* with the process through which the size and composition of the supposed 'pie' are determined."[31]

Gordon Tullock provides a sharp critique of the American state regarding income redistribution. He states that it is "an area where government does not perform well. ... [T]he voters' desire to abdicate active or even visible decision-making is not necessarily irrational from the standpoint of maximizing their utility. The result, however, is that rational thought is almost of necessity banned."[32]

Tullock suggests practical alternatives. He opines, "It seems to me that the object of aid to the poor should be a high level of minimum income together with no leisure for the people who are on whatever subsidy we give. In other words, relief clients should continue working even if they do not produce very much." He further adds, "It would seem to be highly desirable to try to experiment with the use of private rather than government bodies here. Traditionally, there was a great deal of aid to the poor given through private charity."[33]

Capitalism, despite some volatile characteristics, has clearly benefited humankind. It has produced growing material abundance almost everywhere around the world. This abundance creates the potential for significant examples of voluntary acts of social justice in the United States and other advanced nations. Yet current American policy focuses instead on material redistribution.

Intersection: A Better Approach to Social Justice

In considering Catholicism, citizenship, and capitalism, we can logically create a set of principles that will lead to a better and improved approach to genuine social justice in the United States. The views of Leo XIII, John Paul II, the Founding Fathers, Adam Smith, and contemporary free-market thinkers create a degree of linkage between these three traditions. For one thing, they all convey an optimistic view of the potential of human nature. Humankind is capable of personal virtue and of valuing the human experience beyond materialism.

The very best of what true social justice can be involves a dual relationship between the individuals who provide justice and those who benefit from it. The closer these activities can entail involvement on a personal level, the greater the "good" that all parties take away. A great number of "microjustice" events, when added together, is the best conduit to achieving substantive "macrojustice" change.

In this context, the common linkages between Catholicism, citizenship, and capitalism are best exemplified in the concepts of "agency," "virtue," and "subsidiarity." These concepts speak to human activity at a "ground" level and seek to elevate individual human experience through self-development and specific actions.

Agency speaks to human individuals voluntarily taking part in actions with intentional consequences. As an example, the Catholic tradition has a longstanding tradition of "alms," whereby individual acts of charity are praised.

The papal encyclicals, specifically *Rerum novarum*, call for such charitable activities. The American social contract deriving from the Declaration of Independence and the Constitution affirms the dignity of citizens. Individuals within this framework are free to act by their own choice to assist and benefit fellow citizens. Consistent with this principle, the concepts of "utility" and "subjective value" found in classical economic theory acknowledge that doing "good" for others can represent a rational economic choice.

The papal encyclicals, the Founding Fathers, and liberal economic thought extol individual *virtue*. In the Christian example, individual virtue represents the opportunity to self-actualize on a spiritual level. In the case of politics, it creates the pathway to a well-informed and well-acting citizenry. In the world of economic activity, virtuous behavior leads to well-functioning markets.

A crucial consideration is the Catholic concept of *subsidiarity*, which advocates that actions, activities, decisions, and a host of other possibilities should occur at the lowest possible level. For example, subsidiarity suggests that school governance decisions are likely to be better if made at a school district level than at the national level. The acts of charity praised in *Rerum novarum* are based on the principle of subsidiarity. The U.S. Constitution was ratified only after several states conditioned their approval with a commitment to passing the Bill of Rights, which sought to limit the federal government's ability to intrude into the activities of individual citizens. Adam Smith's "invisible hand" is premised on the belief that proper economic activity is grounded in the individual, at a microlevel rather than a macrolevel.

It is time to return to the original contrast between Novak's and Gutiérrez's views of social justice. Novak's interpretation is broader, encompassing both material and nonmaterial elements into his understanding of what social justice entails. He suggests that social justice is an egalitarian experience that encompasses an individual's legal and social status in a society of individual citizens, all of whom possess both rights and responsibilities, and where work is recognized as beneficial and dignified. These views fully embrace agency, virtue, and subsidiarity.

In sharp contrast, Gutiérrez views social justice as properly accomplished at a macrolevel. The state rather than the individual should take responsibility for dispensing social justice. The objective is to involuntarily redistribute material wealth. There is an absence of agency, virtue, and subsidiarity in

Gutiérrez's social justice. In short, it can be argued that this form of social justice lacks a soul!

Unfortunately, the ideal of social justice through public-sector policy is problematic. The existing system partially achieves the breadth and depth that certain liberation theologians such as Gutiérrez prefer, but through totally unacceptable means. First, the American system of assistance to citizens in need is based on economic redistribution of wealth that is not voluntary. Second, the process is directed largely at the federal and state levels, a faceless process that contradicts the principle of subsidiarity. Third, the economic redistributions often occur with little or no consideration to the dignity of work.

Given the caveat in the previous paragraph, the most effective way for the United States to achieve social justice that will fully actualize both the individual providers and the recipients of social justice initiatives is to incorporate the guiding principles from the Christian tradition, develop the sense of proper citizenship, and harness the beneficial attributes of free markets. Social justice must embrace the concept of subsidiarity. The American tradition is replete with many examples of effective and successful examples of charity and assistance at the individual and local levels prior to the Progressive Era. Social justice must prioritize agency, which suggests that there ought to be a much greater voluntary element within the process on the part of providers and a great level of respect toward encouraging work as a dignified outcome for recipients. These principles, appropriately executed, will promote virtue throughout American society, with resulting civic and cultural benefits.

Ultimately, social justice must be premised upon facilitating opportunities for human happiness, which is best achieved through each citizen's self-actualization to the best of his or her potential. This will always be an aspirational goal because individuals in a free society are certainly free to elect not to achieve either fulfillment or happiness. That reality, however, does not negate the fact that a combination of agency, subsidiarity, and virtue—built upon a foundation that incorporates the personal generosity of alms, acknowledges both the rights and responsibilities of citizens, and produces the bountiful economic returns of a capitalist system—is likely to be the best pathway to true social justice.

Social justice involves a just balance in relationships between individuals and societies. A society that celebrates the superior economic gains from capitalism must accept the disruptions that Schumpeter identifies. A society that respects the natural rights espoused in the Declaration of Independence will respect property and accept that the voluntary nature of social justice raises dignity and virtue across all elements of society. A right-ordered sense of American social justice can change the "isness" that Martin Luther King Jr. observed to a cultural "oughtness" that will deliver "three meals a day for their bodies, education and culture for their minds, and dignity, equality and freedom for their spirits" to all of those citizens who have such a need.[34]

Social Justice or Preferential Option for the Poor?

Martin Schlag*

Introduction

ANYONE WHO IS acquainted with the history of Catholic social teaching will have read the following words in Pope Francis's social encyclical *Laudato Sí* with surprise: "the principle of the common good immediately becomes ... a preferential option for the poorest."[1] Right up to that statement, Francis is quite traditional in his wording: the common good is based on respect for human dignity and subsidiarity; it aims at the "overall welfare of society," especially the family; even the "intermediate groups" (quite an old-fashioned term) are mentioned; there is an appeal to distributive justice.[2]

What is surprising is that Pius XI and traditional Catholic social teaching would have called this commitment to the common good "social justice." Actually, Pius XI expressed very similar, if not identical, concerns as Francis. He scourged exclusion, the "winner-gets-all" principle, inequality, violence and extremism, and other social evils.[3] And this Pius XI called the "law or norm of social justice": "The public institutions themselves ... ought to make all human society conform to the needs of the common good; that is, to the norm of social justice."[4]

Francis does not: he calls it the "preferential option for the poor(est)." Francis speaks a lot about justice, and in one passage also of *social* justice in combination with concern for the poor.[5] However, "social justice" is not his standard buzzword.

---

*Martin Schlag is the Alan W. Moss Endowed Chair for Catholic Social Thought of the John A. Ryan Institute in the Center for Catholic Studies at the University of St. Thomas.

Is this a mere change in terminology that comes and goes like the waves of the sea? A meaningless fad? Or, perhaps, are we once again witnessing the phenomenon of "social magisterial composting": earlier texts of Catholic social teaching serve as the compost in which more recent applications can grow, which adapt better to changing historical circumstances? Or is there more to it than that? Is there a hermeneutical shift?

In order to find an answer to this question, I would like to first analyze the concepts of social justice and the preferential option for the poor.

Social Justice

This concept is elusive because it is not immediately evident what the notion of *social* justice could add to the virtue and principle of justice, which by its essence concerns others and is thus social. Commutative justice, even though it aims at creating an equilibrium in exchange among individuals, presupposes the notion of fairness and thus also of equal bargaining power between the partners in an exchange. Where this does not obtain (e.g., because of exploitation and overbearing economic power on one side), commutative justice requires correction and the establishment of balance. Distributive and legal justice aim at distributing the benefits and burdens proportionally to the needs, possibilities, capacities, and so forth of individuals vis-à-vis the common good of the community, and thus express what social justice wishes to convey. It is telling that the *Compendium of the Social Doctrine of the Church* formulates its description of social justice in vague terms: "Ever greater importance has been given to *social justice*, which represents a real development in *general justice*, the justice that regulates social relationships according to the criterion of observance of the *law*."[6] Definitions like that in the *Dizionario* to the *Compendium* confuse more than they clarify: "Social justice is the constant and firm will to further the common good in as far as it is the social condition for the development of the integral dignity of all human persons."[7] Such a definition does not add anything to legal justice. The one given by the *Oxford English Dictionary* is much better: "justice at the level of a society or state as regards the possession of wealth, commodities, opportunities, and privileges. ... Much of the debate surrounding social justice has been concerned with the precise nature of fair distribution, and to what extent this may conflict with individual rights of acquisition and ownership."[8]

However, the *Oxford Dictionary* too refers to distributive justice as key to the notion of social justice.

What does seem to be clear is that the rise of social justice as a concept of social ethics and of Catholic social teaching was a reaction to particular challenges of justice, created by modernity and globalization, in the economic, political, and social fields. Breaking the molds of a merely individualistic conception of ethics, social justice highlights the need to not only fulfill established duties in an existing deontological framework but also to reflect on the structures themselves. In this sense, the notion of social justice is a typical achievement of the nascent social sciences of the nineteenth century, which increasingly became aware in a reflexive sense that social reality is malleable. The mission of science was seen not only in describing society but also in transforming it. Therefore, it is correct that social justice adds a structural dimension to all other subcategories of justice.[9] However, its particular use refers to the role of government and public authorities in general regarding social affairs. Social justice requires the state to become active in the social field with the aim of creating a balance between the social classes. This understanding is rooted in the Latin use of the concept as a relationship between the *socii*, the allies of Rome. It was still the dominant interpretation in the eighteenth century, when Alexander Hamilton referred to it in the context of the relationships and rivalries between the various states of the Confederation.[10] From there it was a short step to apply it to the relationships between social classes.

The novelty of the notion of social justice for the Catholic tradition was that it called on the state to care for the poor and cope with the social problem of masses of disenfranchised and miserable people. This was new because the Catholic Church had traditionally opposed public interference with charity, almsgiving, and poor relief, considering this her own prerogative. For example, Wilhelm Emmanuel von Ketteler, the celebrated doyen of Catholic social thought in Germany, rejected state reforms and activism, and sought the solution in Christian charity alone.[11] Leo XIII did not mention social justice in his encyclical *Rerum Novarum*, perhaps also because he was aware of its use and connotations in Bismarck's Germany, where the chancellor who had introduced social policies in the name of social justice also had brutally persecuted the Catholic Church. In reality, the tension that underlay this rejection by the church was very similar to the modern one manifested in the debate between social models that favor entitlement and those that prefer voluntary charity and beneficence. In this debate, the church traditionally had come down very clearly on the side of voluntary charity and almsgiving, viewing state agency in the social field with disfavor. It goes right back to the Protestant Reformation, in the course of which Martin Luther had ascribed the responsibility for poor relief to the commune as an exercise of the common priesthood of all baptized. Each town and local circumscription was to have a common chest, from which the deserving poor were to be sustained. In return, law forbade public begging.[12] This solution was generally not implemented in Catholic countries, not only because it was too closely associated with the suppression of the monasteries and the mendicant orders, which had been decisive benefactors of the poor up to the Reformation, but also because the prohibition on public begging was seen as a rejection of the poor and curtailment of their freedom to appeal to Christian compassion. The paradigmatic confrontation between the two schools of thought took place between Domingo de Soto, cofounder of the School of Salamanca, and Juan de Robles. Domingo de Soto, whose position was to prevail, defended the right of the (deserving) poor to beg and opposed their criminalization and extradition, while at the same time condemning vagabondism.[13] Help was to be sought in the generous donations of the rich, not in deporting the poor or transferring responsibility for their sustenance to the public authorities.

Social justice in the modern sense, to the contrary, demands public social measures. The massive increase in wage labor and its connected social problems simply required a different approach than in the sixteenth century. The shift of attitude in the magisterium was initiated by Luigi Taparelli d'Azeglio, SJ (1793–1862).[14] Through his *Saggio Teoretico di Dritto Naturale Appoggiato sul Fatto*[15] and his role as one of the founding editors of *La Civiltà Cattolica*, this Jesuit can be considered as the true forerunner of modern Catholic social doctrine. In his writings he uses a terminology that was modern for his times (for instance, he distinguished the social from the political) and combines it with Thomism. Pius XI was an ardent admirer of Luigi Taparelli,[16] and thus it is not surprising that the pope used the terminology of Taparelli for his own social documents. Taparelli was the first moral theologian to explicitly use the expression *social justice*. However, his definition is disappointing: "*Social justice for us is justice between man and man [sic]*."[17] Once again, a definition that does not seem to add anything to what general justice is. However, Taparelli does specify that this form of justice demands equality of all persons in their human rights, leaving intact the natural inequalities among men. This position was certainly in accordance with modern sensibility.[18] We find the modern implications of social justice under a different title, which we would nowadays call subsidiarity. Taparelli calls it the "hypotactic right" (*dritto ipotattico*). He anticipates Pius XI's teaching on subsidiarity by writing that society is composed of many smaller units, called "minor societies" or "consortia."[19] These smaller units and individual people have the right to seek "social subsidy" (*sussidio sociale*) from the larger entities,[20] thus creating a functioning "organic division" (*divisione organica*).[21] Smaller and larger units must conserve their own identities without destroying one another.[22]

Pius XI echoed these words when he referred to "social justice" and "social charity" as the supreme structural elements in the economy; these two principles, not unrestricted competition, were to be the steering wheels of the economy.[23] He also introduced the principle of subsidiarity into Catholic social doctrine. Not since that time have the terms *social justice* and *social charity* been used with such immediacy and clarity. Benedict XVI draws on the language of *Quadragesimo anno* in his social encyclical *Caritas in veritate*.

As stated at the outset, Pope Francis expresses the aims formerly covered by social justice in terms of the preferential option for the poor. It is therefore time to turn to our second concept.

The Preferential Option for the Poor

The term *preferential option for the poor* originated in Latin America, specifically in the theology of liberation. Since then, two major currents of interpretation of this principle have formed.[24] One interpretation is that of the theology of liberation. Another one is the position taken by the magisterium, especially by the papal magisterium[25] that Pope Francis has developed and modified, nevertheless remaining in the range of the precedential magisterial texts, as I will try to show.

Liberation theology affirms that without the prior preferential commitment to the poor (in the widest sense of the word, including the underprivileged and the endangered), we are far from the Kingdom of God.[26] This implies that the first and overarching condition for the possibility of theology is that the theologian participates in liberating action. "Before we can do theology we have to 'do' liberation," say the Boff brothers.[27] Liberating practice comes first because liberation theology is the critical reflection on the practice of liberation in the light of the Word of God.[28] Therefore, hope for and praxis of improvement of the human condition on Earth in liberation theology logically precede the comprehension of Christ. In Sobrino's formulation, hope and praxis are hermeneutical settings for knowing Christ.[29]

In such a view, the preferential option for the poor is not just an aspect of love for those in need but presents itself as the universal precondition for any reflection on faith. Class conversion is seen as a hermeneutical requisite for the correct understanding of revelation.[30] Liberation theology's interpretation of the preferential option for the poor thus moves outside the bounds of traditional Catholic social thought. Jon Sobrino has expressed it in a radical fashion: the massive, unjust, and lethal misery in the world is the only setting from where it is relevant to speak about God and Christ. The world of the poor is what makes us ponder, what enables us to think, and teaches us to reflect.[31]

The magisterium understands the preferential option for the poor differently. After notional forerunners in *Gaudium et Spes* and *Evangelii Nuntiandi*, as well as in the two documents of the Congregation for the Doctrine of the Faith, *Libertatis Nuntius*[32] and *Libertatis Conscientia*,[33] and the Conclusions of the Extraordinary Bishops' Synod 1985,[34] from 1986 onward St. John Paul II consistently used the expression "option or love of preference for the poor" in many of his documents. He defined this attitude as "an option or a special form of primacy in the exercise of Christian charity."[35] This official formulation was the one that was received into the *Compendium of the Social Doctrine of the Church*, where it is situated as a subtitle in the chapter on the universal destination of goods, one of the principles of Catholic social thought.[36]

Rohan Curnow has pointed out that John Paul II did not use the preferential option for the poor in the same sense that liberation theology does. The pope spoke of the preferential option for the poor in terms of love, not in the sense of a necessary precondition for the possibility of reformulating the whole of theology. He thus did not "invoke the conversional and hermeneutical emphases" given to the preferential option for the poor by liberation theology.[37] In this sense, he positioned the preferential option for the poor among the other principles and elements of Catholic social thought, not as its overarching and paramount foundation.[38] This is the reason why we have distinguished between two lines of interpretation of the idea of the preferential option for the poor.

Notwithstanding the above, the urgency with which both John Paul II and Benedict XVI formulated their writings on the preferential option for the poor leave no doubts about the priority they gave to love for the poor and suffering, the oppressed and downtrodden, and those whose human rights have been denied.

I distinguish Pope Francis's interpretation from the one given by liberation theology for reasons of clarity and intellectual honesty. Pope Francis has never called himself a theologian of liberation but a "son of the theology of the people."[39] The theology of the people is a variant of the theology of liberation that goes back to the work of Lucio Gera, Juan Carlos Scannone, and others like Alberto Methol Ferré.[40] The theology of the people puts the emphasis on culture instead of socioeconomic structures.[41] That is why I prefer not to simply identify the theology of the people with liberation theology.[42]

The point of departure for the theology of the people is not directly and immediately the poor but the people, in which the poor play a preeminent role. The people are the faithful, humble, and simple persons who possess an evangelical instinct,[43] or in the words of Pope Francis "*el santo pueblo fiel de Dios*" (the holy faithful people of God), which is "a vaccine against the prevailing ideologies and political violence."[44] The people are the subject of a history (not of *the* history or of history in general) and of a culture. The theology of the people includes everyone in the notion of people, also the rich, unless he or she rejects the common good by oppressing others. The poor have a preferential position among the people because they are more aware of their lack of power and thus of their need for commonality. "In a preferential way we call the multitude of the poor a people."[45] In a certain way the preferential option for the poor in this theological interpretation is mediated through the notion of the people.[46]

In accordance with the theology of the people, Pope Francis rejects Marxism,[47] and has opted for the social market economy or social economy as the model of social and economic organization. This was also apparent in his work in the Episcopal Conference of Latin America (CELAM).[48]

At Aparecida in 2007, Archbishop Bergoglio was entrusted with drafting the concluding document. In a chapter dedicated entirely to the preferential option for the poor, the bishops refer to it as one of "the distinguishing features of our Latin American and Caribbean church."[49] They therefore give it a central function in pastoral care: "That it is preferential means that it should permeate all our pastoral structures and priorities."[50] However, there is no hint at class struggle; to the contrary, Aparecida includes the world of business and finance in the preferential option for the poor: "The preferential option for the poor demands that we devote special attention to those Catholic professional people who are responsible for the finances of nations, those who promote employment, and politicians who must create conditions for the economic development of countries, so as to give them ethical guidelines consistent with their faith."[51]

Pope Francis has reinforced the church's message of inclusion of the poor, advocating for structural reforms that place the human person—not money—at the center of the economy. Forcefully, he has highlighted that Christian culture begins with the love of the poor:

> The proclamation of the Gospel is destined for the poor first of all, for all those who all too often lack what they need to live a dignified life. … Go to the poor first of all: this is the priority. … Some, however, may think that Jesus' message is for those who have no cultural background. No! No! … The Church has always been present in places where culture is worked out. But the first step is always the priority for the poor. …

> The Gospel is for everyone! This reaching out to the poor does not mean we must become champions of poverty or, as it were, "spiritual tramps"! No, no this is not what it means! It means we must reach out to the flesh of Jesus that is suffering, but also suffering is the flesh of Jesus of those who do not know it with their study, with their intelligence, with their culture.[52]

Francis's version of the preferential option for the poor is very clearly presented in these words: it is linked to charity and to evangelization without any form of exclusion. He also constantly repeats that all his teachings on society and the economy remain in the limits of Catholic social doctrine. The pope thus continues the theological line of the assemblies of CELAM in Santo Domingo and Aparecida.

Pope Francis understands poverty in the broad sense of exclusion: "Moreover there is no worse material poverty, I am keen to stress, than the poverty which prevents people from earning their bread and deprives them of the dignity of work."[53]

Conclusion

Francis's positive constructive vision for a remedy is a social (market) economy "that invests in persons by creating jobs and providing training."[54] Pope Francis wants the poor included in the market economy, not dependent on government handouts:

> The need to resolve the structural causes of poverty cannot be delayed. ... Welfare projects, which meet certain urgent needs, should be considered merely temporary responses. As long as the problems of the poor are not radically resolved by rejecting the absolute autonomy of markets and financial speculation and by attacking the structural causes of inequality, no solution will be found for the world's problems or, for that matter, to any problems. Inequality (Spanish original: *inequidad*) is the root of social ills.[55]

This is where I spot the difference and the reason why Francis speaks of the preferential option for the poor rather than "social justice": he does not appeal only or foremost to the "public authorities" as Pius XI did, but "to the people," to civil society as a whole, including the political elites. Francis wants a different cultural paradigm, a "bold cultural revolution,"[56] a "new lifestyle"[57] that places the human person, including the poor, at the center, and sees everything else as an instrument; this requires overcoming what the pope calls the "technocratic paradigm" that excludes ethics.[58] He calls for integral development[59] and another kind of progress that is "healthier, more human, more social, more integral."[60] He does not believe in the top-down approach, in the leadership of the elites, but seeks help in the periphery, in the holy and faithful people of God.

It is sad and counterproductive that the preferential option for the poor has long been perceived as anti-capitalist and antibusiness. The concentration on systemic and structural reform, which is undeniably important, has led to a neglect of what businesses and corporations can do to overcome poverty and improve the economic system.[61] Pope Francis, to the contrary, sees the potential of business and the role it must play in the preferential option for the poor: "Business is a noble vocation, directed to producing wealth and improving our world. It can be a fruitful source of prosperity for the areas in which it operates, especially if it sees the creation of jobs as an essential part of its service to the common good."[62]

This is the way forward for the implementation of the preferential option for the poor that really creates and distributes wealth in a just and equitable manner. Therefore, the change in terminology is not just a fad or an example of "social magisterial composting," but a wise hermeneutical shift.

13

Biblical Christianity and Social Justice

D. Eric Schansberg*

AN INTEREST IN justice is universal, from the child who pro-
tests *"that's not fair"* to the woman who contemplates the fairness of life, and
to the man who shakes his fist at the heavens.[1] The concept of justice easily
extends into the realm of public policy, but views about justice differ widely.
For example, psychologist Jonathan Haidt finds that those on "the Left" see
fairness as "equality" and on "the Right" as "proportionality."[2] Some are fond
of harnessing the coercive power of government as an ethical and practical
means to just ends; others are repulsed by efforts to use government or are
skeptical of its ability to be effective. James Schall points to the subjective
weights and definitions of justice, noting that its use can be noble or twisted.
Without roots in a greater system of the good, "justice" often "introduces an
unsettling utopianism" and can be "the most terrible of virtues."[3]

What does Christianity offer that might be more stable and helpful? This
chapter will describe what Christianity rooted in the biblical tradition teaches
and implies in the realm of economic justice and public policy. But a few
caveats are in order.

First, my discussion of Christianity does not inherently preclude what
other religious traditions might bring to the table.[4] But an analysis of all religions—or even a single additional religion—would expand the scope of this
project too far and take us into areas beyond this author's purview of research.

Second, my insistence on "biblical" Christianity will focus our attention
on the authoritative text(s) of the faith. By contrast, I will not rely on much

---

*D. Eric Schansberg is professor of economics at Indiana University, New Albany.

input from Christian tradition or Christian views that are not particularly rooted in Scripture.[5] This is not to dismiss the value of such efforts, but to narrow the scope of this study. In addition, I will not weigh the impact of the more cultural forms of Christianity in syncretic combination with deism, patriotism, nationalism, consumerism, various "social gospels," and so on.

Third, a call to consider all types of "social justice" would also be too broad for this chapter. Social justice could easily imply an interest in explicitly social issues where justice is clearly involved—most notably abortion, civil rights, and rights such as freedom of speech and religion. So, I will narrow the field further to concentrate on its common conception as "economic justice." Again, this is not to downplay social justice in "noneconomic" issues, but to reduce the chapter to a manageable size and to rely on my areas of study.[6]

Fourth, we need a working sense of what turns out to be a slippery term. Paul Heyne notes that "[j]ustice is notoriously hard to define in any way that goes much beyond platitude and still commands wide assent."[7] Still, for want of a term and given its popular use, we must persist. We can start by noting that there are many types of justice: *commutative* (defining fair economic processes—e.g., exchange with minimal fraud and coercion), *distributive* (equitable outcomes and allocation, independent of process), *procedural* (e.g., legal processes are equitable and contracts are honored), *remedial* or retributive (e.g., punishment for misdeeds and compensation for victims), and so on.[8] In this chapter, with a focus on economic justice, I will mostly discuss commutative and distributive justice—and injustice.[9]

Moreover, it is insufficient to define and describe justice with respect to "consequentialist" outcomes but to ignore justice in terms of the chosen means to those ends. The concept of justice can be applied to concerns about both process and outcomes. Here, I will discuss the use of government policy as a just means to just ends.

Fifth, it should not be overlooked that justice can be pursued through private action or through public policy. The former is noteworthy—whether the efforts of a heroic individual or the impressive work of a group of private actors. Heyne notes that "[i]n the Kingdom of law, [the Christian] pursues the goals of order, minimization of conflict, reasonable equity, and the preservation of life. ... This is justice. In the kingdom of the Gospel, however, mere justice gives way to the life of love."[10] It is tempting to imagine justice as purely in the realm of public policy, but it is also a matter of everyday life. Hebrew Bible scholar Walter Brueggemann observes that "[t]he issues of God's freedom and his will for justice are not always and need not be expressed primarily in the big issues of the day. They can be discerned wherever people try to live together."[11] I will honor Brueggeman's sentiment by acknowledging the tremendous role of private actors and roles within the smaller issues of public policy.

Sixth, although bureaucrats, the executive, and the judicial are key components of the implementation of government policies, my terminology will bow to common usage and emphasize the legislative part of the process. *Legislating* will describe the process by which government uses its power to restrict or motivate behavior through law—prohibitions, mandates, taxes, and subsidies. By extension, this focus includes efforts by outside parties to promote government activity.

Legislating Justice versus Legislating Morality

One other key distinction remains—what I will describe as justice and morality.

"Legislating morality" (henceforth LM) can be categorized in two strands. The first is an effort to regulate and restrict consensual but "bad" acts by an adult or between two adults in which no significant, direct costs are imposed on others. Examples of this would include sex outside of marriage, drug abuse, and worshiping within a false religion. Although decisions to do these activities are made willingly, since they are "sins," Christians believe that the choices are harmful on net. But the behavior is voluntary for all parties and they expect to benefit—what economists call "mutually beneficial trade."

The second category is the use of government to mandate or subsidize "good" behaviors, such as prayer in K–12 schools and charitable activity. Here, a failure to act is a sin of omission. As a sin, the failure to act is assumed to cause net harm—to the one who decides to abstain, and often, to others as well.

In contrast, "justice" issues are those in which someone's rights are directly and significantly violated. Examples of this include murder, rape, and theft. One party uses significant force of some type to directly harm another party; someone benefits directly at the expense of another. It follows that "legislating justice" (henceforth LJ) is a change in government policy in an attempt to improve justice or reduce unjust processes and outcomes. LJ could entail more government—or less government, if the status quo is using unjust methods or reaching unjust outcomes.

Thus, the key distinctions between justice and morality are the extent of the earthly consequences of the offense ("sin") and whether those costs are imposed directly on others or not. Pope John Paul II draws the same line: "each individual's sin in some way affects others. ... Some sins, by their very matter, constitute a direct attack on one's neighbor."[12] Spooner distinguishes between vices ("those acts by which a man harms himself or his property") and crimes ("those acts by which one man harms the person or property of another").[13] Reed makes a similar distinction when he concludes that "the best standard for government is still John Stuart Mill's principle of allowing the greatest liberty possible until someone else's life or liberty is jeopardized."[14] And Rawls argues that "liberty can be restricted only for the sake of liberty."[15]

A few points of further clarification are needed before moving on. First, morality and justice are certainly intertwined to some extent: to act justly is a matter of morality, and the morality of one's actions often determines the justice of the subsequent outcome.[16] Still, there are important distinctions, so that distinguishing between the two is more beneficial than conflating them.

Second, both justice and morality issues involve costs imposed on others. Proponents of LM often argue that other parties are indirectly harmed by gambling, prostitution, and so forth, and thus that government activism is warranted. Of course, everything we do (or don't do) imposes costs of some sort on others. So, we're left with noting or ignoring the extent of those costs. At the least, this framework is helpful in distinguishing between more/less significant and direct costs—from murder to secondhand cigarette smoke.

In *Just Capitalism*, Waters defines justice in terms of freedom to pursue human flourishing.[17] When my freedom is used in ways that are inconsistent with the freedom of others, using government to restrict my freedom becomes more coherent. But, what happens when my choices are clearly or debatably consistent with my own flourishing?

Note that the size and type of the costs vary between offenses—for example, not being charitable to the needy, driving too fast, supporting the central tenets of a false and harmful religion, being a serial rapist, and eating an extra piece of pie. Should the state legislate on all of these? When do the costs become significant enough to allow Christians to righteously invoke government solutions? As the costs become larger and more direct, there is a greater potential ethical role for government activism. And on a practical level, it will be easier to strive for improvements in justice with the reduction of costs that are larger, clearer, and more direct.

What Does the Biblical Tradition Say about Justice?

What follows is a brief (and highly simplified) survey of what the Hebrew Bible and New Testament Scriptures seem to indicate about justice and standards of justice, according to a broadly Christian orientation.

Christians worship a God of justice and righteousness; "righteousness and justice are the foundation of His throne," writes the Psalmist.[18] God does not show favoritism,[19] repeatedly condemns oppression,[20] and defends the poor and needy in the face of affliction and oppression.[21]

As a result, leaders placed in positions of authority by God are instructed to judge between the rich and poor fairly.[22] They should not oppress others, but are to establish "rules that are just."[23] Moreover, they are to enforce these rules and promote justice—for the ruler "does not bear the sword for nothing."[24] As an example of a theocratic king representing the government of God, David did what was "just and right"—at least early in his reign.[25] And his son followed in his footsteps as king: "the Lord was pleased that Solomon had asked for … discernment in administering justice."[26]

Counter to the world's norms, believers are not supposed to show favoritism.[27] They are supposed to defend the poor, the needy, and the defenseless.[28] They are instructed not to oppress others.[29] Christians are encouraged to do good, to be generous, and to lend freely.[30] Moreover, believers are told that God values justice over rituals of sacrifice and thus that we should "follow justice and justice alone."[31] Other passages also point to justice as a top priority. Proverbs 16:8 says, "Better a little [gain] with righteousness than much gain with injustice," and the very purpose of the book of Proverbs as defined in 1:3 is to do "what is right and fair."[32]

In addition, Scripture often defines the pursuit of justice as a matter of character: "The righteous care about justice for the poor"; "when justice is done, it brings joy to the righteous"; and "the righteous give generously."[33] "The wife of noble character" in Proverbs 31:20 "opens her arms to the poor and extends her hands to the needy." Proverbs also relates our behavior toward others to our attitude toward God: one "who oppresses the poor shows contempt for their Maker, but whoever is kind to the needy honors God"; and "he who is kind to the poor lends to the Lord."[34] But Micah 6:8 probably best sums up what God wants from us: "[t]o act justly and to love mercy and to walk humbly with [our] God."

How Did Jesus Christ Deal with Injustice?

Jeremiah had prophesied that the Messiah would "reign wisely and do what is just and right."[35] His ministry was largely centered on reaching the poor and those outside of power.[36] He was remembered as being critical of the Pharisees for giving a tenth of their spices but failing to follow "the more important matters of the Law—justice, mercy, and faithfulness."[37]

Christ suffered, endured, and tolerated tremendous personal injustices. His ministry threatened the power of the religious leaders of his day, eventually resulting in his crucifixion. Even after his death, Matthew 28:11–15 records a bribe to the guards at the tomb in order to try to protect the status quo. And perhaps most noteworthy, in arranging arguably the greatest act of injustice in history, Judas betrayed him to the chief priests and the officers of the temple guard—in a political market, Christ was taken by force, for a bribe of thirty silver pieces.[38]

In stark contrast to the injustices done to him, Christ was far less tolerant of injustices done to others. In Luke 4:18, he quotes (or, in the view of non-conservative and/or non-Christian scholars, is *remembered* quoting) Isaiah to describe part of his mission—"to release the oppressed."[39] Mark 10:14 records Christ becoming "indignant" when the disciples tried to keep the children away from him. In Matthew 18:6, he promised severe punishment for one "who causes one of these little ones to sin." When the Pharisees were bothered that he healed a man on the Sabbath, Mark 3:5 records that he "looked around at them in anger and [was] deeply distressed at their stubborn hearts." Concerning his numerous healings on the Sabbath, he flaunted the timing of these miracles to show that loving others often runs counter to the norms of the religious establishment.

The Gospel accounts of Christ clearing the temple combine his anger when the rights of the relatively powerless were violated by the powerful and when God's name was maligned by the behavior of religious people.[40] Among other sins, the religious leaders had allowed those who exchanged currencies ("money-changers") and vendors ("those who sold doves") to turn the temple into "a den of robbers."[41] To "rob" the people, customers must have been forced to buy currency and doves at too high of a price. If sellers had been charging competitive prices, they would have been merely providing a valuable service (cf. Dt 14:24–26). As with government today, the governing authorities of the temple probably sold exclusive rights to operate in the temple area, allowing sellers to exploit the resulting monopoly power by charging high prices and providing unfavorable exchange rates—thus "robbing" the people. In particular, since doves were the usual offering of the poor (Leviticus 5:7), the effects of this monopoly power would have been disproportionately borne by the poor.[42]

Why Is Legislating Justice Preferable to Legislating Morality?

Followers of God should treat others with dignity, respect, and justice—and they should hope for (and perhaps work toward) a government that does the same. But, in my perspective, the Bible also describes a God of perfect morality as well. Does this provide license to use the government to pursue greater "morality"?

Francis Beckwith argues that "[a] Christian's moral obligation to do justice may also involve concern for the public culture and how it affects the virtue of its citizens. ... And yet, the Christian must exercise care in the extent to which the government uses its power to protect a community's moral ecology."[43] Christianity is concerned with both private and public spheres. But the use of government to mediate private spheres requires "care."

For a variety of reasons that I develop at length elsewhere, LM is an inappropriate tool for Christians on ethical and biblical grounds.[44] But to note one important aspect, Christ showed that anger in the name of justice—in defense of the rights of others—can be ethical. He verbally defended the rights of others in matters of "social justice," especially the powerless. However, he did not restrict the freedom of non-followers in matters of "social morality" by using human government.

The pursuit of social justice, rather than social morality, can produce better results. Attempts to LM are always fraught with unfortunate costs, but attempts to LJ (if done well) will have a number of beneficial by-products. First, with LJ, Christians set themselves apart as "servants"—in ministering to others, defending the defenseless, and so on. In other words, it is easier to be seen as "the light of the world." Those who LM are inevitably seen as prudes and busybodies who are trying to keep people from doing what they think is best.

Second, to the extent that Christians are critical of injustices, those who benefit from, or are responsible for, the injustices are usually the only ones who will view LJ efforts negatively. For example, if the poor are being exploited in some way, arguing against the injustice is likely to raise the sympathies of objective observers, not rankle them.[45]

Third, the pursuit of justice gives Christians an opportunity to be *for* something—and for something greater. Christians, especially in North America, are often known for what they are *against*. Libertarians are in a similar position—often perceived as focused on niche rights (e.g., legal prostitution and pot), rather than for broader rights, especially for the oppressed. In addition to its merits, the pursuit of justice for the poor and oppressed will typically be perceived well.

Conflating Justice and Oppression with Poverty

Scripture often mentions "the poor and the oppressed"; thus, the two terms are often connected.[46] However, since some other texts also distinguish between the two, there can also be a distinction between them. Many people believe that the rich often oppress the poor to gain their wealth. Although more prevalent in biblical times, it is unusual today—at least without help from unjust government policies. Schneider writes that "we now know beyond controversy that modern high-tech economies do not work in the same way that the ancient orders did. ... Nor do they work in the ways that the capitalism observed by Wesley, Marx, and Weber did. ... [It] works primarily by means of the creation of wealth, not by its seizure from others."[47]

To oppress, as *Webster's Dictionary* describes, is "to keep down by the cruel or unjust use of power or authority; to trample down; the imposition of unreasonable burdens ... [through] excessively rigorous government." In other words, oppression stems from a use of force that makes others worse off.[48] This would seem to occur much more frequently through government policy than economic activity. Economic markets feature voluntary transactions and mutually beneficial trades that enhance wealth and well-being. But wealth can be gained through the use of force, theft, extortion, and bribes. For example, political markets often involve the use of government power to make some better off at the expense of others.

To the extent that oppression occurs in any realm, it is wrong. However, the primary causes of poverty today are poor decisions by individuals and poor policies by their governments. As Chilton notes, "God is against certain poor people": sluggards (Proverbs 6:6–11), law-breakers (Proverbs 28:6), those who covet and then curse God (Proverbs 30:7–9), and so on.[49] Thus, Christians should seek to educate others about the consequences of poor decisions and oppose unjust policies.

Redistribution, Bribes, and Justice

After reading a pointed description of redistribution, the first problem that may come to mind for Christians is that it seems to violate the Eighth Commandment: "Do not steal."[50] In criticizing attempts to LJ through government redistribution, Chilton argues that "[t]he mark of a Christian movement is its willingness to submit to the demands of Scripture. ... 'You shall not steal,' for instance ... must not be relativized on the mere excuse that the thief has no bread."[51] Likewise, Bandow argues that "the political process has become a system of legalized theft, with personal gain rather than public interest becoming the standard for government action."[52] Pursuing godly goals with ungodly methods is not a godly option.

This use of force cannot be motivated from a Christian perspective, unless perhaps the government spending is for the "general interest" or the "common good"—a narrow set of examples when economic markets do not function efficiently (e.g., some "public goods" and externalities). But it is not even clear whether Christians should vocally endorse those efforts. And certainly, Christians should eschew the use of government to appropriate funds from the general public to benefit "special interests" or, especially, themselves.[53]

Biblical texts are active in condemning bribery as injustice. In wisdom literature, Proverbs 17:23 says that "a wicked man accepts a bribe in secret to pervert the course of justice." In the Torah, the Israelites were told not to "accept a bribe, for a bribe blinds those who see and twists the words of the righteous."[54] In establishing Israelite government under God, the selection process for judges included that they should "hate dishonest gain."[55] Thus, I Samuel 8:3 notes when Samuel's sons unfortunately "turned aside after dishonest gain and accepted bribes and perverted justice." And Samuel's farewell sermon included his declaration and the people's affirmation that he had not cheated or oppressed anyone, and had not taken any bribes.[56]

In moving from the historical writings to the prophetic literature, two prophets noticeably explicitly tie together the themes of bribery and justice. Isaiah 1:21–23 reads, "See how the faithful city has become a harlot! She once was full of justice; righteousness used to dwell in her ... (now) your rulers are rebels, companions of thieves; they all love bribes and chase after gifts." And in Amos's treatise on justice, he accuses the people, and especially, the leaders: "You trample on the poor and force them to give you grain. ... I know how many are your offenses and how great are your sins. You oppress the righteous and take bribes and you deprive the poor of justice in the courts."[57]

What does such bribery and injustice look like today? For one, special interest groups use money to influence outcomes in political institutions. In less-developed countries, the stereotype of these transactions is political graft on a national scale, or the $20 paid to a customs officer to make his inspection less thorough or a tariff less burdensome. In the United States, bribes are less frequent—or, at least, more subtle.[58] Campaign contributions are the most prominent example of legal political influence. They are not inherently evil. But to the extent that they influence justice negatively, they are a cause for great concern.

Policy Applications

Given a biblical license to pursue LJ, what would constitute a godly agenda for justice and which prescriptions will have the intended results? In theory, LJ could involve additional government intervention. But in practice, the available data indicate that LJ will typically involve less government activity—or, at the least, different policies.

In biblical tradition, government appears to be portrayed at its best as "a necessary evil" to restrain evil (Romans 13:1–7). Otherwise, biblical perspectives on government appear quite pessimistic from Genesis to Revelation. The first mention of a city has an ominous origin, with the jealous and murderous Cain as its founder.[59] The first detailed description of a city includes Babel's troubling civic agenda (Genesis 11). As the Israelites clamor for what an earthly king will do *for* them, God memorably warns them about what government will do *to* them (I Samuel 8:10–22).[60] The state is certainly rough on Jesus and the early church, from persecution to martyrdom. And in John's marvelous apocalyptic, the state's evils are broadly described in colorful terms as the first Beast (Revelation 13:1–10). From the many examples of bad government in the Scriptures, one can only worry and be wary about the potential for evil overreach.

From economic theory—Public Choice economics and Austrian economics in particular—one shouldn't be surprised to find that government activism is fraught with corruption and incompetence. And from any study of world history, it is clear that many government policies—economic, social, and military—have been unjust means toward unjust ends.[61]

The first requirements of an effective agenda for LJ would probably require satisfying the concerns of Public Choice and Austrian economics. Policy should be reasonably well-intentioned—and based on sufficient knowledge of how the economies and human behavior are known to work, rather than merely good intentions. A full accounting of troubling economic policies would require a full book and is well beyond the scope of this chapter.[62] But a few key, quick examples can be briefly traced out.

First, consider the use of government to try to help the poor. Ethically, welfare programs are troubling, since they forcibly take money from one party to give to someone else. Practically, these programs face the inherent disincentives and moral hazard problems of any effort to render assistance. These concerns are likely exacerbated by impersonal government agents who are spending someone else's money.[63] And government can hardly be expected to ably address more than material well-being, when any holistic understanding of the human person recognizes that there's much more in play. In sum, such efforts can be no better than a mixed bag in practical terms.

Unfortunately, many Christians actively advocate government welfare programs—out of general ignorance or a misunderstanding of the Scriptures. In particular, those on the religious left point to the communal living of the early church—as depicted in Acts 2 and Acts 4—and extrapolate from a small voluntary arrangement to large coercive policies such as welfare or even state socialism. Although helping the poor on a voluntary basis—individually or through a group like the church—is laudable if done well, there is no biblical license to advocate the force of government to redistribute income, even to the poor.

Second, consider the use of government to help special interest groups in a way that oppresses by imposing costs on others, especially the poor.[64] Sometimes the redistribution is direct, but usually it's indirect and more subtle—as government restricts competition, redistributing wealth from consumers and workers to those in politically powerful interest groups. Koyzis argues that we "are justified in appreciating constitutional democracy. ... Yet we must avoid the assumption that democracy is identical to just government. ... Western democracies routinely pervert justice, albeit in less overtly destructive ways."[65]

Such policy outcomes are initially surprising to imagine in a democracy. The majority should easily outvote what most would consider an unjust outcome—often a form of "reversing Robin Hood," in redistributing from common folk to the wealthy and politically connected.[66] Compare the subtle, small-per-person costs borne by members of the general public who are "rationally ignorant and apathetic"—with the concentrated benefits pocketed by a motivated interest group—to understand and explain the winning political calculus. Koyzis notes that "it is simplistic to assert that one side favors justice while the other does not. It is more accurate to observe that each party wants to see justice done but that each conceives of it differently. ..."[67] This is true to some extent. But one wonders how often those pursuing their own interests are able to fool themselves into imagining that the outcomes fall under a robust and coherent sense of "justice." In any case, an objective view of justice will find difficulty in this approach, reducing justice to a purely subjective preference.

This redistributive mechanism describes a vast array of government policies. Government increases the price of food, clothing, and shelter. It often insists on providing K–12 education through public-sector entities with tremendous monopoly power, especially over the poor. Its War on Drugs foists costs onto a range of innocents, particularly in the inner city. It locks less-skilled workers out of some labor markets through occupational licensing—and makes them more expensive to hire through minimum wages and mandated benefits. If they have a job, many state governments have income taxes on the working poor, while the federal government imposes its remarkably oppressive FICA taxes on every dollar they earn. Social Security has a rate of return near zero—the only nest egg for most poor people. And so on.

Many of these policies redistribute income to the *non*poor at the expense of the poor. Presumably, these efforts are not designed to hurt the poor; their harm is merely a by-product or an indirect effect of policies with other goals. Unfortunately, neither the methods nor the outcome can be considered just. But this laundry list provides a wealth of opportunities for those who want to pursue LJ through less government intervention.

Conclusion

Brueggemann warns us not to focus too much on a laundry list of "concrete issues" and miss "the dominant crisis."[68] Woodiwiss concurs from a different angle: "[T]he church of Christ exists not as the institution for the eradication of poverty, but rather as God's emblematic institution for how the poor are to be treated, welcomed, cared for, and respected. ... There simply cannot be a Christian *theory* of justice. There can only be local, particular, ecclesial efforts to be the church."[69]

As such, Christians should share the concern of God toward the poor and oppressed, have the passion of Christ for justice, and use methods consistent with biblical principles in dealing with oppression and injustice. In this context, knowledgeable Christians should be willing to stand up in the public square—especially for the poor, who are disproportionately harmed by many forms of government activism. Where government is limited or deeply flawed, the call to minister to the poor and oppressed is still relevant.

When we fail to do so, "justice is driven back, and righteousness stands at a distance; truth has stumbled in the streets, honesty cannot enter. The Lord looked and was displeased that there was no justice. He saw that there was no one, he was appalled that there was no one to intervene."[70] We should respond to God's call to promote justice and righteousness.

Often, the motives to help are there, but the knowledge about how to do so, ethically and practically, is lacking. Guinness draws an analogy to the Tin Man in *The Wizard of Oz*. In one scene, Scarecrow reasons, "I shall ask for brains instead of a heart; for a fool would not know what to do with a heart if he had one." But the Tin Man replies, "I shall take the heart; for brains do not make one happy, and happiness is the best thing in the world."[71] Of course, the optimal strategy is to use one's heart and brains, with zeal and knowledge, to love the Lord our God with our heart *and* our mind—in pursuit of social justice for others.

B.

Let People Build a Just Society on Their Own—and Reform Flawed Public Policies

14

The Myth of Social Justice

Pascal Salin*

AS IS WELL known, Friedrich Hayek wrote an outstanding book—*Law, Legislation, and Liberty*—and the title of its second volume is *The Mirage of Social Justice*. Hayek explains in a convincing way that the expression *social justice* is meaningless. Thus, he writes in the preface to this volume: "To demonstrate that a universally used expression which to many people embodies a quasi-religious belief has no content whatever and serves merely to insinuate that we ought to consent to a demand of some particular group, is much more difficult than to show that a conception is wrong." Hayek succeeds splendidly in providing a very rigorous demonstration of the inanity of the concept of social justice, and one may think that there is no more to say on the subject and that debate is useless. I will certainly not criticize what has been written by Hayek, nor try to summarize his book. But I believe that this topic is so complex and so important that it may be possible to add some remarks to what has been authoritatively written by Friedrich Hayek.

It is obvious that there is not one single definition of social justice. This term is much used—particularly as regards political problems and policies—but often with divergent implicit meanings. However, one thing is certain: when speaking of "social justice," all people rightly interpret it as an ethical concept. Therefore, in order to better understand its meaning, it may be useful to begin with a broader approach, namely considering what is exactly meant by "ethics." From this point of view, it seems justified to make a basic distinction between two kinds of ethics, which I think useful to label "universal ethics" and "personal ethics."

---

*Pascal Salin is professor of economics at the Université Paris-Dauphine in France.

Universal ethics is unfortunately not universally recognized in our time; perhaps I should call it "universalizable ethics." It can be defined as a set of moral principles that are potentially acceptable to all individuals of the world, without contradictions and conflicts between these principles and other actions. Therefore, it seems that only one definition of universal ethics is possible: namely, respecting the legitimate rights of individuals (i.e., legitimately obtained rights to their own person and property).

Personal ethics consist of choosing how one wants to behave toward others and toward whom one wants to practice altruism. Insofar as it is obviously not possible to be altruistic toward all people of the world, each one must choose toward whom he desires to be altruistic and in which forms. Thus, he chooses simultaneously to exclude other people from his altruistic activities (or "egalitarian" activities). Therefore, if an individual prefers to help his children rather than a person who lives miserably because this person does not want to do any work and/or because he prefers to live at the expense of others, why should a policy aimed at reducing inequalities require that this individual make choices that he does not desire? Such a policy creates new conflicts between those who consider it respectful of their personal morality and those who do not agree.

This distinction between universal ethics and personal ethics helps us to understand what is meant by social justice. In fact, there are two very different definitions of social justice. The first one is concerned with universal ethics—namely, respecting individual rights. On the other hand, personal ethics inspires the second definition of social justice: it consists in comparing the actual situation of individuals and deciding subjectively whether the differences are fair. This second definition is the most widely accepted one, and usually, when speaking of social justice, people care mainly about the monetary income of individuals. According to a personal judgment—more or less shared by a great number of people—the differences between individual incomes must be diminished to some degree. Now, some more characteristics of both definitions must be clarified in order to present a rigorous analysis of this problem.

Let us consider the first definition of social justice, which is in fact a mere application of universal ethics. I just mentioned that it means that individual rights are respected by everyone. But it is not sufficient to care about respecting rights because individual rights must be ethically founded for such respect to be justified. In fact, let us assume that there is a society in which most properties have been obtained by stealing; it is obvious that, in such a case, there is no justification for respecting property rights! This means that it is important to determine in which cases property rights are legitimate.

The basic principle of ethics consists in claiming that individuals are free, which means that they are not subject to constraint by other people; that is, they are the owners of themselves. But one does not own himself if ever he is not the owner of the goods and services he creates by using his mind and physical labor. Therefore, it must be considered that legitimate property rights are those obtained by acts of creation (and, obviously, by exchanging goods and services that have been created by parties to the exchange).

Thus, the first definition of social justice is potentially acceptable to everyone all over the world, at least if people agree about the legitimacy of property rights. But as regards the second definition of social justice—a comparison of the standard of life of individuals in a society—each individual has a different definition of what he considers socially fair. There is therefore a very important problem of the coherence between these different opinions. As it is very likely that all individuals have different opinions about "solidarity," there cannot be a universal criterion for what should be considered as social justice in the fair distribution of resources. It is then assumed that social justice in the distribution of income can be defined by a majority of votes in a democratic system. Nowadays, social justice is taken to mean solidarity or, rather, redistributive activities implemented using social policy, which refers to the second meaning of social justice. It is assumed that social justice implies a reduction in inequality. In the term *equality* or *inequality* there is an implicit value judgment, leading to the reduction of inequality being viewed as a morally justified policy.

Libertarians are frequently critical of egalitarian policies, so it is often claimed that they promote selfishness, and that libertarianism must be challenged for ethical reasons. But human beings are characterized by their diversity and this is why one should, on the one hand, talk about diversity rather than inequality and, on the other hand, respect this diversity inherent in human nature. The term *inequality* would be justified if the fate of all individuals—and in particular their standard of living—were determined by a central authority owning all resources and able to distribute them more or less equally. But fortunately, that is not the case in a free society, and that is why the expression "income redistribution" is totally misleading.

However, contrary to what is often claimed, libertarianism does not support the freedom of anyone to do anything, but the freedom to act while respecting the legitimate rights of others. This freedom to act implies the freedom to implement one's own personal ethics, but only if legitimate and respectful of universal ethics. It is the case if someone who holds legitimate property rights to certain resources uses a portion of those resources to help another person; his acts are then in accordance with his personal morality without damaging universal morality. This behavior is totally moral and respectable. But someone who steals goods from a person to give the loot to another person—because his personal morality induces him to help the latter—violates the property rights of the first person and therefore universal morality.

Now, it is exactly the same with "inequality policies": statesmen (politicians and bureaucrats) levy, thanks to coercion, resources from some people (known as citizens) to give them to others. In doing so, they undermine universal morality, and therefore we must accept the idea that a policy aimed at reducing inequalities is immoral in principle. Although statesmen use their monopoly on legal constraint so that this coercion is legal, it is however immoral because it is an attack on legitimate property rights (and this is why one must consider it a moral duty to cut taxes as much as possible). It may be that in doing so, some statesmen try to implement their own personal morality, but in any event they infringe on universal morality. On the other hand, it is well known that in so doing they often pursue personal goals: thus, to be elected or reelected they transfer resources to a large number of voters at the expense of a minority. It is for this reason that the progressive tax—immoral and unequal by nature—exists. And the fact that they are elected by a majority of voters does not give them legitimacy, since one can always find a majority to violate the legitimate rights of a minority as far as the exercise of legal constraint is possible.

Furthermore, equality is defined arbitrarily from a single criterion, namely income at some point in time. However, the objectives of individuals vary (they do not concern only monetary income), their ages differ and therefore their experience and their capital (which are the sources of their income). Even were all individuals identical, there would still be an inequality in income according to each person's age.

Of course, some are victims of physical or mental disabilities, and human history shows that charity has always existed in such cases. This charity, decided personally by each individual, corresponds to personal morality and is worthy of respect, unlike so-called public charity (which, moreover, is vulnerable to electoral change, potentially leading to new inequalities between those who come into power—claiming to take charge of poverty—and those who must depend on public welfare).

Let me stress again, it is totally wrong to pretend that libertarians advocate selfishness because they do not agree with egalitarian policies. They respect all human beings—rich or poor, young or old—and they respect deeply universal morality but also all personal morals. And that is why it is not wrong to say not only that libertarianism is humanistic, but even that only libertarianism is humanistic. Basically, libertarians are confident in the capacities of individuals rather than treating them as one would a machine. They know that individuals are capable of generosity and also that they are able, if necessary, to invent processes to bring relief to others. This is the case, for instance, with insurance that helps the victims of some unlucky events to benefit from compensation. We could, from this perspective, imagine that in a society without egalitarian policies, parents would receive insurance benefits even before the birth of their children to enable them to live decently, even if they were suffering from a physical or mental disability that would prevent them from providing for their needs.

It is therefore for moral reasons that one should be critical of egalitarian policies, but there are also utilitarian reasons. Thus, if a minimum wage is made compulsory by law in a country, it is supposed to allow all employees to receive the same salary, at least. But the consequence is that it excludes some individuals—especially the youngest ones—from the labor market and it prevents them from improving their lives thanks to their own efforts and from gaining knowledge they might otherwise accumulate. It is also a so-called concern of egalitarianism, which is given to justify a strong progressive tax on income. But a consequence of this unequal policy is to punish and discourage those who are the most innovative, the hardest working, the most able to take risks. The result is the existence of obstacles to economic progress, which is detrimental for everyone. And this policy also pushes into exile some individuals who are victims of the creation of inequality between individuals.

Let us also take the case of inheritance taxes. It is quite often assumed that it is not "fair" that some people obtain more resources than others thanks to inheritance and that it is fair to redistribute what they have received. Let us assume that Jack and Martin have earned exactly the same amount of money throughout their lives, that they die at the same age, and that they have exactly the same number of children who inherit from them. But let us also assume that Jack has constantly accepted the sacrifice of spending less than his income in order to accumulate capital and transfer it to his children after his death, whereas Martin preferred to spend all of his income. Both will have paid the same amount of taxes during their lives, at least as regards income tax, although there may have been an overtaxation of capital gains. It is certainly not fair that inheritance taxes imply that after their lives are over, more taxes will be levied on the resources earned by Jack than on those by Martin. Once more, a social justice policy creates a very important injustice.

The idea that there are unbearable inequalities—for example, in the *distribution* of income or inheritance—comes from a formidable confusion between a purely statistical concept and a moral concept. The very notion of a distribution of income or wealth is meaningless, insofar as someone can redistribute only what belongs to him. Income and wealth exist insofar as they are created, and they are created only because they are owned. Statistical disparities thus only reflect the disparity in the abilities and preferences of individuals. In other words, statistical disparities in income or wealth are nothing other than the *result* of human activity.

Certainly, individuals are equal in their rights (for example, the right to be free and therefore the right to own the fruits of one's labors), but they are not the same, and it is this equal dignity that creates cohesion between them. Individualism, which is frequently criticized as advocating withdrawal from relations with others, is instead based on the recognition of social connections between individuals because it stresses the unique character of each individual along with his *equal* dignity. And this does not exclude, of course, acts of voluntary generosity: the persistence of family ties through history and civilizations is the most striking testimony.

However, as soon as one accepts changing the results of individual activities, the source of these activities is damaged—that is, individual rights. A policy of compulsory transfers, under the pretext of equalizing the results of human activity, consists in taking by force resources from those who have created them to give to those who have not created them. Unlike what happens in voluntary donation or free exchange, in which both parties are winning, in the forced transfer there is a winner and a loser, and no test will allow us to say if there is a "social gain." The evaluation of this transfer is purely subjective, and no one can demonstrate that the fight against statistical inequalities leads to improvement. Thus, a policy of reducing inequalities necessarily means the introduction of arbitrariness in relationships between people.

Modern societies—those that have allowed the largest number of people to gain material resources, culture, or health—are complex societies where everyone plays a specific role and benefits, through exchange, from the activities of others. The miracle of exchange is that it is the creator of value for both parties. It is neither a simple transfer of value nor a zero-sum game, but the *creation* of wealth. In a free exchange there is equality between the market value of what is sold and what is purchased (I sell $10 of tomatoes for $10 of wheat). And yet, what I buy is more valuable to *me* than what I am selling. What each of us seeks, in his dealings with others, is an inequality in subjective values. And one can achieve his own objectives, incommunicable to others, only because individuals are not the same—they do not have the same scales of value, they are unequal from the point of view of their capabilities, their preferences, and their information. Human beings derive their specificity and even their dignity from their differences.

According to the classic conception of law, and as remarkably explained by Friedrich Hayek, equality in law between individuals implies that a rule be general (i.e., that it does not impose a specific result), be universal (i.e., that all citizens are equal before the law), and be certain. With the law thus defined—often invoked, but also often misunderstood—no one can know in advance what will be the precise result of the application of general rules (for instance, the rule according to which "the contract is the law of the participants"). However, claims of equality focus on *result* (concerning, for instance, citizens' incomes) and are incompatible with this conception of justice. If the spontaneous game of human activities under general and universal rules does not lead to the result desired by those who monopolize the power of constraint, their intervention destroys the general, universal, and certain character of the law, which is the foundation of a free society.

To take a simple example, who could dare to claim that it is morally justified to take money from an individual who has been courageously working to give it to a lazy individual? And should we not honestly acknowledge that a progressive tax is unfair because it falls short of the universality that ought to characterize a rule of justice? Far from creating equality between people, a progressive tax introduces discrimination and is unfair. It prevents citizens from being equal before the law. Governments of many countries—developed or less developed, socialist or conservative—have recently reduced the progressivity of the income tax for reasons of efficiency, which are obvious. But one should go further and recognize its deeply immoral character because the inefficiency of progressive taxation is only a logical consequence of its immorality. It is also clear that a progressive tax exists only because, in a system based on democratic absolutism (that is, in fact, a tyranny of the majority), it is always possible to find a majority to oppress a minority and achieve income transfers by force under the pretext of reducing inequalities.

In a society based on free trade, one who owns more is the one who creates more value *for others*. It is not the case in a society based on constraint, in which the inequalities of resources are partly the product of arbitrary processes. A vicious circle may then develop: inequalities based less on the exercise of individual rights appear more arbitrary and are more likely to be changed by constraint.

The notion of equality of results is reductive: it is evaluated, for instance, by monetary incomes. However, if an individual prefers to live modestly in the countryside and admire nature, instead of working continuously to get the income that his capabilities would allow him to earn, he will be considered as "disadvantaged" from the point of view of the statistical criterion of the distribution of monetary incomes, and other individuals will eventually be forced to transfer resources to him. But why is he not obliged to transfer to other people part of the privileges he enjoys as a result of his pleasant life? Because it is more difficult, which means that an equality policy is very reductive in comparison with the subtlety of the choices made in every human life. And were the equalization of living standards ever obtained—which is the dream of egalitarian utopians—it would obviously lead to totalitarianism. There is in fact no *logical* difference between the claim for a greater equality of results and the eventual claim for a more totalitarian society.

In complex societies, how do we know how to direct people to the jobs where they are most useful to others? By the system of remuneration and, more generally, by all the characteristics of a job: prestige, attractiveness, safety, and so forth. In trying to equalize some of these characteristics—for example, income or assets—one takes into account only a part of a very complex set of choices and relationships. And if all the members of a society were exactly in the same condition, regardless of their efforts, merits, or capabilities, not only would there be no more incentives for them to make choices that would bring the most benefit to themselves and to *others*, but even the most generous of them would not have the means of *knowing* which of his actions are the most profitable to others. Inequality thus means not that some are making profits at the expense of others but, on the contrary, that they provide services to others. In this sense the inequalities are "requested"—they are even the condition for social cooperation between people.

But, one may say, it is not necessary when speaking of inequality to use force to completely equalize conditions of life for all people. But how do we define what is tolerable on the path toward totalitarianism? Each person has his own definition, so that the degree of tolerable equality is necessarily determined by the balance of powers. While free exchange and free gifts are of a peaceful nature, the equalization of resources is necessarily violent. It implies that some people can impose their conception of the tolerable level of totalitarianism on others. And the violence is not less so because it is legal.

An individual has enough awareness of the requirements of his own nature to spontaneously condemn theft, because it is an attack on the freedom of action of individuals. How could a theft become legitimate because it is legalized through arbitrary procedures—for instance, the rule of majority decision—in the name of a certain conception of equality? Even the theme of inequality is in fact nothing more than the expression of democratic tyranny. It means claiming that some people have rights to the fruits of the labor of others, beyond what those others wish to give or exchange. What is the ethical foundation of this incredible claim? It does not exist.

The obsession with equality becomes destructive of civilization, and it is not surprising that revolutions on behalf of equality lead to the worst inequalities—those coming from the inequality of power. The enrichment by exploitation of others replaces the enrichment gained by serving others. There are two ways to differentiate oneself from others; but one is harmful, the other not. This means that it is absurd to consider only the result of the social game, instead of looking at the *process* and wondering if it gives some the possibility of stealing from others legally.

The collapse of socialism all over the world is not surprising. While its legitimacy came essentially from its requirements of equality, it could exist only thanks to arbitrariness and tyranny—that is, by creating inequalities regarding the rules of law. And when we learn that this or that country converts from socialism to liberalism, it does not mean that there was a series of historical accidents, but that there was an inconsistency in the existing system that was so deep that it necessarily became intolerable.

The only real inequality is the one that exists between those who live thanks to their own efforts and those who live thanks to constraint, legalized or not. This is the essential drama of our time. Through state violence, we return to a situation of the struggle of all against all. The so-called fight against inequality has created an arbitrary world without rules, without respect for others, a huge machine to destroy people—even, and perhaps especially, the bravest, the most honest, the most generous. The real inequality is the unequal right to freedom.

Bleeding Heart Libertarianism and the Social Justice or Injustice of Economic Inequality

Andrew Jason Cohen*

WE LIVE IN a market system with much economic inequality.[1] This may not be an essential characteristic of market systems but seems historically inevitable. How we should evaluate it, on the other hand, is contentious. I propose that bleeding heart libertarianism provides the best diagnosis and prescription.

I begin by explaining "bleeding heart libertarianism" (hereafter, "BHL"). Next, I indicate why, as a matter of theory, a market generally includes economic inequality. I then step away from theory to comment on real-world market systems—and indicate the real moral problems often associated with the inequality therein. Finally, I explain that although inequality that arises in a *libertarian market* is morally acceptable, the inequality of *our market* system is often not. While some claim inequality requires government intervention, I suggest the key difference between our market system and a libertarian market system is precisely routine government intervention.

Bleeding Heart Libertarianism

BHL is a form of libertarianism. If anything distinguishes it from other forms of libertarianism, it is that bleeding heart *libertarians* are explicitly *bleeding hearts*—concern for the plight of the less fortunate is central to our project.

*Andrew Jason Cohen is professor of philosophy and founding coordinator of the Interdisciplinary Studies Program in Philosophy, Politics, and Economics at Georgia State University.

In short, BHL is a family of libertarian (and hence liberal) views that take suffering to be a moral problem. Like all libertarians, however, we recognize that not all moral problems require state action—and, indeed, that state action sometimes causes the problem.[2]

The BHL concern for the less fortunate does not mean we endorse socialism or increased redistributive welfare policies.[3] It means we think the social world should be set up in a way such that the least well-off (whoever they are) are as well-off as possible, consistent with ensuring liberty for all. This may be why some consider BHL "Rawlsekianism," combining John Rawls—who made famous the idea that we ought to allow inequalities that are to the advantage of the least well-off—with Friedrich Hayek, the famous libertarian.

That said, whether there is anything distinctive in BHL remains an open question. Historically, many that we now call "libertarian" shared our concern with those living in poverty. Even Herbert Spencer, the supposed father of "social Darwinism," was concerned to not make the poor worse off than they were.[4] The stereotype of the "coldhearted" libertarian may have arisen for good reason—if so, I hope BHL corrects it—but is not fairly attributed to all libertarians.[5] This does not mean BHLs merely seek to make an unpopular view palatable. BHLs want, in part, to show that libertarianism is not unpalatable in the first place.

Perhaps it is worth noting that BHLs endorse the free market but are eager to consider what empirical economic science—as well as economic theory—has to teach us. The emphasis on empirical evidence is significant. BHLs will look at the effects of particular government policies before judging them. We likely all oppose redistributive policies in principle, but may endorse some, in specific circumstances, that actually help the poor. We all oppose policies that redistribute resources from poor to rich or that otherwise place unfair burdens on poorer people. In this, we are similar to Spencer when he condemns the "sins of responsible legislators seen in the long list of laws made in the interests of dominant classes." As Spencer notes, for example, the corn-laws—which limited the importation of corn into England—"ensure[d] high rents" for landowners while ensuring "that multitudes should hunger."[6] "High rents" are essentially profits artificially created by government intervention without creating value for others. Given a lack of imported corn, British landowners were able to sell their corn at higher prices. That hurt the poor.

While law is meant to protect, Frédéric Bastiat noted that it is often "perverted through the influence of two very different causes—naked greed and misconceived philanthropy."[7] The naked greed of those with power encourages them to use the law to take from the poor and others; this is "legal plunder."[8] Misconceived philanthropy starts with the good intention of helping, but imposes a view about what is good for people that some may not share and encourages ill-feeling between citizens, as well as other problems. By contrast, "When law and force keep a man within the bounds of justice, they ... only oblige him to abstain from doing harm."[9] More simply, individuals should be free to trade with one another as they wish, without interference, but never *forced* to trade with each other. Markets where such freedom is present require no force except that needed to prevent or rectify harm—where harm is not merely being hurt but being hurt by the wrongful action of another.[10] Force used to help the poor (which often has perverse effects that are harmful) that does not rectify such harm, or to help the wealthy at the expense of the poor, is impermissible on this view.[11]

BHL is a family of views that take some form of negative liberty (freedom from interference) to be a normatively primary and guiding value in the organization of a just state, insisting it must be present for all (this is "classical liberalism") but that *also* share a deep concern to prevent suffering (and perhaps promote at least minimal individual well-being).[12] Some in this camp may approve of limited government interventions to end suffering; all agree that allowing individuals extensive (negative) liberty is likely to create the least suffering possible. Put simply, we believe that ensuring negative freedom as a matter of law will also allow people the most de facto positive freedom (freedom to do as one wants)—and we value that positive freedom. By contrast, socialists seek to ensure positive freedom as a matter of law, believing that will allow most people extensive de facto negative freedom. Rawlsians and other left-leaning liberals who favor redistributive welfare schemes, by contrast, seek to ensure both positive and negative liberty as a matter of law. Other libertarians might be thought of as concentrating on negative liberty without any concern with positive liberty.[13]

As with other political views, including other libertarianisms, there are different ways the view can be morally defended. One might defend BHL on the basis of natural rights, eudaimonism, consequentialism, public reason, or some combination thereof. Investigating this is not our topic here.

Markets Bring Inequality but …

The history of the world is a history almost entirely of subsistence. It is not until the nineteenth century and the Industrial Revolution that we see substantial accumulation of wealth. In what some call "the Great Divergence,"[14] Europe and the United States saw a growth in wealth completely anomalous with all of preceding history (and, at that time, the rest of the world). In the twentieth century, such growth continued throughout the world. To take just one example, as late as 1981, 90 percent of the people in China lived in poverty; in 2018, under 7 percent did. This is a truly phenomenal change that means the number of people in the group that is the least well-off has been dramatically reduced. This is a clear gain that should not be understated. The Brookings Institution expected the world "to reduce extreme poverty by 38 million people [in 2017], slightly faster than in 2016 when an estimated 34 million escaped poverty."[15] According to the World Bank, the world "cut the 1990 poverty rate in half by 2015" as "[n]early 1.1 billion people have moved out of extreme poverty."[16] While there are still too many living with poverty, the numbers are good—and not only has poverty been reduced, but the rest of us have gotten wealthier.

Historically speaking, poverty was the norm; wealth, the anomaly. Though there are many factors that contributed to the tremendous growth in wealth in the last two hundred years—while in the previous two thousand years, humankind languished—freer and more extensive trade is clearly the single biggest factor.[17] The accumulation of capital and the continuing tremendous reduction of poverty is a direct result of the market system and property rights that make such a system possible.[18] This, more than anything else, likely explains why BHLs take trade so seriously. Indeed, it may be that the single clearest difference between BHLs and other libertarians is that while other libertarians start with economic freedom as a value and thus support markets, BHLs are concerned with human welfare, see that markets improve human welfare, and thus support economic freedom and the markets it enables.[19]

Trade is good because it brings wealth, and wealth means improved human welfare. Wealth should not be conceived of as mere money. Wealth is the means that one has to do as one wishes. As a form of wealth, money allows one to buy the goods and services one needs or wishes to use. Increasing wealth (as money or otherwise) means increasing one's ability to live as one wishes. It means improving one's life. Of course, increased wealth does not mean all lives are equally improved. The "Great Divergence" was, after all, a period in which the lives of some—primarily in Europe and the United States—were improved at a vastly quicker rate than those elsewhere. Within Europe and the United States, we also see differential gains, with some doing exponentially better than others.[20] There is, no doubt, economic inequality in developed markets.[21] Let us step back for a moment to consider where the inequality comes from.

According to Adam Smith, "there is a natural propensity in human nature ... to truck, barter, and exchange one thing for another."[22] If this is not inherent in human nature, it is certainly widespread. Say I have four sticks and two stones and prefer a third stone to two of the four sticks; meanwhile, you have two sticks and five stones and prefer more sticks. We trade and are both happier for doing so. Say I prefer to spend my days reading political philosophy, political science, and economics; you prefer to spend your days raising cattle or apples. You might not want to trade your meat or fruit for my reading (or explaining what I read), but I can find buyers for my teaching, accepting some relatively stable currency (through the intermediary of the university) and then trade some of that currency for your meat or fruit.

Importantly, I might be a better farmer than you if I decided to dedicate myself to it. I might, that is, have an absolute advantage over you in regard to farming. Why, then, don't I farm? In part, this is simply my preference, but it is also related to the fact that while I might be able to more efficiently produce food than you, doing so would not be the most efficient use of my time because I can produce teaching more efficiently than I can produce food. My opportunity cost of producing food is higher than yours (assume you have no other talents). You have a comparative advantage in food production. Though I could produce food more efficiently than you, doing so would leave me less well-off than producing teaching and trading with you for the food. This is an instantiation of the principle of comparative advantage.[23]

The principle of comparative advantage shows that even someone with an absolute advantage in producing a good may be better off trading for that good from someone else. Having trading partners with comparative advantages producing most of the goods and services we value benefits us. Having more trading partners—indeed, having more trading partners with more diverse skill sets—improves our ability to trade for goods and services we value. So long as we also produce goods or services valued by others, we do better than trying to produce all we value ourselves.[24]

Given the propensity to trade and the principle of comparative advantage, we do better to extensively divide labor. The division of labor, as Smith notes, results in increased productivity and wealth due to the increased dexterity (itself due to increased simplicity of tasks), the time we save by not having to switch tasks, and the increased use of machinery.[25] It is unlikely this increased productivity and wealth would be spread equally. Some will be more generally skilled and talented than others; they will have absolute advantages in a greater array of tasks and thus be able to choose from that greater array in a way that they benefit more than others, earning a greater income and accumulating more wealth.

Economic inequality is thus to be expected in markets where people freely sell their labor or the goods and services they produce. Still, there are economic gains to all because in all but the rarest cases, even those with relatively few absolute advantages will find themselves with a comparative advantage in something. This may be some form of menial labor, but that labor will be productive and valuable to the overall market system and its participants. Markets work, in part, by incentivizing people to take responsibility for production. When individuals can trade as they wish and benefit in the process—rather than receiving what someone else declares sufficient—they have incentive to produce. In the process, all do better.[26]

Importantly, the advantage of market systems is not merely the economic wealth they produce. Given the need to trade with people with a wide array of skill sets, markets open the door for each of us to meet many more people than we would if we continued to live the subsistence lives our ancestors lived. We have more contact with others—some similar to us, but many different—and thus more opportunity to find compatible friends and even spouses than we would otherwise. We have more chances to choose a different way to live—including with different people, different jobs, different churches, and so forth.[27]

To summarize: markets bring more wealth for all because individuals invest themselves in their work to create more as a means of promoting their own welfare. Markets also bring more contact with others, some who become friends and family. Markets also likely bring inequality. This inequality is a factor of all doing better, though some more than others. This is not necessarily something to bemoan.

The Inequality in Our Market System and the Real Problems

Thus far, we have seen that property rights and the market systems they make possible provide great benefits for all—especially increased wealth and more social ties—but do so unequally. Inequality on its own, though, is not a problem. To see this, imagine there is a society with rising income and rising inequality, such that

- at Time 1, 90 percent of the population has an income of $10,000/year and 10 percent has an income of $50,000/year; and
- at later Time 2, 90 percent of the population has an income of $50,000/year and 10 percent has an income of $500,000/year.

At the earlier time, each member of the smaller and richer tenth of the population earns five times the amount of those in the larger and poorer nine-tenths. At the later time, they earn ten times their poorer compatriots. Income inequality has increased. Why we should be concerned about this is less clear. Of course, if the wealthy became wealthy by exploiting or stealing from the others, we should be concerned—but the concern would be with the exploitation or theft rather than the inequality itself.

To make the point starker, consider a later date:

- at Time 3, 95 percent of the population has an income of $100,000/year and 5 percent has an income of $5 million/year.

Now those in the richer twentieth earn fifty times what their poorer compatriots do. More drastic inequality, but at this later date, it is unreasonable to think anyone is poor (holding the value of dollars constant). That fact—that no one is poor—is significant.[28] As Harry Frankfurt says, "From the point of view of morality, it is not important that everyone should have *the same*. What is morally important is that each should have *enough*."[29] "Enough" is *"what is needed for the kind of life a person would most sensibly and appropriately seek for himself."*[30]

Frankfurt's view captures an important intuition very well: what we care about is suffering. We find suffering morally bad without need for argument (though arguments can be made), and we tend to think that where there is inequality, those with the least will suffer. Historically, this may have been the case. Given the general subsistence level of wealth throughout the world, being on the lower end of income or wealth meant always being close to death. But that is a contingent fact. As shown above, inequality can easily exist even where no one is poor or suffering. We can thus be morally unconcerned with inequality and exceedingly concerned with poverty and suffering. That is the BHL stance.

To be clear, there are two contingent but real moral problems associated with inequality. One is poverty or other suffering on the low end of the spectrum of economic inequality, as just discussed. The other is the abuse (e.g., exploitation) those on the high end can engage in. Specifically, those on the high end can use their wealth to influence government in ways that improve their lot at the expense of others—what economists call "rent-seeking" behavior. This is the legal plunder I discussed earlier.

In their recent book, *The Captured Economy*,[31] Brink Lindsey and Steven Teles provide a nice summary of some of the ways the problem is instantiated in the United States today. Lindsey and Teles do not try to discuss all of the ways the wealthy seek to use government power to their benefit—a gargantuan task that would require several hundreds of pages. They concentrate on four areas: finance, intellectual property, licensing, and land use regulations. We won't delve into these in any detail and will only, and briefly, consider two. Lindsey and Teles's conclusion is straightforward: we have seen a "rise of policies that deliver maximum benefit for a favored few while inflicting maximum harm on everybody else."[32]

Consider, first, occupational licensing. The stated intention for licensing is usually protection of consumers. Most cannot determine if someone is a qualified health care provider, for example, so we require licenses believing this will rule out the unqualified. Of course, such requirements usually intend only to guarantee a minimal level of quality, but even that is problematic. First, some may prefer care from individuals not well practiced in methods approved by the existing authorities (e.g., allopathic medicine).[33] Indeed, some may refuse all medical care if they cannot get it from someone they trust, but who is not versed in the standards accepted for licensing. Second, some may well be very good according to those standards but be poor test takers and thus not able to receive a license—though they would have provided a good service at a comparatively low cost. Obviously, the tighter the licensing requirements, the fewer that will receive the license—and the fewer that can legally provide the service, the more they can charge for their services. The wealthy, of course, will pay for such services. The poor, though, will suffer without them.

Licensing is not just about medicine. In the United States, "[t]he percentage of workers subject to a licensing requirement jumped from 10 percent [in 1970] to almost 30 percent" today.[34] Consumers pay for this because "prices for licensed services are inflated anywhere from 5 percent to 33 percent, with the cost to consumers amounting to some $203 billion a year."[35] It is not just increased prices that matter, of course. The fact is, this results in underconsumption of the service in question and "widens the gap between rich and poor by squelching employment opportunities for people at the lower end of the socioeconomic scale and by inflating the compensation of highly skilled professionals at the top of that scale."[36] It is important to realize that licensing requirements *always* impose costs—on those who seek licenses and those who seek services from those with licenses. Medical school is costly, of course, but so too is having to attend school to braid hair or apprentice with someone already licensed.

Our second example from *The Captured Economy* is the finance industry. Lindsey and Teles rightly point out that the way homeownership is encouraged is problematic and involves much redistribution to the wealthy. "Instead of subsidizing home ownership directly … policymakers elected instead to subsidize mortgage credit by bestowing special favors on the businesses that

214 | *How to Do (Social) Justice Right*

provide it."[37] Several federal agencies offer guarantees on mortgage loans—meaning that the financial firms providing the loans cannot lose their investment. Such policies leave financial firms willing to take risks they would not otherwise, including lending money to those unlikely to repay the debt. Financial firms are basically enabled to make and keep profits but foist their losses onto government (and taxpayers). While these loans may serve a good purpose, they may also encourage poor people to take on debt they cannot afford—which can result in them losing more than they invested.[38]

The two examples just discussed are recent, but not new—and far from exhaustive of the many ways the wealthy use the power of government to their advantage and the disadvantage of others. There are other examples that are worth considering in this light, including the entire institution of slavery (which benefited wealthy white landowners) and, more recently, in the United States, overcriminalization and overincarceration (which benefit the entrenched elite in various law enforcement agencies and the businesses that serve them at the expense of poor people, especially minorities).

In her book *The New Jim Crow*,[39] while discussing the "drug war" in the United States, Michelle Alexander notes that "[b]etween 1980 and 1984, FBI antidrug funding increased from $8 million to $95 million. Department of Defense antidrug allocations increased from $33 million in 1981 to $1,042 million in 1991. During that same period, DEA antidrug spending grew from $86 to $1,026 million, and FBI antidrug allocations grew from $38 to $181 million."[40] It is hard to read about these increases and not think rent seeking on behalf of these agencies greatly influenced policy. Indeed, when Alexander discusses the rise of civil asset forfeiture, she notes that "local police departments, as well as state and federal law enforcement agencies ... have a direct pecuniary interest in the profitability and longevity of the drug war."[41] She goes on to show how the drug war disproportionately affects minorities—in extremely serious ways. Indeed, these examples of rent seeking are more pernicious than those Lindsey and Teles discuss because they involve widespread and massive violations of individual rights, resulting in harms to millions of people.[42]

What we have seen here is that the sort of inequality that exists in the contemporary Western world is morally problematic, not because people earn different amounts or have unequal wealth, but because some suffer and some use their wealth to warp government policy in their favor while causing harm to others. Obviously, this is not a new problem. The attempt "to enrich all classes at the expense of each other" that Bastiat found so rightly concerning is always seductive.[43]

Government Intervention Is the Cause, Not the Answer

Inequality matters when it includes suffering by those who are not well-off and it matters when those who are well-off use their positions to inflict their desires on others. What we want is a system wherein people live by mutual cooperation, a system wherein no one systematically and wrongfully hurts others. To be clear, what matters is *not* inequality per se, but two possible phenomena that are often (but not necessarily) correlated with inequality. As we saw above, even substantial inequality might be unproblematic if all are doing well.

Some might object that I seem to believe that real-world markets work in ways that are required in economic theory without realizing that the latter idealizes in its models. However, I am not blind to the fact that real markets are not ideal markets; I simply also realize that we should not be blind to the fact that real governments are not ideal governments. We should not think we can replace the very flawed real markets we live in with ideal government programs.[44] The question we ought to be concerned with is "why do markets go awry?"

From the perspective of BHL, the main cause of markets misfiring is the perversion of law, as discussed above, and which Lindsey and Teles so admirably demonstrate. The idea that some professional services should be licensed so as to protect consumers will likely meet with widespread approval. The problem comes when some use licensing laws to their advantage at the expense of others. When licensing primarily enriches those who are licensed but adds little to no value to consumers or, worse, removes value by making it impossible to purchase the service at a lower cost—a pervasive feature of licensing—law is perverse. Similarly, helping people buy their own homes may be laudable, and laws set to help in this way are likely to be approved of by many. The problem again comes when some use that power to enrich themselves at the expense of others. Yet this too is pervasive—and perverse.

When law is perverted, some—usually those already well-off—use it to enrich themselves at the expense of others—often the less well-off—without their agreement. This is the opposite of what BHLs—indeed, any libertarians—want. We want a free market in which, as already discussed, no one is coerced to trade with anyone else. A genuinely free market is one in which each is free to do as she wishes, trading with whomever will freely trade with her, on terms they both find beneficial. When this is what happens, we have a system wherein people flourish by providing value for others. This is obviously morally permissible. It would be a mistake to consider it selfless or altruistic, but it is a system in which people do better by doing well for others.

When government interferes, some manage to do well for themselves by seeking and receiving rents from government action. They might receive higher pay because they have few competitors due to licensing requirements. They might receive their pay even if their investments fail in predictable ways. That pay comes from others, forced to pay taxes to support bad bets of those who can get the government to cover their risks. They might be able to charge more for their goods because they convinced the government to impose tariffs on competition from elsewhere. When this is the case, we have immorality built into a hybrid market system. While some trades may be freely entered into and mutually beneficial, others are forced—either literally or by the artificial limiting of options by government power, or via other factors that make genuine informed consent in various trades impossible.

The point here is simple: when government interferes, it renders mutual benefit through consent impossible. When it does that, there is immorality in the system. The inequality that results is immoral and likely to be more extreme than otherwise. To make this vivid, imagine you want to marry Donna.[45] Donna does not want to marry you. You are hurt by her rejection, but nothing immoral has occurred; she married me, and you went on and found someone else (we hope). Imagine, though, that the reason Donna married me is that I convinced the government to require a "Donna marrying license" that allowed only one license per decade and I, knowing it was being instituted, got to the licensing board first. Or imagine she married me because I managed to get the government to make your travel to her hometown illegal. Or to make your profession illegal. Or to subsidize mine. In such situations, you would rightly be aggrieved. You failed to marry who you wanted but only because of unjust interference by the government on my behalf. Now imagine this example multiplied by a million—that is, with government determining the outcome in millions of cases, leaving it impossible for millions to do what they wish.

Recognizing that every market transaction has winners and losers, one should worry about having an agency that operates in ways that determine the winners and losers. If I win Donna because of my superior charm, humor, intellect, looks, or what have you, it is one thing; if I win her because of undue interference on my behalf, it is another. If Microsoft, Apple, Google, or whoever sells the most software because it makes the most desirable software, it is one thing. If it sells the most software because of undue interference, it is another. If medical doctors earn more money than professors because they work harder or longer, or are simply deemed to provide a more valuable service by most people, it is one thing. If they earn more money because of undue limits on their competition, it is another.

Import tariffs, immigration restrictions, agricultural and industrial subsidies, licensing requirements, government grants of monopolies, real estate zoning laws, among other measures, are all ways that the government aids some at the expense of others. These are all ways that markets are made less free and less fair.[46] Importantly, it is worse than it may thus far seem—because we are not likely to have government determining the winner of a single transaction in isolation from all other transactions. More likely, if the government sets things so that I win and you lose in one transaction, it will set things so that I win in a lot of transactions (and perhaps that you lose in a lot of transactions) because the winner of a transaction will seek to persuade government to continue setting things in his favor and, by virtue of earlier "wins," will have the resources to do so, offering compensation to government officials that help him.

The objection raised earlier might now be restated: I remain blind to the problems of markets unimpeded by government interference. Of course, government does interfere and (most) BHLs want government to interfere—if only to protect property rights and the consensual actions of market participants. The claim might be that this always occurs, and I have provided little reason to think interfering to ensure market transactions are consensual is anything more than aiding one group of market participants at the expense of others. Those protected, after all, will be benefited at the cost of those they are protected against (as well as those who pay taxes to support the system). The response here can be made straightforwardly, even if its defense would need to be more extensive. Protecting those who consensually trade with others is protecting them from harm by those who would unjustly seek to set back their interests. It is justified by that injustice. By contrast, interfering on behalf of some who are not the subjects of unjust attempts to set back their interests is interference not justified by injustice. It is itself an unjust use of force. Protecting consensual trade—and allowing the inequalities that come with it—is the core of social justice.

Classical Liberalism as the Fulfillment of the Egalitarian Ideal

Axel Kaiser*

Liberalism is distinguished from socialism, which likewise professes to strive for the good of all, not by the goal at which it aims, but by the means that it chooses to attain that goal.

—Ludwig von Mises

Socialism, Exploitation, and Inequality

WHAT POLITICAL PHILOSOPHY understands by "distributive justice," which in essence attempts to shed light on how much each individual is entitled to receive in terms of material goods, welfare, and status within a given political community, would make no sense in a world of unlimited resources, because in that case the redistribution of goods and opportunities would not be necessary. It is solely the shortage of resources that sparks concerns about economic inequality, which is then attributed to social hierarchies. Thus, any attempt to reduce material inequality for reasons of fairness must be based on a vision about the functioning of the economic and institutional system that generates or preserves it. In other words, the outcomes of a system S shall be unfair if its operation O is not in line with principles P. Failure to do so would imply the a priori condemnation of inequality, which would transform egalitarianism into a sort of religious creed beyond rational discussion. In the words of John Rawls, "a redistribution

---

*Axel Kaiser is president of Fundación Para el Progreso and director of the Friedrich Hayek Chair at the Adolfo Ibáñez University in Santiago, Chile.

cannot be judged in isolation from the system of which it is the outcome,"[1] so there cannot be an answer to the uncontextualized question of whether a given distribution is fair or not. This idea is shared by Robert Nozick, who suggests a conception of fairness in which the confirmation of economic and social inequality does not suffice because it is also necessary to examine the processes that give rise to it.[2] This is the only reasonable starting point for discussing the ideal of distributive fairness in a scheme of social cooperation. Whatever principle is applied, economic analysis—that is, the analysis of the system's overall operation—is unavoidable to assessing the ethical nature of its outcomes.

Both Marx and Rousseau, two of the fathers of modern egalitarian doctrine, condemned economic and social inequality on the grounds that it was nothing more than the expression of an economic system that turned some individuals into the slaves of others. The great fraud, according to Rousseau, began when we forgot that "the fruits of the earth belong to all of us."[3] Order based on private property is unfair because it establishes a system of inequality that destroys men's liberty and subdues them in ways that result in "each man becom[ing] the slave of another," which is the origin of competition, conflicts of interest, and the desire to benefit at the expense of others. According to Rousseau, all these evils are the "first effects of property, and the inseparable attendants of growing inequality."[4] What is more, Rousseau claims that the institution of political society

> bound new fetters on the poor and gave new powers to the rich; which
> irretrievably destroyed natural liberty, eternally fixed the law of prop-
> erty and inequality, converted clever usurpation into unalterable right,
> and, for the advantage of a few ambitious individuals, subjected all
> mankind to perpetual labor, slavery and wretchedness.[5]

Rousseau's economic vision—according to which private property is a form of robbing the community because it is founded on an unequal, unjust, and exploitative system that annihilates freedom, as well as the idea that love for the whole should replace individual interest—formed the cornerstone of the theoretical construction of socialism.[6] According to Marx:

> the man who possesses no other property than his labor power must,
> in all conditions of society and culture, be the slave of other men who

have made themselves the owners of the material conditions of labor. He can only work with their permission, hence live only with their permission.[7]

Thus, for Marx, the rule of private property over the means of production was a source of unjust inequalities because it was based on a form of slavery that created a zero-sum game. Marx states:

> Since labor is the source of all wealth, no one in society can appropriate wealth except as the product of labor. Therefore, if he himself does not work, he lives by the labor of others and also acquires his culture at the expense of the labor of others.[8]

And Engels would add that "every progress of production is at the same time a retrogression in the condition of the oppressed class, that is, of the great majority. Every benefit for one class is necessarily an evil for the other."[9]

The arguments presented above lead to an inevitable conclusion: if the socialist economic analysis is wrong, as was shown by Eugen von Böhm-Bawerk and Ludwig von Mises, among others, then the condemnatory verdict on inequality is unsustainable.[10] To put it another way, if the economic operation of the system of private property is neither thieving nor the source of exploitation and misery that Marx, Rousseau, and other socialists denounced, but is a source of universal prosperity and the expression of the freedom of the members of the community, then market or capitalist inequality cannot be considered unjust under the same socialist logic. Without exploitation: economic argument; the immorality of the system disappears: ethical conclusion.

The Market as Source of Justice as Fairness

We have seen that, like Nozick, Rawls thought that inequality cannot be condemned without prior examination of the process that originates it. But unlike Nozick, who placed the emphasis on individual rights, Rawls focused on an economic criterion to determine whether income distribution in a given community is fair or not. According to this view, the social division of benefits—the central point of Rawlsian contractualist theory—must take place according to principles selected under a veil of ignorance; that is, a situation in which the contractors are totally unaware of their specific characteristics and social position. Under these conditions, Rawls argues that two principles of justice are agreed on: the first one, which has to do with equality of basic liberties and duties; and the second, which implies that inequalities in wealth and authority should be considered fair only if they benefit everyone, particularly the less privileged of society.[11] Specifically, Rawls argues that social and economic inequalities must (1) benefit the least privileged and (2) be related to positions open to all under conditions of *fair equality of opportunities*.[12] According to Rawls, "there is no injustice in the greater benefits earned by a few provided that the situation of persons not so fortunate is thereby improved."[13] If the market order should indeed constitute a system of exploitation in which one gains what another loses, as Marx and Rousseau thought, it would be totally incompatible with the theory of Rawlsian justice. Rawls says: "Injustice, then, is simply inequalities that are not to the benefit of all."[14] That said, whether the content of the index of primary goods proposed by the second Rawlsian principle—essentially wealth, opportunities, and the basis of self-respect—is distributed in a way that benefits one and all is a question that only economic theory and evidence can answer. Contrary to Otfried Höffe's interpretation of Rawls, without prior economic analysis it is impossible to say that the difference principle implies a commitment to the "social state" [*Sozialstaat*].[15] The truth is that economic science offers enough theoretical and empirical arguments to support the thesis that a system in which the means of production are private property, and in which competitive markets and limited government prevail, is the most beneficial to the less privileged of society in the sense conceived by Rawls. As Deirdre McCloskey has explained, "the poor have been the chief beneficiaries of capitalism."[16] The benefits that come from innovation in an open market in line with liberal institutions, says McCloskey, first go to the rich who generated them. However, what historical evidence shows is that they ultimately benefit the less privileged by causing prices to drop in relation to wages, generating more job opportunities and greater social mobility and, consequently, leading to a better distribution of income.[17] Thus, natural and social inequalities, when they occur within the framework of liberal institutions, allow the most privileged to benefit the less privileged; even though, as F. A. Hayek explained, this process of general progress does not necessarily benefit in the first place those that most deserve it.[18] To deny the enjoyment of advantages to a few on the grounds of lack of merit would lead, according to Hayek, to a standstill in the entire process of opportunity and income improvement for the more disadvantaged.[19] The result would be the opposite of what Rawls intended: less well-being, fewer jobs, fewer socially valued opportunities, and fewer sources of self-respect. David Schmidtz has raised this point, saying that if we are aware that minor differences in economic growth rates have gigantic impacts on the chances of improvement of the poorest in the medium and long term, and at the same time we support Rawls's difference principle, we probably should not encourage distributive policies that reduce economic growth.[20] This first limit to the redistribution of wealth set by the difference principle is a *redistributive limit.* A second limit, directly related to the first, is that the principle of difference does not claim that any amount of sacrifice by the most privileged to benefit the less privileged is fair. Making a rich man's assets plummet by a billion dollars to benefit a poor man by one cent is rejected by the second principle of justice. As Schmidtz himself has noted, the principle should not be taken to such improbable extremes.[21] This second restriction is a *viability limit.*

A third limit set on state intervention by the difference principle is what we can call a *limit of general systemic sustainability.* Provision by the state of basic goods to the less privileged must be economically sustainable. Confirmation that the welfare state is, in the words of Niklas Luhmann, an illusion with an unsustainable desire to compensate all those considered victims of social interaction,[22] thus finds (at least in part) an answer in the Rawlsian difference principle, even though Rawls himself was not fully aware of this. As explained by Richard Epstein, Rawls intended to reduce individual risk without considering that by doing so, the risk of failure of the system as a whole increased.[23] In other words if, as Epstein himself has argued, the progressive institutions are economically unsustainable and incubate the potential to severely undermine and even destroy democratic coexistence and social peace, then according to the Rawlsian difference principle there would be no alternative but a classic liberal institutional framework. This would not only be more effective in increasing wealth by generating greater opportunities for the most disadvantaged, but would also resist better the pressures of groups and factions of political interest that jeopardize the subsistence of the system as a whole.[24] A classical liberal scheme would thus prevent the appearance of what Milton and Rose Friedman called the "iron triangle" formed by the beneficiaries of government programs, bureaucrats, and politicians who reap benefits at the expense of others in a zero-sum game.[25] Therefore, Epstein reminds us that "the best solution to the problem of unequal wealth distribution is economic growth that reduces the size of the problem by expanding the size of the pie."[26] Only thus, by cutting back on redistribution except for cases of extreme need, is it possible to prevent redistribution from being captured by political pressures.[27] In the words of Luigi Zingales:

> When the government is small and relatively weak, the most efficient way to make money is to start a successful private-sector business. But the larger the size and scope of government spending, the easier it is to make money by diverting public resources.[28]

The fourth limit to redistribution set by the difference principle, which we shall call *entrepreneurial limit*, is that a system of transfers should not destroy the incentives of the less privileged of society to succeed by their own means, condemning them to a "poverty trap" or dependency. Sweden is an example of the application of social-democratic policies incompatible with the second Rawlsian principle, since they led to less entrepreneurship, higher unemployment, fewer opportunities, erosion of the values associated with work, and less integration of the most disadvantaged members of Swedish society—namely, the immigrants.[29]

This last point is directly related to economic freedom as one of the essential sources of human dignity and self-esteem that were crucial to Rawls. When John Tomasi developed his conception of free-market fairness, he observed that many of the things that people need in order to feel personal attainment and self-respect are only found in economic activity in the private sector; that is, in market relations: obstacles to overcome, success, being self-funded and able to fund dependents, and so forth.[30] It appears that the ability to sort out economic problems allows individuals to develop moral capacities, essential to their self-determination and self-esteem. This has to do not only with their dependent others living well, but also with being acknowledged as the source of that well-being. For parents, being able to provide for their children is not a nuisance, but a source of dignity, respect, and self-fulfillment.[31]

Meritocracy and Cosmic Justice

Modern egalitarianism in general advocates forms of official redistribution to reach an ideal of justice based on "meritocracy." According to this view, merit is the criterion par excellence used to assess the fairness of a given distribution. John Stuart Mill, in his essays on socialism, regretted that "the very idea of distributive justice, or any proportionality between success and merit" is "manifestly chimerical as to be relegated to the regions of romance."[32] Long before Rawls, Mill stated that "the most powerful of all the determining circumstances is birth,"[33] confirming his idea that rewards should depend on some sort of merit in order to be just. This view, according to which property rights are legitimate insofar as they respond to a notion of merit, is incompatible with a society of free people. As David Hume observed, a social order in which possessions are distributed in proportion to virtues or merits requires "an omniscient superior being of infinite intelligence who only acts questing after good."[34] In a society of humans, however, the same rule would cause "the total dissolution of society" because "so great is the uncertainty of merit, both from its natural obscurity, and from the self-conceit of each individual, that no determinate rule of conduct would ever result from it."[35]

Rawls's vision of organizing the basic structure of society so that inequalities not stemming from merit should be compensated[36] is destined to end in an actual "paternalistic meritocracy," because if we insist on the idea of considering a distribution just only when it stems from merit, we must then establish a radical policy of equal opportunities that eliminates or compensates for any undeserved privilege of one person over others. In this case, Hayek notes, the state would need to control the entire physical and social environment in order to guarantee equal options and control any circumstance affecting the welfare of the people.[37] In other words, a strict structure of equal opportunities based on merit, instead of the provision of a sufficient minimum, would demand a "homogenization" policy that would result in the annihilation of the individual, denounced by Nietzsche as the aspiration of socialism.[38] Wilhelm Röpke, validating Nietzsche's point, explained that egalitarianism, even if it only sought equal opportunity, would inevitably push the government toward a "totalitarian functionalization of society."[39] The aftermath would be the loss of everything that is pre-state, para-state, and super-state, which would be relinquished for the sake of greater mathematical equality among individuals. Consequently, "the idea of 'placing' each individual according to their 'merits' and 'talents' involves a Welfare State which will differ from the totalitarian state in name only" because the system will respond to a "craving for uniformity" that will result in "a centralized, coercive and uniform state education."[40] Moreover, a system of equal opportunity would be inclined to incubate "intolerance towards those who diverge from the abstract 'common man' not only vertically because they have a higher social position, but also horizontally because they differ somehow on the same social level."[41] Röpke emphasizes that equal opportunity is impossible without totally equal economic outcomes and social status because inequality of outcomes and status in the parents engenders unequal opportunities for their children.[42] Röpke also refers to another fundamental issue: there is no reason to consider personal capabilities less legitimate than any other type of possession, including those acquired by merit.[43]

The Rawlsian view of equality of opportunity, achieved by means of an institutional design that compensates individuals for any type of disadvantage, can be seen as "a revolt against nature"[44] and its aim has less to do with social justice than with getting what Thomas Sowell calls "cosmic justice."[45] Rawls's fellow traveler, Thomas Nagel, offers a clear example of this quest for "cosmic justice." According to Nagel, equality of opportunity assumes that society must compensate for those inequalities that arise from factors "beyond the control of the individual," including those derived from economic status, type of nurturing environment, education of parents, genetic endowment, culture, geography, and history—among many other aspects. In his words, "from a moral point of view it is to some extent arbitrary how benefits—intelligence, education, genetic endowment, etc.—are distributed, and therefore, there is nothing wrong with the State tinkering with that distribution."[46] Following the same logic, Ronald Dworkin argues that egalitarians should not consider inequalities in the distribution of wealth as fair, if they result from differences in capabilities that have been inherited or are the product of fortuitous advantages.[47]

For Nagel, as well as for Rawls and Dworkin, everything created by the laws of the universe that benefits one over another is morally "arbitrary" and the state must fix it. It is evident, as already mentioned, that a program aimed at correcting all existing inequalities not stemming from "merit" demands a sort of knowledge that, as Hume stated, and Sowell reaffirmed, is "superhuman" and thus impossible to acquire,[48] because the truth is that we do not know how to identify and quantify merit.[49] Dworkin himself admits that it is impossible to determine, even in principle, which aspects of a person's economic position stem from that person's own decisions and which advantages or disadvantages do not.[50] Thus, we shall never be able to tell how much of a person's success or failure is due to their own merit and how much to genetics, intelligence, effort, education, experience, luck, culture, and so forth. There is no preestablished criterion to determine advantages and disadvantages. The examples of the uncertain nature of advantages and disadvantages are endless, and thus it is impossible to establish a rule based on merit—let alone determine a formula based on such rule—to compensate those who presumably are at a disadvantage.

Complexity, Liberty, and Capabilities

The previously mentioned idea of social complexity also makes the ideal of social justice based on capabilities, proposed by Amartya Sen and Martha Nussbaum, counterproductive. According to Sen, equality of capabilities aims at giving "substantial freedom" to allow people to get what they really want.[51] Thus, Sen understands freedom as the effective power to obtain what a person intends to achieve and not as the absence of arbitrary coercion by third parties, as proposed by classical liberalism. In Sen's view, there is no freedom in the absence of material conditions that support its actual exercise. The poor, for instance, have neither the freedom nor the capability to create wealth and require state assistance to do so. This has been widely refuted by authors such as Jagdish Bhagwati and Arvind Panagariya, who have shown that reforms that promote economic freedom—and not capabilities created by government policies—were the cause of the growth of underdeveloped countries such as India.[52] Along the same lines, refuting Sen's idea that, by definition, the poor cannot get ahead without state assistance, as well as Piketty's argument that "the poorest half of the population still owns nothing,"[53] Hernando de Soto has shown that the poorest of the world have managed to create and accumulate extraordinary levels of wealth that cannot be transformed into actual assets due to institutional problems—mainly, failure of the state to ensure property rights.[54]

But the definition of freedom as power proposed by Sen not only is refuted in its economic application but also distorts the political sense of the word. Freedom is a social concept that refers to the limits set to the actions of individuals with respect to other individuals.[55] John Locke, the founding father of this classical tradition, argued that freedom consists in "disposing and ordering in any way he wants of his person, his actions, his possessions, and his whole property ... within whatever limits that are set by the laws that he is under"; that is to say, without being subjected "to the arbitrary will of anyone else but freely to follow his own will."[56] As this is a social or political concept it makes no sense to speak of Robinson Crusoe's lack of freedom on the island due to the fact that he had nothing to eat. As Isaiah Berlin claims, the absence of political freedom means being "prevented by others from doing what I could otherwise do."[57] Sen, on the contrary, endorses "positive freedom," which as Berlin himself explains, involves a liberator gifted with privileged knowledge to free a person who struggles with internal or external obstacles that prevent them from answering the call of their "true self."[58] In a broad interpretation of this approach, the state should not only restrict itself to the primary goods suggested by Rawls as the basis of his difference principle, but also remove or compensate for all obstacles in life, including malnutrition, disabilities, limitations due to old age or gender, psychological problems, unfavorable looks, and many other factors that impede a person's self-fulfillment. That is exactly Sen's aim, even though he makes it clear that "the state may have better grounds for offering support to a person for overcoming hunger or illness than for helping him to build a monument to the person's hero."[59] However, the idea that building a statue to somebody's hero is at least theoretically considered by the capabilities thesis shows the interventionist hyperinflation to which this proposal potentially may lead. Nussbaum confirms this when she explains that capabilities are as multiple and diverse in quantity and quality as the number of human beings. Therefore, it is not possible to come up with a capabilities scale, according to which the state must provide capabilities to "improve the quality of life for all people."[60] Thus, on the one hand Nussbaum acknowledges it is impossible to identify accurately the capabilities required, and on the other, she claims that the state must provide or compensate for them to attain social justice.

But even if we accept the capabilities approach, a market system in a classical liberal context would come closer to achieving the ideal of social justice proposed by Sen and Nussbaum, given its advantage over centralized mechanisms in processing the required information and the absence of the problem of public choice inherent to bureaucratic organizations. As Ingrid Robeyns puts it:

> The question of what, if anything, the government ought to do depends on the … answer to the question of whether we need the government to deliver those goods and what can realistically be expected from a government. Just as we need to take people as they are, we need not work with an unrealistic utopian account of government. It may be that the capabilitarian ideal society is better reached by a coordinated commitment to individual action or by relying on market mechanisms.[61]

Factual Egalitarianism, Moral Alienation, and Progress

The proponents of what we might call "factic" equality, who advocate material equality instead of mere equality before the law, must admit that their proposal is incompatible with the strict safeguard of what is known as negative freedom. Given that organized violence is the means par excellence of materializing the egalitarian program, such a program is not entirely compatible with institutions that hold the utmost respect for the life projects of the people. When Hayek argued that "this equality of the general rules of law and conduct" was "the only kind of equality conducive to liberty and the only equality which we can secure without destroying liberty," he was accounting for this inevitable and unsolvable conflict between ethical and factic egalitarianism.[62] For if we respect the equality of all, insofar as they are moral agents responsible for their actions, we cannot judge the results of those same actions as unjust as long as they have followed fair rules of conduct. Equality before the law is the inevitable result of moral equality, and equality through the law is the inevitable consequence of the impossible quest for cosmic justice.

The second, and perhaps the most fundamental, problem of egalitarianism is that it simply does not and cannot achieve the results proposed. If we consider the state as it actually is (and not an idealized vision), we cannot but conclude that the ideals of social justice pursued by all the varieties of egalitarianism, from the classical socialist to the Rawlsian and even the capabilities versions, are better served by a classical liberal structure with little state intervention, extensive markets, and a sufficient minimum for those who fail to become part of the development process promoted by this system.

The greatest mistake of egalitarians has always been to believe that centralized rather than decentralized systems allow for the best possible use of the knowledge scattered throughout society to achieve universal well-being and higher levels of meaningful equality. Probably this inclination for state intervention stems from the fact that the egalitarian doctrine generates, in the words of Harry Frankfurt, true moral alienation.[63] By focusing on the differences in wealth among people instead of what is relevant to each individual in terms of their actual position in the world, egalitarianism diverts the discussion from the most relevant issue—that each should have enough, regardless of the gaps between them—to a morally irrelevant issue such as determining how much more than another a given person has.[64] The objective of improving the fate of those who have less, which undoubtedly motivates all forms of egalitarianism, is transmuted into seeking to eliminate large differences between human beings.

The moral alienation of egalitarianism consists precisely in denying individual well-being for the sake of political preferences for relative positions, whose motivation may be directly associated with envy,[65] because not even the argument of maximizing aggregate utility in a society can justify egalitarian redistributions.[66] The problem is even more serious because given that wealth and resources do not exist in nature, but must be created, their equal distribution on the grounds that if there is not enough for everyone nobody should have more than another, would lead to a complete social disaster.[67] Therefore, the egalitarian argument faces an insurmountable contradiction: on the one hand, it posits as its ideal a society in which everyone has enough; on the other, it focuses redistribution of wealth on the idea of some being worse off than others, thus completely ignoring the crucial question of how wealth for everyone is created in the first place.

The fact that the ultimate goal of egalitarianism is not "equality of re-sources"—as Dworkin mistakenly argues—but wealth, becomes clear when we wonder whether egalitarians think that equality in misery is morally pref-erable to inequality in wealth. Actually, what egalitarians seek and what shocks them is that some do not have enough, and not that some should not have more than others (herewith the origin of the sufficiency doctrine).[68] A society in which no one lacks anything relevant for a satisfactory quality of life can be very unequal. In that case, discussion around social justice becomes meaningless. This point is apparently controversial, but it is interesting to note that in pursuit of his ideal, an egalitarian like Dworkin is very close to a libertarian like Friedman, precisely because Dworkin's concern is not—ulti-mately—equality, but sufficiency.[69] Dworkin himself discards a welfare state that controls services and transfers if they prove to be inefficient. According to Dworkin, a negative income tax could prove "more efficient and fair" to achieve "equality of resources" than a welfare scheme.[70] Friedman in turn argues that a negative income tax "is directed specifically at the problem of poverty."[71]

The difference between libertarians and egalitarians lies, as we can see, in the language they use. Dworkin speaks of "levelling income," arguing that his goal is equality—which could also be achieved by confiscatory marginal tax rates—yet in fact, his goal is identical to Friedman's and consists in achieving a sufficient minimum. Thus, the discussion is not first and foremost about objectives but about methods; although egalitarianism generally falls into a moral alienation that prevents it from admitting the aims originally intended. If the classical liberal formula of open and extensive markets, property rights, and respect for individual liberties has proven to be the most successful in raising the level of well-being of the masses and improving the lives of the less privileged, it is because it has proposed the best methods. Egalitarians must re-flect on this point because if their ideal of social justice is universal abundance, as Marx envisioned; or the greatest possible progress for the less privileged, as Rawls and Nagel wished for; or the greatest number of tools for personal fulfillment, as Sen and Nussbaum proposed; or sufficient resources for all, as Dworkin intended; or any other form of universal progress, then there is no doubt that such ideals will be better served by the theoretical framework provided by classical liberalism. For not only does classical liberalism ensure respect for the negative liberties that are essential for the different forms of modern egalitarianism, but it also provides the best theoretical and empirical instruments that permit the stock of assets valued by humankind to increase.

17

Social Justice, Public Goods, and Rent Seeking in Narratives

Vincent J. Geloso and Phillip W. Magness*

SOCIAL JUSTICE, AS a concept, has long been considered in-
imical to the classical liberal tradition.[1] To be fair, there is much to criticize
about the concept. The definitional fluidity of the term *social justice* and its
frequent deployment for "activist" political endeavors cast doubt upon its
scholarly rigor.[2] However, where there is chaff, there is wheat and thus the
possibility of salvaging some parts of the social justice concept to serve both
normative and positive ends.[3] Sorting the wheat from the chaff is the aim of
this chapter. To do so, we introduce the concept of "rent seeking in narratives," which, as we argue, takes the best concepts from the literature on social
justice to make it a relevant tool for social science and classical liberal thought.

Throughout the chapter, we assume that abstract and general rules that
apply equally to all are the most conducive to improvements in all forms of
liberty and living standards.[4] General rules constitute a form of open orders
that are normatively superior to closed-access orders. The concept of rent
seeking in narratives starts with the assumption that the creation of rules
of cooperation is a public good. The rules fall on a spectrum between the
extremes of open-access orders and closed-access orders.[5] However, we argue
there can be competition for the production of a certain set of general societal
rules in a way that favors a given coalition of interest. The more this practice
occurs, the more opportunities will exist for rent seeking. Once a given set of
rules is established, narratives can then be built to increase the cost of replac-

*Vincent J. Geloso is visiting professor of economics at Bates College. Phillip W. Magness
is senior research fellow at the American Institute for Economic Research.

ing the given set of rules or acting in ways that fully dissipate the existing rent for the beneficiary group.[6]

This structure in part salvages the idea of relational equality and fully conserves its close cousin "euvoluntary exchange."[7] Because these concepts are taken to be equals of F. A. Hayek's claims that we need general and abstract rules that apply equally to all so as to permit welfare-enhancing social cooperation, deviations from these rules reduce well-being. Rent seeking to shape rules in ways to benefit one group is *by definition* a deviation.[8] The rent-seeking groups can see their rents dissipated by other groups who push either for general rules or for rules to their own benefit. They must thus resist this push by increasing the cost to others of contesting the established rules. One way of doing so is to shape social discourse so as to increase the cost of holding views that fall outside of the existing general rules.[9]

Distributive Justice, Relational Equality, and the Generality Ideal

When during the 1960s and 1970s classical scholars criticized the concept of social justice, they equated it with distributive justice in the sense of greater equality of outcomes.[10] This distributive justice, they argued, would generate the seeds to its own destruction as agency on the part of individuals would create deviations. The criticisms assembled were deemed convincing to a degree sufficient to warrant a restatement of what social justice meant.[11] The reply that has emerged is that social justice is about relational equality.[12] Simply put, relational equality holds that the way in which one individual is treated ought to extend to all other individuals. Differential treatment, positive or negative, invites stigma that may have persistent effects.[13] The main value of this restatement is that relational *in*equality can persist in spite of legal equality even if there are interconnections between the two.[14] Thus, invisible forces at play lead to lesser outcomes for certain groups (e.g., de jure racial equality accompanied by de facto inequality in practice). Moreover, because relational inequality fosters stigma, it discourages the development of self-respect (i.e., independence).[15]

Described as such, relational equality resembles Hayek's generality principle whereby rules ought to be abstract and general and apply to all.[16] It also bears great similarity to the "open-access" orders described by Douglass North, John Wallis, and Barry Weingast.[17] In open-access orders, "all citizens have access to the political and economic systems, and they have the right to form organizations," which in turn sustains "impersonal exchange and allow[s] all citizens to compete for political control and for economic rents, which are continuously eroded as a result of this political and economic competition."[18] In contrast, in "limited-access orders" relations are between the powerful, who create a hierarchy in which they, at the top of the hierarchy, extract rents that cannot be dissipated by political and economic competition. Both the generality rule and the open-access orders are conducive to widespread improvements in living standards. Limited-access orders and discriminatory rules are less conducive to economic growth.[19] "Relational equality" entails, at the very least, a legal equality to contest arbitrary hierarchies—thus a similarity with the open-access orders. At the very least, it also shares similarities with the generality rule because all must receive equal treatment.

Relational equality does not necessarily entail redistributive efforts, however. To be fair, most of those who invoke the concept do so to justify *some* redistribution.[20] Thus, it does differ modestly from Hayek's generality principle and North, Wallis, and Weingast's "open-access orders," on which classical liberals rely. However, there are steps that generate a marginally more equal society in relational terms but do not require redistribution and would allow classical liberals to follow in a similar direction until a crossroad is reached. Relational equality can fit within a classical liberal policy course of "first, do no harm" with regard to inequality.[21] This type of policy approach requires the removal of any form of regressive redistribution whereby one group is treated differentially in a nefarious way (e.g., through tariffs, regressive taxation and regulations, corporate welfare, and also directly oppressive measures such as racial segregation). As a consequence, a policy that eliminates an existing regressive redistribution will marginally move us closer to more relational equality. Thus, there is some mileage to be done between those who are reluctant to adopt redistributive policies but want relational equality and those who argue for relational equality as the end of redistributive policies. The very first step toward relational equality is the elimination of the policies that formalize relational inequality. There is some wheat with the chaff.

More importantly, relational equality has a quality whereby it links the individual to the society. Uneven treatment of individuals (i.e., relational *in*equality) limits heterogeneous individuals' ability to make contact. Obviously, contractual restrictions imposed on one particular set of individuals (e.g., black Americans during segregation, women before the twentieth century, Jews in the medieval era) will restrict the ability of this set of individuals to make contact with individuals who are in different sets. Although less extreme, other measures that deprive individuals of certain options will nevertheless restrict contact (e.g., trade tariffs falling predominantly on goods consumed by the poor prevent them from engaging in a larger number of exchanges, which could have brought them in contact with others). In turn, restricting contact creates stigma toward the unevenly treated set of individuals. Stigma is social distance, and social distance is a source of transaction costs—the greater the social distance, the greater the transaction costs, the smaller the size of the market, and the lesser the gains from specialization.[22] Thus, the stigma reinforces the institutional restrictions and may generate persistent outcomes well after the restrictions are removed. In other words, in a world where individuals of a disfavored set earn no mutual respect from preferred groups, it is harder to build self-respect—an outcome that may persist for a long period.

This ability to speak to the persistent effects of relational *in*equality is a serious advantage that allows more wheat to be sorted from the chaff. Not only are we able to see that those in the classical liberal tradition can support an agenda that removes policies that create relational inequality, but we can explain why even after bad institutions are removed, the long shadow of their detrimental effects can persist. For that reason alone, classical liberals should be amenable to attempts to salvage part of the new discourse on social justice. However, the best reason for sorting the wheat from the chaff is that relational inequality allows classical liberals to develop a well-rounded (positive) explanation of the persistent effects of state intervention.

Rules as Public Goods and Rent Seeking in Narratives

In order to produce this explanation, it is best to think of social rules as public goods[23]—not in the sense of the public/private dichotomy, but rather in the sense of collective action deployed to create the rules of the game that allow a stable environment in which to reap the gains from trade. The publicness of these rules and norms that govern exchange means that "opportunities exist for political entrepreneurship" and rent seeking.[24] This political entrepreneurship leads to rules that benefit a concentrated interest group at a cost that, although diffused throughout the whole society, is, on the whole, greater for society.

However, once the rules are in place, other groups can contest them. The changes proposed may either enhance or inhibit efficiency, but this is irrelevant here as anticipated changes in rules incite groups to engage in rent seeking.[25] In the contest, the incumbents must defend the rent they earn from the established set of rules. The resources they expend in the defense dissipate their gains from the rents. Thus, to preserve their rents, the incumbents must find a way to increase the cost of contest for others, which will also dissipate part of the incumbents' rent because they need to expend further resources on defensive action. However, as long as the costs are subjectively greater to contesters, the incumbents will remain unchallenged.

Hindering relational equality is one way of generating a rent-preserving entry barrier. If a stigma is associated with one of the groups being excluded from the rent, other (and possibly less) excluded groups see a greater cost to forming a coalition to contest the rent beneficiary. It deters them from contesting because the total cost is greater to them than the benefits of ending their disadvantaged situation.

This formulation is very similar to the one proposed by Jennifer Roback,[26] who models racism as rent seeking. By conceiving of social norms—including discriminatory social norms associated with racism—as collective action aimed at producing a public good, Roback shows that sharply defining relations between groups reduces the odds of a collapse of a rent-seeking outcome. She states that this sharper definition benefits one group by "effectively enforcing an economic cartel arrangement amongst its members."[27] Although she is referring to reducing defection *within* the rent-beneficiary group, her conclusion can easily be extended to other groups who might form a contesting coalition with the excluded group. The sharply defined stigma (i.e., the cementing of relational *in*equality) protects the rent-seeking outcome. This sharpening of definitions, meant to crystalize relational inequality, is rent seeking. However, it is what we call "rent seeking in narratives." The aim is to invest in a social discourse, an intellectual narrative, that increases the cost of contesting an established rent extraction.

Here, the concept of preference falsification developed by Timur Kuran is particularly useful. *Preference falsification* refers to the idea that we try to "manipulate the perceptions of others regarding our own motivations and dispositions."[28] We "live a lie" because the benefits of expressing our true disposition are small and the costs are uncertain and potentially larger than the benefits. The "public" preference is determined by the incentives generated by the institutional context that surrounds public life. However, in the privacy of our homes we exert our true preferences. The gap between what is done in private and what is done in public depends entirely on the institutional setting in public. Preference falsification is a "barrier to social change"[29] as long as the institutional context establishes strong penalties for defecting from the established narratives. Groups with strong, concentrated interests may constitute a minority, but majorities may be deterred from revolting (or from contesting established rules by collectively organizing) by social pressures that make them unwilling to express their true preference. Simultaneously, this lack of open expression of true preferences entails that individual members of a potential majority coalition do not identify their allies and thus fail to organize. According to Kuran, preference falsification is particularly damaging because it generates "widespread ignorance of the status quo's disadvantages."[30]

Rent seeking in narratives is simply a different take on preference falsification, whereby the rent seeker also establishes a discourse that creates the inability to organize. The concept of rent seeking in narratives, however, clarifies that adding stigma to one hierarchically inferior group creates an unwillingness to organize because the cementing of relational *in*equality increases the perceived costs to forming a contesting coalition.

It is worth noting here the other bit of wheat to be sorted from the chaff. Here, we see that the protection of a limited-access order can be served by creating relational inequality, which also means deviating from general and abstract rules that apply equally to all.[31] The concept of relational equality, if articulated within the broader story of rent seeking, thus offers the possibility to explain the persistence of discriminatory and impoverishing outcomes.

Examples of Rent Seeking in Narratives

Two examples illustrate and make the case for this concept of rent seeking in narratives. The first speaks directly to racism toward black Americans in the nineteenth century, and the second speaks to discrimination aimed at the French Canadian majority population of Quebec in Canada. We selected these examples because they allow us to illustrate that cementing relational *in*equality may work against both minorities *and* majorities.

Antebellum Slavery

The economic history of the antebellum South suggests that nonslaveholding whites were not beneficiaries of chattel slavery.[32] Slaveholders used the political process to delegate the costs of the system onto the larger public, North and South, while preserving and reaping the benefits of slave-based production. One potent illustration of this point is the slave patrols. Slaveholders should have had to expend their own resources to prevent slaves from running away because this cost was associated specifically with the preservation of slavery. However, because the slaveholders constituted a concentrated interest group, they organized successfully to convince the states to take over the task of policing slaves at public expense—thus the slave patrols. Divided over the entire population of the country, this expense appeared smaller, but it constituted an important increase in profitability for slaveholders. The cost of the slave patrols in 1850, according to Jeffrey Hummel's computations,[33] was more than fifty cents per person (including slaves, but slightly less than one dollar per person when computed over the free white population). The slave patrols entailed a burden of 0.3 percent of annual per capita income in the South—quite a large cost for such a "small" policy. Totaling all the costs for nonslaveholding whites, Hummel concludes that it is unlikely that they gained economically from slavery.[34]

Poor whites in the South did not gain from slavery—they carried a burden that made them poorer than they otherwise would have been absent slavery. However, forming a coalition with abolitionists or with politically excluded slaves to end slavery was out of the question for them.[35] Jeffrey Grynaviski and Michael Munger[36] argue that this option was unavailable to them because of the stigma associated with blacks, who were deemed lesser humans. Similar stigmas associated Northern abolitionism with sedition and its proponents with contemporary events that had devolved into mass bloodshed, such as the Haitian revolution. This stigmatization of antislavery and the slaves themselves grew more pronounced from the time of the American Revolution to the time of the Civil War. The institution of slavery was initially seen as a necessary evil that would have to be eradicated eventually. However, this view gradually changed. Slaves began to be considered lesser human beings unable to take command of their lives, and, thus, slavery became associated with a positive good. Grynaviski and Munger emphasize that this "redefinition of the personhood of slaves" was meant to "co-opt dissent"[37] through an exercise of legitimation, which preserved the rent-seeking structures. This legitimation was complemented, as Hummel[38] notes, by a series of laws and edicts preventing the education of slaves and voluntary manumission so as to preserve a rationalization for the notion of blacks' lesser personhood.[39]

All of these circumstances constitute a willful construction of relational inequality between groups of excluded persons so as to prevent rebellion against an established set of rules. Antebellum slavery benefited from a rent-seeking narrative that limited the ability of antislavery campaigners to convince poor whites to side with slaves. Even challenging the existence of slavery could be deemed "seditious," as with antebellum attempts to censor the mail, in particular abolitionist literature. By hindering relational equality between poor whites and black slaves, slaveholders created a barrier to contesting the extracted rents that the public subsidization of slavery provided them.

When slavery was ended, the ideological construct that was supporting the slaveholders' rent-seeking efforts did not disappear. It remained more or less intact and thus allowed the emergence of a lesser but nonetheless tragic form of legal discrimination against black Americans.[40] If segregation, as Roback[41] argues, was rent seeking, then the narratives set to protect rents under slavery were used to partially restore them after the Reconstruction era.

French Canadians to 1960

Black Americans were a disempowered minority facing a discriminatory majority. The reverse, a majority discriminated against by a minority, can also occur. This was the case for French Canadians in their home province, Quebec, where they constituted more than 80 percent of the population. To be sure, the French Canadians never suffered legal discrimination nearly as intense as black Americans. However, most historians agree that from the mid-nineteenth century to the 1960s French Canadian society was noticeably poorer than English Canadian society.[42] Even within the municipalities of Quebec, French Canadians and English Canadians lived separately.

One important contributor of this relative isolation of both groups was the Catholic Church. In the buildup to the British North America Act of 1867 (which made Canada into a country), the Catholic Church lobbied hard to secure a constitutional arrangement that allowed it a strong role in the provision of education and social services such as health care. This arrangement was meant to protect the church's market from religious competition.[43] In exchange, the church supported the conservative agenda of protectionism[44] with the now well-known statement "le ciel est bleu et l'enfer est rouge": the skies are blue (referring to the Conservative Party colors), and hell is red (referring to the colors of the Liberal Party, which was ill disposed toward the church and protectionism).

Through a de facto monopoly on education, the Catholic Church had the ability to enlist schooling to the advantage of its position. The church thought that the English Canadians wanted to assimilate the French Canadians, that capitalism and markets were the prerogatives of the English Canadians, and that French Canadians were better off as farmers or small entrepreneurs.[45] To preserve its rents, the church cemented a discourse that created a relational inequality (a stigma) between French and English Canadians. More research should be allocated to this topic, but in general it can be said that the emergence of this discourse occurred at the same time as an income convergence between French and English Canadians observed up to the mid-nineteenth century so that the gap started to widen again.[46]

To some extent, this narrative cementing relational inequality has had a long half-life. Even though the Catholic Church has since the 1960s lost its influence and French Canadians' living standards have converged rapidly toward English Canadians' living standards,[47] the narrative survives. In the 1950s and 1960s, a new, more secular nationalism emerged in Quebec and retained many of the distinctions between the French and the English. It led to the passage of acts that targeted the English-speaking minority in Quebec and the redistribution of state favors from English Canadians to French Canadian secular nationalists.[48]

Conclusion

The implications from this sorting of the wheat and the chaff are manifold. Relational equality allows us to understand, regardless of ideological predispositions, how limited-access orders are persistent. The cementing of unequal rules of treatment that violates Hayek's generality principle allows rent-seeking coalitions to prevent the formation of contesting coalitions who propose different rules of the game (which may be welfare improving by being more open-access and following the generality principle).

This sorting also allows those who share in the classical liberal predisposition to assemble a policy agenda. One step in the direction of relational equality can be taken by removing restrictions to contact between groups. Although this removal will not erase stigmas that amplify the effect of the restrictions, it will make things marginally better for everyone. This policy of "first, do no harm" is not likely to constitute a full resolution of the issue of stigmatization of certain groups. However, it offers a chance for classical liberals to cooperate with progressives and conservatives in the direction of marginal improvements. As long as the roads lead in the same direction, there is no point in not following them. Unavoidably, of course, there is a point ahead where the paths will diverge. But it is better to grasp the improvements of a "first, do no harm" policy than to reject them on the basis of a fork in the road.

18

Is Social Justice a Mirage?

Stefanie Haeffele and Virgil Henry Storr*

THERE IS BOTH popular and scholarly concern that the current socioeconomic systems in the United States and other Western democracies are not working, especially for the least advantaged.[1] Discrimination based on race, ethnicity, gender, sexual orientation, and age has declined in recent decades, but some worry that discrimination on these margins is still too prevalent.[2] Issues such as inequality and lack of social mobility are frequently debated, but there is no consensus around the nature or extent of or solutions to these social problems. The least advantaged certainly lack economic power and political capital. In response, there have been widespread demands for social justice usually motivated by genuine concern for the least advantaged.

Social justice is about the fair distribution of power and wealth in society.[3] Demands for social justice thus hope to correct the inequalities brought about by the interaction between powerful market participants and government officials. Proponents of social justice often call for increased equality through equal rights to opportunities or equal distribution of wealth based on merit or the redistribution of wealth.[4] Policy and social work—through both government welfare programs and private charity—became the major mechanisms for achieving these goals.[5]

Developments in the late twentieth century "expand[ed] the range of social justice concerns beyond distributive mechanisms by drawing in issues

*Stefanie Haeffele is senior research fellow and the deputy director of Academic and Student Programs in the Mercatus Center at George Mason University. Virgil Henry Storr is associate professor of economics at George Mason University.

around recognition, representation, identity, a focus on process alongside outcomes, and inculcating an obligation to challenge the normative dominant governing, economic, and belief systems in which power, privilege, and oppression are enacted."[6] This view of social justice is not only about redistribution but also about examining the underlying institutions and the dynamics between the privileged and disadvantaged, between the elite and the rest of society. It is no longer primarily about the potential abuses of capitalism, but also about a recognition of discrimination in all aspects of social life.[7] Therefore, values of social justice today include equality as well as inclusivity, diversity, and multiculturalism.[8]

Given the ambitious aims of the proponents of social justice, it is difficult to understand exactly what social justice might look like in practice. Although much of the literature advocates for government intervention to ensure rights and to redistribute income, and many efforts to do so have been enacted, our society still has social injustices. So how can we adjust the current system to effectively address the needs of the disadvantaged? Can we constrain profit and still make progress (i.e., balance the conflicting values of equality and liberty)? Can we constrain special interests from obtaining privileges from government and still provide a broad array of public services (i.e., diminish the power of elites in order to benefit the masses)? Any reforms that attempt to address these issues must arguably be developed from an understanding of (1) the institutional systems that shape our society, (2) the incentives and limitations that influence action, and (3) the unintended consequences that may arise.

F. A. Hayek's critique of social justice, developed in *The Mirage of Social Justice*, the second volume of of *Law, Legislation, and Liberty*, is perhaps one of the most compelling critiques because it attempts to address the three aspects mentioned in the previous paragraph. Hayek argues that the outcomes of market activity (wealth inequality) cannot be deemed just or unjust. The outcome of the game (who wins or loses) is not an issue of justice, though individuals' actions within the game may be.[9] However, redress against individual actors is the realm of justice rather than of social justice. For Hayek, justice can be carried out only against individuals or individuals gathered in organizations, but not against society and social institutions. Hayek goes on to express that many calls for reform in the name of social justice have led to special interests seeking privileges from government, often in an attempt to keep their current social positions rather than to help the least advantaged. He argues that government should instead stick to universal, generalizable rules (such as the protection of private property and the freedom to pursue one's own goals and interests) that apply to everyone and ensure the functioning of a liberal social order.

Hayek highlights many concerns regarding social justice, but there are tensions or inconsistencies in his approach.[10] Here we argue that although the outcome of a game cannot generally be deemed just or unjust, the referees of the game may be.[11] We also argue that there is at least one scenario where it would be appropriate to call even a fairly played and refereed game unjust. When the rules of the socioeconomic game or the referees favor the powerful, the chances that the least advantaged will rise to the top is thwarted. In this scenario, it is worth reexamining the role and functions of these social institutions, attempting to reform them where possible, and providing redress for the disadvantaged where it makes sense to do so.

In this chapter, we examine the concept of social justice by critiquing and expanding upon Hayek's view. Because his critique focuses on the social justice concerns regarding economic outcomes, we limit our discussion to this aspect of social justice. In the next section, we examine that critique, including the notion that the outcomes of a game can be neither just nor unjust. In the second section, we explore how the rules of a game, the officials empowered to interpret and enforce those rules, and even the results of a game that is fairly played and refereed may in fact be just or unjust and highlight how this argument relates to current calls for social justice and the social institutions involved. We conclude by briefly speculating on what social justice might demand and the potential institutions that can remedy injustices.

The Outcomes of Games Are Neither Just nor Unjust

In *The Mirage of Social Justice*, Hayek lays out how the market functions, the principles and rules necessary for the maintenance of the market order, and a critique against calls for social justice that interfere with the workings of the market.

For Hayek, the market order is the result of a process whereby individuals come together to buy and sell goods and services in the pursuit of their own interests. The local baker does not get up early to bake fresh bread because he wants to make us happy but because he wants to receive income in order to provide for himself and his family and can do so by providing sustenance to others in his community; it is a bonus that he also makes us happy.[12] If, however, we stop buying his baked goods (because our tastes for baked goods change or another bakery offers a higher quality at a lower price), he will suffer losses and eventually go out of business. He will have to find another way to make a living. This process of interpreting the feedback of the market, learning about one's own skills and the needs of others, and adapting in order to make a living is what drives the market and the progress that has come along with it.[13]

In order for this coordination to be possible, Hayek contends that society needs enforceable rules of just conduct (generalizable rules that protect property, ensure freedoms, and restrict harms from others).[14] These rules allow for the proper functioning of the market order by enabling individual action and constraining the chances of harm from others. However, they do not eliminate failure and loss within the market order. As Hayek states, "[T]his manner of coordinating individual actions will secure a high degree of coincidence of expectations and an effective utilization of knowledge and skills of the several members only at the price of a constant disappointment of some expectations."[15] Although individuals are free to decide what occupations and activities they want to pursue, they also must deal with the market's feedback (their peers' satisfaction or dissatisfaction) and adjust or fail to adjust accordingly. Hayek understands that these losses may not be based on merit.[16] Individuals may work hard, learn new techniques, treat others fairly, but still not succeed. The local baker may receive losses because he slacks on the job, he is not a good baker, an even better baker moved into town, or many people in the community take up gluten-free diets. Some of these types of losses are not based on merit, and all are unfortunate for the baker and his family, yet they are the cost of a system that generally brings about progress and ensures individual freedom.

From this reasoning, Hayek views calls for social justice—defined as redistribution to remedy economic injustices—as incompatible with a free society (specifically the institutions of the market and a limited government that enforces the rules of just conduct). His critique focuses on two major grounds: (1) the concept of social justice has no real meaning within the context of a free society, and (2) advancing reforms based on social justice will undermine a free society and the progress that has come along with it.[17]

First, Hayek argues that social justice in a free society is meaningless. Claims for social justice are based on the perception of systematic injustices against people owing to the structure or process of social life. However, Hayek notes that actions and outcomes are unjust (and can be remedied) only when you can pinpoint who precisely is acting unjustly. He compares "the general feeling of injustice about the distribution of material goods in a society of free men" to the misfortune of fate, such as when "a succession of calamities befalls one family while another steadily prospers, when a meritorious effort is frustrated by some unforeseeable accident."[18] According to Hayek, "Though we are in this case less ready to admit it, our complaints about the outcome of the market as unjust do not really assert that somebody has been unjust; and there is no answer to the question of *who* has been unjust. ... There is no individual and no cooperating group of people against which the sufferer would have a just complaint, and there are no conceivable rules of just individual conduct which would at the same time secure a functioning order and prevent such disappointments."[19] The cost of disappointed expectations is the price paid for living in a society where we can choose our occupations and pursue our own goals and interests. In this system, Hayek argues, "the fates of the different individuals are not distributed according to some recognizable principle of justice."[20]

Further, according to Hayek, the market order can be viewed as a game with rules of conduct as well as winners and losers. He states that the market

> is wholly analogous to a game, namely a game partly of skill and partly of chance. ... It proceeds, like all games, according to rules guiding the actions of individual participants whose aims, skills, and knowledge are different, with the consequence that the outcome will be unpredictable and that there will regularly be winners and losers. And while, as in a game, we are right in insisting that it be fair and that nobody cheat, it would be nonsensical to demand that the results for the different players be just. They will of necessity be determined

partly by skill and partly by luck. Some of the circumstances which make the services of a person more or less valuable to his fellows, or which may make it desirable that he change the direction of his efforts, are not of human design or foreseeable by men.[21]

For Hayek, as long as players do not cheat, the outcome of the game cannot be called just or unjust even though the players' success or failure may not necessarily be a result of superior skill or effort.[22] If the players do cheat, there is someone to pinpoint as acting unjustly who can be dealt with under the rules of conduct.

Consider the game of basketball. The team that scores the most points may not be the one with the most skilled players or the hardest-working players; the winning team may have practiced less than their opponents and may have been more lucky than good. Although we may complain that the worse team has won against the more deserving one, the winning team has not acted unjustly, and the outcome of the contest is not unjust. However, if members of the winning team took steroids or tampered with the ball or net, they have acted unjustly. It would be appropriate to kick them out of the game or have them pay a fine for their misdeeds and to declare that the results of the game are void. According to Hayek, the same is true of the market. However, as we argue in the next section, under some circumstances the results of a game might be fairly described as unjust even though none of the participants broke the rules and the referees impartially enforced the rules.

Second, for Hayek, attempts to bring about social justice will undermine a free society by expanding laws beyond the rules of just conduct and by increasing government's command on people's actions and livelihoods. In other words, according to Hayek, equality of wealth can be achieved only at the expense of liberty. If social justice does have meaning and our institutional settings can provide insight into how social justice may be achieved, however, it is possible that reforms can be made that do not undermine the values and existence of a free society. We discuss this possibility further in a later section.

But Some Games Are Unjust

Actual socioeconomic systems in the United States and other Western democracies differ in at least two ways from the idealized game(s) that Hayek uses in his critique of social justice. First, although all games favor players with certain skill sets, this in and of itself does not raise any justice concerns because there are countless games that individuals can and do play that favor individuals with different skill sets. Stated another way, we do not worry that some individuals will almost always be winners and some will almost always be losers in some particular game because there are likely to be other games where the pattern of winners and losers is likely to be very different. There is a sense, however, that there is only one economic game (i.e., one set of rules governing economic life) in any real-world context. If there are individuals who cannot or are unlikely to ever be able to win this game, for whatever reason, then it might make sense to call this game unjust.

Second, the referees in Hayek's idealized game are fair. In real-world contexts, there are many instances in which the referees are not fair. Referees of the game can be partial to certain players over others or stand to benefit from one outcome over another, and so their monitoring and enforcement of the rules of the game may not be neutral. In this case, it would be reasonable to say that the game is or at least the referees are unjust. Further, specific individuals have acted unjustly. It would thus make sense to hold those biased referees accountable for their actions and either remove them from the game or require that they provide redress to those they have harmed.

Consider again the game of basketball. In basketball, it is widely accepted that players who exhibit exceptional height, speed, and hand–eye coordination are more likely to succeed and that players who are slow and short will be disadvantaged. Because of this, all the successful players are likely to display the characteristics that lead to success. This is not cause for concern because there are other games that can be won even if you are shorter and slower— games that advantage individuals with other characteristics (e.g., chess). There are even multiple types of games for the tallest, fastest, and most coordinated in society (e.g., football, volleyball). These options mean that even if you fail as a basketball player, you can still succeed by playing a different game that privileges your characteristics and skills.

Now imagine that basketball is the only game people are permitted to play or, further, that everyone is forced to play basketball. The rules and structure of the game would still be the same, but the alternative options would be missing. In this scenario, there would be permanent winners and losers; the tallest, fastest, and most coordinated would consistently beat the rest of the players.[23] In this instance, you could say that anyone who insists on basketball being the only game and perhaps even anyone who benefits from it being the only game has committed an injustice against the rest of the members of a society (i.e., the permanent losers of this game). It would be appropriate to call the results of this solitary and mandatory game unjust precisely because this game is the only one and mandatory. The game and its results may be thought to be unjust even though no one associated with the game has committed an unjust act. Social justice thus might have meaning even when assessing the results of a game that is fairly played and refereed.

In fairness, Hayek likely views the market order as a constellation of games instead of as one single game and certainly not as a game that everyone must play. And he would probably reject the notion that there is anything like per-manent winners and losers in markets, as he envisioned them. Nevertheless, there are actual markets where the rules and the referees favor big, established businesses over new, small competitors. There are market environments where big businesses receive government bailouts during financial downturns, se-cure tax breaks for opening new ventures, and succeed in getting regulations passed that make it harder for other businesses to compete. In those cases, the referees (government agents) alter the rules of the game to rig the outcome to benefit big business. Rent-seeking firms petition government agents for favors, and the government agents may benefit in turn from campaign contributions, expert insight into the industry, future job prospects, or other favors (that range from mundane benefits to outright bribes).

Many market societies (almost all real-world market societies) are forms of political capitalism. Political capitalism, Randall Holcombe explains, is a unique system (or game) where the rules are created and refereed in such a way that elites win at the expense of the rest of society.[24] Likewise, Joseph Stiglitz similarly notes that "[w]e have a political system that gives inordinate power to those at the top, and they have used that power not only to limit the extent of redistribution but also to shape the game in their favor." "It's one thing to win a 'fair' game," he states. "It's quite another to be able to write the rules of the game—and to write them in ways that enhance one's prospects of winning. And it's even worse when you can choose your own referees."[25]

Interestingly, Hayek argues that although the concept of social justice would support merit-based reforms, in practice reforms under the guise of social justice are often advanced by groups insisting on protecting their accustomed positions in society:

> The satisfaction of such claims by particular groups would thus not be just but eminently unjust, because it would involve the denial to some of the changes to which those who make this claim owe their position. For this reason it has always been conceded only to some powerfully organized groups who were in the position to enforce their demands. Much of what is today done in the name of "social justice" is thus not only unjust but also highly unsocial in the true sense of the word: it amounts simply to the protection of entrenched interests.[26]

Of course, groups of players (special interests) attempting to sway the referees (the government) existed long before the concept of social justice was developed or utilized as another way of gaining favor.[27]

Even if we were to grant that social justice is a mirage when looking at the results of a game that is fairly played and refereed, social justice is not without meaning when evaluating the results of an unfair game. Of course, a game where the same players always win and other players always lose might still be a fair game. But when the distribution of rewards seems skewed, it would not be inappropriate to examine the rules or the nature of the play that they engender or the types of players that they systematically reward to determine if the rules promote fair or unfair outcomes. Rather than being meaningless, the concept of social justice can be useful in assessing political capitalism.

Some Speculation on What Social Justice Demands

Social justice is a meaningful concept.[28] To the extent that the socioeconomic system in a country favors some and not others, either because it systematically rewards some characteristics (e.g., hard work, inventiveness, intelligence, etc.) that are not equally distributed or it privileges some groups (e.g., based on economic power, political capital, demographic characteristics, etc.), it is appropriate to question the justness of the system and its results. The question of what to do to promote social justice, however, remains an open question.[29] If the concern is that some simply lack the skills to ever win the socioeconomic game, then social justice might demand that we ensure that these permanent losers have the resources to live a reasonably decent life.[30] David Johnston, for instance, advocates for indirect efforts at social justice.[31] Similarly, Hayek recommends providing a minimum income for the least advantaged.[32]

However, if the concern is that elites have gained and maintained their socioeconomic power through altering the rules of the game and choosing the referees, then relying on government to remedy social injustice is an untenable option.[33] To be sure, ending political capitalism (i.e., eliminating the rules that favor some groups over others) is the first best solution to the problems associated with political capitalism.[34] But political capitalism is likely to resist reform for the same reasons that it evolved in the first place.

The market process, however, might offer alternative opportunities to remedy social injustices. Hayek argues that the market and civil society (through liberty, competition, and coordination) can provide opportunities and remedies to social injustices that the government cannot.[35] Indeed, the transaction-cost revolution is not just a radicalization of the way we distribute and consume goods and services, but a fundamental challenge to existing socioeconomic privilege.[36]

This approach to conceiving of social justice allows for both recognizing social justice concerns about the least advantaged as legitimate and determining the appropriate responses to and the likely paths through which we might remedy social injustices.

19

Social Justice, Antiracism, and Public Policy

Robert M. Whaples*

WE ALL HUNGER to live in a just world. Most of us work constantly, in ways great and small, to promote justice.[1] But how does racism relate to justice? What is racism? What is antiracism? How can one justly combat racism?

This chapter seeks to tentatively answer these questions by taking new concepts about racism and antiracism seriously. The definitions of racism and antiracism that it considers are drawn from Ibram Kendi's influential bestseller *How to Be an Antiracist* (2019). Even if the reader does not accept all of Kendi's arguments about racism or antiracism, it is hoped that sincerely addressing them can prove fruitful.[2]

Kendi sees no middle ground when it comes to racism, stipulating that "there is no such thing as a not-racist idea, only racist ideas and antiracist ideas." "A racist idea is any idea that suggests one racial group is inferior or superior to another racial group in any way," while "an antiracist idea is any idea that suggests the racial groups are equal in all their apparent differences—that there is nothing right or wrong with any racial group."[3] More concretely for our purposes, Kendi argues that "a racist policy is any measure that produces or sustains racial inequity between racial groups. An antiracist policy is any measure that produces or sustains racial equity between racial groups. ... Racial inequity is when two or more racial groups are not standing on approximately equal footing."[4]

---

*Robert M. Whaples is professor of economics at Wake Forest University and editor of *The Independent Review*.

Thus, the litmus test of social and economic arrangements and policies is whether they foster the result of all groups standing on an approximately equal footing. Policies create the political and economic landscape, and antiracists believe that "political and economic conditions, not the people, in poor Black neighborhoods are pathological."[5] Policy derives from power. "The problem of race has always been at its core the problem of power, not the problem of immorality or ignorance."[6] Policy is paramount. But racist ideas "manipulate us into seeing people as the problem, instead of the policies that ensnare them."[7] Success is achieved when and where "equal opportunities and thus outcomes exist between the equal groups. Where people blame policy, not people, for societal problems."[8]

Ultimately, the challenge goes well beyond government policy. It also embraces institutions like societal and individual norms—what is going on in people's heads and hearts. The struggle is "to be fully human and to see that others are fully human."[9] The struggle is to fulfill the antiracist belief that people are "entirely capable of ruling themselves."[10] The struggle is to recognize people as individuals, not as representatives of groups: "To be antiracist is to think nothing is behaviorally wrong or right—inferior or superior—with any of the racial groups. Whenever the antiracist sees individuals behaving positively or negatively, the antiracist sees exactly that: *individuals* behaving positively or negatively, not *representatives* of whole races."[11]

Potential Policy Implications of Antiracism

So, what policies, institutions, and ideas can help put all groups on an equal footing?

Kendi sees racism and capitalism as "conjoined twins," which grew out of the transatlantic slave trade.[12] This is a very selective reading of history, which does not fit the facts well and ignores generations of research by economic historians and others.[13] As a result, he advocates "anti-capitalist" policies.[14] Unfortunately, the principal modern alternative to capitalism—socialism and central planning—has a very bleak track record in terms of both economic prosperity and the kinds of freedoms that antiracists clearly espouse.[15] People and groups living under socialist regimes are not on an equal footing with those living in capitalist democracies and often risk their lives to escape from these societies. The capitalist system does not solve every problem well, but it does help solve immensely important problems like generating wealth and eliminating absolute poverty. It incentivizes people to serve others productively, increase and share knowledge, and think for the long term—while harnessing cooperation and minimizing the use of force.[16]

Because the goal is to achieve an equal footing by letting all flourish, rather than by leveling people and groups downward, it may be more useful to think about more modest changes that can redirect markets and government policies to better achieve antiracist goals, such as the long-term trend toward convergence in racial incomes in the American economy.[17] Kendi suggests some of these policies himself. Many of the other ideas that I discuss below are drawn from articles published in *The Independent Review*. None can solve these persistent problems alone. Policy makers and their critics must act in a spirit of humility, rather than claiming powers beyond their abilities or forcing their prescriptions on others.

Education. Kendi's detestation of the American education system is palpable.[18] He recounts many racist incidents in his own schooling and recalls that he didn't put in much effort: "I was checked out—following the lead of most of the teachers, administrators, and politicians who were ostensibly in charge of my education." By most accounts, the American educational system as a whole fails the antiracist policy test of significantly helping all groups to stand on approximately equal footing—and fails in many other ways, as well. Contrary to many expectations, however, this is probably not due to funding inequalities. A recent Brookings Institution study reports that "on average, poor and minority students receive between 1–2 percent *more* resources than non-poor or white students in their districts" and that "average levels and variation in spending inequality between districts [are] nearly identical to the [small] within-district inequalities."[19]

What would antiracist school reform look like? Most likely, it would be a polycentric system, such as the one described by Michael Strong.[20] It might involve the separation of education and state to a large degree. It would put more power into the hands of those who care the most about students in every group—their parents—via meaningful school choice. It would capitalize on the successes of many charter school innovations in closing racial achievement gaps.[21] It would encourage genuine experimentation and learning about what makes students in all groups learn most effectively. It would make education an enjoyable, fulfilling exploration. It could probably personalize the learning experience, putting students in the driver's seat. It could "follow the child" with respect to the timing of introducing various materials and content. In short, it might follow the Montessori model described by Strong—although there are many other models that might achieve the antiracist goal. An objection might be that such schools are too expensive. With tuition averaging around $1,500 per month and a ten-month school year, the annual cost of a Montessori school is around $15,000,[22] which is roughly 20 percent higher than expenditures per pupil in public schools, which averaged $12,612 in 2018.[23]

Health Care. What would an antiracist health care system look like? Kendi observes that "White lives matter to the tune of 3.5 additional years over Black lives in the United States, which is just the most glaring of a host of health disparities, starting from infancy."[24] However, a more complete picture shows that the life expectancy in the United States is 75.0 years for blacks, 77.4 for American Indians, 78.6 for whites, 81.9 for Hispanics, and 86.3 for Asians.[25] Hispanic and Asian Americans live *longer* than whites. More importantly, when it comes to blacks, the picture is far bleaker than Kendi's statistics suggest. The difference in health outcomes begins *before* infancy. The Centers for Disease Control and Prevention show that the abortion rate is almost four times higher for black women than for white women.[26] In their report "Perceiving and Addressing the Pervasive Racial Disparity in Abortion," Studnicki, Fisher, and Sherley show that this gap has persisted for at least the past three decades.[27] Using Pennsylvania data from 2018, they estimate that abortions were 23.9 percent of white deaths and 62.7 percent of black deaths. Abortions were responsible for 53.8 percent of years of potential life lost (YPLL) among whites and 82.4 percent of YPLL among blacks. Antiracist policies should surely aim to eliminate this gap—and, ultimately, all abortions.

Health care expenditures in the United States are extraordinarily high in comparison to other countries. Part of this is because health care is a normal good, so that wealthier countries spend a greater share of their income on it. However, despite this extra spending, life expectancy in the United States is lower than in many other wealthy nations and many people receive inadequate health care. As John Goodman explains in *A Better Choice*, the subsidies in the current health care system encourage wasteful spending, crowd out wage increases, discourage job creation, and are riddled with mandates benefiting special interests.[28] Following his proposal, an antiracist health insurance system could move people from every group to a much more equal footing. The wealthy would not receive huge subsidies for expensive and wasteful health insurance through policies that exempt employers' health care packages from taxation. Goodman proposes replacing current mandates and subsidies with a *universal* tax credit that is the same for all individuals and groups—regardless of income level. The tax credit would be used to purchase Medicaid or whatever private health insurance the individual felt best met their needs at the same cost.[29] The tax credit would be refundable, so even those who don't have a federal tax liability could use it to purchase health insurance. This portable insurance would help decouple health insurance from the workplace and reduce overall labor costs, thereby boosting wages and encouraging employers to expand hiring, especially for low-wage workers. The reform could be accompanied by rules that require providers to be transparent about their prices and policies that lower the barriers to entry in medical fields. These proposals would encourage health care providers to compete in terms of price and quality to offer the best product to all their customers, unlike the current system.

Crime. Policing has the potential to make everyone safer and to reduce crime. The homicide rate in the United States peaked between the mid-1970s and early 1990s and fell to less than half its peak in 2014,[30] with the rate among black males falling by an even larger percentage. However, it has risen noticeably since 2014, and 2020 saw the largest percentage increase in homicides in American history.[31] Proactive policing practices have been successful in reducing crime and disorder,[32] but police mistreatment of blacks has become a national concern, spotlighted by the death of George Floyd in May 2020. Kendi argues that white police officers are "far and away more likely to be racist" than black officers, citing a survey in which "only 6 percent of White officers co-signed the antiracist idea that 'our country needs to continue making changes to give Blacks equal rights with Whites'" versus 92 percent who answered that "'our country has made the changes needed to give Blacks equal rights with Whites.'"[33]

Not all will agree with his conclusion, but everyone agrees that the public needs to be protected from racist police officers and *all* police officers who abuse their authority. Tate Fegley demonstrates that unionized departments have been more successful than their nonunionized counterparts in protecting officers from liability for misconduct—undermining the ability to hold police officers accountable for wrongdoing.[34] These protections afforded to police officers have the potential to impede criminal investigations against them, protect them from civil liability and forestall civilian oversight of police departments. These policies need to be reformed. Fegley questions the desirability of having a single police bureaucracy serve diverse urban populations with heterogeneous preferences, citing empirical research that suggests returns to scale in policing are maximized when serving relatively small populations.

The "War on Drugs" fits Kendi's definition of a racist policy when it disproportionately harms blacks. In their article "Inequality: First, Do No Harm," Vincent Geloso and Steven Horwitz argue that

> among the policies that harm the poorest, the war on drugs probably has the largest effect. ... [T]he vast majority of America's large penal population is composed of younger members of ethnic minorities. ... [B]ecause the majority of these individuals are young, prison time impairs them considerably on the labor market in the long run. The wage penalty is considerable relative to both pre-incarceration income and potential earnings had incarceration not occurred. ... When these individuals exit prisons, they are more likely to be unemployed and unmarried. ... As a consequence, the rate of wage growth for former inmates is slower. ... Repealing drug prohibition would reduce the incarceration of many currently poor Americans, increase the income they earn, and thereby reduce inequality, with no harm to others and with positive effects on economic growth.[35]

Jobs, Housing, and Income Guarantees. "Antiracists," explains Kendi, "say Black people, like all people, need more higher-paying jobs within their reach," especially those groups with the highest unemployment rates.[36] Creating good jobs for everyone is antiracist. Therefore, dismantling policies that make it more difficult for people to enter good jobs can help put all racial groups on an equal footing—rent-creating occupational licenses, especially those to enter low-wage positions—can be a significant hurdle in obtaining better jobs.[37] Even more daunting are zoning rules that function to keep the poor out of rich neighborhoods and away from higher-productivity areas and higher wages. Restrictive zoning laws drive up the price of housing in dynamic areas like California's Bay Area and New York City, driving the poor away and reducing their real earnings. Peter Ganong and Daniel Shoag find that income convergence has continued in less-regulated housing markets, while it has mostly stopped in places with more regulation. They estimate that poor workers' limited mobility is sufficient to explain 10 percent of the increase in inequality from 1980 to 2010.[38]

Some policies explicitly designed to increase wages of those with low incomes work better than others. Increasing the minimum wage, for instance, reduces the number of jobs, while subsidizing low-income earners—for example, as done through the Earned Income Tax Credit—works much better to encourage employment. Michael Munger argues that eliminating the minimum wage would open up more jobs to those who want them—especially young black males—and that getting rid of all work penalties in welfare programs would encourage more people to look for jobs. He proposes a thoroughgoing antiracist policy, replacing all welfare programs with a Basic Income Guarantee (BIG, also called a universal basic income) of $16,000 per person to put all groups on an approximately equal footing, freeing everyone to make decisions about how to run their own lives.[39] "Baby bonds" are a similar policy. Rather than giving a lifetime of payments, a Children's Saving Account (CSA) is a one-time payment at birth put into a long-term asset-building account, which is then available at age eighteen for purposes such as paying for higher education, buying a home, or funding a business. Sullivan and colleagues estimate that if a universal CSA program had been established in 1979, with public investment reaching $7,500 for low-wealth households and incremental reductions to $1,250 for the highest-wealth households, "the wealth gap between Black and White households for young adults would have decreased by 23%, while the wealth gap between White and Latino households for young adults would have declined by 28%."[40] ($7,500 in 1979 corresponds to about $29,000 in 2021 dollars.) In practice, a BIG of $16,000 per year could add over $1.3 trillion to the national debt each year,[41] although a smaller BIG could be revenue neutral. A CSA starting at $29,000 given to the 3.8 million babies born each year would cost around $100 billion per year.

However, the fact that national debt now exceeds GDP—and continues to rise—means that current generations are consistently favored over future generations by public policies that "fleece the young," as Loren Lomasky puts it.[42] A ballooning national debt harms future generations because it slows economic growth and necessitates higher taxes in the future—a future in which whites are likely to be a smaller fraction of the population. Had the Social Security system been established as a program to invest in equities, rather than as a pay-as-you-go system, racial wealth gaps would probably be much smaller today, as Social Security wealth would grow more rapidly and would be inheritable.[43]

Energy, Food, and Climate Change. Although Kendi fleetingly notes that racists "refuse to acknowledge that climate change is having a disastrous impact on the earth,"[44] it is likely that many of the policies advertised as combating global warming would be rejected by an antiracist. This is because policies designed to replace traditional fossil fuels and nuclear power with renewable energy push up energy costs substantially, harming the poor. The "green" energy policies of European countries, such as Germany, make electricity almost three times as expensive as it is in the United States, for example.[45] As Bjorn Lomborg explains, these policies—including subsidies for renewables, carbon taxes, and cap-and-trade programs—won't do much at all to change the temperature trend in the United States or the developing world, as they increase energy and food prices.[46] JunJie Wu and Christian Langpap estimate that biofuel mandates and subsidies have increased the price of corn by 25 to 40 percent.[47] An antiracist food policy would eliminate programs that subsidize wealthy agricultural producers, while harming producers in poor developing countries, for example, the cotton subsidy that harms millions of farmers in Africa.[48]

The fracking revolution, on the other hand, has had clear benefits to the poor. Ilia Murtazashvili and Ennio Piano explain that fracking has pushed natural gas prices down considerably, saving consumers as a whole about $74 billion per year.[49] Fracking reduces heating bills, which comprise a larger share of expenditures for the poor. Chirakijja, Jayachandran, and Ong estimate that as the price of natural gas relative to electricity fell by 42 percent between 2005 and 2010, the price decline caused a 1.6 percent decrease in the winter mortality rate for households using natural gas for heating. Cheaper natural gas lowered the U.S. winter mortality rate by 0.9 percent, totaling over 11,000 deaths per year. Across the board, their estimates suggest larger effects among the poor.[50] As a side effect, relatively clean-burning natural gas has pushed dirty coal from the market, reducing airborne pollutants and total greenhouse gas emissions. An antiracist energy policy would embrace developments like fracking and reject mandates with a poor track record of helping the environment, while harming the poor.

Technology. The antiracist paradigm argues that racism is rooted in power. This would suggest that policy should aim to diffuse power. Modern technology has diffused power in many ways, for example, as social media has supplanted the more centralized traditional media, allowing numerous racist acts to go viral and pushing concerns about racial inequity to the center of national debates. However, modern technology has also concentrated power. Money is power—and a handful of tech entrepreneurs including Elon Musk, Jeff Bezos, Bill Gates, Larry Ellison, Mark Zuckerberg, Larry Page, and Sergey Brin have each amassed a net worth exceeding $75 billion.[51] With more technological breakthroughs on the horizon, the ranks of the world's billionaires are likely to swell.[52] The antiracist will think about how to rein in this power, which may entail efforts to reduce the economies of scale that often lie at its roots, although this can come at the price of poorer-quality products and higher prices. Technological progress can mean that older products are pushed from the market. A recent example is the rise of digital transactions and the "war against cash."[53] An antiracist would warn that the victims of this push to eliminate cash include those who cannot afford banking services and undocumented workers, while the winners in the war include large financial companies that charge fees for electronic transactions.

Corporate Welfare and Trade. Antiracists, like Kendi, are quick to denounce rich people who benefit from "government contracts, hookups, and bailouts."[54] Rightly so. The problem of crony capitalism is endemic. Fighting it is difficult, because executives who don't spend corporate resources in lobbying and rent seeking will generally earn lower profits than their competitors.[55] There are no proven remedies to crony capitalism, especially in a society that expects the government to step in as a third party in almost every economic transaction. Cronyism is largely a *by-product* of big government,[56] so shrinking government is necessary to root it out. Other potential solutions include empowering the independent judiciary (which may be less prone to the seductions of crony capitalists), a cultural consensus that crony capitalism is unacceptable, and greater competition among jurisdictions, so that those favoring crony capitalism give it up lest they fall behind those that don't.[57] This competition can also take the form of freer international trade. Fajgelbaum and Khandelwal conclude that the poor are generally the greatest beneficiaries of international trade. They estimate that Americans at the tenth percentile in the income distribution see a 69 percent gain from trade, while those at the ninetieth percentile have a gain of only 4 percent—part of a "pro-poor bias of trade" seen in every country.[58]

In avoiding crony capitalism and bailouts, the subprime mortgage bubble and crash is a cautionary tale. Putatively antiracist government policies designed to increase homeownership and wealth in poor and minority populations misfired as easy financing terms to those with poor credit ratings pushed excessive borrowing, which was often followed by defaults and a loss of housing equity, threatening the entire financial system. The homeownership rate among blacks rose from 42.3 percent in 1994 to 49.1 percent in 2004, then fell sharply after the housing bubble burst in 2007, declining to 41.6 percent by 2016.[59]

Conclusion

The policy suggestions above—including reforming education, discouraging abortion, implementing a universal health care tax credit, taming police unions, eliminating restrictive zoning laws, funding a basic income guarantee or baby bonds, ending agricultural subsidies, encouraging fracking, and forswearing corporate bailouts and crony capitalism—have the potential to reduce racism in American society, but they all have substantial limits.

At its best, the antiracist movement for social justice aims for all "to be fully human and to see that others are fully human."[60] Humanity is much too divided. Well-crafted policies can help overcome these divisions, but the challenge goes well beyond government policy. It also embraces the thoughts and stirrings of people's heads and hearts. My experience is that the quest to see every person as fully human can flourish most completely when people of all groups believe that they have something in common that unites them despite all their differences. This happens when they recognize that they are all made in the image of God, that they are all children of the same God, who has created them to love one another as brothers and sisters.[61] This happens when everyone rejects the idea that one group or one individual is superior to another—recognizing this idea for the sin that it is.

Notes

Foreword, Peterson

1. Nietzsche, *Thus Spake Zarathustra*, 47.

Introduction, Whaples

1. Justinian, *Corpus*.
2. Sowell, *Quest*, 77.
3. See the symposium of crony capitalism in the Winter 2018–19 issue of *The Independent Review*.
4. Novak, "Social Justice," 13.

Chapter 1, Guerrière

1. Feagin, "Social Justice and Sociology," 12a.
2. Feagin, "Social Justice and Sociology," 5a.
3. Feagin, "Social Justice and Sociology," 11b.
4. Feagin, "Social Justice and Sociology," 16b.
5. Kekes, *Illusions*.
6. Voegelin, *Order and History*.
7. Greene, *Moira*; Havelock, *The Greek Concept of Justice*; Voegelin, *Order and History*.
8. Carr and Mahalingam, *Companion Encyclopedia*; Assmann, *Herrschaft und Heil*; Snell, *Companion*.
9. Schmid, *Gerechtigkeit als Weltordnung*; Knight, "Cosmology."
10. Buck, *Dictionary*, 16.73, 21.11–12.
11. Aristotle, *Nicomachean Ethics*.
12. Vinogradoff, *Jurisprudence*.
13. Aristotle, *Nicomachean Ethics*, 5.5.1132b21–25.
14. Plato, *The Republic*, 580D–592B, 611A–613B.
15. Asma, *Against Fairness*.
16. Aristotle, *Nicomachean Ethics*, 5.1.
17. Aristotle, *Nicomachean Ethics*, 5.2–5.
18. Aristotle, *Nicomachean Ethics*, 5.6.

19. Aristotle, *Nicomachean Ethics*, 5.3.

20. Aristotle, *Nicomachean Ethics*, 5.4.

21. Aristotle, *Nicomachean Ethics*, 5.5.

22. Balot, *Greed and Injustice.*

23. Aristotle, *Politics*, 3.9.1280b2–1281a6.

24. Aristotle, *Nicomachean Ethics*, 5.3.1131a29–32.

25. Aristotle, *Nicomachean Ethics*, 5.3.1131a22.

26. Aristotle, *Nicomachean Ethics*, 5.3.1131a24.

27. Aristotle, *Nicomachean Ethics*, 5.3.1131b5–6.

28. Aristotle, *Nicomachean Ethics*, 5.3.1131b8–12.

29. Aristotle, *Nicomachean Ethics*, 5.4.1132a3–7.

30. Aristotle, *Nicomachean Ethics*, 5.4.1132a21.

31. Aristotle, *Nicomachean Ethics*, 5.4.1132a1–2.

32. Aristotle, *Nicomachean Ethics*, 5.4.1132a8–10.

33. Aristotle, *Nicomachean Ethics*, 5.4.1132a14–19.

34. Aristotle, *Nicomachean Ethics*, 5.5.1133a2.

35. Gat, *War*, 3–322.

36. Aristotle, *Nicomachean Ethics*, 5.51132b2–4.

37. Aristotle, *Nicomachean Ethics*, 5.5.1133a12–13.

38. Aristotle, *Nicomachean Ethics*, 5.5.1133a10–11.

39. Aristotle, *Nicomachean Ethics*, 5.10.

40. Plato, "Statesman," 294A.

41. Aristotle, *Nicomachean Ethics*, 5.10.1137b13–20.

42. Aristotle, *Nicomachean Ethics*, 5.10.1137b32–33.

43. Aristotle, *Nicomachean Ethics*, 5.10.1138a3.

44. Vinogradoff, *Jurisprudence*, 63–69.

45. Cicero, *De re publica*, 3.25; Cicero, *De finibus*, 5.67.

46. Justinian, *Novellae institutiones*, I.1.

47. Aquinas, *Justice*, q. 57, a. 4, and q. 58, a. 1.

48. Chenu, *L'éveil*; Morris, *Discovery*; Burridge, *Someone, No One*; Dumont, *Essays*, 23–112, 279–80; Gurewich, *Origins*; Siedentop, *Inventing the Individual*.

49. Scheidel, *The Great Leveler*.

50. Novak, *The Catholic Ethic*, 62–88; Zięba, *Papal Economics*, 7–60.

51. Plato, *The Republic*, 427D–434D.

52. Novak, *The Catholic Ethic*, 7–86.

Chapter 2, Smith

1. Thomas Sowell distinguishes two types of discrimination. One is the ability to discern differences in the qualities of peoples and things (e.g., which cell phone to purchase), on the basis of which we then choose accordingly. This is not moral discrimination. However, immoral discrimination treats "people negatively, based on arbitrary assumptions or aversions concerning individuals of a particular race, sex, etc." (Sowell, *Disparities*, 21).

2. Horkheimer, *Critical Theory*, 246.

3. Bohman, "Critical Theory."

4. Thornhill, "Historicism."

5. Horkheimer, *Critical Theory*, 24.

6. Bohman, "Critical Theory."

7. Hobbes, *Leviathan*, 16 and chaps. 1–6.

8. Smith, *In Search*, chap. 4.

9. Hume, *Treatise*, bk. II, part III, sec. iii.

10. Kant, "Critique," 25.

11. Sellars, *Naturalism*.

12. Schacht, "Nietzsche," 615 (emphasis added).

13. Korsgaard, *Sources*, 4–5.

14. MacIntyre, *Whose Justice?*, 356–57.

15. MacIntyre, *Whose Justice?*, 357–58.

16. See Bacon, "New Organon," bk. 2, no. 2; Osler, "Boyle's Philosophy," 185–86; Sepkoski, "Nominalism," 36.

17. By "naturalism," I mean the ontological view that, roughly, all that exists is natural; there is no supernatural realm.

18. Smith, *In Search*.

19. In contrast, economics had typically been treated as part of moral philosophy.

20. *Economist*, "Economics at Cambridge."

21. As explained in O'Donnell, "J. M. Keynes," 334 (emphasis in original).

22. Garrigou-LaGrange, *Reality*, 28.

23. However, see, for example, Moreland 2001.

Chapter 3, Martin

1. Hayek, *Mirage*, chap. 9.

2. Hayek, *Rules and Order*, chap. 2.

3. Hayek, "What Is 'Social'?," 242.

4. Hayek, *Mirage*, 78.

5. See Martin, "Egalitarianism."

6. All searches conducted December 10, 2018.

7. Rawls, *Justice*, xiii.

8. Tomasi, *Fairness*, 155.

9. Tomasi, *Fairness*, 158 (emphasis added).

10. Tomasi, *Fairness*, 153.

11. Rawls, *Justice*, 4.

12. Hayek, *Rules and Order*, 46.

13. Hayek, *Rules and Order*, chap. 4.

14. Wagner, *Human Action*.

15. Gaus, "Liberalism," 38–39.

16. See Hayek, *Mirage*, 100.

17. Gaus, "Liberalism," 44–47.

18. Hayek, *Mirage*, chap. 8.

19. Hayek, *Liberty*, 318.

20. Crawford and Ostrom, "Grammar."

21. Note that I am not claiming that Brennan holds this view, only that this view is compatible with the argument as presented. Brennan, *Libertarianism*, 279–89.

22. Hardin, *Morality*, 38–41.

23. Smith, *Moral Sentiments*, II.ii.I.5.

24. Smith, *Moral Sentiments*, III.II.

25. Crawford and Ostrom, "Grammar."

26. Gaus, "Liberalism."

27. See, e.g., Smith, *Moral Sentiments*; McCloskey, *Bourgeois Virtues*; Haidt, *Righteous Mind*.

28. Hardin, *Morality*.

29. Hayek, "Scientism."

30. However, individuals do experience the articulation and enforcement of particular social rules. As argued earlier, there is nothing incoherent about calling such rules unjust on Hayekian grounds.

31. Smith, *Moral Sentiments*, II.ii.I.4.

32. Fehr and Gächter, "Altruistic Punishment."

33. Smith and Wilson, "Fair and Impartial Spectators."

34. Smith, *Moral Sentiments*, II.ii.III.

35. Kiel, "Whiteness"; Bailey, "On Anger."

36. Rognlie, *Accumulation or Scarcity?*

37. Ostrom, *Meaning of Democracy*, 294.

Chapter 4, Levy

1. Hayek, *Mirage*. See also Hayek, *Fatal Conceit*.

2. Hayek, *Mirage*, xiii.

3. Johnston, "Hayek's Attack"; Lukes, "Social Justice"; and, in less depth, Fleischacker, *Distributive Justice*.

4. Tomasi, *Fairness*.

5. Brennan and Tomasi, "Classical Liberalism," 115. I should note here that Brennan and Tomasi identify me as a member of this emerging school, along with David Schmidtz, Gerald Gaus, Matt Zwolinski, and Charles Griswold. This is, in the lawyers' sense, a constructive grouping, not one that tracks either self-identification or explicit discussion of the particular questions at hand. Zwolinski has identified himself with the label *neoclassical liberal* and its views, but I am not sure that any of the other listed people have. For my part, the present chapter is my first piece of writing on the problem of social justice. Although I reach a number of conclusions similar to those reached by Tomasi and the others, "social justice" is not a concept that does much work in my path to them, and so I do not recognize myself in the description.

6. The usage of the term *social justice* as a way to talk primarily about the kinds of wrongs generated by racism or sexism rather than about problems of purely economic distribution is decades old in some academic disciplines and activist circles. What I mean here is that as re-

cently as the early 2010s that usage had not spread to other disciplines or become ubiquitous in popular discourse. In 2012, a political theorist such as Tomasi could reasonably assume that his readers would understand that the term *social justice* refers primarily to the problems of distributive justice that arguably divided Rawls and Hayek, and thus he would never mention this alternative. In 2019, that assumption would be hard to imagine.

7. Young, *Justice*; Taylor, *Multiculturalism*; see Fraser, *Justice Interruptus*, for an important work that helped develop the idea that social justice encompasses both redistribution and recognition.

8. De Jasay, "Justice," 162.

9. Plato, *The Republic*, Book I, 331C, 7.

10. Aristotle somewhat confusingly prioritized the *corrective* character of this branch of justice—that is, the duty to make restitution of the appropriate kind after a wrong has been committed. In modern common-law language, he foregrounded remedies over the rights whose violations need to be remedied, such that it appears justice is a matter of, for example, punishing a criminal and making whole the victim of a contract breach rather than refraining from crime and honoring contracts in the first place. On the one hand, we could look at this emphasis on remedies and think that it really reaffirms the core sense of justice; Aristotle seemed to take the underlying rights so thoroughly for granted as to find them less important to discuss than remedial questions. On the other hand, this emphasis on remedies usefully reminds us of the legalism of justice—in other words, its close relationship to judicial proceedings. I also think here, as in the evolution of the common law, in which writs and remedies preceded full legal articulation of the rights they vindicated, we see some of the wisdom in the conceptual emphasis Adam Smith and Judith Shklar later put on the term *injustice*. I return to this point in the conclusion. See Levy, "Political Libertarianism." Aristotle, *Nicomachean Ethics*, pp. 81–84.

11. Aquinas, *Political Writings*, 168.

12. Smith, *Moral Sentiments*, 82.

13. Beever, *Forgotten Justice*.

14. Cohen, *Rescuing Justice*.

15. Cohen, *Rescuing Justice*.

16. I discuss this issue further in Levy, "Review," and Levy, "Ideal Theory."

17. See Fleischacker, "Distributive Justice."

18. Hayek, *Mirage*, 102.

19. Nozick, *Anarchy*, 160.

20. Hayek, *Rules and Order*, 89.

21. Smith, *Wealth of Nations*, 157.

22. Shklar, *Injustice*.

23. Smith, *Moral Sentiments*, 390.

24. Schelling, "Models," 488.

25. Young, *Justice*.

26. I make the case for the value of synthesizing Hayek and Shklar in Levy, "Political Libertarianism," and Levy, "Who's Afraid?"

Chapter 5, Vallier

1. Hayek, *Mirage*, 78.

2. Rawls, *Justice*.

3. Hayek, *Justice*, 100. The reference is not to Rawls's *A Theory of Justice*, but to his "Constitutional Liberty and the Concept of Justice" (Rawls, "Constitutional Liberty," 102).

4. Rawls, *Fairness*, 120.

5. Hayek, *Rules and Order*, 94–123.

6. I understand social rules as social norms and legal norms and legal rules as laws. Hayek appeals to both in his work.

7. Hayek, *Mirage*, 78.

8. Tomasi, *Fairness*, 160; my emphasis.

9. Hayek, *Mirage*, my emphasis; quoting Rawls, "Constitutional Liberty," 102.

10. There are those, however, who interpret Rawls along these reformist lines. See, for example, James, "Constructing Justice."

11. Hayek, *Fatal Conceit*, 69.

12. Gaus, "Hayekian," 35.

13. Hayek, *Mirage*; and Hayek, *Constitution*, 112.

14. Hayek, *Mirage*, 15.

15. Hayek, *Mirage*, 28.

16. Hayek, *Mirage*, 24, 29.

17. Sugden, "Normative."

18. Hayek, *Mirage*, 3.

19. Hayek, *Mirage*, 3.

20. Hayek also does not opt for alternative approaches, such as virtue ethics or natural rights.

21. Hayek, *Mirage*, 122.

22. Hayek, *Mirage*, 132.

23. Buchanan and Tullock may have influenced Hayek's position. See Buchanan and Tullock, *Calculus*, 78.

24. Hayek, *Rules and Order*, 94–123.

25. Hayek, *Mirage*, 25.

26. Hayek, *Mirage*, 32.

27. In *Justice as Fairness*, Rawls defines the principle of restricted utility, though he includes in the definition that average utility is maximized first by guaranteeing "equal basic liberties (including their fair value) and fair equality of opportunity" (*Fairness*, 120). I use the idea of "restricted utility" simply to refer to maximizing average utility with a utility floor. Hayek's view seems closer to the earlier contractarian approach advanced by John Harsanyi (Harsanyi, "Cardinal Welfare").

28. Hayek, *Mirage*, 114.

29. Hayek, *Mirage*, 129.

30. Hayek, *Mirage*, 130.

31. Hayek, *Mirage*, 122.

32. Hayek, *Political Order*, 55.

33. See Peter, "Political Legitimacy."

34. Hayek, *Constitution*, 29; also see Caldwell, *Challenge*, 347.

35. Hayek, *Constitution*, 156–57.

36. Hayek, *Constitution*, 156–57. One might read Hayek as adopting a republican understanding of negative liberty, where we should protect persons from arbitrary interference; certain parts of *The Constitution of Liberty* read this way.

37. Caldwell, *Challenge*, 289.

38. Hayek, *Constitution*, 193.

39. For "inefficiency," see Hayek, "Use"; for "social conflict," see Hayek, 1979, 193; Hayek, *Road*, 109, 166; for "abuses of power," see Hayek, *Mirage*.

40. Hayek, *Political Order*, 13.

41. Hayek, *Political Order*, 137.

42. Hayek, *Political Order*, 5.

43. Hayek, *Road*, 111–12.

44. Hayek, *Constitution*, 106, 116.

45. Hayek, *Road*, 22, 43, 44, 133–35, 217. See the discussion in Burgin, *Great Persuasion*.

46. Hayek, *Constitution*, 264, 276, 286, 294, 379.

47. Hayek, *Constitution*, 231. This was a consistent theme elsewhere in Hayek's work. See Hayek, *Rules and Order*, 62; Hayek, *Political Order*, 41; and Hayek, *Road*, 71.

48. Caldwell, *Challenge*, 291.

Chapter 6, D'Amico

1. There is some archival evidence of Hayek sharing positive impressions of Rawls's earlier works with economist colleague James Buchanan, but Buchanan ("Rawls") wrote a similarly delayed but critical review of Rawls in which he reversed much of his initial positive impression.

2. Hayek, *Constitution*.

3. See Briggs, *Never in Anger*; Brody, *People's Land*; Matthiasson, *Living*.

4. Tomasi, *Fairness*.

5. Capaldi and Lloyd, *Two Narratives*.

6. Harsanyi, "Maxim in Principle."

7. Frohlich, Oppenheimer, and Eavey, "Laboratory Results."

8. Hayek, *Mirage*, 188–89.

9. Posner, "Theory"; Benson, "Legal Evolution."

10. Gambetta, *Sicilian Mafia*; Leeson, *Invisible Hook*; Skarbek, *Social Order*.

11. Ellickson, *Order*; Anderson and Hill, *Not So Wild*.

12. Matthiasson, *Living*, 24–34.

13. Boas, *Handbook*.

14. Hoebel, "Eskimo."

15. Billson and Mancini, *Inuit Women*.

16. La Porta, Lopez-de-Silanes, and Shleifer, "Economic Consequences."

Chapter 7, Watkins Jr.

1. Int'l Forum, *Social Justice*, vii.
2. Int'l Forum, *Social Justice*, 2.
3. Int'l Forum, *Social Justice*, 7.
4. Int'l Forum, *Social Justice*, 6.
5. Int'l Forum, *Social Justice*, 13.
6. Herzog, *Short History*, 13.
7. Calvin, *Institutes*, I.1.1.1.
8. Calvin, *Institutes*, I.1.1.3.
9. Justinian, *Digest*, D.1.1.10.
10. Calvin, *Institutes*, I.4.2.
11. Calvin, *Institutes*, I.4.2.
12. Calvin, *Institutes*, I.4.2.
13. Exod. 22:1 (ESV).
14. Luke 19:8.
15. Needham, *2000 Years*, 165.
16. Stein, *Roman Law*, 40.
17. Stein, *Roman Law*, 41.
18. Richards, "Property," 603–4.
19. Stark, *Christianity*, 5.
20. Perry, *Puritanism*, 83.
21. Calvin, *Institutes*, 258.
22. Calvin, *Institutes*, 258.
23. Calvin, *Institutes*, 259.
24. Calvin, *Institutes*, 259.
25. New Hampshire Constitution, Art. 2.
26. Ely, *Guardian*, 30.
27. Presser, *Law Professors*, 244.
28. Rawls, *Justice*, vii.
29. Dworkin, "Justice," 6.
30. Dworkin, *Law's Empire*, 164.
31. Dworkin, *Law's Empire*, 164.
32. Dworkin, *Law's Empire*, 165.
33. Hart, *Concept*, 240.
34. Hart, *Concept*, 251.
35. Hart, *Concept*, 250.
36. Finnis, *Natural Law*, 12.
37. Finnis, *Natural Law*, 12.
38. Dworkin, *Law's Empire*, 36.
39. Dworkin, *Law's Empire*, 263.
40. Dworkin, *Law's Empire*, 338–39.
41. Nozick, *Anarchy*, 149.
42. Nozick, *Anarchy*, 149.

43. Nozick, *Anarchy*, 149.
44. Nozick, *Anarchy*, 153.
45. Nozick, *Anarchy*, 163.
46. Hayek, *Constitution*, 99.
47. Hayek, *Mirage*, 64.
48. Hayek, *Mirage*, 33.
49. Hayek, *Constitution*, 100.
50. In *The Mirage of Social Justice*, Hayek states that he has "no basic quarrel" with Rawls, although he finds Rawls's use of social justice confusing (Hayek, *Mirage*, 100). It appears Hayek was indeed confused, inasmuch as his body of work is at odds with Rawls's.
51. Raico, *Prussian Aristocrat*, 10.
52. Humboldt, *Limits*, xviii.
53. Humboldt, *Limits*, 10.
54. Humboldt, *Limits*, 10.
55. Humboldt, *Limits*, 21.
56. Humboldt, *Limits*, 33.
57. Bastiat, *Law*, 1.
58. Bastiat, *Law*, 1.
59. Bastiat, *Law*, 2.

Chapter 8, Gill

1. I beg the reader for my poetic license here, acknowledging that Crusoe first sees Friday being attacked by cannibals and decides to rescue him, thus putting Friday in a position of owing his life to Crusoe and, one might say, "thankful subordination." Nonetheless, economists have often used the Crusoe/Friday example as a metaphor for a simplified economy to develop notions of trade (see Buchanan, *Limits*, 118–20; Varian, *Microeconomics*, 628–32). I thank Robert Whaples for this insight.

2. One can imagine an obvious critique of the first question facing Crusoe and Friday. If Friday comes upon an incapacitated Crusoe who needs assistance (e.g., water to avoid dying of thirst), is it Friday's moral duty to provide such aid even if Crusoe is unable to agree to assistance? An earlier draft of this chapter addressed this question, but space considerations make it necessary to hold this question aside for now.

3. See Rawls, *Justice*.

4. Economics is typically taught to students with the examples of exchanges of goods (e.g., bushels of wheat) or services (e.g., insurance protection). However, a more expanded understanding of economics includes any sort of exchange, such as a willingness to spend time with another person (see, e.g., Becker, "Theory"). There are opportunity costs, not to mention declining marginal utility calculations, associated with the choice of spending time with a friend over coffee. For our two islanders—Crusoe and Friday—the first economic decision they must make is whether to spend the time to interact with one another at all.

5. See Munger, "Euvoluntary."

6. Schlee, "Buyer."

7. Gill, Anthony. 2018. "An Economic and Pedagogical Defense of Gratuities." *Journal of Private Enterprise Education* 33(1): 79–102.

8. It may be the case that one party has a higher utility for signaling generosity and will insist on distributing more of the gains from trade to the other person, but this situation could be construed as one in which an individual has a "thicker" preference in the exchange—that is, not merely for fish, but for fish plus "the warm fuzzy feeling of giving" or for fish plus a reputation for generosity among one's broader set of peers.

9. Mauss, *Gift*.

10. Smith, *Moral Sentiments*.

11. Taylor, *Community*.

12. Skyrms, *Evolution*.

13. In terms of anonymity, societies can become "large" very quickly. The work of the anthropologist Robin Dunbar (Dunbar, "Neocortex") on primates, extrapolated to human societies by Malcolm Gladwell (Gladwell, *Tipping Point*, 179–87), indicates that it is possible to know the preferences of only about 150 or so people before significant amounts of anonymity and uncertainty set in.

14. Perry, "General Public."

15. Hayek, "Use"; Akerloff, "Market."

16. Such price discrimination could be achieved by making a routine product "extra special" via a "limited edition," or the seller could set the price to the highest reserve price and then offer coupon discounts.

17. Part of this uncertainty may be reflected in the common behavior of individuals who feel they are being "ripped off" by a retailer but continue regularly to purchase the product. See Bolton, Warlop, and Alba, "Consumer Perceptions," for an overview of the perceptions of price fairness.

18. See Schoeck, *Envy*.

19. Kirzner, *Competition*.

20. Smith, *Wealth of Nations*, 25.

21. Smith, *Wealth of Nations*.

Chapter 9, Otteson

1. Hayek, *Mirage*, 62, 78.

2. Plato, *Euthyphro*, 5, 5a.

3. See, for example, Plato, *Republic*, bk. 5, 122–56.

4. This distinction is a very old one. Aristotle would have said that the first calls for an "efficient" cause, whereas the second calls for a "final" cause (Aristotle, *Physics*, 332–34). W. K. C. Guthrie (Guthrie, *Greek Philosophers*) not atypically calls the former a "materialist" explanation and the latter a "teleological" explanation.

5. See Shermer, *People*; and Thaler, *Misbehaving*.

6. Maureen Linker, for example, argues that social justice involves the removal of undeserved "social privilege," such as living in a country that officially recognizes one's own (Christian) religion's holidays or that presumes as "normal" or as a default one's own sexual (heterosexual) orientation (Linker, *Empathy*, 45, 64–65). Ozlem Sensoy and Robin DiAngelo

define social justice as "the principles of 'fairness' and 'equality' for all people and respect for their basic human rights," connect social injustice to "racism, sexism, and homophobia," and then offer a list of opinions about these topics that they assert "are predictable, simplistic, and misinformed," including "People should be judged by what they do, not the color of their skin" (Sensoy and de Angelo, *Everyone*, xix, 3). Brian Barry claims that "[s]ocial justice is about the treatment of inequalities of all kinds" (Barry, *Social Justice*, 10), both those that arise by deliberate human agency and those that arise from chance, luck, or contingency. See also Tomasi, *Fairness*, esp. chap. 8, and Piketty, *Capital*, esp. 479–81.

7. See Otteson, "Misuse."

8. See, for example, Sunstein, *Free Markets*; and Sandel, *Money*.

9. Hume, "Refinement," 269.

10. Hume, "Refinement," 270.

11. Hume, "Refinement," 271.

12. Hume, "Refinement," 271.

13. Hume, "Refinement," 271.

14. Hume, "Refinement," 271; italics in original.

15. Hume, "Interest," 301–2.

16. Hume, "Refinement," 272; italics in original.

17. Hume, "Jealousy," 331; capitalization in the original.

18. Hume, "Jealousy," 331.

19. Smith, *Wealth of Nations*, 456.

20. Smith, *Moral Sentiments*, 84.

21. Smith, *Wealth of Nations*, 456.

22. See Sandel, *Money*; and Satz, *Moral Limits*.

23. See Schor, *Born*; Ubel, *Free Market*; and Conly, *Autonomy*.

24. See Olson, *Logic*; and Hardin, "Tragedy."

25. See Piketty, *Capital*; and Mazzucato, *Value*.

26. See Schumpeter, *Capitalism*; Cohen, *Socialism*; and Deneen, *Liberalism*.

27. See McCloskey, *Equality*; Pinker, *Enlightenment*; and Rosling, Rosling, and Rönnlund, *Factfulness*.

28. See Ridley, *Optimist*.

29. In its online list of "the world's billionaires," *Forbes* ("Billionaires") estimates Bezos's current net worth at $112 billion.

30. My position is thus consistent with a plausible interpretation of Rawls's first principle of justice and its lexical priority over his second principle. See Rawls, *Justice*.

31. See Satz, *Moral Limits*.

Chapter 10, Stoner Jr.

1. Kraynak, "Origins," 25.

2. Shils, "Virtue."

3. Aristotle, *Politics*, 1252a24–1253a20.

4. Aristotle, *Politics*, 1253b15–1255b40.

5. Aristotle, *Politics*, 1256a1–1258b8.

6. Aristotle, *Politics*, 1258b10, 1259a23.

7. Aristotle, *Politics*, 1253a19.

8. Aristotle, *Politics*; Aristotle, *Ethics*, 1132b21–1133b29.

9. Shulsky, "'Infrastructure,'" 105–11.

10. Smith, *Wealth of Nations*.

11. Marx, "Manifesto."

12. Locke, *Two Treatises*.

13. Hegel, *Philosophy*.

14. Hegel, *Philosophy*, 110–22.

15. Hegel, *Philosophy*, 155–223.

16. Hegel, *Philosophy*, 266.

17. Hegel, *Philosophy*, 123.

18. Hegel, *Philosophy*, 123.

19. Hegel, *Philosophy*, 147.

20. Hegel, *Philosophy*, 150.

21. Hegel, *Philosophy*, 151.

22. Hegel, *Philosophy*, 155, 160.

23. Marx, *Critique*.

24. Rosmini, *Constitution*.

25. Rosmini, *Philosophy*.

26. Leo XIII, *Rerum novarum*.

27. Leo XIII, *Rerum novarum*, 1. Parenthetical citations to the papal encyclicals refer to paragraphs, not to pages.

28. Stoner Jr., "Property."

29. Leo XIII, *Rerum novarum*, 51.

30. Pius XI, *Quadragesimo anno*.

31. See also Fortin, "Natural Law."

32. John Paul II, *Centesimus annus*, 32, 34.

33. John Paul II, *Centesimus annus*, 35.

34. Francis, *Laudato Sí*; Whaples, "Economics."

35. Walzer, "Better Vision," 315.

Chapter 11, Moore

1. Novak, "Social Justice," 13.

2. Novak, "Social Justice," 1.

3. Gutiérrez, *Theology*, 116.

4. Aristotle, *Ethics*.

5. Boethius, *Consolation*.

6. Leo XIII, *Rerum novarum*, 3–5. Citations to the papal encyclicals refer to paragraph numbers rather than to page numbers.

7. Leo XIII, *Rerum novarum*, 17.

8. Leo XIII, *Rerum novarum*, 21–22.

9. Leo XIII, *Rerum novarum*, 22.

10. Leo XIII, *Rerum novarum*, 23.

11. Leo XIII, *Rerum novarum*, 24.

12. John Paul II, *Laborem exercens*.

13. John Paul II, *Laborem exercens*, intro, 1–2; emphasis in original.

14. John Paul II, *Laborem exercens*, 5; emphasis in original.

15. John Paul II, *Laborem exercens*, 7; emphasis in original.

16. Francis, *Evangelii gaudium*.

17. Tornielli and Galeazzi, *Economy*, 36–37.

18. Tornielli and Galeazzi, *Economy*, 36–37.

19. Sibley, *Catholic Economics*, 9.

20. Zięba, *Papal Economics*, 83.

21. Zięba, *Papal Economics*, 83, 104.

22. Martinez, "Playing Fields," 81.

23. Wood, *Creation*, 65.

24. Wood, *Creation*, 68.

25. Smith, *Moral Sentiments*, VI.iii.9.

26. Locke, *Second Treatise*.

27. Schumacher, *Small*, 28–29.

28. Schumacher, *Small*, 29.

29. Schumpeter, *Capitalism*.

30. McCloskey, *Bourgeois Virtues*.

31. Kirzner, *Discovery*, 11–12; emphasis in the original.

32. Tullock, *Economics*, 351.

33. Tullock, *Economics*, 357.

34. King Jr., Nobel speech.

Chapter 12, Schlag

1. Francis, *Laudato Sí*, n. 158.

2. Francis, *Laudato Sí*, n. 157.

3. See, e.g., Pius XI, *Quadragesimo Anno*, n. 57.

4. Pius XI, *Quadragesimo Anno*, n. 110.

5. See Francis, *Evangelii Gaudium*, n. 201: "none of us can think we are exempt from concern for the poor and for social justice."

6. Pontifical Council for Justice and Peace, *Compendium*, n. 201 (emphasis in the original). Here the *Compendium* references the *Catechism of the Catholic Church*, 1928–42, 2425–49, 2832; Pius XI, *Divini Redemptoris*, 92.

7. See Pontificio Consiglio della Giustizia e della Pace, *Giustizia*, 375–82, 377: "la costante e ferma volontà di favorire il bene comune in quanto condizione sociale per sviluppare la dignità integrale di tutti gli uomini." (My English translation in text above.)

8. *Oxford English Dictionary*, online resource, accessed August 25, 2022.

9. See Langhorst, "Soziale Gerechtigkeit," 758f.

10. See Hamilton, Madison, and Jay, *Federalist Papers*, 60, n. 7.

11. See von Ketteler, *Die Arbeiterfrage*, 79–120; Kracht, *von Ketteler*, 66f.

12. See Berman, *Law and Revolution*, 189–92; of special interest also footnote 59 on p. 449f.

13. See Sierra, *El gran debate*, 11–40.

14. See Dianin, *Taparelli*, 11–82.

15. First published in 1840–43 in Palermo, Italy. I have used the 8th edition in two volumes, edited by La Civiltà Cattolica.

16. See the remark of Pius XI in his encyclical *Divini Illius Magistri* on Taparelli's *Saggio Teoretico*: "a work never sufficiently praised and recommended to university students"; https://www.vatican.va/content/pius-xi/en/encyclicals/documents/hf_p-xi_enc_31121929_divini-illius-magistri.html.

17. Taparelli, *Saggio Teoretico*, 183 n. 354: "La giustizia *sociale* è per noi giustizia *fra uomo e uomo*." (Emphasis in the original.)

18. Taparelli, *Saggio Teoretico*, 183–88, nn. 355–64.

19. Taparelli, *Saggio Teoretico*, 398, n. 686.

20. Taparelli, *Saggio Teoretico*, 400f, n. 691.

21. Taparelli, *Saggio Teoretico*, 401, n. 692.

22. Taparelli, *Saggio Teoretico*, 402, n. 694.

23. Pius XI, *Quadragesimo Anno*, n. 89. For further analysis see Schlag, "'Iustitia Est Amor.'"

24. See Curnow, "Which Preferential Option."

25. For the time up until nearly the end of the pontificate of John Paul II, see Twomey, *"Preferential Option for the Poor."*

26. See Gutiérrez, *Teología*, 37.

27. Boff and Boff, *Liberation Theology*, 22.

28. See Gutiérrez, *Teología*, 32.

29. See Sobrino, *Jesucristo*, 35.

30. See Gutiérrez, *Teología*, 245.

31. See Sobrino, *Jesucristo*, 52–56. This statement (and others) by Sobrino has been criticized by the Congregation for the Doctrine of the Faith (CDF) on the grounds of incorrect methodology. See Congregation for the Doctrine of the Faith, "Notification on the Works of Father Jon Sobrino, SJ"; and CDF, "Explanatory Note on the Notification on the Works of Father Jon Sobrino, SJ."

32. Published in 1984 by the CDF under the English title, "Instruction on Certain Aspects of the 'Theology of Liberation.'"

33. See CDF, "Instruction on Christian Freedom and Liberation *Libertatis Conscientia*," n. 68.

34. See the *relatio finalis* of December 8, 1985, http://romana.org/art/1_2.6_1.

35. See John Paul II, *Sollicitudo Rei Socialis*, n. 42; *Centesimus Annus*, n. 11; but also in documents on topics that are not directly social in nature, like *Redemptoris Mater*, n. 37; *Ecclesia in America*, nn. 18 and 58; *Tertio Millennio Adveniente*, n. 51; *Novo Millennio Ineunte*, n. 49f; *Vita Consecrata*, nn. 82 and 90.

36. Pontifical Council for Justice and Peace, *Compendium*, n. 182. There is another mention of the preferential option for the poor in n. 449.

37. See Curnow, "Which Preferential Option," 44.

38. Gustavo Gutiérrez does not make these distinctions but simply affirms that the popes have accepted the preferential option for the poor; see Gutiérrez, *Teología*, 28f.

39. See Scannone, *Quando il popolo*, 45. Scannone is careful to note that Bergoglio is not a "theologian" of the people, but in his pastoral work he has been inspired by the theology of the people, in particular by the preferential option for the poor; see pages 47 and 54.

40. See Ferré and Metalli, *Il Papa e il Filosofo*.

41. See Scannone, *Quando il popolo*, 26f.

42. I am aware of the fact that one of its founders does consider the theology of the people as part of liberation theology; see Scannone, *Quando il popolo*, 5.

43. See Scannone, *Teologia*, 61.

44. See Ivereigh, *The Great Reformer*, 116.

45. Gera, "Pueblo," 717–44, 731.

46. See Scannone, *Teologia*, 61–66; Gera, "Cultura," 605–59; Gera, "Pueblo," 717–44, 729.

47. "The Marxist ideology is wrong. However, during my life I have known many Marxists who were good persons, that is why I don't feel offended" (at being called a Marxist), in Francesco, *Interviste*, 119 (my translation). See Gregg, "Understanding Pope Francis," 51–68.

48. CELAM, Aparecida Document.

49. CELAM, Aparecida Document, n. 391.

50. CELAM, Aparecida Document, n. 396.

51. CELAM, Aparecida Document, n. 395.

52. Francis, "Address to Participants in the Ecclesial Convention of the Diocese of Rome."

53. Francis, "Address to the Centesimus Annus Pro Pontifice Foundation."

54. Francis, "Address during the Conferral of the Charlemagne Prize."

55. Francis, *Evangelii Gaudium*, n. 202.

56. Francis, *Laudato Sí*, n. 114.

57. Francis, *Laudato Sí*, n. 203.

58. Francis, *Laudato Sí*, nn. 108–10.

59. Francis, *Laudato Sí*, n. 102f.

60. Francis, *Laudato Sí*, n. 112.

61. See the insightful essay by Georges Enderle, "The Option for the Poor and Business Ethics," 28–46.

62. Francis, *Laudato Sí*, n. 129.

Chapter 13, Schansberg

1. This chapter was originally published as "Biblical Christianity and Legislating Economic Justice," *Christian Libertarian Review* 3 (2020): 89–111. Reprinted with permission of the publisher, with minor stylistic changes.

2. Haidt, *The Righteous Mind*. Haidt also notes that there is more to morality than harm and fairness, so an overarching emphasis on fairness or justice is not helpful. Sowell distinguishes between two "visions," including thoughts of justice as process and rules versus outcomes and opportunity. Sowell, *Vision*, 105.

3. Schall, "Justice." Asma argues that fairness is not a morally central concern and even argues for favoritism. Asma, *Fairness*. Especially given the ease with which fairness can be invoked, it can crowd out other virtues and easily devolve into destructive envy.

4. As an example, for an impressive essay on justice from a Jewish perspective, see Biren, "The Market."

5. As such, this largely ignores the vast and impressive historical commentaries on Scripture. For particularly Catholic angles on religion and government, see Woods, *The Church and the Market*; and England, *Free Is Beautiful*.

6. Recognizing the broad, common, and sloppy use of vague terms such as a *justice* and *social justice*, Teevan argues for the term *integrated justice*. He notes that "justice is claimed by many who unjustly want the broad benefits of that term." Teevan, *Integrated Justice*, 12.

7. Heyne, *Are Economists Basically Immoral?*, 151. All persons (I would contend) believe that justice exists, but the "devil is in the details." Lewis relies on the universal appeal to justice and moral standards (however defined)—at least when we believe we've been wronged—to make his case for the existence of a God who transcends this world. Lewis, *Mere Christianity*.

8. Stapleford discusses different types of justice in abstract terms and relates it to public policies. Stapleford, *Bulls*, 26, 48–50, 86–88. Lebacqz provides a useful overview in her engagement with the concepts from various utilitarian and Christian angles. Lebacqz, *Six Theories*. Finkel writes at length to distinguish between injustice, unfairness, and misfortune. He argues that justice is used to imply greater objectivity and authority—whereas fairness is more subjective and the more appropriate term for use in daily life. Finkel, *Not Fair!*

9. Heyne in *Are Economists Basically Immoral?*, 152, also observes that "[t]he problem of talking clearly and sensibly about justice diminishes considerably, however, when we shift our focus and talk about *injustice*." He then quotes Aristotle in encouraging his readers to focus on injustice as a negative instead of justice as a positive.

10. Heyne, *Are Economists Basically Immoral?*, 135.

11. Brueggemann, *The Prophetic Imagination*, 110.

12. John Paul II, *Reconciliatio et Paenitentia*, no. 16.

13. Spooner, *Vices Are Not Crimes*, chap. I.

14. Reed, *Active Faith*, 278.

15. Rawls, *Justice*, 250.

16. Machan notes another overlap. In distinguishing between "the Right's idealism"—seeking to regulate "spiritual or mental actions" ("the crafting of people's souls")—and "the Left's materialism"—seeking to regulate "economic or material actions," he notes that the two intersect "since body and soul aren't ever sharply divided." He then cites examples of this overlap—the Right seeking "blue laws" and affecting commerce and the Left restricting free speech and thought at the expense of social freedoms. Machan, "Libertarianism."

17. Waters, *Just Capitalism*, 187.

18. Ps 89:14. See also Job 37:23; Ps 9:16, 11:11, 33:5; Is 9:7, 28:17, 30:18, 61:8; Jer 9:24; I Jn 1:9; Rev 15:3. All Scriptures are from the NIV.

19. Prov 22:2, Rom 2:11, Eph 6:9, Col 3:25.

20. Dt 27:19; Is 10:1–3; Jer 5:26–29, 7:5–7; Ez 18:12, 45:9–10; Amos 2:7, 4:1, 5:11, 8:4–7; Jas 5:1–6.

21. Ex 3:7–8, 6:5–7; Dt 10:18, 26:6–8; Job 5:15–16; Ps 10:15–18, 12:5, 68:5, 72:4, 107:41, 140:12, 146:7; Is 25:4; Mal 3:5; Lk 1:53.

22. Ex 23:3,6; Lev 19:15; Dt 1:17, 16:18–20.

23. Pr 8:15, Is 3:14–15, Jer 21:12, Dan 4:27, Amos 5:15. See also Ps 72 and Ez 34.

24. Rom 13:4. See also Rom 13:2, Prov 21:15, 28:5.

25. II Sam 8:15, I Chron 18:14. Cf. Ps 71:1, Lk 3:10–14; and Hübner, review of Halbertal and Holmes, *The Beginning of Politics*.

26. I Kings 3:9–11. In I Kings 10:9, the Queen of Sheba later told him that God had made him king to "maintain justice and righteousness." Unfortunately, Solomon failed to live up to this standard; even the wisest man in the world was responsible for some very poor policy. See the forced labor and high taxation of I Kings 5:13–18—and the polygamy and idolatry of I Kings 11. Friedman notes that Solomon imposed a disproportionate tax burden on the Northern tribes (land and money) while disproportionately building up military defenses in the South. Friedman, *Who Wrote the Bible?*, 44–45. Ironically, these events follow God's "measureless" provision of wisdom to Solomon in I Kings 4:29–34. An extension of Solomon's unjust "heavy yoke" by his son Rehoboam (I Kings 12:4) eventually led to the division of his kingdom.

27. I Tim 5:21, Jas 2:1,9. Solomon warned, "If you see the poor oppressed … and justice and rights denied, do not be surprised at such things" (Eccl 5:8).

28. Ps 82:2–4; Pr 17:5, 31:8–9; Is 1:17, 58:3, 6–11; Jer 22:3–5, 13–17.

29. Ps 52:7; Pr 22:22; Is 3:14; Ez 22:29, 45:9; Amos 2:7, 5:11–12, 8:4–6; Mic 2:1–2, 6:10–12; Zech 7:9–10; Jas 2:6.

30. Ps 112:5, Pr 19:17, I Tim 6:18–19, I Jn 3:17.

31. Pr 21:3, Amos 5:21–24, Mic 6:7; Dt 16:20.

32. Scripture often equates the seriousness of these issues with sexual sins. In discussing the "sin of Sodom," Ez 16:49–50 lists arrogance, being overfed, and having no concern for the poor and needy—along with "detestable practices." And given its reference to Sodom and Gomorrah, Is 1:10–17 places a greater emphasis on shedding blood and oppressing the poor than on "carnal" sins.

33. Pr 29:7, 21:15; Ps 37:21. See also Job 29:12–17, Pr 22:9.

34. Pr 14:31, 19:17.

35. Jer 23:5.

36. Christ's teachings and ministry seem to favor the poor. (See Lk 16:19–31's parable of the rich man and Lazarus, Mt 19:23's pithy analogy, Lk 6:24's "woe," Lk 12:21's parable of the rich fool, and Lk 21:1's account of the widow's offering. See also Lk 4:18b, 7:22b; Jas 2:1–5, 5:1–6.) Why? At the least, Christ was dealing with a contemporary religious bias in favor of the wealthy—e.g., given the Old Testament's tight correlation between obedience and blessings. Many Jesus scholars highlight this economic aspect of Jesus's ministry and setting.

37. Mt 23:23.

38. Lk 22:4–6.

39. Cf. Lk 4:25–29.

40. Mt 21:12–13, Mk 11:15–17, Lk 19:45–46, Jn 2:14–16. On whether his use of a whip was "violent," see N. Clayton Croy, "The Messianic Whippersnapper," *Journal of Biblical Literature* 128, no. 3 (Fall 2009): 555–68.

41. Matthew, Mark, and Luke record this, while John's account has Christ critical of turning his "Father's house into a market."

42. For an excellent discussion of this topic, see Horsley, *Covenant Economics*.

43. Beckwith, *Politics for Christians*, 68, 70.

44. See Schansberg, "Common Ground" and *Turn Neither to the Right nor to the Left*. Cf. Bandow, *Beyond Good Intentions*, and Hübner, "Christian Libertarianism."

45. An exception to this would be when a majority of (powerful) people benefit from an injustice. Even in these cases, Christians should value justice highly.

46. Motyer notes that "Both dal (poor) and ani (oppressed) have the same general ambience. … The latter, however, also includes the sense of 'humiliated, downtrodden'—not only uninfluential but because uninfluential, manipulated by the authorities as existing only for others' advantage." Motyer, *Isaiah*.

47. Schneider, "Affluence," 6–8. He argues helpfully that this theological response should be based on the doctrine of the Creation (how to use resources wisely) and the Exodus (a focus on freedom from oppression and poverty in a land of "milk and honey").

48. For example, James critiques those who withhold wages rather than criticizing the wage rate itself (Jas 5:4). Ironically, the government forces employers to "withhold" wages by mandating that they collect income and payroll taxes from workers, even the working poor.

49. Chilton, *Productive Christians*, 80–5.

50. The Tenth Commandment, injunctions against moving boundary stones (Dt 19:14, Pr 23:10, Hos 5:10), and the concepts of tithing and sacrifice (out of what one owns and controls) also support strong property rights. See also Mic 4:4, Mt 25:14–30, and the narrative in Genesis 3, which includes taking God's stuff.

51. Chilton, *Productive Christians*, 5.

52. Bandow, "Limited Government," 51. Cf. Schlossberg, *Idols for Destruction*, 118: "Since government produces no goods, it can distribute only what it takes from others. This process is indistinguishable from theft." Note also Eccl 4:1, 5:8–9. Augustine said that the only difference between the state and a band of highwaymen is its justice and supposed legitimacy: "Justice being taken away, then, what are kingdoms but great robberies? But what are robberies themselves, but little kingdoms? The band itself is made up of men; it is ruled by the authority of a prince; it is knit together by the pact of the confederacy; the booty is divided by the law agreed upon" (cited in Bandow, "Limited Government," 147).

53. An interesting potential counterexample is in the Israelites accepting money from the Persian king in rebuilding the temple (Ezra 6:4,8–9, 7:15). But note that the money was volunteered, not requested, and God might have considered it a form of "back pay" (as Ex 12:35–36).

54. Ex 23:8. See also Dt 10:17, 16:19, 28:25; Job 15:34–35, 36:18; Ps 15:5, 26:9–10; Pr 15:28; Eccl 7:7; Is 5:23; Mic 3:9–12.

55. Ex 18:21.

56. I Sam 12:3–4.

57. Amos 5:11–12. One can draw a moral distinction between taking and paying bribes. See Schansberg, "The Ethics of Tax Evasion," 156.

58. Cases of excessive corruption are prosecuted on occasion. And a provision in campaign finance laws that allowed retiring U.S. representatives to pocket excess campaign contributions in 1992 was uncomfortably close to bribery.

59. Gen 4:17. Ironically, Cain's twisted sense of justice led to the impulses behind the murder.

60. Hübner, "Israel's History," argues that the Enneateuch as a whole exhibits an antipolitical bias by the postexile scribes, and provides more internarrative reasons for this conclusion.

61. Cf. Higgs, *Delusions of Power*.

62. See Schansberg, *Poor Policy*.

63. Corbett and Fikkert point to the difficulties of even doing private charity, despite with the best of intentions. Corbett and Fikkert, *When Helping Hurts*. For the societal implications of these problems, see Murray, *Coming Apart*.

64. Note Hübner's review article of Waters's *Just Capitalism*, which deconstructs the "market-state" (market democratic socialism) as being "exploitative," not so much parental.

65. Koyzis, *Political Visions and Illusions*, 151, 250.

66. Some have argued that this phenomenon occurred during the Trump presidency. For example, see Christopher Ingraham, "For the First Time in History, U.S. Billionaires Paid a Lower Tax Rate than the Working Class Last Year," *Washington Post*, October 8, 2019.

67. Koyzis, *Political Visions and Illusions*, 250.

68. Brueggemann, *The Prophetic Imagination*, 13.

69. Woodiwiss, "Christian Economic Justice," 141, 143.

70. Is 59:14–16.

71. Guinness, *Fit Bodies, Fat Minds*, 30.

Chapter 15, Cohen

1. This is a slightly abbreviated and lightly edited version of my "Bleeding Heart Libertarian View of Inequality" in *Ethics in Practice*, 5th ed., edited by Hugh LaFollette (Hoboken, NJ: Wiley, 2020), 598–610, and is being used with permission of the editor. I am indebted to Anna Jane Parrill and others at The Foundation for Economic Education, who asked me to speak about this topic in recent years and to Hugh LaFollette, Michael C. Munger, Daniel Shapiro, and Kevin Vallier for valuable feedback on earlier versions of this chapter.

2. For a concise description of prominent political philosophies and the relation of BHL to these, see http://bleedingheartlibertarians.com/2011/12/our-family-a-possible-taxonomy/.

3. Regarding socialism, see Brennan, *Why Not Capitalism?*, itself a response to Cohen, *Why Not Socialism?*

4. See, e.g., Zwolinksi, "Social Darwinism and Social Justice."

5. For a discussion on "Stoney hearted or bleeding heart liberaltarianism?," see http://bleedingheartlibertarians.com/2013/12/stoney-hearted-libertarianism-or-bleeding-heart-libertarianism/.

6. Spencer, "The Sins of Legislators."

7. Bastiat, *The Law,* 5.

8. Bastiat, *The Law,* 17.

9. Bastiat, *The Law,* 19.

10. See my *Toleration*, chap. 3.

11. BHLs might be receptive to forced taxation that would help the poor without having any perverse effects but would be concerned with the certainty of such.

12. Some BHLs are more pluralistic than others about the sorts of liberty that are of value.

13. For more on the positive liberty–negative liberty distinction, see Carter, "Positive and Negative Liberty."

14. See Pomeranz, *The Great Divergence.* See also Jones, *The European Miracle.* The central claim is made at least as early as 1905 by Max Weber in his *Protestant Ethics*, though Weber attributes the divergence primarily to a religious difference. See also Mokyr's underappreciated *The Lever of Riches*; and, more recently, McCloskey's excellent trilogy, *Bourgeois Virtues.*

15. This was in November 2017. See https://www.brookings.edu/blog/future-development /2017/11/07/global-poverty-is-declining-but-not-fast-enough/.

16. See http://www.worldbank.org/en/topic/poverty/overview. Some raise concerns with the numbers (see, e.g., https://www.aljazeera.com/indepth/opinion/2014/08/exposing-great -poverty-reductio-201481211590729809.html), but the overall prognosis is clearly positive.

17. Why trade was able to blossom in and after the nineteenth century (some would say it started earlier) is not a question we can answer here, but see note 14 above.

18. Property rights provide one way to protect economic freedom. If I am able to own a car—meaning, minimally, that I can use the car, exclude others from using it, and earn money with it (renting it, using it for a service, selling it, etc.), I have economic freedom—I can use my resources as I see fit without interference by others.

19. Some BHLs also treat economic freedom as a central value of political thinking independent of its contribution to welfare. We all agree *at least part of its value* is in its relation to human welfare.

20. See Piketty, *Capital*; and his earlier, but recently translated, *Economics of Inequality.* Piketty's central thesis—that gains to accumulated wealth accrue more quickly than the economy grows—has been challenged. See, e.g., Acemoglu and Robinson, "Rise and Decline"; and Blume and Durlauf, "*Capital in the Twenty-First Century.*" Also of interest are McCloskey's "Measured," *Erasmus Journal for Philosophy and Economics*; and Cowen's "Capital Punishment."

21. It is worth noting that despite the prevalence of significant economic inequality, we now largely enjoy political equality, that many who might be considered poor nonetheless have regular access to food and shelter, and that, generally speaking, no one has to bow to anyone. (Two concerns worth noting about the United States: First, inner-city youth, especially African American males, are far too often subject to unwelcome encounters with police that might come close to including legally required subservience. Second, homelessness among children is a significant issue.)

22. Smith, *Wealth of Nations*, I.II.1.

23. For the original argument, see Ricardo, *Political Economy*, especially chap. 19.1.

24. See my *Toleration,* chap. 4. See also Muldoon, *Social Contract*, chap. 5.

25. Smith, *Wealth of Nations*, I.I.5–8.

26. Property rights, that is, allow us to prevent tragedies of the commons. See Schmidtz, "Institution of Property"; and Schmidtz, "Property and Justice."

27. See note 24 above.

28. Also significant is the fact that the group of people that is "poor" changes over time. As David Schmidtz points out, looking at the distribution of goods (income, wealth, or resources) at a single instant is misguided. College students often have no income and substantially negative wealth (due to college loans), without being badly off. Generally, many of those in the lower quintiles of income earners move up those quintiles as they age (becoming earners, improving their ability to earn, etc.). Their children might move further up (or move down!). We do not live in a caste society where people have to live at the same income or wealth level their parents did. Moreover, those in the lower half, for example, of the income distribution do considerably better today than did those in the lower half of the income distribution a century ago—indeed, almost all of us are materially better off today than people were a century ago. (This is true even though there are, obviously and unfortunately, some today who are as badly off as anyone ever was—homeless children in particular seem "left behind.") See Schmidtz, *Elements of Justice*, 126–39. See also Horwitz, "Inequality."

29. Frankfurt, *On Inequality*, 7.

30. Frankfurt, *On Inequality*, 11. I should note that I am not here fully endorsing Frankfurt's *sufficientarianism*, where once each has enough sufficient to lead the sort of life that is good for one, there is no further concern with inequality at all. Neither that nor *prioritarianism*, the view that the least well-off must always be given priority of some sort, is quite right, though both follow from important insights. A number of BHLs, though, are sufficientarian. On prioritarianism, see Cohen, "Democratic Equality," and Arneson, "Luck."

31. Lindsey and Teles, *Economy*.

32. Lindsey and Teles, *Economy*, 126.

33. Worth considering in this light is the role (in the United States) of the Flexner Report of 1910. See https://www.ncbi.nlm.nih.gov/pmc/articles/PMC3178858/. Part of what this did was judge medical schools in terms of how they trained medical students and whether that method was in line with the methods used at Johns Hopkins University but without concern for how the resulting doctors succeeded. Schools that performed poorly on this score (roughly one-third of the total number of medical schools at the time) ended up closing.

34. Lindsey and Teles, *Economy*, 92.

35. Lindsey and Teles, *Economy*, 95.

36. Lindsey and Teles, *Economy*, 96 and 97. For those worried that, absent licensing, people will have no way to tell who is qualified to perform a service, it is worth noting that there are private certification programs (Consumer Reports, Angie's List, Underwriters Laboratory, etc.) and college and university degrees (MDs, JDs, etc.) that provide much the same information without coercively required licenses.

37. Lindsey and Teles, *Economy*, 39.

38. Lindsey and Teles also discuss securitization that also encouraged financial firms to make risky loans (see Lindsay and Teles, *Economy*, 40–42). See also my discussion of collateralized debt obligations in my *Toleration*, 106.

39. Alexander, *Jim Crow*.

40. Alexander, *Jim Crow*, 49.

41. Alexander, *Jim Crow*, 83.

42. The problem of overincarceration is predominately an issue for the United States, which has vastly higher incarceration rates than the rest of the developed world. See https://www.prisonpolicy.org/global/2018.html.

43. Bastiat, *The Law*, 14. For a recent argument that free markets help society by encouraging positive-sum activity, see Freiman, *Unequivocal Justice*, chap. 6.

44. As others (especially Public Choice economists) have pointed out, it is unfair to compare real (very flawed) markets with ideal governments; we must recognize a symmetry. See Shapiro, *Welfare State*, 2–8. Governments—including their efforts to reduce inequality—are themselves flawed. Comparing real market activity with real government activity is fair. Some of what I say here is meant to be suggestive of the sort of considerations needed. See Keech and Munger, "Anatomy." Also see Long, "Left-Libertarianism."

45. Nozick has a similar case. See Nozick, *Anarchy*, 237.

46. Consider again the extreme example of the U.S. federal government not merely allowing but actually enforcing slavery. This clearly gave an unjust benefit to some while harming others. This may make reparations due. See Boonin, *Race*, chaps. 2 and 3.

Chapter 16, Kaiser

1. Rawls, *Justice*, 88.

2. Nozick, *Anarchy*, 232.

3. Rousseau, *The Social Contract*, 207.

4. Rousseau, *The Social Contract*, 218.

5. Rousseau, *The Social Contract*, 221.

6. Cf. de Jouvenel, *Die Ethik*, 31.

7. Marx, *Critique*.

8. Marx, *Critique*, 9.

9. Engels, *El origen*.

10. Von Böhm-Bawerk, *Karl Marx*; and von Mises, *Socialism*.

11. Rawls, *Justice*, 14–15.

12. Rawls, *Justice*, 83.

13. Rawls, *Justice*, 15.

14. Rawls, *Justice*, 62.

15. Höffe, *Gerechtigkeit*, 67.

16. McCloskey, *Bourgeois Dignity*, 70.

17. McCloskey, *Bourgeois Dignity*, 70.

18. Hayek, *Constitution*, 196.

19. Hayek, *Constitution*, 196.

20. Schmidtz, *Elements*, 139.

21. Schmidtz, *Elements*, 189.

22. Luhmann, *Politische Theorie*, 147.

23. Epstein, "John Rawls."

24. Epstein, *Progressive Institutions*, 56.
25. Friedman and Friedman, *Tyranny*, 157.
26. Epstein, *Design*, 143.
27. Epstein, *Design*, 143.
28. Zingales, *Capitalism*, 6.
29. Sanandaji, "Surprising Ingredients."
30. Tomasi, *Fairness*, 193–94.
31. Tomasi, *Fairness*, 184.
32. Mill, *Collected Works*, 5:714.
33. Mill, *Collected Works*, 5:714.
34. Hume, *Enquiries*, 118.
35. Hume, *Enquiries*, 118.
36. Rawls, *Justice*, 7.
37. Hayek, *Law*, 31.
38. Nietzsche, *Gesammelte Werke*, 308–9.
39. Röpke, "Malady."
40. Röpke, "Malady."
41. Röpke, "Malady."
42. Röpke, "Malady."
43. Röpke, "Malady."
44. Rothbard, *Egalitarianism*.
45. Sowell, *Cosmic Justice*.
46. Nagel, "Meaning," 28.
47. Dworkin, "Equality."
48. Sowell, *Cosmic Justice*, 13.
49. Sowell, *Cosmic Justice*, 22.
50. Dworkin, "Equality."
51. Sen, *Idea*, 253.
52. Bhagwati and Panagariya, *Why Growth Matters*.
53. Piketty, *Capital*, 377.
54. De Soto, *Mystery*, 34.
55. Smith, *System of Liberty*, 136.
56. Locke, *Second Treatise*, 46.
57. Berlin, *Four Essays*, 3.
58. Berlin, *Four Essays*, 3.
59. Sen, *Idea*, 288.
60. Nussbaum, *Creating Capabilities*, 19.
61. Robeyns, "Capabilitarianism."
62. Hayek, *Constitution*, 75.
63. Frankfurt, "Moral Ideal," 23.
64. Frankfurt, "Moral Ideal," 23.

65. Helmut Schöck explained, for instance, that a progressive tax punishes the most successful, and is triggered by the envy that characterized the institutions of primitive communities. See Schöck, *Envy*, 390.

66. Frankfurt, "Moral Ideal," 24ff. See also Schmidtz, *Elements*, 140ff.

67. Frankfurt, "Moral Ideal," 31.

68. Frankfurt, "Moral Ideal," 33.

69. Frankfurt, "Moral Ideal," 34.

70. Dworkin, "Equality."

71. Friedman, *Capitalism and Freedom*, 192.

Chapter 17, Geloso and Magness

1. Nozick, "Justice"; Nozick, *Anarchy*; Hayek, *Mirage*.

2. Hayek, "Atavism."

3. Tomasi, *Fairness*, xvii–xx.

4. Hutt, "Unanimity"; Hayek, *Mirage*; Hayek, *Fatal Conceit*; Schmidtz and Brennan, *Liberty*.

5. North, Wallis, and Weingast, *Violence*.

6. Sam Peltzman, Michael Levine, and Roger Noll identify two scenarios in which rent dissipation can occur: "(1) the gap between the regulated equilibrium and the one plausibly characterizing deregulation of the industry narrows, so continued regulation becomes pointless, or (2) the wealth available for redistribution becomes too small to provide the requisite political payoff to regulation" (Peltzman, Levine, and Noll, *Economic Theory*, 20). A rent-seeking narrative may be thought of as a strategy to forestall these circumstances.

7. For "relation equality" see Anderson, "Equality." For "euvoluntary exchange" see Munger, "Euvoluntary"; Munger, "Objections"; Guzmán and Munger, "Euvoluntariness."

8. Tullock, "Welfare Costs"; Krueger, "Political Economy."

9. Roback, "Racism"; Kuran, *Private Truths*; Grynaviski and Munger, "Reconstructing Racism."

10. Nozick, "Justice"; Nozick, *Anarchy*; Hayek, *Mirage*.

11. Sen, "Social Justice," 68–69.

12. Anderson, "Equality"; Schemmel, "Equality."

13. Kim and Loury, "Collective Reputation."

14. Reeves, *A Little Respect*.

15. Reeves, *A Little Respect*.

16. Hayek, *Fatal Conceit*; see also the restatement in Martin, "Egalitarianism."

17. North, Wallis, and Weingast, *Violence*.

18. Van Bavel, Ansink, and Van Besouw, "Economics," 111.

19. See, notably, Mahoney, "Common Law," for an empirical example.

20. This redistribution would include economic redistribution (Sen, "Social Justice") and the redistribution of rights and privileges emphasized by more modern social justice literature (Tyler and Smith, "Social Justice").

21. Geloso and Horwitz, "Inequality"; Geloso, "Inequality"; Novak, *Inequality*.

22. Kim and Loury, "Collective Reputation."

23. Roback, "Racism," 662.

24. Roback, "Racism," 679.

25. As Roback emphasizes, resources can be expended to change rules in welfare-improving ways. She cites the example of a move from common property to private property wherein the contest dissipates the gains of the shift (Roback, "Racism," 671).

26. Roback, "Racism."

27. Roback, "Racism," 672.

28. Kuran, *Private Truths*, 4.

29. Kuran, *Private Truths*, 8.

30. Kuran, *Private Truths*, 19.

31. For "protection of a limited-access order" see North, Wallis, and Weingast, *Violence*. See also Hayek, *Fatal Conceit*.

32. Hummel, *Emancipating Slaves*; Hummel, "Deadweight Loss"; Wright, *Poverty*.

33. Hummel, "Deadweight Loss," 123.

34. Hummel, "Deadweight Loss," 222.

35. Many abolitionists such as John Brown explicitly tried to foment a coalition between slaves and nonslaveholding whites in the South, and some abolitionist literature (e.g., Spooner, "Plan") proposed an antislavery rebellion on similar lines. Even outwardly racist forms of antislavery activism, such as Hinton Rowan Helper's pamphlet *The Impending Crisis of the South* (1857), written as an appeal to poor whites' self-interest with little expressed concern for the slaves, met with vigorous suppression and censorship in the late antebellum period. This would also explain why individuals such as William Stevenson (who would later be governor of West Virginia) were accused of criminal acts for circulating Helper's treatise and why Ohio representative John Sherman's public praise for the book politically undermined his bid for U.S. Speaker of the House in 1859. The Southern slaveholders' reaction to each suggests a strong investment in the stigmatizing power of the rent-seeking narrative around slavery.

36. Grynaviski and Munger, "Reconstructing Racism."

37. Grynaviski and Munger, "Reconstructing Racism," 162.

38. Hummel, *Emancipating Slaves*; Hummel, "Deadweight Loss."

39. Tullock, "Economics." Gordon Tullock elaborates on these observations in an unpublished memorandum on slavery (box 94, folder 8, Gordon Tullock Papers, Hoover Institution, Stanford, CA). In his little-studied writings on slavery, Tullock makes the important point that stigmatizing and preventing the emergence of free populations of color also served to reduce the costs of slave enforcement, thereby preserving the enforcement rents for slave owners. Free populations of color made it harder for slave patrols to enforce slavery on strictly racial lines and provided a point of refuge for escapees. This is why antimanumission laws and even forced exile such as colonization became so popular (Magness, "American System"; Magness, "Paradox").

40. Egerton, *Reconstruction*.

41. Roback, "Racism"; Roback, "Separation."

42. MacKinnon, "Unilingues"; Geloso, "Inequality."

43. Stark and Iannaccone, "Response." Rodney Stark and Laurence Iannaccone emphasize that the Catholic Church, given its monopoly, was able to preserve its monopoly rents and high attendance simultaneously only because it acted as an "organizational vehicle ... for social conflict" ("Response," 267)—that is, the tension between French Canadians and English Canadians. Thus, the narrative served to prevent rents from being dissipated.

44. Bellavance, *Québec*.

45. See, notably, Taylor, "French Canadians"; Couture, *Le mythe*.

46. Baker and Hamilton, "Écarts salariaux"; MacKinnon, "Unilingues."

47. Albouy, "Wage Gap," 2008.

48. Breton, "Nationalism"; Geloso, *Rethinking*.

Chapter 18, Haeffele and Storr

1. Wendy Duff and her colleagues (Duff et al., "Social Justice Impact") find that scholarly articles on social justice have increased over time along with studies on civil rights and human rights. For articles on the conceptual history and cultural origins of social justice, see Reisch, "Defining Social Justice"; Jackson, "Conceptual History"; and Bankston, "Social Justice."

2. See Blau and Ferber, "Discrimination"; Omi and Winant, *Racial Formation*.

3. Duff et al., "Social Justice Impact," 321.

4. See Reisch, "Defining Social Justice"; Jackson, "Conceptual History"; Duffy, "Citizenship Theory."

5. See Reisch, "Defining Social Justice"; Duffy, "Citizenship Theory."

6. Duff et al., "Social Justice Impact," 321–22.

7. Duff et al., "Social Justice Impact."

8. Reisch, "Defining Social Justice."

9. See Lister, "'Mirage,'" on where Hayek and Rawls stand on the infeasibility of merit-based income distribution in markets as well as where they differ on short-run redistribution. See Jackson and Palm, "Limits," for a modern account of the infeasibility of egalitarianism in a free society. And see Radnitzky, "Anthony de Jasay," on linking this view with that of the work by Anthony de Jasay.

10. Others have criticized Hayek's view that social justice requires coercion, which will undermine a free society, as being simplistic and too optimistic of markets. They also criticize how his policy concessions (specifically supporting a minimum income) weaken his claims. For this debate, see Feser, "Reply to Lukes and Johnston"; Feser, "Reply to Johnston"; Johnston, "Hayek's Attack"; Johnston, "Idea"; Lukes, "Social Justice"; and Tebble, "Hayek."

11. This approach to critiquing Hayek's claim that social justice is meaningless or infeasible because it would require identifying the individuals who or the organization of individuals that have acted unjustly is slightly different from the approach taken by Steven Lukes (Lukes, "Social Justice") or David Johnston (Johnston, "Idea").

12. Smith, *Wealth of Nations*, 26–27.

13. Hayek, "Use of Knowledge."

14. Hayek, *Mirage*, 35–42. Hayek notes that these rules of just conduct are less restrictive than the rules for small groups or communities, but as the market grows, so does the need

to minimize the number of rules to those necessary for it to function (*Mirage*, 88–91). Our desire for more restrictive rules is part of the atavism argument Adam James Tebble (Tebble, "Hayek") discusses.

15. Hayek, *Mirage*, 107.

16. See Lister, "'Mirage,'" for how Hayek's understanding of merit is similar to Rawls's.

17. Hayek, *Mirage*, 68. Tebble further classifies the critique to cover "meaningfulness, atavism, feasibility and compatibility" (Tebble, "Hayek," 582). For our purposes, we focus on meaningfulness as part of the first critique and on feasibility and compatibility as part of the second.

18. Hayek, *Mirage*, 68–69.

19. Hayek, *Mirage*, 69.

20. Hayek, *Mirage*, 69–70.

21. Hayek, *Mirage*, 71.

22. Hayek, *Mirage*, 72.

23. Of course, even if the rules remain fixed (which they rarely do), the strategies and types of players who dominate a game often change over time.

24. Holcombe, *Political Capitalism*; see also Wagner, *Politics*.

25. Stiglitz, *Inequality*, 39–40, 59.

26. Hayek, *Mirage*, 95–96.

27. See Smith, *Wealth of Nations*, 710.

28. This view of meaningfulness is different from the view in other critiques of Hayek (such as Johnston, "Hayek's Attack"; Johnston, "Idea"; and Lukes, "Social Justice"). Tebble summarizes: "The core of the objection that it is not meaningless to predicate (in)justice of catallactic outcomes is that even if no single agent or group of agents acting in concert can be said to have intentionally brought them about that does not mean that, as a (political) society, we cannot hold ourselves responsible for them" (Tebble, "Hayek," 591). Our argument, rather, is that by looking at the referees of the game, we can determine if social institutions lead to injustices.

29. Further research on this approach can examine (1) the causes of social justice issues, (2) the limitations in government remedies, and (3) how society (through markets and civil society) can provide remedies or alternative opportunities to the least advantaged.

30. Hayek interestingly writes about the appropriateness of exploring reparations for past injustices but ultimately argues against them because of the challenges involved in identifying the victims and the uncertainties of time—that is, how recently or long ago the injustice took place (Hayek, *Mirage*, 131).

31. Johnston, "Hayek's Attack"; Johnston, "Idea."

32. Hayek, *Mirage*, 87. In "Hayek," Tebble identifies this concession as a major contradiction in Hayek's claim of infeasibility. For a recent discussion of a basic-income guarantee, see the debate edited by Michael C. Munger in Munger, *Tomorrow 3.0*.

33. Not only is it unlikely that the elites will want to remedy these injustices, but any attempts they make to do so are also unlikely to be successful due to the knowledge and incentive problems prevalent in central planning (see Hayek, *Mirage*, 99; Coyne, *Doing Bad*).

34. See Wagner, *Politics*; Holcombe, *Political Capitalism*.

35. See Tebble, "Hayek"; Tomasi, *Fairness*.

36. Munger, *Tomorrow 3.0*.

Chapter 19, Whaples

1. Thomas Aquinas aptly defines justice as "the perpetual and constant will to render to each one his right" (Aquinas, *Summa Theologiae*, Second Part of the Second Part, Question 58, Article 1).

2. Kendi's definition of racism contrasts with older concepts, such as racism as "prejudice plus power" (Fiske, "Racism," 549). I do not accept many of Kendi's arguments about racism and antiracism. However, even though his unguarded anger and his judgment calls on what is racist and antiracist may dissuade some readers from taking his point of view seriously, I take his framework about the nature of racism, antiracism, and public policy to be in earnest and a potentially useful tool for pursuing justice.

3. Kendi, *Antiracist*, 20.

4. Kendi, *Antiracist*, 18.

5. Kendi, *Antiracist*, 153.

6. Kendi, *Antiracist*, 208.

7. Kendi, *Antiracist*, 8.

8. Kendi, *Antiracist*, 218.

9. Kendi, *Antiracist*, 11.

10. Kendi, *Antiracist*, 30. Kendi's full quote is about the antiracist belief that "Black people [are] entirely capable of ruling themselves." I hope I haven't misinterpreted him in suggesting that he holds this view for all races.

11. Kendi, *Antiracist*, 105; emphasis added.

12. Kendi, *Antiracist*, 157.

13. See, for example, Coclanis, "Capitalism."

14. Kendi, *Antiracist*, 159.

15. Lawson and Powell, *Socialism Sucks*.

16. Whaples, "Pope Francis." Markets generally promote toleration and punish prejudice too. Perhaps as a result, people who live in market societies are significantly less likely to be prejudiced than people who live in nonmarket societies (Storr and Choi, *Markets*, 173–74).

17. In "Four Centuries," Vedder cites census data that show black incomes as a percentage of white incomes have almost doubled since 1950, although this rise has stalled in the last two decades.

18. Kendi, *Antiracist*, 80.

19. Shores and Ejdemyr, "School Districts"; emphasis in the original.

20. Strong, "U.S. Education."

21. Sowell, *Charter Schools*.

22. Mack, "Montessori School."

23. U.S. Census, "Spending."

24. Kendi, *Antiracist*, 22.

25. Figures from Wikipedia, "Race and Health."

26. Jatlaoui et al., "Abortion Surveillance."

27. Studnicki, Fisher, and Sherley, "Perceiving."

28. Goodman, *A Better Choice*.

29. Goodman's preferred tax credit would equal about $2,800 per person in today's dollars or $9,000 for a family of four. However, Medicaid spending per beneficiary exceeds these amounts, with the latest figures at $3,600 per child and $5,200 per adult aged 20 to 64 (Centers for Medicare and Medicaid Services, "Facts and Figures").

30. CDC, Table 29.

31. Mac Donald, "Taking Stock," A17.

32. Weisburd et al., "Proactive Policing," 1.

33. Kendi, *Antiracist*, 148.

34. Fegley, "Police Unions."

35. Geloso and Horwitz, "Inequality," 130.

36. Kendi, *Antiracist*, 80.

37. Carpenter et al., "Regulating Work."

38. Ganong and Shoag, "Regional Income."

39. Munger, "One and One-Half Cheers."

40. Sullivan et al., "Equitable Investments."

41. Henderson, "Philosophical."

42. Lomasky, "Fleecing."

43. World Bank, *Averting*.

44. Kendi, *Antiracist*, 132.

45. Darwall, *Green Tyranny*.

46. Lomborg, *False Alarm*.

47. Wu and Langpap, "Price."

48. Lincicome, "Examining."

49. Murtazashvili and Piano, "More Boon."

50. Chirakijja, Jayachandran, and Ong, *Inexpensive Heating*.

51. *Forbes*, "Billionaires."

52. Whaples, "Economic Future."

53. Clark, *War*.

54. Kendi, *Antiracist*, 154.

55. Munger and Villarreal-Diaz, "Road."

56. Holcombe, "Crony Capitalism."

57. Whaples, "Road."

58. Fajgelbaum and Khandelwal, "Measuring," 1152–53.

59. U.S. Census, "Homeownership."

60. Kendi, *Antiracist*, 10. At its worst, it can serve as a fig leaf for the same kind of rent seeking that it decries and banish individual responsibility by attributing too much to socioeconomic conditions and government policies, while ignoring its own affirmation that people are "entirely capable of ruling themselves." Jason L. Riley ("Race Relations," A17) labels Kendi a "professional polemicist."

61. This is what drove the abolitionist movement and spurred the reduction of racism during the civil rights era. Note also that religious attendance promotes human well-being

in other ways. Rodney Stark and Jared Maier (Stark and Maier, "Faith") find that frequent churchgoers (attending weekly or more) in the United States were more likely to report being "very happy" than others. The happiness advantage of weekly attenders versus never attenders is found among every group and is especially large for blacks. Gaps are found for men (+18 percentage points), women (+13), whites (+15), blacks (+30), married (+14), single (+13), divorced (+6), and widowed (+11). (Blacks attend religious services more frequently than whites [Dehejia, DeLeire, and Luttmer, "Insuring"].)

Bibliography

Foreword, Peterson

Nietzsche, Friedrich. *Thus Spake Zarathustra: A Book for All and None.* Edited by Anthony Uyl. Translated by Thomas Common. Woodstock, Canada: Devoted Publishing, 2017.

Introduction, Whaples

Hayek, F. A. *The Mirage of Social Justice.* Vol. 2, *Law, Legislation, and Liberty: A New Statement of the Liberal Principles of Justice and Political Economy.* Chicago: University of Chicago Press, 1976.

Justinian. Quotations from *Corpus juris civilis.* N.d. Accessed February 26, 2019. https:// en.wikiquote.org/wiki/Corpus_Juris_Civilis.

Kendi, Ibram X. *How to Be an Antiracist.* New York: One World, 2019.

Novak, Michael. "Defining Social Justice." *First Things,* December 2000. https://www .firstthings.com/article/2000/12/defining-social-justice.

Rawls, John. *A Theory of Justice.* Cambridge, MA: Harvard University Press, 1971.

Sowell, Thomas. *The Quest for Cosmic Justice.* New York: Free Press, 1999.

Whaples, Robert M., Michael C. Munger, and Christopher J. Coyne, eds. "The Road to Crony Capitalism." *The Independent Review* 23, no. 3 (2018).

Chapter 1, Guerrière

Aquinas, Thomas. *Justice.* Vol. 37, *Summa theologiae.* Latin text plus English translation by Thomas Gilby. New York: Blackfriars/McGraw-Hill, 1975.

Aristotle. *Nicomachean Ethics.* Rev. ed. Edited and translated by H. Rackham. Loeb Classical Library. Cambridge, MA: Harvard University Press, [1934] 1963.

———. *Politics.* Corrected ed. Edited and translated by H. Rackham. Loeb Classical Library. Cambridge, MA: Harvard University Press, 1944.

Asma, Stephen T. *Against Fairness.* Chicago: University of Chicago Press, 2013.

Assmann, Jan. *Herrschaft und Heil: Politische Theologie in Altägypten, Israel, und Europa*. Munich, Germany: Carl Hanser, 2000.

Balot, Ryan K. *Greed and Injustice in Classical Athens*. Princeton, NJ: Princeton University Press, 2001.

Buck, Carl Darling. *A Dictionary of Selected Synonyms in the Principal IndoEuropean Languages*. Chicago: University of Chicago Press, [1949] 1988.

Burridge, Kenelm. *Someone, No One: An Essay on Individuality*. Princeton, NJ: Princeton University Press, 1979.

Carr, Brian, and Indira Mahalingam, eds. *Companion Encyclopedia of Asian Philosophy*. New York: Routledge, 1997.

Chenu, Marie-Dominique. *L'éveil de la conscience dans la civilisation médiévale*. Paris: Vrin, 1969.

Cicero. *De finibus bonorum et malorum*. 2nd ed. Edited and translated by H. Rackham. Loeb Classical Library. Cambridge, MA: Harvard University Press, [1931] 1999.

———. *De re publica. De legibus*. Edited and translated by Clinton Walker Keyes. Loeb Classical Library. Cambridge, MA: Harvard University Press, [1928] 1977.

Dumont, Louis. *Essays in Individualism: Modern Ideology in Anthropological Perspective*. Chicago: University of Chicago Press, 1986.

Feagin, Joe R. "Social Justice and Sociology: Agendas for the Twenty-First Century (Presidential Address)." *American Sociological Review* 66 (2001): 1–20.

Gat, Azar. *War in Human Civilization*. Oxford: Oxford University Press, 2006.

Greene, William Chase. *Moira: Fate, Good, and Evil in Greek Thought*. New York: Harper & Row, [1944] 1963.

Gurewich, Aaron. *The Origins of European Individualism*. Translated by Katharine Judelson. Oxford: Blackwell, 1995.

Havelock, Eric A. *The Greek Concept of Justice: From Its Shadow in Homer to Its Substance in Plato*. Cambridge, MA: Harvard University Press, 1978.

Justinian. *Novellae institutiones*. Vol. 1, *Corpus juris civilis*. Edited by Paulus Krueger. Hildesheim, Germany: Weidmann, 2000.

Kekes, John. *The Illusions of Egalitarianism*. Ithaca, NY: Cornell University Press, 2003.

Knight, Douglas A. "Cosmology and Order in the Hebrew Tradition." In *Cosmology and Ethical Order*, edited by Robin W. Lovin and Frank E. Reynolds, 133–57. Chicago: University of Chicago Press, 1985.

Morris, Colin. *The Discovery of the Individual, 1050–1200*. London: SPCK, 1972.

Novak, Michael. *The Catholic Ethic and the Spirit of Capitalism*. New York: Free Press, 1993.

Plato. *The Republic.* 2 vols. Edited and translated by Chris Emlyn Jones and William Preddy. Loeb Classical Library. Cambridge, MA: Harvard University Press, [1925] 2013.

————. "Statesman." In *Statesman—Philebus—Ion.* Edited and translated by Harold North Fowler, 1–196. Loeb Classical Library. Cambridge, MA: Harvard University Press, 1925.

Scheidel, Walter. *The Great Leveler: Violence and the History of Inequality from the Stone Age to the Twenty-First Century.* Princeton, NJ: Princeton University Press, 2017.

Schmid, Hans Heinrich. *Gerechtigkeit als Weltordnung: Hintergrund und Geschichte des alttestamentischen Gerechtigkeitsbegriffes.* Tubingen, Germany: J. C. B. Mohr (Paul Siebeck), 1968.

Siedentop, Larry. *Inventing the Individual: The Origins of Western Liberalism.* Cambridge, MA: Belknap Press of Harvard University Press, 2014.

Snell, Daniel C., ed. *A Companion to the Ancient Near East.* Oxford: Blackwell, 2000.

Vinogradoff, Paul. *Outlines of Historical Jurisprudence,* II: *The Jurisprudence of the Greek City.* London: Oxford University Press, 1922.

Voegelin, Eric. *Order and History,* III: *Plato and Aristotle.* Baton Rouge: Louisiana State University Press, 1956–57.

Zięba, Maciej. *Papal Economics: The Catholic Church on Democratic Capitalism.* Wilmington, DE: ISI Books, 2013.

Chapter 2, Smith

Bacon, Francis. "The New Organon [Novum organum]." In *The Works of Francis Bacon,* vol. 8. Translated by James Spedding, Robert Leslie Ellis, and Douglas Denon Heath. Boston: Taggard and Thompson, [1620] 1863. http://www.constitution.org/bacon /nov_org.htm. Accessed December 7, 2018.

Bohman, James. "Critical Theory." In *Stanford Encyclopedia of Philosophy.* Stanford, CA: Stanford University Press, 2005. https://plato.stanford.edu/entries/critical-theory/.

Economist. "The Art and Science of Economics at Cambridge." December 24, 2016. https://www.economist.com/christmas-specials/2016/12/24/the-art-and-science -of-economicsat-cambridge.

Garrigou-LaGrange, Reginald. *Reality: A Synthesis of Thomistic Thought.* South Bend, IN: Ex Fontibus, 2015.

Hobbes, Thomas. *Leviathan.* Edited by Francis B. Randall. New York: Washington Square Press, [1651] 1964.

Horkheimer, Max. *Critical Theory: Selected Essays.* New York: Continuum, [1972] 1982.

Hume, David. *A Treatise of Human Nature.* 1738. http://www.gutenberg.org/files/4705 /4705-h/4705-h.htm. Accessed December 11, 2018.

Kant, Immanuel. "The Critique of Pure Reason." In *The Philosophy of Kant: Immanuel Kant's Moral and Political Writings*, 25–42, translated and edited by Carl J. Friedrich. New York: Modern Library, 1993.

Korsgaard, Christine. *The Sources of Normativity*. Cambridge: Cambridge University Press, 1996.

MacIntyre, Alasdair. *Whose Justice? Which Rationality?* Notre Dame, IN: University of Notre Dame Press, 1988.

Moreland, J. P. *Universals*. Central Problems in Philosophy series, edited by John Shand. Montreal, Canada: McGill-Queen's University Press, 2001.

O'Donnell, Rod. "The Epistemology of J. M. Keynes." *British Journal for the Philosophy of Science* 41, no. 3 (1990): 333–50.

Osler, Margaret. "Boyle's Philosophy of Nature." In *Philosophy, Science, and Religion in England, 1640–1700*, edited by Richard W. F. Kroll, Richard Ashcraft, and Perez Zagorin, 178–98. Cambridge: Cambridge University Press, 1992.

Schacht, Richard. "Nietzsche, Friedrich Wilhelm." In *The Cambridge Dictionary of Philosophy*, 2nd ed., edited by Robert Audi, 613–17. New York: Cambridge University Press, 1999.

Sellars, Wilfrid. *Naturalism and Ontology*. Atascadero, CA: Ridgeview, 1979.

Sepkoski, David. "Nominalism and Constructivism in Seventeenth-Century Mathematical Philosophy." *Historia Mathematica* 32 (2005): 33–59.

Smith, R. Scott. *In Search of Moral Knowledge*. Downers Grove, IL: InterVarsity Press, 2014.

———. "Rethinking the Fact–Value Split: A Place for Religion in the Public Square?" In *Multiculturalism and the Convergence of Faith and Practical Wisdom in Modern Society*, edited by Ana-Maria Pascal, 63–80. Hershey, PA: IGI Global, 2016.

Sowell, Thomas. *Disparities and Discrimination*. New York: Basic Books, 2018.

Thornhill, Christopher. "Historicism." In *Routledge Encyclopedia of Philosophy*. Abingdon-on-Thames, UK: Routledge, 1998.

Chapter 3, Martin

Bailey, Alison. "On Anger, Silence, and Epistemic Injustice." *Royal Institute of Philosophy Supplements* 84 (2018): 93–115.

Brennan, Jason. *Libertarianism: What Everyone Needs to Know*. Oxford: Oxford University Press, 2012.

Crawford, Sue, and Elinor Ostrom. "A Grammar of Institutions." *American Political Science Review* 89, no. 3 (1995): 582–600.

Fehr, Ernst, and Simon Gächter. "Altruistic Punishment in Humans." *Nature* 415 (2002): 137–40.

Gaus, Gerald. "Hayekian 'Classical' Liberalism." In *The Routledge Handbook of Libertarianism*, edited by Jason Brennan, Bas van der Vossen, and David Schmidtz, 34–52. New York: Routledge, 2018.

Haidt, Jonathan. *The Righteous Mind: Why Good People Are Divided by Politics and Religion*. New York: Pantheon, 2012.

Hardin, Russell. *Morality within the Limits of Reason*. Chicago: University of Chicago Press, 1988.

Hayek, F. A. *The Constitution of Liberty: The Definitive Edition*. Edited by Ronald Hamowy. Chicago: University of Chicago Press, [1960] 2011.

———. *The Mirage of Social Justice*. Vol. 2, *Law, Legislation, and Liberty: A New Statement of the Liberal Principles of Justice and Political Economy*. Chicago: University of Chicago Press, 1976.

———. *Rules and Order*. Vol. 1, *Law, Legislation, and Liberty: A New Statement of the Liberal Principles of Justice and Political Economy*. Chicago: University of Chicago Press, 1973.

———. "Scientism and the Study of Society." *Economica* 9, no. 35 (1942): 267–91.

———. "What Is 'Social'? What Does It Mean?" In *Studies in Philosophy, Politics, and Economics*, 237–47. Chicago: University of Chicago Press, 1967.

Kiel, Doug. "Whiteness and the Lengthening Arc toward Justice." *Cultural Anthropology: Hot Spots*, January 18, 2017. https://culanth.org/fieldsights/whiteness-and-the-lengthening-arc-toward-justice.

Martin, Adam. "The New Egalitarianism." *The Independent Review* 22, no. 1 (Summer 2017): 15–25.

McCloskey, Deirdre N. *The Bourgeois Virtues: Ethics for an Age of Commerce*. Chicago: University of Chicago Press, 2006.

Ostrom, Vincent. *The Meaning of Democracy and the Vulnerability of Democracies*. Ann Arbor: University of Michigan Press, 1997.

Rawls, John. *A Theory of Justice*. Cambridge, MA: Harvard University Press, 1971.

Rognlie, Matthew. *Deciphering the Fall and Rise in the Net Capital Share: Accumulation or Scarcity?* Brookings Papers on Economic Activity. Washington, DC: Brookings Institution, 2015.

Smith, Adam. *The Theory of Moral Sentiments*. Indianapolis, IN: Liberty Fund, [1759] 1982.

Smith, Vernon L., and Bart J. Wilson. "Fair and Impartial Spectators in Experimental Economic Behavior." *Review of Behavioral Economics* 1, nos. 1–2 (2014): 1–26.

Tomasi, John. *Free Market Fairness*. Princeton, NJ: Princeton University Press, 2012.

Wagner, Richard. *Mind, Society, and Human Action*. New York: Routledge, 2010.

Chapter 4, Levy

Aristotle. *Nicomachean Ethics*. Translated by Joe Sachs. Newburyport, MA: Focus Publishing, 2002.

Aquinas, Thomas. *Aquinas: Political Writings*. R. W. Dyson, ed. Cambridge, UK: Cambridge University Press, 2002.

Beever, Allan. *Forgotten Justice*. Oxford: Oxford University Press, 2013.

Brennan, Jason, and John Tomasi. "Classical Liberalism." In *The Oxford Handbook of Political Philosophy*, edited by David Estlund, 115–32. Oxford: Oxford University Press, 2012.

Cohen, G. A. *Rescuing Justice and Equality*. Cambridge, MA: Harvard University Press, 2008.

De Jasay, Anthony. "Justice as Something Else." *Cato Journal* 16, no. 2 (1996): 161–73.

Fleischacker, Samuel. *A Short History of Distributive Justice*. Cambridge, MA: Harvard University Press, 2004.

Fraser, Nancy. *Justice Interruptus: Reflections on the "Postsocialist" Condition*. New York: Routledge, 1996.

Hayek, F. A. *The Fatal Conceit: The Errors of Socialism*. Chicago: University of Chicago Press, 1988.

———. *The Mirage of Social Justice*. Vol. 2, *Law, Legislation, and Liberty: A New Statement of the Liberal Principles of Justice and Political Economy*. Chicago: University of Chicago Press, 1976.

———. *Rules and Order*. Vol. 1, *Law, Legislation, and Liberty: A New Statement of the Liberal Principles of Justice and Political Economy*. Chicago: University of Chicago Press, 1973.

Johnston, David. "Hayek's Attack on Social Justice." *Critical Review* 11, no. 1 (1997): 81–100.

Levy, Jacob T. "Political Libertarianism." In *The Cambridge Handbook of Classical Liberal Thought*, edited by M. Todd Henderson, 153–75. Cambridge: Cambridge University Press, 2018.

———. "Review: *Rescuing Justice and Equality* by G. A. Cohen." *Political Theory* 38, no. 4 (2010): 593–96.

———. "There Is No Such Thing as Ideal Theory." *Social Philosophy and Policy* 33, nos. 1–2 (2016): 312–33.

———. "Who's Afraid of Judith Shklar?" *Foreign Policy*, July 2018. https://foreignpolicy.com/2018/07/16/whos-afraid-of-judith-shklar-liberalism/.

Lukes, Steven. "Social Justice: The Hayekian Challenge." *Critical Review* 11, no. 1 (1997): 65–80.

Nozick, Robert. *Anarchy, State, and Utopia*. New York: Basic Books, 1974.

Rawls, John. *A Theory of Justice.* Cambridge, MA: Harvard University Press, 1971.

Plato. *The Republic of Plato.* Allan Bloom, and Adam Kirsch, eds. 3rd ed. New York, NY: Basic Books, 2016.

Schelling, Thomas. "Models of Segregation." *American Economic Review* 59, no. 2 (1969): 488–93.

Shklar, Judith. *The Faces of Injustice.* New Haven, CT: Yale University Press, 1990.

Smith, Adam. *An Inquiry into the Nature and Causes of the Wealth of Nations.* 2 vols. Indianapolis, IN: Liberty Fund, [1776] 1982.

―――. *The Theory of Moral Sentiments.* Indianapolis, IN: Liberty Fund, [1759] 1976.

Taylor, Charles. *Multiculturalism and the Politics of Recognition.* Princeton, NJ: Princeton University Press, 1993.

Tomasi, John. *Free Market Fairness.* Princeton, NJ: Princeton University Press, 2012.

Young, Iris Marion. *Justice and the Politics of Difference.* Princeton, NJ: Princeton University Press, 1989.

Chapter 5, Vallier

Buchanan, James, and Gordon Tullock. *The Calculus of Consent.* Ann Arbor: University of Michigan Press, 1962.

Burgin, Angus. *The Great Persuasion: Reinventing Markets since the Depression.* Cambridge, MA: Harvard University Press, 2012.

Caldwell, Bruce. *Hayek's Challenge: An Intellectual Biography of F. A. Hayek.* Chicago: University of Chicago Press, 2004.

Gaus, Gerald. "Hayekian 'Classical' Liberalism." In *The Routledge Handbook of Libertarianism,* edited by Jason Brennan, Bas van der Vossen, and David Schmidtz, 34–52. New York: Routledge, 2018.

Harsanyi, John. "Cardinal Welfare, Individualistic Ethics, and Interpersonal Comparisons of Utility." *Journal of Political Economy* 63 (1955): 309–21.

Hayek, F. A. *The Constitution of Liberty: The Definitive Edition.* Edited by Ronald Hamowy. Chicago: University of Chicago Press, [1960] 2011.

―――. *The Fatal Conceit: The Errors of Socialism.* Chicago: University of Chicago Press, [1988] 1991.

―――. *The Mirage of Social Justice.* Vol. 2, *Law, Legislation, and Liberty: A New Statement of the Liberal Principles of Justice and Political Economy.* Chicago: University of Chicago Press, 1978.

―――. *The Political Order of a Free People.* Vol. 3, *Law, Legislation, and Liberty: A New Statement of the Liberal Principles of Justice and Political Economy.* Chicago: University of Chicago Press, 1979.

————. *The Road to Serfdom: The Definitive Edition*. Edited by Bruce Caldwell. London: Routledge, 2007.

————. *Rules and Order*. Vol. 1, *Law, Legislation, and Liberty: A New Statement of the Liberal Principles of Justice and Political Economy*. Chicago: University of Chicago Press, 1973.

————. "The Use of Knowledge in Society." *American Economic Review* 35, no. 4 (1945): 519–30.

James, Aaron. "Constructing Justice for Existing Practice: Rawls and the Status Quo." *Philosophy and Public Affairs* 33, no. 3 (2005): 281–316.

Peter, Fabienne. "Political Legitimacy." *Stanford Encyclopedia of Philosophy* Archive, April 29, 2010, revised April 24, 2017. https://plato.stanford.edu/archives/sum2017/entries/legitimacy/.

Rawls, John. "Constitutional Liberty and the Concept of Justice." In *Nomos VI: Justice*, edited by C. J. Friedrich and John Chapman, 98–125. New York: Atherton Press, 1963.

————. *Justice as Fairness: A Restatement*. Edited by Erin Kelly. New Delhi: Universal Law, 2001.

————. *A Theory of Justice*. Rev. ed. Cambridge, MA: Belknap Press of Harvard University Press, [1971] 1999.

Sugden, Robert. "Normative Judgments and Spontaneous Order: The Contractarian Element in Hayek's Thought." *Constitutional Political Economy* 4, no. 3 (1993): 393–424.

Tomasi, John. *Free Market Fairness*. Princeton, NJ: Princeton University Press, 2012.

Chapter 6, D'Amico

Anderson, Terry L., and Peter J. Hill. *The Not So Wild, Wild West: Property Rights on the Frontier*. Stanford, CA: Stanford University Press, 2004.

Benson, Bruce. "Legal Evolution in Primitive Societies." *Journal of Institutional and Theoretical Economics* 144, no. 5 (1988): 772–88.

Billson, Janet, and Kyra Mancini. *Inuit Women: Their Powerful Spirit in a Century of Change*. Lanham, MD: Rowman & Littlefield, 2007.

Boas, Franz. *Handbook of American Indian Languages*. Vol. 2. Cambridge: Cambridge University Press, [1922] 2013.

Briggs, Jean L. *Never in Anger: Portrait of an Eskimo Family*. Cambridge, MA: Harvard University Press, 1971.

Brody, Hugh. *The People's Land: Eskimos and Whites in the Eastern Arctic*. New York: Penguin Books, 1977.

Buchanan, James. "Rawls on Justice as Fairness." *Public Choice* 13 (1972): 123–28.

Capaldi, Nicholas, and Gordon Lloyd. *The Two Narratives of Political Economy*. Hoboken, NJ: Wiley, 2009.

Ellickson, Robert C. *Order without Law: How Neighbors Settle Disputes*. Cambridge, MA: Harvard University Press, 1994.

Frohlich, Norman, Joe A. Oppenheimer, and Cheryl L. Eavey. "Laboratory Results on Rawls's Distributive Justice." *British Journal of Political Science* 17, no. 1 (1987): 1–21.

Gambetta, Diego. *The Sicilian Mafia: The Business of Private Protection*. Cambridge, MA: Harvard University Press, 1996.

Harsanyi, John. "Can the Maximin Principle Serve as the Basis for Morality?" *American Political Science Review* 69, no. 2 (1975): 594–606.

Hayek, F. A. *The Constitution of Liberty*. Chicago: University of Chicago Press, 1960.

———. *The Mirage of Social Justice*. Vol. 2, *Law, Legislation, and Liberty: A New Statement of the Liberal Principles of Justice and Political Economy*. Chicago: University of Chicago Press, 1978.

Hoebel, E. "The Eskimo: Rudimentary Law in a Primitive Anarchy." In *The Law of Primitive Man: A Study in Comparative Legal Dynamics*, 67–99. Cambridge, MA: Harvard University Press, 1954.

La Porta, Rafael, Florencio Lopez-de-Silanes, and Andrei Shleifer. "The Economic Consequences of Legal Origins." *Journal of Economic Literature* 46, no. 2 (2008): 285–332.

Leeson, Peter. *The Invisible Hook: The Hidden Economics of Pirates*. Princeton, NJ: Princeton University Press, 2011.

Matthiasson, John S. *Living on the Land: Change among the Inuit of Baffin Island*. Toronto: University of Toronto Press, 1992.

Posner, Richard A. "A Theory of Primitive Society, with Special Reference to Law." *Journal of Law and Economics* 23, no. 1 (1980): 1–53.

Rawls, John. *A Theory of Justice*. Cambridge, MA: Harvard University Press, 1971.

Skarbek, David. *The Social Order of the Underworld: How Prison Gangs Govern the American Penal System*. Oxford: Oxford University Press, 2014.

Tomasi, John. *Free Market Fairness*. Princeton, NJ: Princeton University Press, 2012.

Chapter 7, Watkins Jr.

Bastiat, Frédéric. *The Law*. Auburn, AL: Ludwig von Mises Institute, [1850] 2007.

Calvin, John. *Institutes of the Christian Religion*. Peabody, MA: Hendrickson Publishers, Inc., [1559] 2008.

Dworkin, Ronald. "Justice and the Good Life." Lecture presented at the University of Kansas, Lawrence, April 1990.

———. *Law's Empire*. Portland, OR: Hart Publishing, 1986.

Ely, James W. Jr. *The Guardian of Every Other Right*. New York: Oxford University Press, 1992.

Finnis, John. *Natural Law and Natural Rights*. Oxford: Clarendon Press, 1980.

Hart, H. L. A. *The Concept of Law*. New York: Oxford University Press, 1997.

Hayek, F. A. *The Constitution of Liberty*. Chicago: University of Chicago Press, 1960.

———. *The Mirage of Social Justice*. Vol. 2, *Law, Legislation, and Liberty: A New Statement of the Liberal Principles of Justice and Political Economy*. Chicago: University of Chicago Press, 1976.

Herzog, Tamar. *A Short History of European Law*. Cambridge, MA: Harvard University Press, 2018.

Humboldt, Wilhelm von. *The Limits of State Action*. Indianapolis, IN: Liberty Fund, [1854] 1993.

The International Forum for Social Development. *Social Justice in an Open World: The Role of the United Nations*. New York: United Nations, 2006.

Justinian. *The Digest of Justinian*. Translated by Theodor Mommsen, Paul Krueger, and Alan Watson. Philadelphia: University of Pennsylvania Press, 1985.

Needham, N. R. *2000 Years of Christ's Power*. Vol 1. London: Grace Publications Trust, 1997.

New Hampshire Constitution. 1784. https://www.nh.gov/glance/constitution.htm.

Nozick, Robert. *Anarchy, State, and Utopia*. New York: Basic Books, 1974.

Perry, Ralph Barton. *Puritanism and Democracy*. New York: Vanguard Press, 1944.

Presser, Stephen B. *Law Professors: Three Centuries of Shaping American Law*. St. Paul, MN: West Academic, 2017.

Raico, Ralph. *The Prussian Aristocrat Who Spoke Out for Liberty*. Irvington-on-Hudson, NY: The Foundation for Economic Education, 2016. https://fee.org/articles/the-prussian-aristocrat-who-spoke-out-for-liberty/.

Rawls, John. *A Theory of Justice*. Cambridge, MA: Harvard University Press, 1971.

Richards, Peter Judson. "Property and Epikeia: Theory, Life and Practice in the Western Christian Tradition." *University of Detroit Mercy Law Review* 82 (2004): 599–647.

Stark, Rodney. *How Christianity Led to Freedom, Capitalism, and the Success of the West*. Oakland, CA: Independent Institute, 2005. http://www.independent.org/news/article.asp?id=1809.

Stein, Peter. *Roman Law in European History*. Cambridge: Cambridge University Press, 1999.

Chapter 8, Gill

Akerloff, George A. "The Market for 'Lemons': Quality Uncertainty and the Market Mechanism." *Quarterly Journal of Economics* 84, no. 3 (1970): 488–500.

Becker, Gary. "A Theory of Marriage: Part I." *Journal of Political Economy* 81, no. 4 (1973): 813–46.

Bolton, Lisa E., Luk Warlop, and Joseph W. Alba. "Consumer Perceptions of Price (Un) Fairness." *Journal of Consumer Research* 29, no. 4 (2003): 474–91.

Buchanan, James M. *The Limits of Liberty: Between Anarchy and Leviathan.* Indianapolis, IN: Liberty Fund, [1975] 2000.

Dunbar, Robin. "Neocortex Size as a Constraint on Group Size in Primates." *Journal of Human Evolution* 22, no. 6 (1992): 469–93.

Gill, Anthony. "An Economic and Pedagogical Defense of Tipping." *Journal of Private Enterprise* 33, no. 1 (2018): 79–102.

Gladwell, Malcolm. *The Tipping Point: How Little Things Can Make a Big Difference.* Boston: Little, Brown, 2000.

Hayek, F. A. "The Use of Knowledge in Society." *American Economic Review* 35, no. 4 (1945): 519–30.

Kirzner, Israel M. *Competition and Entrepreneurship.* Indianapolis, IN: Liberty Fund, [1973] 2013.

Mauss, Marcel. *The Gift: Forms and Functions of Exchange in Archaic Societies.* Translated by W. D. Halls. New York: Norton, [1950] 2000.

Munger, Michael. "Euvoluntary or Not, Exchange Is Just." *Social Philosophy and Policy* 28, no. 2 (2011): 192–211.

Perry, Mark J. "The General Public Thinks the Average Company Makes a 36% Profit Margin, Which Is about 5X Too High: Part II." *Carpe Diem,* AEI, January 15, 2018. http://www.aei.org/publication/the-public-thinks-the-average-company-makes-a -36-profit-margin-which-is-about-5x-too-high-part-ii/?fbclid5IwAR2uDo6IMYSo qMYzG9hxUH7mqXG9I2MIHF7VZ36w9qty2tdKvC2XtWTKD8.

Rawls, John. *A Theory of Justice.* Cambridge, MA: Harvard University Press, 1971.

Schlee, Edward E. "Buyer Experimentation and Introductory Pricing." *Journal of Economic Behavior & Organization* 44, no. 3 (2001): 347–62.

Schoeck, Helmut. *Envy: A Theory of Social Behavior.* Indianapolis, IN: Liberty Fund, [1966] 1987.

Skyrms, Brian. *Evolution of the Social Contract.* Cambridge: Cambridge University Press, 2014.

Smith, Adam. *An Inquiry into the Nature and Causes of the Wealth of Nations.* Indianapolis, IN: Liberty Fund, [1776] 1976.

———. *The Theory of Moral Sentiments.* Indianapolis, IN: Liberty Fund, [1790] 1976.

Taylor, Michael. *Community, Anarchy, & Liberty.* Cambridge: Cambridge University Press, 1982.

Varian, Hal R. *Intermediate Microeconomics: A Modern Approach*. 9th ed. New York: Norton, 2014.

Chapter 9, Otteson

Aristotle. "Physics." In *The Complete Works of Aristotle: The Revised Oxford Translation*, vol. 1, edited by Jonathan Barnes, 315–446. Princeton, NJ: Princeton University Press, 1984.

Barry, Brian. *Why Social Justice Matters*. Malden, MA: Polity Press, 2005.

Cohen, G. A. *Why Not Socialism?* Princeton, NJ: Princeton University Press, 2009.

Conly, Sarah. *Against Autonomy: Justifying Coercive Paternalism*. New York: Cambridge University Press, 2013.

Deneen, Patrick J. *Why Liberalism Failed*. New Haven, CT: Yale University Press, 2018.

Forbes. "The World's Billionaires." https://www.forbes.com/billionaires/list/. Accessed February 26, 2019.

Guthrie, W. K. C. *The Greek Philosophers from Thales to Aristotle*. New York: Harper & Row, 1975.

Hardin, Garrett. "The Tragedy of the Commons." *Science* 162, no. 3859 (1968): 1243–48.

Hayek, Friedrich A. *The Mirage of Social Justice*. Vol. 2, *Law, Legislation, and Liberty: A New Statement of the Liberal Principles of Justice and Political Economy*. Chicago: University of Chicago Press, 1976.

Hume, David. "Of Interest." In *David Hume: Essays Moral, Political, and Literary*, edited by Eugene F. Miller, 295–307. Indianapolis, IN: Liberty Fund, [1754] 1985.

———. "Of the Jealousy of Trade." In *David Hume: Essays Moral, Political, and Literary*, edited by Eugene F. Miller, 327–31. Indianapolis, IN: Liberty Fund, [1754] 1985.

———. "Of Refinement in the Arts." In *David Hume: Essays Moral, Political, and Literary*, edited by Eugene F. Miller, 268–80. Indianapolis, IN: Liberty Fund, [1754] 1985.

Linker, Maureen. *Intellectual Empathy: Critical Thinking for Social Justice*. Ann Arbor: University of Michigan Press, 2015.

Mazzucato, Mariana. *The Value of Everything: Making and Taking in the Global Economy*. New York: PublicAffairs, 2018.

McCloskey, Deirdre N. *Bourgeois Equality: How Ideas, Not Capital or Institutions, Enriched the World*. Chicago: University of Chicago Press, 2016.

Olson, Mancur. *The Logic of Collective Action: Public Goods and the Theory of Groups*. Cambridge, MA: Harvard University Press, 1965.

Otteson, James R. "The Misuse of Egalitarianism in Society." *The Independent Review* 22, no. 1 (Summer 2017): 37–47.

Piketty, Thomas. *Capital in the Twenty-First Century*. Cambridge, MA: Harvard University Press, 2014.

Pinker, Steven. *Enlightenment Now: The Case for Reason, Science, Humanism, and Progress.* New York: Viking, 2018.

Plato. *Euthyphro.* In *Five Dialogues: Euthyphro, Apology, Crito, Meno, Phaedo,* 2nd ed., translated by G. M. A. Grube, revised by John M. Cooper, 2–20. Indianapolis, IN: Hackett, 2002.

————. *Republic.* Translated by G. M. A. Grube, revised by C. D. C. Reeve. Indianapolis, IN: Hackett, 1992.

Rawls, John. *A Theory of Justice.* Cambridge, MA: Harvard University Press, 1971.

Ridley, Matt. *The Rational Optimist: How Prosperity Evolves.* New York: Harper, 2010.

Rosling, Hans, Ola Rosling, and Anna Rosling Rönnlund. *Factfulness: Ten Reasons We're Wrong about the World—and Why Things Are Better Than You Think.* New York: Flatiron Books, 2018.

Sandel, Michael. *What Money Can't Buy: The Moral Limits of Markets.* New York: Farrar, Straus and Giroux, 2012.

Satz, Debra. *The Moral Limits of Markets: Why Some Things Should Not Be for Sale.* New York: Oxford University Press, 2012.

Schor, Juliet B. *Born to Buy.* New York: Scribner's, 2004.

Schumpeter, Joseph A. *Capitalism, Socialism, and Democracy.* New York: Harper, 1942.

Sensoy, Ozlem, and Robin DiAngelo. *Is Everyone Really Equal? An Introduction to Key Concepts in Social Justice Education.* 2nd ed. New York: Teachers College Press, 2017.

Shermer, Michael. *Why People Believe Weird Things: Pseudoscience, Superstition, and Other Confusions of Our Time.* New York: Holt, 2002.

Smith, Adam. *An Inquiry into the Nature and Causes of the Wealth of Nations.* Edited by R. H. Campbell and A. S. Skinner. Indianapolis, IN: Liberty Fund, [1776] 1981.

————. *The Theory of Moral Sentiments.* Edited by D. D. Raphael and A. L. Macfie. Indianapolis, IN: Liberty Fund, [1759] 1982.

Sunstein, Cass R. *Free Markets and Social Justice.* New York: Oxford University Press, 1997.

Thaler, Richard H. *Misbehaving: The Making of Behavioral Economics.* New York: Norton, 2015.

Tomasi, John. *Free Market Fairness.* Princeton, NJ: Princeton University Press, 2012.

Ubel, Peter A. *Free Market Madness: Why Human Nature Is at Odds with Economics—and Why It Matters.* Cambridge, MA: Harvard Business Press, 2009.

Chapter 10, Stoner Jr.

Aristotle. *Nicomachean Ethics.* Translated by Robert C. Bartlett and Susan D. Collins. Chicago: University of Chicago Press, 2011.

_____. *Politics*. Translated by Carnes Lord. 2nd ed. Chicago: University of Chicago Press, 2013.

Fortin, Ernest. "Natural Law and Social Justice." In *Classical Christianity and the Political Order: Reflections on the Theological-Political Problem*. Vol. 2, *Ernest L. Fortin: Collected Essays*, edited by J. Brian Benestad, 223–41. Lanham, MD: Rowman & Littlefield, 1996.

Francis. *Laudato Sí: On Care for Our Common Home*. May 24, 2015. Official Vatican translation. http://w2.vatican.va/content/francesco/en/encyclicals/documents/papa-francesco_20150524_enciclica-laudato-si.html.

Hegel, Georg Wilhelm Friedrich. *Philosophy of Right*. Translated by T. M. Knox. Oxford: Oxford University Press, [1821] 1967.

John Paul II. *Centesimus annus: On the Hundredth Anniversary of Rerum novarum*. May 1, 1991. Official Vatican translation. http://w2.vatican.va/content/john-paul-ii/en/encyclicals/documents/hf_jp-ii_enc_01051991_centesimus-annus.html.

Kraynak, Robert. "The Origins of 'Social Justice' in the Natural Law Philosophy of Antonio Rosmini." *Review of Politics* 80, no. 1 (2018): 3–29.

Leo XIII. *Rerum novarum: On Capital and Labor*. May 15, 1891. Official Vatican translation. http://w2.vatican.va/content/leo-xiii/en/encyclicals/documents/hf_l-xiii_enc_15051891_rerum-novarum.html.

Locke, John. *Two Treatises of Government*. Edited by Peter Laslett. Cambridge: Cambridge University Press, [1689] 1988.

Marx, Karl. "The Communist Manifesto." In *The Marx-Engels Reader*, 2nd ed., edited by Robert C. Tucker, 469–500. New York: Norton, [1848] 1978.

_____. *Critique of Hegel's "Philosophy of Right."* Translated by Annette Jolin and Joseph O'Malley. Cambridge: Cambridge University Press, [1843] 1970.

Pius XI. *Quadragesimo anno: On Reconstruction of the Social Order*. May 15, 1931. Official Vatican translation. http://w2.vatican.va/content/pius-xi/en/encyclicals/documents/hf_p-xi_enc_19310515_quadragesimo-anno.html.

Rosmini, Antonio. [1848] 2007. *The Constitution under Social Justice*. Lanham, MD: Lexington Books, [1848] 2007.

_____. *The Philosophy of Right*. 2 vols. Durham, UK: Rosmini House, [1864] 1993.

Shils, Edward. "The Virtue of Civil Society." In *The Civil Society Reader*, edited by Virginia Hodgkinson and Michael W. Foley, 292–305. Medford, MA: Tufts University Press, 1997.

Shulsky, Abram N. "The 'Infrastructure' of Aristotle's *Politics*: Aristotle on Economics and Politics." In *Essays on the Foundations of Aristotelian Political Science*, edited by Carnes Lord and David K. O'Connor, 74–111. Berkeley: University of California Press, 1991.

Smith, Adam. *An Inquiry into the Nature and Causes of the Wealth of Nations*. 2 vols. Indianapolis, IN: Liberty Fund, [1776] 1982.

Stoner, James R. Jr. "Property, Common Law, and John Locke." In *Natural Law and Contemporary Public Policy*, edited by David Forte, 193–218. Washington, DC: Georgetown University Press, 1998.

Walzer, Michael. "A Better Vision: The Idea of Civil Society." In *The Civil Society Reader*, edited by Virginia Hodgkinson and Michael W. Foley, 306–21. Medford, MA: Tufts University Press, 1990.

Whaples, Robert M. "Introduction: The Economics of Pope Francis." In *Pope Francis and the Caring Society*, edited by Robert M. Whaples. Oakland, CA: Independent Institute, 2017.

Chapter 11, Moore

Aristotle. *Nicomachean Ethics*. Norfolk, VA: Createspace, 2012.

Boethius. *The Consolation of Philosophy*. Translated by H. R. James. New York: Barnes and Noble, 2005. (Original written in Latin around 524.)

Francis. *Evangelii gaudium*. 2013. Official Vatican translation. http://w2.vatican.va /content/francesco/en/apost_exhortations/documents/papa-francesco_esortazione-ap_ 20131124_evangelii-gaudium.html.

Gutiérrez, Gustavo. *A Theology of Liberation*. Maryknoll, NY: Orbis Books, 1988.

John Paul II. *Laborem exercens*. September 14, 1981. Official Vatican translation. http://w2.vatican.va/content/john-paul-ii/en/encyclicals/documents/hf_jp-ii_ enc_14091981_laboremexercens.html.

King, Martin Luther Jr. Nobel Peace Prize acceptance speech, December 10, 1964. http:// www.nobelprizes.com/nobel/peace/MLK-nobel.html.

Kirzner, Israel. *Discovery, Capitalism, and Distributive Justice*. Indianapolis, IN: Liberty Fund, 2016.

Leo XIII. *Rerum novarum*. May 15, 1891. Official Vatican translation. http://w2.vatican .va/content/leo-xiii/en/encyclicals/documents/hf_l-xiii_enc_15051891_rerum-novarum.html.

Locke, John. *Second Treatise of Government*. Redditch, UK: Read Books, [1689] 2018.

Martinez, Gabriel. "Uneven Playing Fields: Markets and Oligarchy." In *Pope Francis and the Caring Society*, edited by Robert Whaples, 69–86. Oakland, CA: Independent Institute, 2017.

McCloskey, Deirdre N. *The Bourgeois Virtues: Ethics for an Age of Commerce*. Chicago: University of Chicago Press, 2006.

Novak, Michael. "Defining Social Justice." *First Things*, December 2000. https:// www .firstthings.com/article/2000/12/defining-social-justice.

_____. *Social Justice: Not What You Think It Is*. Washington, DC: Heritage Foundation, 2009. https://www.heritage.org/poverty-and-inequality/report/social-justice-not -what-youthink-it.

Schumacher, E. F. *Small Is Beautiful: A Study of Economics as If People Mattered*. London: Bond and Briggs, 1975.

Schumpeter, Joseph A. *Capitalism, Socialism, and Democracy*. 2nd ed. Floyd, VA: Wilder, 1942.

Sibley, Angus. *Catholic Economics: Alternatives to the Jungle*. Collegeville, MN: Liturgical Press, 2015.

Smith, Adam. *The Theory of Moral Sentiments*. Washington, DC: Regnery, [1759] 1997.

Tornielli, Andrea, and Giacomo Galeazzi. *This Economy Kills: Pope Francis on Capitalism and Social Justice*. Translated by Demetrio S. Yocum. Collegeville, MN: Liturgical Press, 2015.

Tullock, Gordon. *The Economics and Politics of Wealth Redistribution*. Indianapolis, IN: Liberty Fund, 2005.

Wood, Gordon S. *The Creation of the American Republic, 1776–1787*. Chapel Hill: University of North Carolina Press, 1998.

Zięba, Maciej. *Papal Economics: The Catholic Church on Democratic Capitalism, from "Rerum Novarum" to "Caritas in veritate."* Wilmington, DE: ISI Books, 2013.

Chapter 12, Schlag

Benedict XVI. Encyclical *Caritas in veritate*.

Bergoglio, Jorge Mario–Papa Francesco. *Interviste e conversazioni con i giornalisti: Due anni di Pontificato*. Vatican City: LEV, 2015.

Berman, Harold J. *Law and Revolution, II: The Impact of the Protestant Reformations on the Western Legal Tradition*. Cambridge, MA: Harvard University Press, 2003.

Boff, Leonardo, and Clodovis Boff. *Introducing Liberation Theology*. Maryknoll, NY: Orbis Books, [1986] 2015.

CELAM. Aparecida Document. 2007. http://www.celam.org/aparecida/Ingles.pdf.

Congregation for the Doctrine of the Faith. "Explanatory Note on the Notification on the Works of Father Jon Sobrino, SJ." Vatican City, 2006. http://www.vatican.va/roman _curia/congregations/cfaith/documents/rc_con_cfaith_doc_20061126_nota -sobrino_en.html.

_____. "Instruction on Certain Aspects of the 'Theology of Liberation.'" Vatican City, 1984. https://www.vatican.va/roman_curia/congregations/cfaith/documents /rc_con_cfaith_doc_19840806_theology-liberation_en.html.

————. "Instruction on Christian Freedom and Liberation *Libertatis Conscientia*." Vatican City, 1986. http://www.vatican.va/roman_curia/congregations/cfaith /documents/rc_con_cfaith_doc_19860322_freedom-liberation_en.html.

————. "Notification on the Works of Father Jon Sobrino, SJ." Vatican City, 2006. http://www.vatican.va/roman_curia/congregations/cfaith/documents/rc_con _cfaith_doc_20061126_notification-sobrino_en.html.

Curnow, Rohan M. "Which Preferential Option for the Poor? A History of the Doctrine's Bifurcation." *Modern Theology* 31, no. 1 (January 2015): 27–59.

Dianin, Giampaolo. *Luigi Taparelli d'Azeglio (1793–1862): Il significato della sua opera, al tempo del rinnovamento neoscolastico, per l'evoluzione della teologia morale*. Rome, Italy: Pontificio Seminario Lombardo, 2000.

Enderle, Georges. "The Option for the Poor and Business Ethics." In *The Preferential Option for the Poor beyond Theology*, edited by Daniel G. Groody and Gustavo Gutiérrez. Notre Dame, IN: University of Notre Dame Press, 2014.

Ferré, Alberto Methol, and Alver Metalli. *Il Papa e il Filosofo*. Siena, Italy: Cantagalli, 2014.

Francis. "Address during the Conferral of the Charlemagne Prize." http://w2.vatican.va /content/francesco/en/speeches/2016/may/documents/papa-francesco_20160506_ premio-carlo-magno.html.

————. "Address to Participants in the Ecclesial Convention of the Diocese of Rome." June 17, 2013. http://w2.vatican.va/content/francesco/en/speeches/2013/june /documents/papa-francesco_20130617_convegno-diocesano-roma.html.

————. "Address to the Centesimus Annus Pro Pontifice Foundation." May 25, 2013. http://w2.vatican.va/content/francesco/en/speeches/2013/may/documents/papa -francesco_20130525_centesimus-annus-pro-pontifice.html.

————. Apostolic Exhortation *Evangelii Gaudium*.

————. Encyclical *Laudato Sí*.

Gera, Lucio. "Cultura y dependencia a luz de la reflexión teológica." In *Escritos Teológico-Pastorales de Lucio Gera*. Vol. 1, *Del Preconcilio a la Conferencia de Puebla (1956–1981)*, edited by Virginia Raquel Azcuy et al., 605–59. Buenos Aires, Argentina: Agape Libros–Facultad de Teología UCA, 2006.

————. "Pueblo, religión del pueblo e iglesia." In *Escritos Teológico-Pastorales de Lucio Gera*. Vol. 1, *Del Preconcilio a la Conferencia de Puebla (1956–1981)*, edited by Virginia Raquel Azcuy et al., 717–44. Buenos Aires, Argentina: Agape Libros–Facultad de Teología UCA, 2006.

Gregg, Samuel. "Understanding Pope Francis: Argentina, Economic Failure, and the *Teología del Pueblo*." In *Pope Francis and the Caring Society*, edited by Robert M. Whaples. Oakland, CA: Independent Institute, 2017.

Gutiérrez, Gustavo. *Teología de la Liberación*. Salamanca, Spain: Ediciones Sígueme, [1971] 2009. (18th Spanish edition, with an important preface added to the 14th Spanish edition [1990].)

Hamilton, Alexander, James Madison, and John Jay. *The Federalist Papers*. Edited by Clinton Rossiter. New York: Signet Classics, [1787] 2003.

Ivereigh, Austen. *The Great Reformer: Francis and the Making of a Radical Pope*. New York: Holt, 2014.

John Paul II. Apostolic Exhortation *Ecclesia in America*. Vatican City: LEV, 1999.

―――. Apostolic Exhortation *Vita Consecrata*. Vatican City: LEV, 1996.

―――. Apostolic Letter *Novo Millennio Ineunte*. Vatican City: LEV, 2001.

―――. Apostolic Letter *Tertio Millennio Adveniente*. Vatican City: LEV, 1994.

―――. Encyclical *Centesimus Annus*. Vatican City: LEV, 1991.

―――. Encyclical *Redemptoris Mater*. Vatican City: LEV, 1987.

―――. Encyclical *Sollicitudo Rei Socialis*. Vatican City: LEV, 1987.

Kracht, Hermann-Josef Grosse. *Wilhelm Emmanuel von Ketteler: Ein Bischof in den sozialen Debatten seiner Zeit*. Cologne, Germany: Ketteler Verlag, 2011.

Langhorst, Peter. "Soziale Gerechtigkeit." In *Lexikon für Theologie und Kirche*, vol. 9, edited by Walter Kasper and others. Freiburg, Germany: Herder, 2000.

Pius XI. Encyclical *Divini Illius Magistri*.

―――. Encyclical *Divini Redemptoris*.

―――. Encyclical *Quadragesimo Anno*.

Pontifical Council for Justice and Peace. *Compendium of the Social Doctrine of the Church*. Vatican City: LEV, 2004.

Pontificio Consiglio della Giustizia e della Pace. *Dizionario di Dottrina Sociale della Chiesa*. Edited by Giampaolo Crepaldi and Enrique Colom. Rome, Italy: LAS, 2005.

Scannone, Juan Carlos. *Quando il popolo diventa teologo: Protagonisti e percorsi della teología del pueblo*. Bologna, Italy: EMI, 2016.

―――. *Teologia de la Liberación y Doctrina Social de la Iglesia*. Madrid, Spain: Cristiandad, 1987.

Schlag, Martin. "'Iustitia Est Amor': Love as Principle of Social and Economic Life?" *Acta Philosophica* 1, no. 21 (2012): 77–98.

Sierra, Félix Santolaria. *El gran debate sobre los pobres en el siglo XVI: Domingo de Soto y Juan de Robles 1545*. Barcelona, Spain: Ariel Historia, 2003.

Sobrino, Jon. *Jesucristo liberador: Lectura histórico-teológica de Jesús de Nazaret*. Madrid, Spain: Trotta, 1991.

Taparelli d'Azeglio, Luigi. *Saggio Teoretico di Dritto Naturale Appoggiato sul Fatto*. 8th ed. Edited by La Civiltà Cattolica. Palermo, Italy: [1st ed. 1840].

Twomey, Gerald S. *The "Preferential Option for the Poor" in Catholic Social Thought from John XXIII to John Paul II*. Lewiston, ME: Edwin Mellen Press, 2004.

von Ketteler, Wilhelm Emmanuel. *Die Arbeiterfrage und das Christentum*. Mainz, Germany: Franz Kirchheim, [1890] 2013.

Chapter 13, Schansberg

Asma, Stephen. *Against Fairness*. Chicago: University of Chicago Press, 2013.

Bandow, Douglas. *Beyond Good Intentions: A Biblical View of Politics*. Wheaton, IL: Crossway Books, 1988.

———. "The Necessity of Limited Government." In *Caesar's Coin Revisited: Christians and the Limits of Government*, edited by M. Cromartie. Grand Rapids, MI: Eerdmans, 1996.

Beckwith, Francis. *Politics for Christians: Statecraft as Soulcraft*. Downers Grove, IL: InterVarsity Press, 2010.

Biren, Curt. "The Market, Justice, and Charity: A Jewish Perspective." *Transatlantic Blog*. Acton Institute, September 10, 2018. https://acton.org/publications/transatlantic /2018/09/10/market-justice-and-charity-jewish-perspective.

Brueggemann, Walter. *The Prophetic Imagination*. Philadelphia: Fortress Press, 1978.

Chilton, David. *Productive Christians in an Age of Guilt Manipulators: A Biblical Response to Ronald J. Sider*. 3rd ed. Tyler, TX: Institute for Christian Economics, 1985.

Corbett, Steve, and Brian Fikkert. *When Helping Hurts: How to Alleviate Poverty without Hurting the Poor ... and Yourself*. Chicago: Moody, 2009.

England, Randy. *Free Is Beautiful: Why Catholics Should Be Libertarian*. Scotts Valley, CA: CreateSpace, 2012.

Finkel, Norman. *Not Fair! The Typology of Commonsense Unfairness*. Washington, DC: American Psychological Association, 2001.

Friedman, Richard Elliott. *Who Wrote the Bible?* Englewood Cliffs, NJ: Prentice Hall, 1987.

Guinness, Os. *Fit Bodies, Fat Minds: Why Evangelicals Don't Think and What to Do about It*. Grand Rapids, MI: Baker Books, 1994.

Haidt, Jonathan. *The Righteous Mind: Why Good People Are Divided by Politics and Religion*. New York: Vintage Books, 2013.

Halbertal, Moshe, and Stephen Holmes. *The Beginning of Politics: Power in the Biblical Book of Samuel*. Princeton, NJ: Princeton University Press, 2017.

Heyne, Paul. *Are Economists Basically Immoral? And Other Essays on Economics, Ethics, and Religion*. Indianapolis, IN: Liberty Fund, 2008.

Higgs, Robert. *Delusions of Power*. Oakland, CA: Independent Institute, 2012.

The Holy Bible: New International Version, Containing the Old Testament and the New Testament. Grand Rapids, MI: Zondervan, 1978.

Horsley, Richard. *Covenant Economics: A Biblical Vision of Justice for All.* Louisville, KY: Westminster John Knox, 2009.

Hübner, Jamin Andreas. "Christian Libertarianism: An Introduction and Signposts for the Road Ahead." *Christian Libertarian Review* 1 (2017): 15–74.

―――. "Review of Halbertal and Holmes." *Christian Libertarian Review* II (2019): R30–37.

―――. "Israel's History as a Post-Exile Critique of Political Power." Presentation at the "Peace and Violence in Scripture and Theology" Fall Conference of the Canadian-American Theological Association, October 20, 2018. Transcript available at https://independent.academia.edu/JaminH%C3%BCbner.

John Paul II. *Reconciliatio et Paenitentia*, 1984, no. 16. Quoted in *The Social Agenda: A Collection of Magisterial Texts*, edited by Robert Sirico and Maciej Zięba. Vatican City: Pontifical Council for Justice and Peace: 2000.

Koyzis, David. *Political Visions and Illusions: A Survey and Christian Critique of Contemporary Ideologies.* Downers Grove, IL: InterVarsity Press, 2003.

Lebacqz, Karen. *Six Theories of Justice.* Minneapolis, MN: Augsburg, 1986.

Lewis, C. S. *Mere Christianity.* New York: Macmillan, 1952.

Machan, Tibor. "Libertarianism in One Easy Lesson." *The Philosophers' Magazine* 21 (2003): 44–47.

Motyer, Alec. *The Prophecy of Isaiah.* Downers Grove, IL: InterVarsity Press, 1993.

Murray, Charles. *Coming Apart: The State of White America, 1960–2010.* New York: Crown Forum, 2012.

Rawls, John. *A Theory of Justice.* Cambridge, MA: Harvard University Press, 1976.

Reed, Ralph. *Active Faith.* New York: Free Press, 1996.

Schall, James. "Justice: The Most Terrible of the Virtues." *Journal of Markets & Morality* 7, no. 2 (Fall 2004): 409–21.

Schansberg, D. Eric. "Common Ground between the Philosophies of Christianity and Libertarianism." *Journal of Markets and Morality* 5, no. 2 (2002): 439–57.

―――. "The Ethics of Tax Evasion within Biblical Christianity: Are There Limits to 'Rendering unto Caesar'?" In *The Ethics of Tax Evasion*, edited by R. McGee. South Orange, NJ: The Dumont Institute for Public Policy Research, 1998.

―――. *Poor Policy: How Government Harms the Poor.* Boulder, CO: Westview Press, 1996.

―――. *Turn Neither to the Right nor to the Left: A Thinking Christian's Guide to Politics and Public Policy.* Greenville, SC: Alertness Books, 2003.

Schlossberg, Herbert. *Idols for Destruction: The Conflict of Christian Faith and American Culture.* Wheaton, IL: Crossway Books, 1990.

Schneider, John. "The Good of Affluence." *Religion and Liberty* (March/April 2002): 6–8. (Excerpted from *The Good of Affluence: Seeking God in a Culture of Wealth.* Grand Rapids, MI: Eerdmans.

Sowell, Thomas. *The Vision of the Anointed.* New York: Basic Books, 1995.

Spooner, Lysander. *Vices Are Not Crimes: A Vindication of Moral Liberty.* 1875. Available at https://theanarchistlibrary.org/library/lysander-spooner-vices-are-not-crimes -a-vindication-of-moral-liberty.

Stapleford, John. *Bulls, Bears, and Golden Calves: Applying Christian Ethics in Economics.* Downers Grove, IL: InterVarsity Press, 2002.

Teevan, John. *Integrated Justice and Equality: Biblical Wisdom for Those Who Do Good Works.* Grand Rapids, MI: Christian's Library Press, 2014.

Waters, Brent. *Just Capitalism: A Christian Ethic of Economic Globalization.* Louisville, KY: Westminster John Knox Press, 2016.

Woodiwiss, Ashley. "Christian Economic Justice and the Impasse in Political Theory." In *Toward a Just and Caring Society: Christian Responses to Poverty in America*, edited by David Gushee. Grand Rapids, MI: Baker Books, 1999.

Woods, Thomas. *The Church and the Market: A Catholic Defense of the Free Economy.* Lanham, MD: Lexington Books, 2005.

Chapter 15, Cohen

Acemoglu, Daron, and James A. Robinson. "The Rise and Decline of General Laws of Capitalism." *Journal of Economic Perspectives* 29 (2015): 3–28.

Alexander, Michelle. *The New Jim Crow.* New York: The New Press, 2010.

Arneson, Richard. "Luck Egalitarianism and Prioritarianism." *Ethics* 110 (2000): 339–49.

Bastiat, Frédéric. *The Law.* Auburn, AL: Ludwig von Mises Institute, 2007.

Bleeding Heart Libertarians. "Our Family: A Possible Taxonomy." BHL. Accessed January 21, 2022. http://bleedingheartlibertarians.com/2011/12/our-family-a-possible -taxonomy/.

Blume, Lawrence E., and Steven N. Durlauf. "*Capital in the Twenty-First Century*: A Review Essay." *Journal of Political Economy* 123 (2015): 749–77.

Boonin, David. *Should Race Matter?* New York: Cambridge University Press, 2011.

Brennan, Jason. *Why Not Capitalism?* New York: Routledge, 2014.

Carter, Ian. "Positive and Negative Liberty." In *The Stanford Encyclopedia of Philosophy*, edited by Edward N. Zalta, Summer 2018 edition. https://plato.stanford.edu /archives/sum2018/entries/liberty-positive-negative/.

Cohen, Andrew Jason. *Toleration.* London: Polity Press, 2014.

————. *Toleration and Freedom from Harm: Liberalism Reconceived.* London: Routledge, 2018.

Cohen, G. A. *Why Not Socialism?* Princeton, NJ: Princeton University Press, 2009.

Cohen, Joshua. "Democratic Equality." *Ethics* 99 (1989): 727–51.

Cowen, Tyler. "Capital Punishment: Why a Global Tax on the Wealthy Won't End Inequality." *Foreign Affairs*, May/June 2014. https://www.foreignaffairs.com/reviews/review-essay/capital-punishment.

Flexner Report. 1910. https://www.ncbi.nlm.nih.gov/pmc/articles/PMC3178858/.

Frankfurt, Harry. *On Inequality.* Princeton, NJ: Princeton University Press, 2015.

Freiman, Christopher. *Unequivocal Justice.* New York: Routledge, 2017.

Horwitz, Steve. "Inequality, Mobility, and Being Poor in America." *Social Philosophy and Policy* 31 (2015): 70–91.

Jones, Eric. *The European Miracle: Environments, Economies, and Geopolitics in the History of Europe and Asia.* Cambridge: Cambridge University Press, 2003.

Keech, William, and Michael Munger. "The Anatomy of Government Failure." *Public Choice* 164 (2015): 1–42.

Lindsey, Brink, and Steven Teles. *The Captured Economy.* Oxford: Oxford University Press, 2017.

Long, Roderick. "Left-Libertarianism, Market Anarchism, Class Conflict, and Historical Theories of Distributive Justice." *Griffith Law Review* 21 (2012): 413–31.

McCloskey, Deirdre. *Bourgeois Dignity.* Chicago: University of Chicago Press, 2010.

————. *Bourgeois Equality.* Chicago: University of Chicago Press, 2017.

————. *The Bourgeois Virtues.* Chicago: University of Chicago Press, 2007.

————. "Measured, Unmeasured, Mismeasured, and Unjustified Pessimism: A Review Essay of Thomas Piketty's *Capital in the Twenty-First Century.*" *Erasmus Journal for Philosophy and Economics* 7 (2014): 73–115.

Mokyr, Joel. *The Lever of Riches.* Oxford: Oxford University Press, 1992.

Muldoon, Ryan. *Social Contract for a Diverse World.* London: Routledge, 2017.

Nozick, Robert. *Anarchy, State, Utopia.* New York: Basic Books, 1974.

Piketty, Thomas. *Capital in the Twenty-First Century.* Cambridge, MA: Belknap Press, 2014.

————. *The Economics of Inequality.* Cambridge, MA: Belknap Press, 2015.

Pomeranz, Kenneth. *The Great Divergence: China, Europe, and the Making of the Modern World Economy.* Rev. ed. Princeton, NJ: Princeton University Press, 2001.

Ricardo, David. *On the Principles of Political Economy and Taxation.* [1821.]

Schmidtz, David. *The Elements of Justice.* New York: Cambridge University Press, 2006.

————. "The Institution of Property." *Social Philosophy and Policy* 11 (1994): 42–62.

————. "Property and Justice." *Social Philosophy and Policy* 27 (2010): 79–100.

Shapiro, Daniel. *Is the Welfare State Justified?* Cambridge: Cambridge University Press, 2007.

Smith, Adam. *An Inquiry into the Nature and Causes of the Wealth of Nations.* Ed. R. H. Campbell and A. S. Skinner. Indianapolis: Liberty Fund, 1982.

Spencer, Herbert. "The Sins of Legislators." In *The Man Versus the State.* Indianapolis: Liberty Fund, 1982.

Spencer, Herbert. "The Sins of Legislators." In *The Man versus the State.*

Weber, Max. *The Protestant Ethics and the Spirit of Capitalism.* Rev. ed. Oxford: Oxford University Press, [1905] 2010.

Zwolinksi, Matt. "Social Darwinism and Social Justice: Herbert Spencer on Our Duties to the Poor." In *Distributive Justice Debates in Social and Political Thought: Perspectives on Finding a Fair Share,* edited by Camilla Boisen and Matthew Murray, 56–76. New York: Routledge, 2016.

Chapter 16, Kaiser

Berlin, Isaiah. *Four Essays on Liberty.* Oxford: Oxford University Press, 1969.

Bhagwati, Jagdish, and Arvind Panagariya. *Why Growth Matters: How Economic Growth in India Reduced Poverty and the Lessons for Other Developing Countries.* Washington, DC: Public Affairs, 2013.

de Jouvenel, Bertrand. *Die Ethik der Umverteilung.* Munich, Germany: Olzog, 2012.

de Soto, Hernando. *The Mystery of Capital.* London: Black Swan, 2001.

Dworkin, Ronald. "Why Liberals Should Believe in Equality." *New York Review.* February 3, 1983. https://www.nybooks.com/articles/1983/02/03/why-liberals-should -believe-in-equality/.

Engels, Friedrich. *El origen de la familia, la propiedad privada y el Estado.* Madrid, Spain: Fundación Federico Engels, 2006.

Epstein, Richard. *Design for Liberty.* Cambridge, MA: Harvard University Press, 2011.

———. "The Risk-Free World of John Rawls." Forbes.com. http://www.forbes .com/2008/10/13/rawls-risk-system-oped-cx_re_1013epstein.html.

———. *Why Progressive Institutions Are Unsustainable.* New York: Encounter Broadsides, 2001.

Frankfurt, Harry. "Equality as a Moral Ideal." *Ethics* 98, no. 1 (1987): 21–43. https://www .law.upenn.edu/institutes/cerl/conferences/prioritarianism_papers/Session3Franfurt .pdf.

Friedman, Milton. *Capitalism and Freedom.* Chicago: University of Chicago Press, 2002.

Friedman, Milton, and Rose Friedman. *The Tyranny of the Status Quo.* Harmondsworth, UK: Penguin Books, 1985.

Hayek, F. A. *The Constitution of Liberty.* Chicago: University of Chicago Press, 2011.

_____. *Law, Legislation, and Liberty*. London: Routledge & Kegan Paul, 1982.

Höffe, Otfried. *Gerechtigkeit*. Munich, Germany: C. H. Beck, 2001.

Hume, David. *Enquiries concerning the Human Understanding and concerning the Principles of Morals*. Oxford: Clarendon Press, [1748] 1902.

Locke, John. *Second Treatise of Government*. Indianapolis, IN: Hackett, [1690] 1980.

Luhmann, Niklas. *Politische Theorie im Wohlfahrtsstaat*. Munich, Germany: Olzog, 1981.

Marx, Karl. *Critique of the Gotha Programme*. 1875. https://www.marxists.org/archive/marx/works/download/Marx_Critque_of_the_Gotha_Programme.pdf.

McCloskey, Deirdre. *Bourgeois Dignity: Why Economics Can't Explain the Modern World*. Chicago: University of Chicago Press, 2010.

Mill, John Stuart. *Collected Works of John Stuart Mill*. Vol. 5. Indianapolis, IN: Liberty Fund, 2006.

Nagel, Thomas. "The Meaning of Equality." *Washington University Law Quarterly* 1979, no. 1 (1979): 25–31.

Nietzsche, Friedrich. *Gesammelte Werke*. Bindlach, Germany: Gondrom, 2005.

Nozick, Robert. *Anarchy, State, and Utopia*. New York: Basic Books, 1974.

Nussbaum, Martha C. *Creating Capabilities: The Human Development Approach*. Cambridge, MA: Belknap Press, 2011.

Piketty, Thomas. *Capital in the Twenty-First Century*. Cambridge, MA: Harvard University Press, 2014.

Rawls, John. *A Theory of Justice*. Cambridge, MA: Belknap Press, [1971] 2005.

Robeyns, Ingrid. "Capabilitarianism." Human Development and Capability Association. 8th Conference, 2011. http://ssrn.com/abstract=2482007.

Röpke, Wilhelm. "The Malady of Progressivism." *The Freeman*, July 31, 1951, 687–91. https://bradbirzer.com/2014/12/21/the-malady-of-progressivism-1951-by-wilhelm-roepke.

Rothbard, Murray. *Egalitarianism as a Revolt against Nature and Other Essays*. Auburn, AL: Ludwig von Mises Institute, 2012.

Rousseau, Jean-Jacques. *The Social Contract and Discourses*. London: J. M. Dent and Sons, 1923.

Sanandaji, Nima. "The Surprising Ingredients of Swedish Success: Free Markets and Social Cohesion." Institute of Economic Affairs, Discussion Paper No. 41, 2012.

Schmidtz, David. *Elements of Justice*. New York: Cambridge University Press, 2006.

Schöck, Helmut. *Envy: A Theory of Social Behavior*. Indianapolis, IN: Liberty Fund, 1987.

Sen, Amartya. *The Idea of Justice*. London: Penguin Books, 2010.

Smith, George H. *The System of Liberty: Themes in the History of Classical Liberalism*. New York: Cambridge University Press, 2013.

Sowell, Thomas. *The Quest for Cosmic Justice*. New York: Touchstone, 2002.

Tomasi, John. *Free Market Fairness*. Princeton, NJ: Princeton University Press, 2012.

von Böhm-Bawerk, Eugen. *Karl Marx and the Close of His System.* New York: Augustus, [1896] 1949.

von Mises, Ludwig. *La acción humana.* Madrid, Spain: Unión Editorial, 2011.

———. *Socialism.* Indianapolis, IN: Liberty Fund, 1981.

Zingales, Luigi. *A Capitalism for the People.* New York: Basic Books, 2012.

Chapter 17, Geloso and Magness

Albouy, David. "The Wage Gap between Francophones and Anglophones: A Canadian Perspective, 1970–2000." *Canadian Journal of Economics/Revue Canadienne d'Économique* 41, no. 4 (2008): 1211–38.

Anderson, Elizabeth. "What Is the Point of Equality?" *Ethics* 109, no. 2 (1999): 287–337.

Baker, Michael, and Gillian Hamilton. "Écarts salariaux entre francophones et anglophones à Montréal au 19e siècle." *L'Actualité Économique* 76, no. 1 (2000): 75–111.

Bellavance, Marcel. *Le Québec et la confederation —un choix libre? Le clergé et la Constitution de 1867.* Montreal: Éditions du Septentrion, 1992.

Breton, Albert. "The Economics of Nationalism." *Journal of Political Economy* 72, no. 4 (1964): 376–86.

Couture, Claude. *Le mythe de la modernisation du Québec: Des années 1930 à la Révolution tranquille.* Montreal: Editions du Méridien, 1991.

Egerton, Douglas. *The Wars of Reconstruction: The Brief, Violent History of America's Most Progressive Era.* New York: Bloomsbury, 2014.

Geloso, Vincent. "The Fall and Rise of Inequality: Disaggregating Narratives." *Advances in Austrian Economics* 23 (2018): 161–75.

———. *Rethinking Canadian Economic Growth and Development since 1900: The Case of Quebec.* London: Palgrave Macmillan, 2017.

Geloso, Vincent, and Steven Horwitz. "Inequality: First, Do No Harm." *The Independent Review* 22, no. 1 (Summer 2017): 121–34.

Grynaviski, Jeffrey, and Michael Munger. "Reconstructing Racism: Transforming Racial Hierarchy from 'Necessary Evil' into 'Positive Good.'" *Social Philosophy and Policy* 34, no. 1 (2017): 144–63.

Guzmán, Ricardo Andrés, and Michael Munger. "Euvoluntariness and Just Market Exchange: Moral Dilemmas from Locke's 'Venditio.'" *Public Choice* 158, nos. 1–2 (2014): 39–49.

Hayek, F. A. "The Atavism of Social Justice." In *Social Justice, Socialism, and Democracy: Three Australian Lectures,* 3–17. Sydney, Australia: Centre for Independent Studies, 1978.

———. *The Fatal Conceit: The Errors of Socialism.* London: Routledge, 1988.

_____. *The Mirage of Social Justice*. Vol. 2, *Law, Legislation, and Liberty: A New State-ment of the Liberal Principles of Justice and Political Economy*. Chicago: University of Chicago Press, 1976.

Helper, Hinton Rowan. *The Impending Crisis of the South: How to Meet It*. New York: A. B. Burdick, 1857.

Hummel, Jeffrey Rogers. "Deadweight Loss and the American Civil War: The Political Economy of Slavery, Secession, and Emancipation." October 1, 2012. https://ssrn .com/abstract52155362 or http://dx.doi.org/10.2139/ssrn.2155362.

_____. *Emancipating Slaves, Enslaving Free Men: A History of the American Civil War*. Chicago: Open Court, 1996.

Hutt, William Harold. "Unanimity versus Non-discrimination (as Criteria for Con-stitutional Validity)." *South African Journal of Economics* 34, no. 2 (1966): 133–47.

Kim, Young-Chul, and Glenn Loury. "Collective Reputation and the Dynamics of Statistical Discrimination." *International Economic Review* 59, no. 1 (2018): 3–18.

Krueger, Anne. "The Political Economy of the Rent-Seeking Society." *American Economic Review* 64, no. 3 (1974): 291–303.

Kuran, Timur. *Private Truths, Public Lies: The Social Consequences of Preference Falsifica-tion*. Cambridge, MA: Harvard University Press, 1995.

MacKinnon, Mary. "Unilingues ou bilingues? Les Montréalais sur le marché du travail en 1901." *L'Actualité Économique* 76, no. 1 (2000): 137–58.

Magness, Phillip. "The American System and the Political Economy of Black Coloniza-tion." *Journal of the History of Economic Thought* 37, no. 2 (2015): 187–202.

_____. "A Paradox of Secessionism: The Political Economy of Slave Enforcement and the Union." In *Public Choice Analyses of American Economic History*, edited by Joshua Hall and Marcus Witcher, 53–68. Cham, Switzerland: Springer, 2018.

Mahoney, Paul. "The Common Law and Economic Growth: Hayek Might Be Right." *Journal of Legal Studies* 30, no. 2 (2001): 503–25.

Martin, Adam. "The New Egalitarianism." *The Independent Review* 22, no. 1 (Summer 2017): 15–25.

Munger, Michael. "Euvoluntary or Not, Exchange Is Just." *Social Philosophy and Policy* 28, no. 2 (2011): 192–211.

_____. "Objections to Euvoluntary Exchange Do Not Have 'Standing': Extending Markets without Limits." *Journal of Value Inquiry* 51, no. 4 (2017): 619–27.

North, Douglass, John Wallis, and Barry Weingast. *Violence and Social Orders: A Con-ceptual Framework for Interpreting Recorded Human History*. Cambridge: Cambridge University Press, 2009.

Novak, Mikayla. *Inequality: An Entangled Political Economy Perspective*. New York: Springer, 2018.

Nozick, Robert. *Anarchy, State, and Utopia*. New York: Basic Books, 1974.

———. "Distributive Justice." *Philosophy and Public Affairs* 3, no. 1 (1973): 45–126.

Peltzman, Sam, Michael Levine, and Roger Noll. *The Economic Theory of Regulation after a Decade of Deregulation*. Papers on Economic Activity. Washington, DC: Brookings Institution, 1989.

Reeves, Richard. *A Little Respect: Can We Restore Relational Equality?* Washington, DC: Brookings Institution, 2018.

Roback, Jennifer. "Racism as Rent Seeking." *Economic Inquiry* 27, no. 4 (1989): 661–81.

———. "The Separation of Race and State." *Harvard Journal of Law and Public Policy* 14, no. 1 (1991): 58–64.

Schemmel, Christian. "Distributive and Relational Equality." *Politics, Philosophy, and Economics* 11, no. 2 (2012): 123–48.

Schmidtz, David, and Jason Brennan. *A Brief History of Liberty*. Hoboken, NJ: Wiley, 2011.

Sen, Amartya. "Social Justice and the Distribution of Income." In *Handbook of Income Distribution*, vol. 1, edited by A. B. Atkinson and F. Bourguignon, 59–85. Amsterdam: Elsevier Science, 2000.

Spooner, Lysander. "To the Non-slaveholders of the South: A Plan for the Abolition of Slavery." 1858. http://praxeology.net/LS-PAS.htm. Accessed February 19, 2019.

Stark, Rodney, and Laurence Iannaccone. "Response to Lechner: Recent Religious Declines in Quebec, Poland, and the Netherlands. A Theory Vindicated." *Journal for the Scientific Study of Religion* 35, no. 3 (1996): 265–71.

Taylor, Norman. "French Canadians as Industrial Entrepreneurs." *Journal of Political Economy* 68, no. 1 (1960): 37–52.

Tomasi, John. *Free Market Fairness*. Princeton, NJ: Princeton University Press, 2012.

Tullock, Gordon. "The Economics of Slavery." *Left and Right* 3, no. 2 (1967): 5–16.

———. "The Welfare Costs of Tariffs, Monopolies, and Theft." *Western Economic Journal* 5, no. 3 (1967): 224–32.

Tyler, Tom, and Heather Smith. "Social Justice and Social Movements." Working Paper Series. Berkeley: Institute for Research on Labor and Employment, University of California, 1995.

Van Bavel, Bas, Erik Ansink, and Bram Van Besouw. "Understanding the Economics of Limited Access Orders: Incentives, Organizations, and the Chronology of Developments." *Journal of Institutional Economics* 13, no. 1 (2017): 109–31.

Wright, Robert. *The Poverty of Slavery: How Unfree Labor Pollutes the Economy*. New York: Springer, 2017.

Chapter 18, Haeffele and Storr

Aquinas, Thomas. *Summa Theologiae: Second Part of the Second Part.* Question 58. N.d. https://www.newadvent.org/summa/3058.htm#article1.

Bankston, Carl L. III. "Social Justice: Cultural Origins of a Perspective and a Theory." *The Independent Review* 15, no. 2 (Fall 2010): 165–78.

Blau, Francine D., and Marianne A. Ferber. "Discrimination: Empirical Evidence from the United States." *American Economic Review* 77, no. 2 (1987): 316–20.

Coyne, Christopher J. *Doing Bad by Doing Good: Why Humanitarian Action Fails.* Stanford, CA: Stanford University Press, 2013.

Duff, Wendy M., Andrew Flinn, Karen Emily Suurtamm, and David A. Wallace. "Social Justice Impact of Archives: A Preliminary Investigation." *Archival Science* 13, no. 4 (2013): 317–48.

Duffy, Simon. "The Citizenship Theory of Social Justice: Exploring the Meaning of Personalisation for Social Workers." *Journal of Social Work Practice* 24, no. 3 (2010): 253–67.

Feser, Edward. "Hayek on Social Justice: Reply to Lukes and Johnston." *Critical Review* 11, no. 4 (1997): 581–606.

———. "Hayek, Social Justice, and the Market: Reply to Johnston." *Critical Review* 12, no. 3 (1998): 269–81.

Hayek, F. A. *The Mirage of Social Justice.* Vol. 2, *Law, Legislation, and Liberty: A New Statement of the Liberal Principles of Justice and Political Economy.* Chicago: University of Chicago Press, 1976.

———. "The Use of Knowledge in Society." *American Economic Review* 35, no. 4 (1945): 519–30.

Holcombe, Randall G. *Political Capitalism: How Economic and Political Power Is Made and Maintained.* Cambridge: Cambridge University Press, 2018.

Jackson, Ben. "The Conceptual History of Social Justice." *Political Studies Review* 3, no. 3 (2005): 356–73.

Jackson, Jeremy, and Jeffrey Palm. "The Limits of Redistribution and the Impossibility of Egalitarian Ends." *The Independent Review* 22, no. 1 (Summer 2017): 71–81.

Johnston, David. "Hayek's Attack on Social Justice." *Critical Review* 11, no. 1 (1997): 81–100.

———. "Is the Idea of Social Justice Meaningful?" *Critical Review* 11, no. 4 (1997): 607–14.

Lister, Andrew. "The 'Mirage' of Social Justice: Hayek against (and for) Rawls." *Critical Review* 25, nos. 3–4 (2013): 409–44.

Lukes, Steven. "Social Justice: The Hayekian Challenge." *Critical Review* 11, no. 1 (1997): 65–80.

Munger, Michael C. *Tomorrow 3.0: Transaction Costs and the Sharing Economy.* Cambridge: Cambridge University Press, 2018.

Omi, Michael, and Howard Winant. *Racial Formation in the United States.* 3rd ed. New York: Routledge, 2014.

Radnitzky, Gerard. "Anthony de Jasay: A Life in the Service of Liberty." *The Independent Review* 9, no. 1 (Summer 2004): 99–103.

Reisch, Michael. "Defining Social Justice in a Socially Unjust World." *Families in Society* 83, no. 4 (2002): 343–54.

Smith, Adam. *An Inquiry into the Nature and Causes of the Wealth of Nations.* Vol. 1. Indianapolis, IN: Liberty Fund, [1776] 1981.

Stiglitz, Joseph E. *The Price of Inequality: How Today's Divided Society Endangers the Future.* New York: Norton, 2012.

Tebble, Adam James. "Hayek and Social Justice: A Critique." *Critical Review of International Social and Political Philosophy* 12, no. 4 (2009): 581–604.

Tomasi, John. *Free Market Fairness.* Princeton, NJ: Princeton University Press, 2012.

Wagner, Richard E. *Politics as a Peculiar Business: Insights from a Theory of Entangled Political Economy.* Northampton, MA: Edward Elgar, 2016.

Chapter 19, Whaples

Carpenter, Dick M., Lisa Knepper, Angela Erickson, and John Ross. "Regulating Work: Measuring the Scope and Burden of Occupational Licensure among Low- and Moderate-Income Occupations in the United States." *Economic Affairs* 35, no. 1 (2015): 3–20.

Centers for Disease Control and Prevention (CDC). "Table 29—Death Rates for Homicide, by Sex, Race, Hispanic Origin, and Age: United States, Selected Years 1950–2016." 2017. https://www.cdc.gov/nchs/hus/contents2017.htm#029.

Centers for Medicare and Medicaid Services (CMS). "Medicaid Facts and Figures." 2020. https://www.cms.gov/newsroom/fact-sheets/medicaid-facts-and-figures.

Chirakijja, Janjala, Seema Jayachandran, and Pinchuan Ong. *Inexpensive Heating Reduces Winter Mortality.* National Bureau of Economic Research Working Paper no. 25681. Washington, DC: NBER, 2019.

Clark, Ross. *The War against Cash.* Petersfield, UK: Harriman House, 2017.

Coclanis, Peter A. "Capitalism, Slavery, and Matthew Desmond's Low-Road Contribution to the 1619 Project." *The Independent Review* 26, no. 4 (2022): 485–511.

Darwall, Rupert. *Green Tyranny: Exposing the Totalitarian Roots of the Climate Industrial Complex.* New York: Encounter Books, 2017.

Dehejia, Rajeev, Thomas DeLeire, and Erzo Luttmer. "Insuring Consumption and Happiness through Religious Organizations." *Journal of Public Economics* 91, nos. 1–2 (2007): 259–79.

Fajgelbaum, Pablo D., and Amit K. Khandelwal. "Measuring the Unequal Gains from Trade." *Quarterly Journal of Economics* 131, no. 3 (2016): 1113–80.

Fegley, Tate. "Police Unions and Officer Privileges." *The Independent Review* 25, no. 2 (2020): 165–86.

Fiske, Susan. "Racism, Role of Power." In *Encyclopedia of Power*, edited by Keith Dowding. Thousand Oaks, CA: SAGE, 2011.

Forbes. "The World's Real-Time Billionaires." 2021. https://www.forbes.com/real-time -billionaires/#4384424e3d78. Accessed January 14, 2021.

Ganong, Peter, and Daniel Shoag. "Why Has Regional Income Convergence Declined?" *Journal of Urban Economics* 102 (2017): 76–90.

Geloso, Vincent, and Steven Horwitz. "Inequality: First, Do No Harm." *The Independent Review* 22, no. 2 (2017): 121–34.

Goodman, John C. *A Better Choice: Healthcare Solutions for America*. Oakland, CA: Independent Institute, 2015.

Henderson, David. "A Philosophical Economist's Case against a Government-Guaranteed Basic Income." *The Independent Review* 19, no. 4 (2015): 489–502.

Holcombe, Randall G. "Crony Capitalism: A By-product of Big Government." *The Independent Review* 17, no. 4 (2013): 541–59.

Jatlaoui, Tara C., Lindsay Eckhaus, Michele G. Mandel, Antoinette Nguyen, Titilope Oduyebo, Emily Petersen, and Maura K. Whiteman. "Abortion Surveillance—United States, 2016." *Surveillance Summaries* 68, no. 11 (2019): 1–41. https://www .cdc.gov/mmwr/volumes/68/ss/ss6811a1.htm.

Kendi, Ibram X. *How to Be an Antiracist*. New York: One World, 2019.

Lawson, Robert, and Benjamin Powell. *Socialism Sucks: Two Economists Drink Their Way through the Unfree World*. Washington, DC: Regnery, 2019.

Lincicome, Scott. "Examining America's Farm Subsidy Problem." Cato Institute. 2020. https://www.cato.org/publications/commentary/examining-americas-farm -subsidy-problem.

Lomasky, Loren E. "Fleecing the Young." *The Independent Review* 21, no. 1 (2016): 5–28.

Lomborg, Bjorn. *False Alarm: How Climate Change Panic Costs Us Trillions, Hurts the Poor, and Fails to Fix the Planet*. New York: Basic Books, 2020.

Mac Donald, Heather. "Taking Stock of a Most Violent Year." *Wall Street Journal*, January 25, 2021, A17.

Mack, Lindsay E. "Montessori School Tuitions May Be More Affordable Than You Realize." 2020. https://www.romper.com/p/how-much-is-montessori-school-tuition -it-depends-on-these-factors-10012991.

Munger, Michael. "One and One-Half Cheers for a Basic-Income Guarantee: We Could Do Worse, and Already Have." *The Independent Review* 19, no. 4 (2015): 503–13.

Munger, Michael, and Mario Villarreal-Diaz. "The Road to Crony Capitalism." *The Independent Review* 23, no. 3 (2019): 331–44.

Murtazashvili, Ilia, and Ennio E. Piano. "More Boon than Bane: How the U.S. Reaped the Rewards and Avoided the Costs of the Shale Boom." *The Independent Review* 24, no. 2 (2019): 249–72.

Riley, Jason L. "Race Relations in America Are Better than Ever." *Wall Street Journal,* April 28, 2021.

Shores, Kenneth, and Simon Ejdemyr. "Do School Districts Spend Less Money on Poor and Minority Students?" Brookings Institution, 2017. https://www.brookings .edu/blog/brown-center-chalkboard/2017/05/25/do-school-districts-spend-less -money-on-poor-and-minority-students/.

Sowell, Thomas. *Charter Schools and Their Enemies.* New York: Basic Books, 2020.

Stark, Rodney, and Jared Maier. "Faith and Happiness." *Review of Religious Research* 50, 1 (2008): 120–25.

Storr, Virgil Henry, and Ginny Seung Choi. *Do Markets Corrupt Our Morals?* Cham, Switzerland: Palgrave Macmillan, 2019.

Strong, Michael D. "Is the U.S. Education System Adequately Polycentric?" *The Independent Review* 25, no. 2 (2020): 235–48.

Studnicki, James, John W. Fisher, and James L. Sherley. "Perceiving and Addressing the Pervasive Racial Disparity in Abortion." *Health Services Research and Managerial Epidemiology,* 2020. https://www.ncbi.nlm.nih.gov/pmc/articles/PMC7436774/.

Sullivan, Laura, Tatjana Meschede, Thomas Shapiro, Dedrick Asante-Muhammed, and Emanuel Nieves. "Equitable Investments in the Next Generation: Designing Policies to Close the Racial Wealth Gap." Annie E. Casey Foundation, 2016. https:// prosperitynow.org/files/resources/IASP_CFED_Equitable_Investments_in_the_ Next_Generation-FINAL.pdf.

U.S. Census. "Homeownership by Race." 2016. https://www.census.gov/housing/hvs /files/annual16/ann16t_22.xlsx.

U.S. Census. "Spending per Pupil Increased for Sixth Consecutive Year." 2016. https:// www.census.gov/newsroom/press-releases/2020/school-system-finances.html.

Vedder, Richard K. "Four Centuries of Black Economic Progress in America: Ideological Posturing versus Empirical Realities." *The Independent Review* 26, no. 2 (2021): 287–306.

Weisburd, David, Hassan Aden, Anthony Braga, Jim Bueermann, Philip J. Cook, Phillip Atiba Goff, Rachel A. Harmon, et al. "Proactive Policing: Effects on Crime and Communities." National Academy of Sciences, 2017. https://www.nap.edu/resource/24928/Proactive%20Policing.pdf.

Whaples, Robert. "The Economic Future: An Introduction." In *Future: Economic Peril or Prosperity*, edited by Robert M. Whaples, Christopher J. Coyne, and Michael C. Munger. Oakland, CA: Independent Institute, 2016.

——. "The Economics of Pope Francis: An Introduction." *The Independent Review* 21, no. 3 (2017): 325–45.

——. "The Road to Crony Capitalism: An Introduction." *The Independent Review* 23, no. 3 (2019): 325–30.

Wikipedia. "Race and Health in the United States." 2021. https://en.wikipedia.org/wiki/Race_and_health_in_the_United_States. Accessed January 14, 2021.

World Bank. *Averting the Old Age Crisis.* New York: Oxford University Press, 1994.

Wu, JunJie, and Christian Langpap. "The Price and Welfare Effects of Biofuel Mandates and Subsidies." *Environmental and Resource Economics* 62, no. 1 (2015): 35–57.

Index

government, 163, 189–91, 206, 244;
to help the poor, 206; indirect, 190;
and justice, 187–88; limits to, 223–24;
and meritocracy, 225; necessity of, 219;
regressive, 235; and relational equality,
235; to remedy economic injustices,
246; rights and privileges, 288n20;
short-run, 290n9; as theft, 187, 203,
282n52; to the wealthy, 213; *see also*
welfare programs
redistributive limit, 223
Reed, Ralph, 182
relativism: aesthetic, 26; ethical, 34; moral,
26, 88
religion, and the concept of sharing, 116;
see also Christianity; Roman Catholic
Church; theology
rent-seeking, 2, 4, 11, 212, 214, 216, 233–34,
242, 250, 261, 293n60; in narratives,
11, 233, 236–40, 288n6, 289n35; to
shape rules, 233–34
reparations, 286n46, 291n30
republics, 161–62
reputation, 22
Rerum novarum, 149, 150, 158, 160, 166, 171
resentment, 6, 51–55, 119, 122
reserve price: diversity in, 117–21; and
social responsibility, 125; uncertain,
121–24
respect: for diversity, 15, 197; for equality,
229; for human dignity, 40, 169, 185;
for liberties, 231–32; for morality, 198;
mutual 3, 138–39, 236; for property,
168; self-, 148, 222, 223, 224, 234, 236
restitution, 8, 60, 102, 103, 110, 269n10
restricted utility, 73–74, 78–81, 82, 83,
270n27
righteousness, 9, 17–18, 20, 183, 188, 192,
281n26
rights: civil, 291n1; concept of, 67; as creations of the sovereign, 33; equal, 152;
equality with respect to, 25; family,
152–53, 200; human, 152, 162, 175,

290n1; hypotactic, 173; inalienable,
25, 33; individual, 9, 113, 147, 152,
161, 196–97, 201, 214; inherent, 104;
liberal constitutional, 74, 81–82, 83;
to liberty, 152; material-oriented, 163;
natural, 146, 150, 162, 208; negative,
140; niche, 186; to opportunity, 152; of
ownership, 144, 159; property, 10, 46,
58, 82, 104, 152, 196, 197–98, 211, 217,
225, 228, 231, 282n50, 284n18, 285n26;
violation of, 181–82; *see also* liberties
Roback, Jennifer, 237
Robinson Crusoe (literary character), 111,
113–16, 124, 228, 273nn1–2, 273n4
Robles, Juan de, 172
Rognlie, Matthew, 53
Roman Catholic Church: and French
Canadians, 241; Jesuits, 172–73; on
justice, 18; monopoly rents of, 290n43;
papal encyclicals, 149–51, 169, 171,
172, 278n16; and social justice, 149–51,
153, 156–61, 165–66, 169–78; social
teachings of, 9, 144, 171; and subsidiarity, 173; *see also* Christianity
Röpke, Wilhelm, 225, 226
Rosmini, Antonio, 143, 144, 149
Rousseau, Jean-Jacques, 220, 221
rule of law, 47, 81–82

S
Scannone, Juan Carlos, 175
scarcity, 61
Schall, James, 179
Schelling, Thomas, 69
Schmidtz, David, 223
Schneider, John, 186
Scholastics, 35, 145
School of Salamanca, 172
Schumacher, E. F., 163
Schumpeter, Joseph, 64, 164, 168
science: nominalism and, 35–36; probabi-
listic reasoning used by, 38–39
Scientific Revolution, 29, 32, 35

About the Editors and Contributors

About the Editors

Christopher J. Coyne is the F. A. Harper Professor of Economics at George Mason University, senior fellow at the Independent Institute and co-editor of *The Independent Review: A Journal of Political Economy*, co-editor of the *Review of Austrian Economics,* and book review editor at *Public Choice*. His books include *In Search of Monsters to Destroy: The Folly of American Empire and the Paths to Peace*; *Manufacturing Militarism: U.S. Government Propaganda in the War on Terror* (with Abigail R. Hall); *The Economics of Conflict and Peace: History and Applications* (with Shikha Basnet Silwal, Charles H. Anderton, Jurgen Brauer and J. Paul Dunne); *Defense, Peace, and War Economics*; *Tyranny Comes Home: The Domestic Fate of U.S. Militarism* (with Abigail R. Hall); *Doing Bad by Doing Good: Why Humanitarian Action Fails*; *After War: The Political Economy of Exporting Democracy*; *Media, Development, and Institutional Change* (with Peter T. Leeson); *Context Matters: Entrepreneurship and Institutions* (with Peter J. Boettke); and *The Handbook on the Political Economy of War* (with Rachel L. Mathers).

Michael C. Munger is director of the Philosophy, Politics, and Economics Program and professor in the Departments of Political Science and Economics at Duke University, senior fellow at the Independent Institute, and co-editor of *The Independent Review: A Journal of Political Economy*. He has been staff economist at the Federal Trade Commission, president of the Public Choice Society, and president of the North Carolina Political Science Association. His books include *Is Capitalism Sustainable?*; *In All Fairness: Equality,*

Liberty, and the Quest for Human Dignity (co-edited with Robert M. Whaples and Christopher J. Coyne); *Ideology and the Theory of Political Choice* (with Melvin J. Hinich); *Future: Economic Peril or Prosperity?* (co-edited with Robert M. Whaples and Christopher J. Coyne); *The Thing Itself: Essays on Academics and the State*; *Philosophy, Politics, and Economics: An Anthology* (co-edited with Jonathan Anomaly, Geoffrey Brennan, and Geoffrey Sayre-McCord); *Analytical Politics* (with Melvin J. Hinich); *Analyzing Policy: Choices, Conflicts, and Practices*; *Choosing in Groups: Analytical Politics Revisited* (with Kevin M. Munger); *Empirical Studies in Comparative Politics* (co-edited with Melvin J. Hinich); and *Tomorrow 3.0: Transaction Costs and the Sharing Economy*.

Robert M. Whaples is professor of economics at Wake Forest University, senior fellow at the Independent Institute, and editor of *The Independent Review: A Journal of Political Economy*. He is the former director of EH.Net, the recipient of the Allan Nevins Prize and the Jonathan Hughes Prize for Excellence in Teaching Economic History, the author of over 300 articles and reviews in scholarly journals, and the editor of the books *In All Fairness: Equality, Liberty, and the Quest for Human Dignity* (with Christopher J. Coyne and Michael C. Munger); *Pope Francis and the Caring Society*; *Future: Economic Peril or Prosperity?* (with Michael C. Munger and Christopher J. Coyne); *Historical Perspectives on the American Economy: Selected Readings* (with Dianne Betts); *Public Choice Interpretations of American Economic History* (with Jac C. Heckelman and John C. Moorhouse); *The Handbook of Modern Economic History* (with Randall Parker); *The Handbook of Major Events in Economic History* (with Randall Parker); and *The Economic Crisis in Retrospect: Explanations by Great Economists* (with G. Page West III).

About the Contributors

Andrew Jason Cohen is professor of philosophy and founding coordinator of the Interdisciplinary Studies Program in Philosophy, Politics, and Economics at Georgia State University, and he is the author of the book *Toleration and Freedom from Harm: Liberalism Reconceived*.

Daniel J. D'Amico is an associated faculty member at Wabash College and the inaugural director of the Stephenson Institute for Classical Liberalism.

Vincent J. Geloso is an assistant professor of economics at George Mason University, associate editor of *Essays in Economic and Business History*, and the author of *Rethinking Canadian Economic Growth and Development since 1900: The Quebec Case.*

Anthony Gill is professor of political science and adjunct professor of sociology at the University of Washington and a Distinguished Senior Fellow at the Institute for Studies of Religion at Baylor University.

Daniel Guerrière is Professor Emeritus of Philosophy at the California State University, Long Beach. He taught and published widely in Greek philosophy, Hegel, phenomenology, existentialism, metaphysics, the philosophy of religion, and the philosophy of politics. He edited *Phenomenology of the Truth Proper to Religion.*

Stefanie Haeffele is senior research fellow, Senior Program and Operations Director of Academic & Student Programs, and a senior fellow for the F. A. Hayek Program for Advanced Study in Philosophy, Politics and Economics in the Mercatus Center at George Mason University. She is co-author of *Community Revival in the Wake of Disaster: Lessons in Local Entrepreneurship* (with Virgil Henry Storr and Laura E. Grube).

Axel Kaiser is president of Fundación Para el Progreso and director of the Friedrich Hayek Chair at the Adolfo Ibáñez University in Santiago, Chile. His books include *The Fatal Ignorance: The Right-Wing's Cultural Anorexia against the Ideological Advance of Progressive Ideas*, *The Tyranny of Equality*, and *The Populist Deception.*

Jacob T. Levy is the Tomlinson Professor of Political Theory in the Department of Political Science at McGill University in Montreal, Canada, and he is the author of *Rationalism, Pluralism, and Freedom*; *The Multiculturalism of Fear*; *The Oxford Handbook of Classics in Contemporary Political Theory*; *Interpreting Modernity: Essays on the Work of Charles Taylor*; *Nomos LV: Federalism and Subsidiarity*; and *Colonialism and Its Legacies.*

Phillip W. Magness is senior research fellow at the American Institute for Economic Research. His books include *Colonization after Emancipation: Lincoln and the Movement for Black Resettlement* (with Sebastian N. Page); *Rules* *of the Game: How Government Works and Why It Sometimes Doesn't* (with Paul Weissburg), *What Is Classical Liberal History?* (edited with Michael J. Douma); and *Cracks in the Ivory Tower: The Moral Mess of Higher Education* (with Jason Brennan).

Adam G. Martin is political economy research fellow and associate professor of economics at the Free Market Institute and associate professor of agricultural and applied economics in the College of Agricultural Sciences and Natural Resources at Texas Tech University.

John A. Moore is professor of finance at Walsh College, a Certified Public Accountant, and Secretary-Treasurer of the Economic and Business History Society. The recipient of the Colonial Dames Award and the James Soltow Award, he has also served as CFO for numerous private commercial real estate firms holding investments throughout the United States.

James R. Otteson is the John T. Ryan Jr. Professor of Business Ethics at the University of Notre Dame. His books include *The End of Socialism*; *Honorable Business: A Framework for Business in a Just and Humane Society*; *Seven Deadly Economic Sins: Obstacles to Prosperity and Happiness Every Citizen Should Know*; *Adam Smith*; *Adam Smith's Marketplace of Life*; *What Adam Smith Knew: Moral Lessons on Capitalism from Its Greatest Champions and Fiercest Opponents*; and *Actual Ethics*.

Jordan Peterson is a clinical psychologist and professor emeritus at the University of Toronto. He is the international bestselling author of *Beyond Order, 12 Rules for Life: An Antidote to Chaos*, and *Maps of Meaning: The Architecture of Belief*.

Nicholas Rescher is a Distinguished University Professor of Philosophy and former Director of the Center for Philosophy of Science at the University of Pittsburgh. He is also a Member of the Editorial Board for *The Independent Review* and a member of the Board of Advisors for the Center on Culture and Civil Society at the Independent Institute.

Pascal Salin is professor of economics at the Université Paris-Dauphine in France. He is past president of the Mont Pèlerin Society, a Knight of the Légion d'Honneur, and an officer of the Ordre National du Mérite, and his books include *Tax Tyranny*; *Currency Competition and Monetary Union*; *Competition, Coordination and Diversity: From the Firm to Economic Integration*; *L'ordre monétaire Mondial*; *La vérité sur la monnaie*; *Macroéconomie*; *Libre-échange et Protectionnisme*; *Competition and Free Trade*; *La Tyrannie Fiscale*; *Le Vrai Libéralisme: Droite et Gauche Unies dans l'Erreur*; *La concurrence*; *L'Arbitraire Fiscal ou Comment Sortir de la Crise*; and *Liberalism*.

D. Eric Schansberg is professor of economics at Indiana University Southeast, and author of the books *Poor Policy: How Government Harms the Poor* and *Turn Neither to the Right Nor to the Left: A Thinking Christian's Guide to Politics and Public Policy*.

Martin Schlag is the Alan W. Moss Endowed Chair for Catholic Social Thought of the John A. Ryan Institute in the Center for Catholic Studies at the University of St. Thomas, and he is the director of the Program in Church Management at the Pontifical University of the Holy Cross and consultant to the Pontifical Council for Justice and Peace in Rome.

R. Scott Smith is professor of ethics and Christian apologetics in the School of Professional Ethics at Biola University. His books include *Virtue Ethics and Moral Knowledge: Philosophy of Language after MacIntyre and Hauerwas*; *Truth and the New Kind of Christian: The Emerging Effects of Postmodernism in the Church*; *Naturalism and Our Knowledge of Reality: Testing Religious Truth-Claims*; *In Search of Moral Knowledge: Overcoming the Fact-Value Dichotomy*; and *Authentically Emergent: In Search of a Truly Progressive Christianity*.

James R. Stoner Jr. is the Hermann Moyse Jr. Professor and director of the Eric Voegelin Institute in the Department of Political Science at Louisiana State University. His books include *Common-Law Liberty: Rethinking American Constitutionalism* and *Common Law and Liberal Theory: Coke, Hobbes, and the Origins of American Constitutionalism*.

Virgil Henry Storr is vice president of Academic and Student Programs and the Don C. Lavoie Senior Fellow in the F. A. Hayek Program for Advanced Study in Philosophy, Politics, and Economics at the Mercatus Center, as well as associate professor of economics at George Mason University. His books include *Enterprising Slaves & Master Pirates*; *Understanding the Culture of*

Markets; *Community Revival in the Wake of Disaster* (with Stefanie Haeffele and Laura E. Grube); and *Do Markets Corrupt Our Morals?* (with Ginny Seung Choi).

Kevin D. Vallier is associate professor of philosophy at Bowling Green State University, and his books include *Illiberal Perfectionism*; *Trust in a Polarized Age*; *Liberal Politics and Public Faith: Beyond Separation*; and *Must Politics Be War? Restoring Our Trust in the Open Society*.

William J. Watkins Jr. is a research fellow at the Independent Institute, a former law clerk to Judge William B. Traxler Jr. of the U.S. Court of Appeals for the Fourth Circuit, and president of the Greenville, South Carolina, Lawyers Chapter of the Federalist Society. He is the author of the books *Crossroads for Liberty: Recovering the Anti-Federalist Values of America's First Constitution*; *Judicial Monarchs: Court Power and the Case for Restoring Popular Sovereignty in the United States*; *Patent Trolls: Predatory Litigation and the Smothering of Innovation*; and *Reclaiming the American Revolution: The Kentucky and Virginia Resolutions and Their Legacy*.

Robert M. Whaples is professor of economics at Wake Forest University, editor of *The Independent Review*, and editor of several books including *In All Fairness: Equality, Liberty, and the Quest for Human Dignity*; *Pope Francis and the Caring Society*; and *Future: Economic Peril or Prosperity?*

Credits

The following chapters were originally articles published in *The Independent Review* 24, no.1 (Summer 2019), copyright © 2019 by the Independent Institute:

"New Thinking about Social Justice" by Robert M. Whaples originally published as "New Thinking about Social Justice," *The Independent Review* 24, no.1 (Summer 2019): 5–12; "Opting Out: A Defense of Social Justice" by James R. Otteson originally published as "Opting Out: A Defense of Social Justice," *The Independent Review* 24, no.1 (Summer 2019): 13–24; "Social Justice versus Western Justice" by Daniel Guerrière originally published as "Social Justice versus Western Justice," *The Independent Review* 24, no.1(Summer 2019): 25–36; "Social Justice, Public Goods, and Rent Seeking in Narratives" by Vincent J. Geloso and Phillip W. Magness originally published as "Social Justice, Public Goods, and Rent Seeking in Narratives," *The Independent Review* 24, no.1 (Summer 2019): 37–48; "Social Injustice and Spontaneous Orders" by Jacob T. Levy originally published as "Social Injustice and Spontaneous Orders," *The Independent Review* 24, no.1 (Summer 2019): 49–62; "Hayekian Social Justice" by Kevin D. Vallier originally published as "Hayekian Social Justice," *The Independent Review* 24, no.1 (Summer 2019): 63–72; "Knowledge Problems from behind the Veil of Ignorance" by Daniel J. D'Amico originally published as "Knowledge Problems from behind the Veil of Ignorance," *The Independent Review* 24, no.1 (Summer 2019): 73–84; "Civil Society and Social Justice: A Prospectus" by James R. Stoner Jr. originally published as "Civil Society and Social Justice: A Prospectus," *The Independent Review* 24, no.1 (Summer 2019): 85–94; "Social Justice, Economics, and the Implications of Nominalism" by R. Scott Smith originally published as "Social Justice, Economics, and the Implications of Nominalism," *The Independent Review* 24, no.1 (Summer 2019): 95–106; "The Mantle of Justice" by Adam G. Martin originally published as "The Mantle of Justice," *The Independent Review* 24, no.1 (Summer 2019): 107–118; "Social Justice: Intersecting Catholicism, Citizenship, and Capitalism" by John A. Moore originally published as "Social Justice: Intersecting Catholicism, Citizenship, and Capitalism," *The Independent Review* 24, no.1 (Summer 2019): 119–130; "An Exchange Theory of Social Justice: A 'Gains from Trade under Uncertainty' Perspective" by Anthony Gill originally published as "An Exchange Theory of Social Justice: A 'Gains from Trade under Uncertainty' Perspective," *The Independent Review* 24, no.1 (Summer 2019): 131–144;

"Is Social Justice a Mirage?" by Stefanie Haeffele and Virgil Henry Storr originally published as "Is Social Justice a Mirage?," *The Independent Review* 24, no. 1 (Summer 2019): 145–154.

The following chapters were originally published elsewhere and were reprinted with permission from their respective publishers:

"Bleeding Heart Libertarianism and the Social Justice or Injustice of Economic Inequality" by Andrew Jason Cohen originally published as "Bleeding Heart Libertarianism and the Social Justice or Injustice of Economic Inequality" in *Ethics in Practice: An Anthology*, edited by Hugh LaFollette, 5th ed., 624–36 (Hoboken, NJ: Wiley-Blackwell, 2020).

"Biblical Christianity and Social Justice" by D. Eric Schansberg originally published as "Biblical Christianity and Legislating Economic Justice," *Christian Libertarian Review* 3 (2020): 89–111.

Independent Institute Studies in Political Economy

THE ACADEMY IN CRISIS | *edited by John W. Sommer*

AGAINST LEVIATHAN | *by Robert Higgs*

AMERICAN HEALTH CARE |
edited by Roger D. Feldman

AMERICAN SURVEILLANCE | *by Anthony Gregory*

ANARCHY AND THE LAW |
edited by Edward P. Stringham

ANTITRUST AND MONOPOLY |
by D. T. Armentano

AQUANOMICS |
edited by B. Delworth Gardner & Randy T Simmons

ARMS, POLITICS, AND THE ECONOMY |
edited by Robert Higgs

A BETTER CHOICE | *by John C. Goodman*

BEYOND POLITICS | *by Randy T Simmons*

BOOM AND BUST BANKING |
edited by David Beckworth

CALIFORNIA DREAMING | *by Lawrence J. McQuillan*

CAN TEACHERS OWN THEIR OWN SCHOOLS? |
by Richard K. Vedder

THE CHALLENGE OF LIBERTY |
edited by Robert Higgs & Carl P. Close

THE CHE GUEVARA MYTH AND THE FUTURE
OF LIBERTY | *by Alvaro Vargas Llosa*

CHINA'S GREAT MIGRATION | *by Bradley M. Gardner*

CHOICE | *by Robert P. Murphy*

THE CIVILIAN AND THE MILITARY |
by Arthur A. Ekirch, Jr.

CRISIS AND LEVIATHAN, 25TH ANNIVERSARY
EDITION | *by Robert Higgs*

CROSSROADS FOR LIBERTY |
by William J. Watkins, Jr.

CUTTING GREEN TAPE |
edited by Richard L. Stroup & Roger E. Meiners

THE DECLINE OF AMERICAN LIBERALISM |
by Arthur A. Ekirch, Jr.

DELUSIONS OF POWER | *by Robert Higgs*

DEPRESSION, WAR, AND COLD WAR |
by Robert Higgs

THE DIVERSITY MYTH |
by David O. Sacks & Peter A. Thiel

DRUG WAR CRIMES | *by Jeffrey A. Miron*

ELECTRIC CHOICES | *edited by Andrew N. Kleit*

ELEVEN PRESIDENTS | *by Ivan Eland*

THE EMPIRE HAS NO CLOTHES | *by Ivan Eland*

THE ENTERPRISE OF LAW | *by Bruce L. Benson*

ENTREPRENEURIAL ECONOMICS |
edited by Alexander Tabarrok

FAILURE | *by Vicki E. Alger*

FINANCING FAILURE | *by Vern McKinley*

THE FOUNDERS' SECOND AMENDMENT |
by Stephen P. Halbrook

FUTURE | *edited by Robert M. Whaples, Christopher J.
Coyne, & Michael C. Munger*

GLOBAL CROSSINGS | *by Alvaro Vargas Llosa*

GOOD MONEY | *by George Selgin*

GUN CONTROL IN NAZI-OCCUPIED FRANCE |
by Stephen P. Halbrook

GUN CONTROL IN THE THIRD REICH |
by Stephen P. Halbrook

HAZARDOUS TO OUR HEALTH? |
edited by Robert Higgs

HOT TALK, COLD SCIENCE, 3RD ED. | *by
S. Fred Singer with David R. Legates & Anthony R. Lupo*

HOUSING AMERICA |
edited by Randall G. Holcombe & Benjamin Powell

IN ALL FAIRNESS | *edited by Robert M. Whaples,
Christopher J. Coyne, & Michael C. Munger*

IN SEARCH OF MONSTERS TO DESTROY |
by Christopher J. Coyne

JUDGE AND JURY |
by Eric Helland & Alexander Tabarrok

LESSONS FROM THE POOR |
edited by Alvaro Vargas Llosa

LIBERTY FOR LATIN AMERICA |
by Alvaro Vargas Llosa

LIBERTY FOR WOMEN |
edited by by Wendy McElroy

LIBERTY IN PERIL | *by Randall G. Holcombe*

LIVING ECONOMICS | *by Peter J. Boettke*

MAKING POOR NATIONS RICH |
edited by Benjamin Powell

Independent Institute Studies in Political Economy

INDEPENDENT INSTITUTE

100 SWAN WAY, OAKLAND, CA 94621-1428

For further information:
510-632-1366 • orders@independent.org • http://www.independent.org/publications/books/